THE RIDERS OF THE PLAINS

OFFICERS OF THE HEADQUARTERS STAFF, REGINA, 1910.

(STANDING) INSPECTOR J. F. BURNETT. INSPECTOR R. S. KNIGHT.
VETERINARY SURGEON. ADJUTANT.

(SITTING) J. H. McILLREE, LIEUT. COL. A. BOWEN PERRY, C.M.G. G. PEARSON BELL, M.D.
ASSISTANT COMMISSIONER. COMMISSIONER. SURGEON.

THE RIDERS OF THE PLAINS

A RECORD OF THE ROYAL NORTH-WEST
MOUNTED POLICE OF CANADA
1873–1910

BY
A. L. HAYDON

ILLUSTRATED WITH PHOTOGRAPHS, MAPS, AND DIAGRAMS

CHARLES E. TUTTLE COMPANY: PUBLISHERS
Rutland, Vermont & Tokyo, Japan

Representatives
Continental Europe: BOXERBOOKS, INC., *Zurich*
British Isles: PRENTICE-HALL INTERNATIONAL, INC., *London*
Australasia: PAUL FLESCH & CO., PTY. LTD., *Melbourne*
Canada: M. G. HURTIG LTD., *Edmonton*

Published by the Charles E. Tuttle Company, Inc.
of Rutland, Vermont & Tokyo, Japan
with editorial offices at
Suido 1-chome, 2-6, Bunkyo-ku, Tokyo, Japan

© *1971 by M. G. Hurtig Ltd.*

All rights reserved

Library of Congress Catalog Card No. 77-130423

International Standard Book No. 0-8048-0933-X

First Tuttle edition published 1971

HV
8157
.H 35

PRINTED IN JAPAN

Dedicated

TO

THE COMPTROLLER
THE COMMISSIONER
THE ASSISTANT-COMMISSIONERS

AND TO ALL THE OTHER

OFFICERS AND MEN

OF THE

ROYAL NORTH-WEST MOUNTED POLICE

IN WHOLE-HEARTED ADMIRATION

TABLE OF CONTENTS

List of Illustrations	xiii
Introduction to the New Edition . . .	xv
Preface	xxiii

CHAPTER I.

THE NORTH-WEST OF THE PAST.

PAGE

An historical survey—The early explorers—the fur companies—A new administration—The half-breeds' rebellion—Extinction of the bison—Disaffection among the Indians—Illicit traders—Colonel Robertson-Ross's reconnaissance. . . . 1

CHAPTER II.

THE COMING OF THE POLICE.

Sir John Macdonald's scheme—First steps towards organisation—Lieut.-Colonel G. A. French, Commissioner—Recruiting—The march westward, July 1874—At the Forks of the Bow and Belly Rivers—The Sweet Grass Hills—Colonel Macleod and Inspector Walsh in quarters—The return to Dufferin . . 17

CHAPTER III.

OUTPOSTS IN THE WILDERNESS.

Colonel Macleod's great task—Fort Macleod—The first blow at the liquor traffic—Dealings with the Indians—Chief Red Crow—Major-General Selby Smyth—Inspection of the Force—New posts established—Old Fort Walsh—The magic of the red coat—Important changes—Lieut.-Colonel Macleod, second Commissioner 34

TABLE OF CONTENTS

CHAPTER IV.

INDIAN PROBLEMS.

PAGE

The tribes in the north-west—Blackfeet and Crees—Savage warfare—Two sides of the shield—"The Moose that Walks"—Early Indian treaties—The Blackfeet Treaty—Indian oratory—A bloodless revolution 52

CHAPTER V.

"SITTING BULL" AND THE SIOUX INVASION.

Early fugitives (1862)—Settling in the west—The Custer Massacre—First-fruits of Police policy—The Blackfeet stand firm—Negotiations with the Sioux—The Sitting Bull Commission—An anxious time — Sergeant M'Donald — The Bull Elk affair—Sitting Bull's surrender—A contrast in method . . 70

CHAPTER VI.

CHANGES AND DEVELOPMENTS.

Lieut.-Colonel A. G. Irvine, third Commissioner (1880)—Fresh factors in the problem—Augmentation of the Force—New headquarters—Fort Regina—Long distance journeys—"Have done my best"—Notable reforms—Arms and equipment—Horse-stealing—Assisting the Indian Department—Railway pioneers 86

CHAPTER VII.

RAILWAY PROGRESS: A NEW ERA.

The Canadian Pacific Railway—Indian disturbances—Chief Pie-a-pot—Railway strikes—Inspector Steele at Golden—A critical situation—Prohibition duties—A desperado from Idaho—Fort Walsh abandoned—New Fort Macleod—Changes in equipment—The Marquess of Lorne's tour 102

TABLE OF CONTENTS

CHAPTER VIII.

THE NORTH-WEST REBELLION.—I.

PAGE

Completion of the Canadian Pacific Railway—Grievances of the half-breeds — The new land survey — Louis Riel — Signs of trouble—The Bill of Rights—The storm breaks—Fears for an Indian rising—Successful Police manœuvres—The affair at Duck Lake—Superintendent Crozier—At Prince Albert—Wild rumours—Militia troops from the east—General Middleton takes the field 120

CHAPTER IX.

THE NORTH-WEST REBELLION.—II.

The Frog Lake Massacre—Attack on Fort Pitt—Inspector Dickens' gallant defence—Indian raid at Battleford—The siege raised—Colonel Otter's column—Assault on Cut-Knife Hill—Chief Poundmaker—Battle of Batoche's Ferry—Enforced inactivity of the Police—Colonel Irvine's defence—Frenchman's Butte and Loon Lake—Inspector Perry's forced march—An exciting incident—Louis Riel captured—Big Bear—Execution of Riel . 137

CHAPTER X.

TEN YEARS' WORK, 1885-1895.

After the war—Lawlessness among the Indians—Liquor law difficulties—Cattle-killing—A rush of immigrants—Visit of the Marquess of Lansdowne — Lawrence W. Herchmer, Esq., fourth Commissioner—The *personnel* of the Force—A high standard of efficiency—Lord Stanley—Patrolling the border—Prairie fires—Death of Sir John Macdonald—Reduction in strength—Indian progress—A wider sphere of operations—The Earl of Aberdeen, Governor-General—Off to the Yukon . 155

CHAPTER XI.

"ALMIGHTY VOICE," BAD INDIAN.

Sergeant Colebrook shot—Hunt for the murderer—On the trail—Inspector Allan—In a death-trap—Shelling the bluff—The end of the drama—The "Charcoal" case—A long pursuit—Indian aid—Death of Interpreter Jerry Potts 174

TABLE OF CONTENTS

CHAPTER XII.

IN THE YUKON.—I.

Police protection called for—Inspector Constantine—Rush to the gold-fields—Skagway—" Soapy Smith "—A miners' meeting—Lynch law—A gruesome ride—Police posts on the summits—Relief work—Customs officers—Mail-carrying and other duties—A claim-jumping story—" Old man D—— " . . 188

CHAPTER XIII.

IN THE YUKON.—II.

New routes to the Territory—Inspector Routledge's patrol—Inspector Moodie's patrol—Down the Pelly River—Disasters of the trail—Winter travel—Dog sleds—Superintendent Perry in command—Strength of the Force—Dawson City—" Good Samaritans "—Winter clothing—Crime in the Yukon—A case of witchcraft—" Murder Island " mystery—Labelle and Fournier—Smart Police work—Assistant-Commissioner Wood . 207

CHAPTER XIV.

BACK TO THE TERRITORIES.

Foreign immigrants—Doukhobors—Adamites—Dreamers—Mormon settlements—Drains on the Force—Lieut.-Colonel A. Bowen Perry, fifth Commissioner—Increase of strength authorised—A 1300 miles' trip—Indian " Sun Dance "—Medicine Pipe Society—The Great Bond Robbery—An arrest in the Rockies—A Royal visit 229

CHAPTER XV.

AT THE FRONT IN SOUTH AFRICA.

The 1st C.M.R.—N.W.M.P. contributions to the war—Strathcona's Horse—South African Constabulary—Notable performances—Major Sanders' heroism—Lieutenant Chalmers' sad fate—A V.C. exploit—Scouting—An exhibition of riding—Distribution of honours—The death-roll 246

TABLE OF CONTENTS

CHAPTER XVI.

PUSHING NORTHWARD.

In Athabasca—Detachment at Fort Macpherson—In the Arctic Circle—Herschell Island—Eskimo—Inspector Howard—Police posts at Hudson's Bay—"The-place-where-ghosts-chase-women"—Fort Churchill—"On Special Duty"—King Murder Case—Title of "Royal" conferred on the Force—Earl of Minto, Honorary Commissioner—Earl Grey, new Governor-General—Provinces of Alberta and Saskatchewan created—Increase of pay 259

CHAPTER XVII.

A BATCH OF STORIES.

Corporal Smith at Norway House—"Cowboy Jack's" arrest—Fighting a prairie fire—Sergeant Field's trip—Constable Pedley—In charge of a madman—Sergeant Field again—A tragedy of the far north—1788 miles by land and water . 280

CHAPTER XVIII.

HORSE THIEVES AND "CATTLE RUSTLERS."

A prevalent crime—Swift retribution—An American apology—"Mavericks"—Sergeant Egan—Trapping a thief—"Rustler" methods—Need for vigilance—A lost foal—Detecting brands—Patrols on the boundary 295

CHAPTER XIX.

ON A PATROL.

Varieties of patrol work—Nature of reports—A typical instance—Inspector Pelletier's journey—Norway House to Sandy Lake—Cranes and Sucker Indians—A nine months' patrol—Far north—The rough side of Arctic travelling . . . 307

CHAPTER XX.

IN BARRACKS.

To join the R.N.W.M.P.—Taking the oath—At the dépôt, Regina—Riding and drilling—Police horses—A day's routine—Instructional classes—The ideal and the real—Target practice—A special course—General duties—The lighter side—Punishable offences—An attractive life 323

TABLE OF CONTENTS

CHAPTER XXI.
THE POLICE OF TO-DAY.

PAGE

Distribution and strength—Network of posts—A divisional station—More men needed—Multifarious duties—" No complaints "—Present constitution—Comptroller Fred White, C.M.G.—Equipment—Notable changes in uniform—Arms, past and present—Little-known phases of duty—More relief work—In the Yukon again—The north-west to-day—In the future . 336

APPENDIX A.
LIST OF N.W.M.P. OFFICERS EMPLOYED ON THE WESTWARD MARCH OF 1874 355

APPENDIX B.
THE TREATY WITH THE BLACKFEET, NUMBER SEVEN . . 355

APPENDIX C.
LIST OF NON-COMMISSIONED OFFICERS AND MEN OF THE NORTH-WEST MOUNTED POLICE KILLED OR WOUNDED IN THE SUPPRESSION OF THE NORTH-WEST REBELLION 364

APPENDIX D.
LIST OF COMMISSIONERS OF THE R.N.W.M.P., 1873–1910 . . 364

APPENDIX E.
LIST OF OFFICERS OF THE R.N.W.M.P. AT THE BEGINNING OF THE PRESENT YEAR, 1910 365

APPENDIX F.
R.N.W.M.P DISTRICTS AND OFFICERS ATTACHED THERETO . . 366

APPENDIX G.
LIST OF OFFICERS OF THE R.N.W.M.P. WHO HAVE LEFT THE FORCE FOR VARIOUS REASONS BETWEEN 1873 AND 1909 . . 368

APPENDIX H.
HOW TO ENTER THE FORCE 371

APPENDIX I.
DISTRIBUTION STATE OF THE FORCE, BY DIVISIONS, SEPTEMBER 30, 1909 373

APPENDIX J.
STATISTICS OF CRIME UNDER R.N.W.M.P. JURISDICTION . . 379

INDEX 381

LIST OF ILLUSTRATIONS

OFFICERS OF THE HEADQUARTERS STAFF, REGINA, 1910	*Frontispiece*	
A VIEW ON THE BOW RIVER, NEAR BANFF, ALBERTA	*Facing page*	16
TYPES OF UNIFORM, 1874–1885	*Page*	27
OLD FORT MACLEOD	,,	47
SITE OF OLD FORT WALSH	*Facing page*	48
AN INDIAN ENCAMPMENT	,,	56
THE FIRST FOUR COMMISSIONERS	,,	64
A DETACHMENT POST IN THE NORTH-WEST	,,	80
A SEIZURE OF STOLEN HORSES	,,	96
STONY CREEK BRIDGE, BRITISH COLUMBIA	,,	104
PORTRAITS OF COLONEL S. B. STEELE, C.B., M.V.O., AND ASSISTANT-COMMISSIONER Z. T. WOOD	,,	112
12-POUNDER GUNS IN POLICE CAMP AT EDMONTON	,,	128
R.N.W.M.P. HEADQUARTERS POST AT REGINA, FROM THE PRAIRIE	,,	144
THE BARRACKS AT REGINA	,,	160
R.N.W.M.P. POST AT WHITE HORSE, YUKON TERRITORY	,,	176
THE BRITISH FLAG IN THE YUKON	,,	184
CANADIAN CUSTOMS HOUSE ON THE SUMMIT OF CHILKOOT PASS, 1898	,,	192
PLEASANT CAMP POST, ON THE KLEEHINE RIVER, NEAR DALTON TRAIL, YUKON TERRITORY	,,	208
A POLICE DOG TEAM AND SLED	,,	224
A SQUAD OF RECRUITS, REGINA BARRACKS	,,	240
THE RIDING SCHOOL, REGINA BARRACKS	,,	256

LIST OF ILLUSTRATIONS

IN THE FAR NORTH: AFLOAT IN A KAYAK	*Facing page* 264
A POLICE WOOD CAMP ON CHURCHILL RIVER	,, 272
GROUP OF ESKIMO NATIVES, FORT CHURCHILL, HUDSON'S BAY	,, 288
IN WINTER DRESS	,, 296
"REG. NO. 2561." A POLICE TROOP HORSE	,, 304
A "MUSICAL RIDE" SQUAD, REGINA	,, 328
INTERIOR OF CHAPEL, REGINA BARRACKS	,, 336
"NO COMPLAINTS"	,, 352

DIAGRAM AND MAPS.

DIAGRAM OF FORT MACLEOD	*Facing page* 34
SKETCH MAP SHOWING TRAILS LEADING INTO THE YUKON TERRITORY	*Page* 199
SKETCH MAP SHOWING ROUTES OF PATROLS UNDERTAKEN BY INSPECTOR E. A PELLETIER, 1908-9	,, 321
SKETCH MAP OF R.N.W.M.P. DISTRICTS, 1910	*Facing page* 380

INTRODUCTION TO THE NEW EDITION

IF any man wants to feel the sweep of Western Canada's history, and if he wants to get the first glimmer of what the force, in any or all of its three successive names, means to that history, let him travel south of Maple Creek, Saskatchewan, to the Cypress Hills, that geological anomaly of the Great Plains.

Let him climb its steep escarpment and go forward until he stands on the rim of its great dished center. Let him look down on the restored buildings and the front stockade wall of Fort Walsh. The view has changed little since the first fort was built, except that there are today more trees and green woods.

This is rangeland country, and its face has not been lined by the settler's plow. This is the closest one can come today to seeing an early Mounted Police post as it was... seeing Fort Walsh much as it appeared after Superintendent J. M. Walsh and his patrol of thirty men under the indomitable guide, Jerry Potts, came from Fort Macleod to build it in 1875. On this ancient meeting and bartering ground with plentiful wood, grass and water, the Indian nations of the West came to rest, to parley and to trade. Chips of obsidian for arrowheads which came from the Yellowstone far south can still be found. They were brought to trade for the red pipestone found east of the fort.

Walking down the winding road to the fort gate, one finds the little police cemetery on the right. Here, in a grove of trees, rests Constable Grayburn, the first member of the force

INTRODUCTION TO THE NEW EDITION

murdered in the line of duty. Around him lie his comrades, dead of typhoid or other scourges which assailed the fort. One may read their ages—18, 19, 20 and 21—and it will come as something of a shock to recollect that young men, mere youths, led by good officers and made men beyond their years by tough NCO's, saved the West from the bloody wars with the Indians that stained the history of the United States. In so doing, they left no excuse for American troops to cross the Medicine Line into Canada, and prevented the almost certain absorption of most of Western Canada into the United States.

When Sitting Bull, having whipped the cream of the United States 7th Cavalry led by the reckless Custer, crossed into Canada with between four and six thousand braves, Superintendent Walsh confronted him with that seemingly ridiculous little garrison of about 150 men. He saved Western Canada for Canada, saved it despite stupidity by government and threats from Sitting Bull and his victory-proud warriors.

Here was a man who, on one occasion, spun the great warrior around and kicked his backside so that he stumbled and fell in front of his own warriors. Despite this almost unforgivable assault to the dignity of Sitting Bull, Walsh saved his own hair, his garrison, somehow the trust and respect of the chief himself—and above all, the whole Northwest of Canada.

If you are ever in the Cypress Hills, ride a few short miles, three or four, south of Fort Walsh and stand on a long curving ridge as I have done. Look down on meandering Battle Creek, and follow its winding course by the scrub willow that lines its banks. The little trading forts of Moses Solomon and Abe Farwell are to the left and right, rebuilt by the Royal Canadian Mounted Police as a centennial project in 1967. This is the real birthplace of the North West Mounted Police, even though the idea was conceived by John A. Macdonald, who gave Parliament notice of his intent in April 1873.

It is quiet here today. The only sign of man is the rutted

INTRODUCTION TO THE NEW EDITION

prairie trail and the two forts of the free traders. There is the smell of wolf willow in the air.

It was not quiet here on one horrible night in the spring of 1873. About forty lodges of peaceful Assiniboines stood by a grove of trees across Battle Creek from the trading posts. Circles of teepee stones still remain to mark where the lodges stood.

On that infamous night, a party of hunters and wolfers from Montana were whooping it up at the trading post. At least some of the Indians were drinking with them. The wolfers, who had come looking for Indians who had stolen their horses, apparently decided that one dead Indian would serve their purpose as well as another.

In the cold false dawn they took up their positions, crouching in the willow bushes across the creek from the Assiniboines' camp. As soon as there was enough light to sight a rifle, they opened fire on the lodges of the sleeping Indians. It was a slaughter, although the Indians managed to kill one white man, Ed Grace. The wolfers burned Solomon's fort to the ground along with Ed Grace's body, and headed south of the border. Farwell went along, no doubt to save his skin.

The news of that one episode, when it reached Ottawa, crystallized plans to create the police. Born in the Cypress Hills, this birth was duly registered in Ottawa following an act of Parliament on May 23, 1873.

Come away from these historied hills some fifteen hundred miles or more northwest as the crow flies, and God knows how many more by sea and land, to where the gold seekers, in a few short months, built the roaring camp of Dawson City, Yukon Territory, into a city of thirty to forty thousand inhabitants.

Walk today through the relics of its fame and infamy, where several hundred Yukoners still live this life they love. Look at the crumbling false fronts of the old stores, the saloons, parlor houses and the churches. Then visit the museum and study the pictures of the days of '98 and '99,

INTRODUCTION TO THE NEW EDITION

when every night was Saturday night and con men, thieves, killers and painted ladies came from across the world to separate the miner from his gold.

If your mind begins to picture it as Robert W. Service rhymed it, then climb the winding road up the high hill behind Dawson until you find the old cemetery. Most of it is a mass of overgrown graves, slanted rotting wooden crosses, the names long since obliterated. In the midst of this eerie wilderness, you will come upon a freshly white-washed picket fence. Within its enclosure in orderly rows, with clean white crosses and well-kept river gravel paths between, are the graves of the force, and a few of its soldier comrades of the Yukon Field Force. The force remembers its own.

As you read the crosses, once again you are awed at the youthfulness of the men who kept the Queen's peace in this roaring gold camp of Dawson City, or who held the Chilkoot Pass.

Again north and east, just across the Yukon border in the Northwest Territories, in the little church cemetery at Fort MacPherson, the bodies of Inspector Fitzgerald and his patrol, Carter, Kinney and Taylor, rest in a common grave. All perished of exposure when lost on the MacPherson-Dawson patrol of 1911.

Fort Garry, Dufferin, Swan River, Fort Walsh, Whisky Gap, Batoche, Fish Creek, Fort Carleton, Prince Albert, Pile o' Bones, Herschel Island, Wild Horse Creek, Blackfoot Crossing, Standoff, Pincher Creek, Athabasca Landing, Fort Saskatchewan. What names to conjure up the historic events, the sweat and guts and vision and heartache and sacrifice of life itself, which in just about ninety-six years has transformed vast, almost empty, millions of acres of prairie wool!

Great cities now stand where the log forts of the company stood one hundred years ago. Take nothing away from the missionaries, the explorers and the traders who first ventured into this land of nomadic Indian nations, but realize that it

INTRODUCTION TO THE NEW EDITION

was the police who made it possible for the pioneer settler to bring his women and his children into this great lone land in safety. It was the presence of the police that permitted him to dip his plow into the prairie's beneficent earth and garner its rich rewards. Seldom in the history of man has such a fantastic empire of new land been opened to peaceful settlement with so little turmoil, so little corruption and, except for 1885, so little of the violence and bloodshed that followed the passage of other great historic migrations.

Through every inch of the warp and woof of the colorful tapestry of Western Canada's history runs the scarlet thread of the North West Mounted Police, later the Royal North West Mounted Police and, finally, the Royal Canadian Mounted Police.

Its members were not storybook heroes. There were among them ex-soldiers, city boys and boys off eastern farms. Their ranks held the sons of European aristocracy. Indeed, on one early morning behind the stables at Fort Macleod, a German baron and a French count fought a sabre duel, with inexperienced but fascinated Canadian-born constables as their seconds and judges. There were "gentlemen rankers," and Kipling would easily have recognized his Soldiers Three and other of his characters among them.

The truth is that this body of common and uncommon men was mustered and annealed into a force, that when called upon to do the impossible, did just that. In so doing it developed for itself a fierce esprit de corps that only those who have served the force can really comprehend, and it has made Canada synonymous with the Mounted Police the world over.

Its rewards have not always been apparent, particularly to the men in the ranks. Too often a grateful government has shown its appreciation by neglect and forgetfulness.

Nine months after the force left Fort Dufferin in Manitoba on its long hard march west, which was to end with the establishment of Fort Macleod, not a man had received a

INTRODUCTION TO THE NEW EDITION

cent of pay. Uniforms and boots were in tatters or worn through; they were patched with rawhide, canvas or whatever else was available.

When Walsh left Fort Macleod for the Cypress Hills on May 15, 1875, to establish a post there, some of his little troop of thirty-odd men, lacking anything else, were wearing United States Army bluecoats discarded by deserting United States soldiers who had fled into Canada. A party of roving Sioux understandably mistook them for the hated Pony Soldiers of the United States Cavalry and, but for the rapid explanation of Jerry Potts, would undoubtedly have attacked and might well have wiped out the police.

Today a statue to the memory of Louis Riel stands in a place of honor on the grounds of the Saskatchewan legislature. Yet who remembers, or what Canadian school history records the names of the first three constables killed in the first action in the Riel Rebellion?

Although the force fought in the first and every subsequent major engagement of the Riel Rebellion, its men who were in that campaign were denied for years the Rebellion Medal, awarded to all serving troops. Eventually a belated award was allowed to those who remained.

Commissioner Irvine, who saw the force through the rebellion only to suffer unjust criticism in the press and Parliament, also had to face, as a reward for the force's services in the rebellion, a cut in the pay of recruit constables from the princely sum of seventy-five cents a day to forty cents a day. Morale reached an all-time low and many men understandably deserted. Driven to utter frustration by the treatment given the force, Irvine, who had assumed command in 1880, resigned in 1886.

Becoming alarmed at the results of its austerity program, the government retreated . . . but only to the pinnacle of fifty cents a day, where the pay remained until 1905. In 1932, recruit pay had achieved the affluent scale of $1.50 per day. Canada bought its West cheaply in more ways than

INTRODUCTION TO THE NEW EDITION

just the original £300,000 paid to the Hudson's Bay Company.

Of the work of the force during the great rush on the Trail of '98, Superintendent Sam Steele reported: "More than 30,000 persons, every one of whom had received assistance, had passed down the Yukon. Over $150,000 in duty and fees had been collected, more than 30,000,000 pounds of solid food sufficient to feed an army corps for a year had been inspected and passed over by us." Additionally, he reported how the force had cared for the sick, buried the dead and administered their estates to the satisfaction of their relatives. The police had also brought in their own supplies, built their own quarters and maintained the laws of Canada. Only three homicides had occurred. Over seven thousand went downriver during the rush. The force had less than two hundred men in the Yukon to carry out this awesome task and, as Steele said later in his report, "a record which should, and I believe did give satisfaction to the Government of the Dominion."

The government expressed its satisfaction to the underpaid members of the force with a special order-in-council forbidding them to stake claims.

The Riders of the Plains takes the history of the force from its inception, in 1873, to 1918. First published in 1910, it went into five subsequent editions, brought up to date in 1918 by its author, a painstaking and excellent military historian. Its statistical material alone, covering the early distribution of the force's posts and men and the names of its early officers, is of particular interest to the student of Western Canadian history.

In 1920 the force assumed federal duties for all of Canada when its headquarters were removed from the historic Regina site to the capital at Ottawa. It now carries out the functions of a provincial police force as well in all of the provinces but Ontario and Quebec.

A number of excellent personal reminiscences of their

INTRODUCTION TO THE NEW EDITION

own times and life in the force have been written by two commissioners and by other former officers and ex-members. There are other very good histories of some of the later years, but the definitive history of the force since 1920 has yet to be written. It may lack some of the glamor of the frontier scene, but it would, none the less, be a history of great achievement, great expansion, courage and frustration.

The force's efficiency has at times been challenged; its integrity, never. It has sometimes suffered for the mistakes and weaknesses of government, as well as its own errors. Its own ministers have, on occasion, stepped aside and let the force bear the brunt of the criticism they were not prepared to assume for their own faults and weaknesses.

The force has made its mistakes and it will again. Its detractors have howled against it and will again.

It is, however, my firm belief that as long as the force continues to be led by commissioners who are not prepared to allow the principles upon which the force was built to be eroded in the name of expediency—as long as the force remembers its history and keeps faith with those who rode ahead, it will continue to be the finest and most unique force of its kind . . . and it will continue to be the pride of Canada.

> GEO. B. MCCLELLAN
> Commissioner, RCMP (Rtd.)

Edmonton, Alberta
September 30, 1969

PREFACE

TO have had the opportunity of writing the record of the Royal North-West Mounted Police is a great satisfaction and pleasure to me. This fine force, which has maintained the best tradition of the British race in doing its work silently, unostentatiously, and efficiently, has not received its full measure of recognition at the hands of the public. It is a characteristic of the Rider of the Plains that he does not waste words upon his deeds; to this is due the general ignorance of his solid achievements. He has a manly aversion to the sentimentality that marks most of the descriptive magazine articles through which he has been introduced to the world at large, and apart from these I know of only two volumes that purport to give any serious and reliable account of his activities.

It is time that an authoritative history of the Royal North-West Mounted Police should be added to the regimental records of the British Empire. To do this has been my object in the preparation of this book. I have endeavoured to give a faithfully exact presentment of the wearer of the scarlet tunic, of the man and his work, without any more embellishment than he himself indulges in when telling his story unofficially. In addition to seeing the Mounted Policeman in all the varied phases of his life, in barracks and on the open prairie, it has been my good fortune and privilege to be admitted into the confidence of the corps, and thus to acquire exclusive and accurate

PREFACE

information; and by personal and intimate contact with officers and men I have come to realise that the glamour and romance of the far north-west is not a thing of the past, but is still to be read between the lines that separate " I have the honour to report " from " I have the honour to remain " in regimental dispatches. All official records have been placed generously at my disposal, and so far as I am aware my errors are only errors of omission. Should any misstatements of fact, however, be detected, I shall be very grateful for correction.

My dedication is my formal expression of thanks for the hospitality extended to me during my stay at headquarters and other R.N.W.M.P. posts. But in this preface I take the opportunity to acknowledge my particular indebtedness to the Comptroller, Colonel Fred. White, C.M.G., to Commissioner A. Bowen Perry, C.M.G., Assistant-Commissioner J. H. M'Illree, Superintendent G. E. Sanders, D.S.O., Superintendent R. Burton Deane, Inspector J. H. Heffernan, Inspector R. S. Knight, Inspector W. Parker, Inspector A. Allard, Inspector E. A. Pelletier, Assistant-Surgeon S. M. Fraser, and, last but not least, the late Inspector Frank Church, whose sudden and untimely death, which occurred while this book was in the press, I deplore with all his comrades.

I desire to add a separate word of thanks to Major-General Sir George A. French, K.C.M.G., the first Commissioner of the Mounted Police, for placing at my service invaluable material respecting the earliest years of the Force, and for courteously revising the chapters dealing with the history of the corps during his tenure of office.

A. L. HAYDON.

LONDON, *March* 1910.

THE RIDERS OF THE PLAINS

CHAPTER I.

THE NORTH-WEST OF THE PAST.

An historical survey—The early explorers—the fur companies—A new administration—The half-breeds' rebellion—Extinction of the bison—Disaffection among the Indians—Illicit traders—Colonel Robertson-Ross's reconnaissance.

THE great north-west of Canada extends fully nine hundred miles westward in a direct line from the Red River in Manitoba to the foothills of the Rocky Mountains. It comprises the enlarged provinces of Saskatchewan and Alberta (the former provisional districts of Athabasca and Assiniboia having been merged into them), and, to the north, the extensive Yukon territory. In addition there is a great tract of sparsely settled land stretching from the Yukon on the west to the shores of Hudson Bay on the east, and known as the North-West Territories. A truly vast area is this, reaching as it does from the 49th Parallel, the border line on the south, to the Arctic Ocean itself, and the wonder of it is that the maintenance of law and order throughout these many thousands of square miles rests in the hands of a small body of some six hundred men—the Royal North-West Mounted Police of Canada.

THE RIDERS OF THE PLAINS

How this splendid and unique Force has justified its existence in carrying out its remarkable duties, must ever remain one of the romances of our Empire. It is Canada's special pride, and very justly so; no other British colony or dependency can boast of its exact counterpart. But before going on to speak of its origin and history we must glance back to the early days prior to the coming of the Police. To understand properly the magnitude of the work they have performed it is necessary that we ask ourselves the question: what like was the far north-west of the olden time? For our answer we must go back thirty, fifty, a hundred years and more, and see what were the conditions of life in that immense and unexplored land.

For centuries the north-west of the American continent was the home solely of the red man, the bison, and the lesser wild animals native to the country. Without any artificial restriction of boundary lines the Indians roamed at will, north and south, east and west, being divided only into several great families or tribes whose origins are lost in the mists of antiquity. A wild, rugged country it was for the most part, and the means of existence were wrested hardly from it. Like nearly all savage peoples, the red men of the past lived principally upon the chase. The bison, bear, deer, and other creatures furnished them with food, clothing, and the various necessaries they required.

Into this primeval land, with its innumerable leagues of prairie, lake, swamp, and forest, the first white men to venture were the French missionary priests, burning with zeal to convert the heathen, and the fur traders, who speedily saw its potentialities for wealth. The fur trade, indeed, was the pioneer of civilisation in the north-west. As the daring *voyageurs* pushed further and further inland they established forts which served as centres for barter with the Indians, and when in time the two great rival companies, the Hudson's Bay Company and the Great North-West Fur Company, entered the field, these outposts were increased in number and strength. The wild, lone land was still a wilderness, but it was no longer the sealed book that it had been for so many hundreds of years.

To Pierre Radisson and his comrade, the Sieur des Groseilliers, belong the credit of having first penetrated this vast tract of undiscovered country. The story of their adventurous explorations cannot be narrated here: it is a volume in itself. They plunged into the unknown, took the daring leap that all such pioneers are called upon to take, and along the paths they blazed followed a host of others hardly less intrepid. He who would read of the further discovery and exploitation of the north-west of Canada must study the glowing life-stories of Marquette, Jolliet, La Salle, De la Verendrye and Samuel Hearne, among others.

In brief, the opening up of the west is linked with one of those early myths such as that which set Columbus voyaging across the Atlantic to find the Indies and stumble upon America. To the settlers in New France in the eighteenth century there came the fanciful idea that somewhere away to the north-west of their little colony was a great sea lying between America and Japan—not the Pacific Ocean, for that, of course, was already known, but another, scarcely as large though equally important.

In 1731 the Sieur de la Verendrye, as gallant a gentleman as ever sought his fortune in the New World, started gaily from Montreal upon the quest for this great sea. He and his company followed the Red River to its junction with the Assiniboine, pitching their camp at Fort Rouge, where the city of Winnipeg now stands; but no vast expanse of water met their view. They found a sea, in very truth, but it was a sea of waving grass, the illimitable prairie which stretched away to the westward.

Certain Indians at this point, persisting in the rumours of "mighty waters beyond the mountains," lured the Frenchman still further on in his quest. It was the Pacific Ocean of which they spoke, though he knew it not, and so it came to pass that for years he traversed in vain the valleys of the Saskatchewan, Missouri, and other rivers, being at last compelled to turn back baffled after reaching the foot of the Rockies. The formidable barrier of the *Montagnes des Rochers* proved too much for De la Verendrye; it was reserved for a young fur trader of the North-West Company, Alexander Mackenzie by name, to wrest their secret from the mountains, to cross them to the Pacific, and by following the Mackenzie River to its mouth to set at rest the vexed question of a north-west passage between the two oceans.

The two great fur companies that have been referred to claim more than passing attention here. Their history marks an epoch in that of the north-west. The Hudson's Bay Company, which had its origin in the "Honourable Company of Merchants-Adventurers Trading into Hudson's Bay," incorporated in 1670 under Prince Rupert's patronage, owed its inception to the glowing reports brought to England by Radisson and Groseilliers. It held its own successfully for more than a hundred years. Then, in 1784, the Montreal merchants, who had been profiting

THE NORTH-WEST OF THE PAST

considerably in their dealings with the Indians through the agency of the *coureurs de bois*, entered the lists with the North-West Company.

There now began a long and bitter warfare between the two rival associations, many of the conflicts resulting in blood being shed. The crisis was reached in the early years of the nineteenth century, when the French half-breed trappers, the *bois brulés*, rose against the Scottish settlers who had been drafted into the country under Lord Selkirk's scheme, and committed many outrages. In the long-run, the Hudson's Bay Company gained the upper hand, and with its amalgamation of the North-West Company the feud ended.

Through all this ensanguined rivalry, however, the development of the north-west proceeded slowly but surely. Trading posts sprang up in all directions, the more inaccessible parts of the country were penetrated, and many of the little settlements that were thus founded grew in importance.

But although by the end of the eighteenth century so much had been done, and the geography of the western portion of the continent had been more clearly defined, to the world at large the great north-west still remained something of a mystery. It was not the policy of the fur traders to reveal the country's possibilities in any direction. To them it was a lucrative field, and so long as they could maintain a hold upon it their monopoly was assured. We cannot be surprised, therefore, that cartographers of that day represented the centre of North America as one vast inland ocean, the blank space on the maps stretching away up to the Polar seas.

Even such great rivers as the Saskatchewan, the Bow,

the Assiniboine, and the Qu'Appelle, were vaguely sketched for many years. The most noteworthy attempt to investigate the interior, Captain Palliser's expedition of 1857, had failed in its object to find a practical waggon-trail over the continent, and for some time after nothing occurred to awaken public interest in what was assumed, too readily, to be a barren wilderness. Only such travellers as Dr. Grant, the author of *Ocean to Ocean*, and Colonel (now Sir) William Butler could find anything good to say about the "great lone land."

Fifty years ago, when a scheme was projected for forming the Red River and Saskatchewan country into a Crown Colony, a leading British review ridiculed the idea, characterising the district as one of "hailstones, hostile Indians, frosts,—early and late,—rocks and bogs," and declaring that the want of wood and water made settlement impracticable. The grossest ignorance prevailed generally as to the conditions of life in the north-west; the reviewer in question did but voice what popular opinion held to be the truth.

There is no doubt, nevertheless, that the ill name acquired by the Canadian north-west was due somewhat to the reckless methods under which settlements were made. The nature of the country was not sufficiently taken into account. The immigrants who were hurried into the newly opened districts expected to find them Edens, and were too easily discouraged by the set-backs which they received. The hardy Scottish settlers, who were located by the Red River by the Earl of Selkirk in 1811 and 1812, passed through many vicissitudes of fortune before they obtained a secure foothold. Disastrous floods and famines more than once almost wiped them out of existence.

THE NORTH-WEST OF THE PAST

Some time prior to 1869 the need for more effective administration in the north-west had made itself felt. The Government was petitioned on the subject, and as a result of negotiations the whole of the territories belonging to the Hudson's Bay Company, covering over two million square miles, were admitted into the confederation. To the thousands of settlers scattered over the country this was a satisfactory conclusion, but to a certain section of the inhabitants it marked an alarming departure. The French half-breeds now believed themselves about to be deprived forcibly of their lands. The nature of the transfer was not clear to them, and, regarding the manner in which the surrender of the territory was carried through, we may grant that they had a fairly just grievance.

The immediate outcome was what is known in history as the first North-West, or Riel, Rebellion, that of 1869. This short-lived outbreak was suppressed by the expedition under Lord (then Colonel) Wolseley. Louis Riel became a fugitive, seeking shelter in the United States, where he was to lie safe for several years before making his second and final dramatic appearance upon the stage, and his turbulent followers settled down under the new régime. Following upon this came the formation of the Province of Manitoba, marking a new epoch in the history of the north-west.

The foregoing brief historical survey, it is hoped, will give the reader some conception of the sequence of events leading up to the period when the Royal North-West Mounted Police were called into being. It now remains to account for the disturbed state of the country which rendered the intervention of the Government imperative.

THE RIDERS OF THE PLAINS

Two great forces had been at work for some time to bring about considerable unrest among the Indians of the new territories. In the first place the treatment meted out by the United States authorities to the Sioux and other tribes within their borders had led to severe reprisals. The warfare between the red men and the American troops sent into the field against them became incessant, and more and more bands of Indians flocked across the border to seek refuge under the British flag. The presence of these marauders was by no means welcomed by the white population of the north-west. Fresh from scenes of massacre, and full of resentment at their ill-treatment, they could hardly fail to exercise a bad influence upon the Canadian Indians. Of the latter there were nearly seventy thousand, and in its proclamation the Imperial Government had pledged itself to their care and protection.

The second great factor in the situation was the imminent extinction of the bison, the animal upon which the Indian depended almost entirely for his existence. The importance of taking this into account cannot be over-estimated. To the red man of Canada the bison was Heaven's greatest gift. It supplied him at once with food and clothing, with most of the needs and comforts essential to his life. Its skin provided tent as well as garments; the undressed hide was converted into a boat. From the sinews came strings for the bow; from the short, curved horn a powder flask, and from the tanned leather the stout lariat for bridle and rein. Its flesh, either eaten alone or pounded down and mixed with fat into "pemmican," afforded the best of food. From first to last the bison was the Indian's friend in need,

THE NORTH-WEST OF THE PAST

for even when the savage descended into the grave it was a buffalo robe that served him as a shroud.

At the present time, when only a few hundreds of these creatures are alive, carefully guarded in special reservations, it is difficult to comprehend the extent of the immense herds which formerly ranged over the prairies. In bygone days, according to travellers' reports, the plains were literally black with them. It was not unusual for a waggon train to be compelled to camp one or two days to allow a herd of buffalo to pass. One might ride, as once did Colonel Dodge of the U.S.A. Army, through an unbroken line of them for 25 miles. On that day he computed he saw half a million of buffaloes. A restless tide of bison was for ever surging to and fro between the plains of the Saskatchewan and the Assiniboine and those of the Missouri, Mississippi, and Ohio. The great prairies were their principal feeding-grounds; they left these only for the pasture afforded by the gorges of the Rockies.

By the year 1870, following on the completion of the Union Pacific Railway, the once universal herd which roamed across the whole continent had been broken up into two portions, a northern and a southern herd. The former kept to the north-west, the latter to Texas and other western states of America. The war of extermination began almost immediately. Hardly more than four years later the southern herd was blotted out, Indians and whites alike butchering the buffaloes without restraint.

Such noted American hunters as Comstock and Colonel Cody accounted for many thousands. The latter owed his well-known title of " Buffalo Bill " to a remarkable feat. He had entered into a contract to deliver all the buffalo meat that would be needed to feed the huge army of labourers working on the Kansas Pacific Railway while in course of construction. In less than eighteen months he had killed 4280 buffaloes. As further exemplifying Buffalo Bill's deadly skill with the rifle, the story is told of how, in answer to the taunts of some Pawnee Indians who belittled his prowess, he rode into a herd and single-handed shot down forty-eight buffaloes in fifty minutes.

In the Canadian territory the same senseless, wasteful annihilation was going on. Thanks to American traders, the Indians were now armed with breech-loading rifles which did far more deadly execution than their bows and arrows. Moreover, both for meat and for robes cows were shot down in preference to bulls. At this period the northern herd was itself divided. One portion ranged eastward from Regina to the Red River, the other westward from Regina to the base of the Rocky Mountains. The first of these herds came down from the north, following the course of the Assiniboine, and found its way into the Dakotas; the second browsed along the flanks of the mountains in Alberta and as far south as the rich grass lands of Montana, returning to winter in the hills by Calgary.

Although the years 1880–83 were responsible for the greatest wanton slaughter, the decimation of the northern herd had been in progress for some considerable time before. Within a comparatively short period the bison were reduced to an insignificant number. The construction of the Canadian Pacific Railway may be said to have sealed their doom, for by its means the buffalo were made accessible at all points. Eventually only some small isolated bands of the animals escaped, to find refuge in the fastnesses of the mountains or in the "barren lands" north of Athabasca.

As will be understood, the result of this ruthless war of extermination was to place the Indians in a well-nigh hopeless position. They saw themselves about to be bereft of their chief means of sustenance. In addition to this, they were not a little unsettled by the treatment of the neighbouring tribes in the American borders. In the eyes of the United States citizen the only good Indian was a dead Indian, and acting on that opinion the said citizen spared no pains to drive the red man out of his country, or exterminate him altogether. A significant remark was made by a Yankee colonel to Sir William Butler while the latter was on his way to the Red River to join Colonel Wolseley's force. Said this gentleman : " Kill every buffalo you see. Every buffalo dead is an Indian gone."

Large numbers of the disaffected Indians, as has been noted, trooped across the border into British territory, thereby constituting themselves a menace to the peace of their adopted country. They had no precise locations on which to settle, they had no "visible means of subsistence," to use the legal phrase, and, what made matters worse, they were exposed to the insidious wiles of American traders who supplied them freely with intoxicating liquors. In the year following the close of the American Civil War, the western states of the Union had been opened up, and traders had drifted thence northwards to come into contact with the various Indian tribes. The trade in buffalo robes and furs, which were readily bartered for whisky, arms, and ammunition, proceeded at a great pace, until the lamentable results that ensued compelled the Government's attention to this state of affairs.

THE RIDERS OF THE PLAINS

To what a pitch of disorder the Indians were being hastened is made evident in the report of Colonel Robertson-Ross, the Adjutant-General, who was dispatched by the Canadian Government in the summer of 1872 to make "a reconnaissance of the north-west provinces and Indian territories of the Dominion." In this interesting document he gives concise particulars of the methods employed by the illicit American traders to plunder the Indians and supply them with the much-coveted "fire water."

"When at Edmonton and the Rocky Mountain House," he states, "I was informed that a party of American smugglers and traders had established a trading post at the junction of the Bow and the Belly Rivers, about 30 miles due east from the Porcupine Hills, and about 60 miles on the Dominion side of the boundary line. This trading post they have named Fort Hamilton, after a mercantile firm of Fort Benton, Montana, U.S.A., from whom it is said they obtain supplies. It is believed that they number about twenty well-armed men, under the command of a man called John Healy, a notorious character. Here, it appears, they have for some time carried on an extensive trade with the Blackfeet Indians, supplying them with rifles, revolvers, goods of various kinds, whisky and other ardent spirits, in direct opposition to the laws both of the United States and the Dominion of Canada, and without paying any customs duties for the goods introduced into the latter country.

"The demoralisation of the Indians, the danger to the white inhabitants, and injury resulting to the country from this traffic are very great. It is stated upon good authority that during the year 1871 eighty-eight of the Blackfeet Indians were murdered in drunken brawls among themselves, produced by whisky and other spirits supplied to them by those traders. At Fort Edmonton during the past summer whisky was openly sold to the Blackfeet and other Indians trading at the Fort by some smugglers from the United States who derive large profits therefrom, and on these traders being remonstrated with by the gentlemen in charge of the Hudson's Bay Post, they coolly replied that they knew very well that what they were doing was contrary to the laws of both countries, but as there was no force there to prevent them, they would do just as they pleased."

Whisky-drinking and brawling led to offences even more unpardonable. Incited by the illicit traders, the Indians took to horse-stealing on a wide scale. The white population of the north-west can scarcely be excused for assuming that unless a stop was put to this forthwith no man's property, and no man's life, were safe.

To instance the general lawlessness in the north-west, the report proceeds: "It appears that of late years no attempt has been made to assert the supremacy of the law, and the most serious crimes have been allowed to pass unpunished. Hardly a year has gone by without several murders and other crimes of the most grave nature having been committed. During the present year, about three weeks before my arrival at Edmonton, a man, by name Charles Gaudin, a French-speaking half-breed, cruelly murdered his wife at no great distance from the gate of the H.B. Company's Post. I was informed that the criminal might have been arrested, but that there was no power to act. This same man had previously most wantonly and cruelly mutilated an old Indian woman, by severing the sinews of her arm so as to incapacitate her for work.

"At Edmonton there is a notorious murderer, a Cree Indian called Ta-ha-kooch, who has committed several murders, and who should have been apprehended long ago. This man is to be seen openly walking about the Post. Many instances of a similar kind can be adduced, and as a natural result there is a widespread feeling of apprehension. The gentleman in charge of the H.B. Company Post at Fort Pitt, as well as others elsewhere, assured me that of late the Indians have been overbearing in manner, and threatening at times. Indeed, the white men dwelling in the Saskatchewan are at this moment living by sufferance, as it were, entirely at the mercy of the Indians. They dare not venture to introduce cattle or stock into the country, or to cultivate the ground to any extent, for fear of Indian spoliation."

However, the time was now at hand when steps were to be taken to ensure the maintenance of order in this portion of the Queen's domains.

The reconnaissance carried out by Colonel Robertson-Ross was instituted by the then Canadian Premier, Sir John Macdonald, and it had for its main object the consideration of a more or less military force to be established in the north-west.

"I would urge," said the Adjutant-General, "if it be the intention of the Government to retain any military force on duty in Manitoba, that one hundred men of the Provisional Battalion be supplied with horses and equipped as Mounted Riflemen, that an addition of one officer and twenty-five gunners from the School of Gunnery at Kingston be made to the Artillery detachment, and the Artillery

THE NORTH-WEST OF THE PAST

supplied with four of the Horse Artillery guns recently obtained from England. Thus the force would form a small but effective Field Brigade, and its military power be increased. With regard to the necessity for maintaining any military force at Fort Garry, no doubt whatever exists in my mind as to the propriety of doing so, in view of the presence of many bands of Indians, considering the primitive state of society in the Province, the strong political party feeling which exists, and the fact that on both sides of the International Boundary Line restless and reckless characters among both white men and Indians abound.

" It is undoubtedly very desirable to maintain a certain number of Police Constables in the Province under the civil power, some of whom should be mounted, but I feel satisfied that the great security for the preservation of good order, and the peace of the North-West Territories, under the changing state of affairs, will for some years be found to lie in the existence and presence of a disciplined military body, under its own military rules, in addition to, but distinct from, any civil force which it may be thought proper to establish. Whatever feeling may be entertained toward Policemen, animosity is rarely, if ever, felt towards disciplined soldiers wearing her Majesty's uniform in any portion of the British Empire. In the event of serious disturbance a Police Force, acting alone and unsupported by a disciplined military body, would probably be overpowered in a Province of mixed races, where every man is armed, while to maintain a military without any Civil Force is not desirable."

Colonel Robertson-Ross's conclusions led him to suggest that no time should be lost in establishing a chain of military posts from Manitoba to the Rocky Mountains. The appointment of a Stipendiary Magistrate for the Saskatchewan, who should reside at Edmonton and act as Indian Commissioner, was also, he urged, a matter of the first importance. "The individual to fill this post should be one, if possible, already known to the Indians, and one in whom they have confidence. No Indian Commissioner should proceed unaccompanied by a military force. A large force is not required, but the presence of a certain force, I believe, will be found to be indispensable for the security of the country, to prevent bloodshed and preserve peace."

The effect of this report, with its important recommendations, was to bring into being the North-West Mounted Police of Canada, whose advent into the western provinces was to herald a new era of peace and prosperity.

A VIEW ON THE BOW RIVER, NEAR BANFF, ALBERTA.

Photo, Canadian Pacific Railway Co.]

CHAPTER II.

THE COMING OF THE POLICE.

Sir John Macdonald's scheme—First steps towards organisation—Lieut.-Colonel G. A. French, Commissioner—Recruiting—The march westward, July 1874—At the Forks of the Bow and Belly Rivers—The Sweet Grass Hills—Colonel Macleod and Inspector Walsh in quarters—The return to Dufferin.

IN his report to the Government, Colonel Robertson-Ross had particularised the nature of the Force which he considered essential to the security of the north-west. A large military body, as he said, was not required. Comparatively small detachments of "well-armed and disciplined men, judiciously posted throughout the country," were all that were needed to maintain military supremacy. With this in view he recommended the establishment of posts at various points indicated, each of these to be garrisoned with from fifty to a hundred mounted riflemen.

"At Portage de la Prairie, 50 Mounted Riflemen; Fort Ellice, 50 Mounted Riflemen; Fort Carlton, 50 Mounted Riflemen; Fort Pitt, 50 Mounted Riflemen; Fort Victoria, 50 Mounted Riflemen; Fort Edmonton, 100 Mounted Riflemen; Fort Porcupine Hills, 150 Mounted Riflemen; with a proportion of officers and non-commissioned officers. I would further beg to suggest," he wrote, "if it be decided to establish any chain of military posts, that for the first year the soldiers be employed in laying down a telegraphic wire from Manitoba towards British Columbia, if not required to hut themselves." (The Hudson's Bay Company were to be relied upon to provide barrack accommodation and rations at the different posts named.) "From my own knowledge and observation of the country, I think that, if proper energy be used, the very desirable work of establishing telegraphic communications might be accomplished, without exacting too much from the soldiers, in one or two seasons. I would further observe that no time should be lost in making the preliminary arrangements. The men and horses should, if possible, be concentrated at Fort Garry in the month of May or June, their equipment forwarded sooner, and the companies dispatched without delay."

Early in the following year the Dominion Parliament at Ottawa began to discuss the situation seriously. In May, Sir John Macdonald, who had formulated his own scheme from the suggestions offered by the Adjutant-General, gave notice that he intended to introduce a bill respecting "the administration of justice and the establishment of a police force in the North-West Territories." Under the provisions of this Act the new force would consist of a Commissioner, as many Superintendents as were deemed desirable, a paymaster, veterinary surgeon, and sergeants, with constables and sub-constables, to a number not exceeding three hundred. All were to be mounted and efficiently equipped, and, above all, there was to be no ostentatious display. "As little gold lace and fuss and feathers as possible," were Sir John's words. He wanted a plain, working, mobile force, suited to the conditions of the country—a force, in short, of well-trained, hard-bitten men, all good riders and good marksmen.

In effect, the North-West Mounted Police was to be purely a civil force, like the Royal Irish Constabulary, drilled in simple movements taken from the British cavalry regulations, and its interior economy was to be conducted much upon the system of a regular cavalry regiment. It was not to be subject to the Queen's regulations and articles of war, but discipline was to be enforced by virtue of the powers conferred upon certain officers by a very concise and comprehensive section contained in the statute,[1] which provides a maximum punishment of six months' imprisonment with hard labour and the deprivation of one month's pay.

One of the sections of the Act ran thus: "No person shall be appointed to the Police Force unless he be of sound constitution, able to ride, active and able-bodied, of good character, and between the ages of eighteen and forty years; nor unless he be able to read and write either the English or French language."

With regard to payment, the following scale was arranged: For the Commissioner, a salary not exceeding $2600 (£520) a year and not less than $2000; for a Superintendent, not exceeding $1400 and not less than $1000; for a paymaster, not exceeding $900; for a quartermaster, not exceeding $500; for a surgeon, not exceeding $1400 and not less than $1000; for a veterinary surgeon, not

---

[1] The North-West Mounted Police was organised under the Dominion Statute 56 Vict. cap. 35. This Act, as amended by 37 Vict. cap. 22, and 38 Vict. cap. 50, conferred upon members of the Force the powers and functions which they respectively exercise in the North-West Territories, and, if required, in every Province of the Dominion, for the purpose of carrying out the criminal and other laws of the Dominion.

exceeding $600 and not less than $400. Ordinary constables were to be remunerated at the rate of $1.00 per day, and sub-constables at 75 cents per day.

The first steps towards actually organising the new Force were taken in the autumn of 1873. Recruiting officers were then appointed east and west to form the nuclei of the three divisions which it was contemplated to create. Many of these officers came from the active militia, some having seen service in Manitoba, and these were soon successful in attracting men to the ranks. The recruits most desired were time-expired men from the militia force in Manitoba and other branches of the service. Not a few of these answered the call, but the rest were drawn from all classes and conditions.[1]

By October about a hundred and fifty Mounted Policemen had been enrolled and dispatched to the temporary headquarters at Lower Fort Garry, Manitoba. Here the command was taken over by Lieutenant-Colonel George A. French, a Royal Artillery officer who held the posts of Inspector of Artillery and Commandant of A Battery, R.C.A., and the School of Gunnery at Kingston, Ontario. The Commissioner lost no time in taking up his new appointment, though in November of the same year he lost the immediate support of Sir John Macdonald. A political crisis had brought about the resignation of the Ministry, and Sir John had been succeeded in office by the Hon. Alexander Mackenzie. In the Macdonald administration the Police had been placed under the direction of the Minister of Justice, an office held by the Premier. In the

[1] The first man to be enrolled was A. H. Griesbach, who had formerly served in the 15th Hussars and the Cape Mounted Rifles. He was the first Regimental Sergeant-Major of the Force. In November 1903, he retired on pension, with the rank of Superintendent.

THE COMING OF THE POLICE

new Cabinet this portfolio was held by the Hon. A. A. Dorion, who naturally assumed control of the Force.

To a great extent Colonel French was given a free hand in his task. Having proceeded without delay to Manitoba, he made himself acquainted with all the details of the new scheme. Questions of transport and supplies were discussed with various authorities, and everything was done that was possible in the short space of time to ensure success. The expedition westward was arranged for an early date in the spring. There was thus much to be carried out before the actual march began.

In the first place, a survey of the situation convinced Colonel French that a hundred and a half men were too few for the matter in hand. The Force must be brought up to its full strength of 300. This view he pressed upon the authorities at Ottawa, with such good result that a strong effort was made to augment the Force. Some 200 men were enlisted and mobilised at Toronto, where they were quickly put through the preliminary drills. This new body constituted three more divisions, D, E, and F, and altogether brought up the total of the Police to about 280.[1] The recruits themselves were, for the most part, experienced men, the only weak spot being want of practice in riding. There was good time, however, for improvement in this direction before they were actually placed in the field, and it was

---

[1] The strength of the Force in 1874, under the Act and Order in Council, was a Commissioner in command, an Assistant-Commissioner, 6 inspectors, 12 sub-inspectors, 2 surgeons, a paymaster, a quartermaster, a veterinary surgeon, and 300 non-commissioned officers and men, divided into six divisions, each having 3 officers, 1 staff constable, 4 constables, and 4 acting constables, doing duties similar to those performed by captains, subalterns, sergeant-majors, and sergeants and corporals respectively in the regular service.

satisfactory to know that their efficiency in drilling and shooting was fairly high.

A considerable number of the men newly enrolled had served either in her Majesty's regular service, in the Royal Irish Constabulary, or in the schools of gunnery at Kingston and Quebec. There were very few, indeed, states the Commissioner in his report, who had not had some previous military experience. This fact augured well for the future. It was no body of raw, undisciplined recruits which was being drafted into the north-west, but a force of capable, proved soldiers such as Sir John Macdonald had had in his mind's eye. There was no room in the expedition for weaklings or faint hearts. Such were not asked to go, and every opportunity was afforded them to withdraw in time.

On two distinct occasions at Toronto the Commissioner assembled all ranks on parade, and, putting before them plainly the conditions under which they would have to serve, called on any who were not prepared to undergo the probable hardships and privations to fall out and take their discharges. A small number did so, and the Force was thus weeded of an undesirable element.

The three newly formed divisions left Toronto by train *via* Chicago, St. Paul, and Fargo on 6th June 1874. They comprised 16 officers, 201 men, and 244 horses. A large quantity of waggons, stores, and agricultural implements accompanied them in separate cases, the whole making an imposing show when they arrived at their journey's end on the 12th. The Fargo people, it is said, when they saw the assortment of goods emptied from the cars and strewn upon the ground, declared that the Police would not get away under a week. However, they were mistaken.

THE COMING OF THE POLICE

By means of properly organised reliefs of men the expedition was quickly put into shape. The several pieces of waggons, saddlery, and guns were sorted out and put together, so that at five o'clock p.m. on the following day D Division drove out with twenty-nine loaded waggons. E Division took the road two hours later, and by the next afternoon F Division had cleared up everything, with the exception of heavy stores which were to be sent down by steamer. The 14th of June being a Sunday, the Force remained in camp, and the actual start was deferred to the 15th. From that day the rate of progress was a little under 30 miles per diem, the three divisions reaching Dufferin on the 19th without any serious mishap.

At Dufferin were already the A, B, and C Divisions, under the command of the newly appointed Assistant-Commissioner, James Farquharson Macleod, C.M.G. The whole Force now went into camp on the north side of the Boundary Commission ground, preparatory to setting out on its great march westward.

On the night after their arrival one of the most dreadful thunderstorms ever witnessed in the country burst over them. "There was apparently one incessant sheet of lightning from 10 p.m. to 6 a.m.," says the Commissioner in his report. "About midnight two hundred and fifty of our horses stampeded from the corral in which they were placed, breaking halters, picquet ropes, etc., and even knocking over some of the waggons which encircled them. It was a fearful sight; several of our men had the hardihood to attempt to stop some of the horses, but it only resulted in their being knocked over and trampled on, and in this manner six of our pluckiest men got hurt, one of them being seriously injured about the head. On pages

254 and 255 of *Army Life on the Border*, by General Marcy, U.S.A., there is a description and illustration of a stampede—one extract will suffice here : ' Soon after the storm set in one of our herd of three hundred horses and mules broke furiously away from the herdsmen who were guarding them, and in spite of their utmost efforts ran at full speed directly with the wind *for fifty miles before they stopped.* Three of the herdsmen followed them as far as they were able, but soon became exhausted, bewildered, and lost on the prairie.'

" We had the good fortune to recover most of ours within a distance of 35 miles, probably in a great measure due to the freshness having been taken out of them by their 160-mile march from Fargo. Many days were lost in recovering the horses, and much injury done, riding in every direction looking for them. Our loss eventually was reduced to one, and this one was supposed to have been drowned in the Pembina River."

Having recovered from this disaster, the force applied itself to the serious business of getting ready for the march. The first three divisions being somewhat below their proper strength, fifty men more were transferred from D, E, and F to make good the deficiency. Then uniforms, clothing, arms and ammunition, saddlery, harness, and general stores were served out, to be packed in waggons and ox-carts. Every one was hard at work, either in the camp or engaged in such other duties as herding horses upon the prairie.

As at Toronto, so at Dufferin, there was still some purging of the Force to be undergone. Badly cooked food (and it must be admitted that the regimental bakers did not do their duty in this respect), mosquitoes, and

THE COMING OF THE POLICE

alarming reports of Indian atrocities that came in, such as the Sioux murders at St. Ives, only 30 miles distant, turned the scale for the few chicken-hearted ones who were left. The proximity to the boundary line was too tempting, and one by one they slunk out of the lines and decamped. As the Commissioner had anticipated their desertion, and had had the foresight to bring with him twenty spare men, the Force was not short-handed after all.

The march to the west began on the 10th of July, the two previous days having been occupied in moving to a fresh camp a few miles from Dufferin, more with a view to seeing that all was right than with the idea of making a start.[1] On the first day 10 miles were covered. The expeditionary train was undoubtedly the largest ever seen in those parts. When closed up to a proper interval it was $1\frac{1}{2}$ miles long; but from advanced to rear guard it more usually extended from 4 to 5 miles, owing to the uneven rate of travel of horses and oxen, and to the frequent breaking of axles and wheels of that " imposition of the country," the Red River cart.

The column *en route* presented a fine, and at the same time an astonishing, appearance. In the van came A Division, with their splendid dark bays, and thirteen waggons. After them followed B Division, with dark brown horses; C, with light chestnuts, drawing the guns and gun and small-arm ammunition; D, with their greys; E, with their black horses; and lastly F, with their light bays. In the rear of the six divisions came a motley

[1] Marching-out state, Dufferin, 8th July 1874: Officers, 21; constables, 254; horses, 310; guides and half-breeds, 20; field guns, 2; mortars, 2; working oxen, 142; cattle, 93; waggons (double), 73; ox-carts, 114. The balance of the men (37) and horses (27) were left " on command " at Fort Ellice and Dufferin. See Appendix A.

string of ox-carts, waggons, cattle for slaughter, cows, calves, etc., and a variety of mowing machines and other agricultural appliances. These last represented the more peaceable side of the expedition. In addition to the fighting that would be necessary, the little Force had to establish posts in the far north-west—to take upon itself, in fact, the duties of a coloniser.

The presence of a large quantity of live cattle accompanying the Police was in accordance with the conclusion arrived at by Commissioner French after his preliminary investigations. In reporting to the Government in January 1874, he had advised that the stores and provisions for the force should be transported westwards by their own horses and oxen, and that cattle for slaughter should be driven on foot, instead of pork or pemmican being carried in large quantities.

To the observer's eye the Police troopers made a striking picture as they rode along. Sir John Macdonald had been insistent that the dominant note in the uniform should be scarlet, this colour conveying the strongest impression to the mind of the Indian through his respect for "the Queen's soldiers." It was desirable that the military side of the Force should be emphasised, and that the men should be distinguishable from the American blue-coated soldiers. On this point, too, Colonel Robertson-Ross had been explicit in his report. "During my inspection in the north-west," he said, "I ascertained that some prejudice existed among the Indians against the colour of the uniform worn by the men of the Provisional Battalion. Many of them had said: 'Who are those soldiers at Red River wearing dark clothes ? Our old brothers who formerly lived there' (meaning H.M. 6th Regiment) wore red coats,'

TYPES OF UNIFORM, 1874–1885.

adding, 'we know that the soldiers of our Great Mother wear red coats and are our friends.'"

The uniform, therefore, consisted of scarlet Norfolk jackets without facings, brown leather belts and haversacks, white helmets with showy brass spikes and chin-scales (decorated in the case of officers with long plumes), breeches of steel-grey cloth, and brown jack-boots. Officers' breeches were of yellow cord. In undress a round forage-cap was worn. Later on, the grey breeches of the men gave place to blue cloth ones, having a broad yellow stripe down the side, and these have remained a distinctive feature of the uniform to the present day.

Fatigue dress was of brown duck, much of the same nature as is now worn. In winter fur caps, coats of buffalo skin (to be superseded by black Russian lambskin), buckskin mitts, moosehide moccasins, and long woollen stockings were the order of the day. The military button adorning the uniform originally bore a crown; this was afterwards replaced by one bearing a buffalo's head, surmounted by a crown, and a label with the letters "N.W.M.P. Canada."

For arms the rank and file were equipped with Snider carbines and revolvers, the cartridges for these being carried in brown leather bandoliers and waist-belts. Only the officers and sergeants were allowed to wear swords. The saddle used was the old "Universal" one, but this proved less serviceable in later years, and was replaced by the high-peaked "Californian." It was found to be too heavy and too much cumbered with buckles and straps.

To return to the march westward, the Force covered the 270 miles to Roche Percée in good order, grass and water having been fairly plentiful along the line of route. The Boundary Commission Road was followed for the most

THE COMING OF THE POLICE

part. At Roche Percée the Commissioner broke up the train, detailing a number of horses, waggons, carts, oxen, and cows with their calves, together with a dozen men from A Division, as many half-breeds, and six men on the sick list, to proceed to Fort Ellice under Inspector Jarvis. This depletion of men, horses, and stores was necessitated by the cancelling of the previous arrangements for leaving men on the Bow and Belly Rivers. That it did not seriously diminish the column as a fighting force is evident from the Commissioner's report, only the weakest of the horses being sent away.

From Roche Percée the Boundary Road struck southwards into United States territory, so the Police were compelled to make a road for themselves. Some days later they were once more on the Road, " the Coteau of the Missouri looming up to our left, bare, parched, and uninviting looking," but soon after they were on rough, unbroken ground again. The heavy going at this point told considerably upon the horses, and a fortnight later some twenty-eight of these, with cattle, stores, and several waggons under a guard of men, were left at a dépôt known as Cripple Camp.

Thus lightened, the force now made better progress, and on 24th August sighted the Cypress Hills. They were now in the country of the Plains Indians, many parties of whom occasionally visited the soldiers. Buffalo, also, were seen for the first time. Other visitors to the camp were half-breeds, who regaled the newcomers with " tall " stories relative to the doings of the whisky traders. One of their toughest yarns was that five hundred of these gentry had been working at their forts all the summer, constructing underground galleries into which to retire when the big guns were brought to bear upon them. To these reports, however, the Police paid little attention.

By the 6th of September the Saskatchewan was reached. The objective of the force was the Forks made by the Bow and Belly Rivers, not far distant to the south-west, and this point was at last attained, though not until the Commissioner had ignored his guide's advice and trusted to his own observations. Owing to the buffalo having eaten up all the grass, this district proved to be " little better than a desert." Not a tree was to be seen, the ground was poor, and wherever there had been a little swamp it was destroyed. From the entries in the Commissioner's diary it may be gathered that he considered his position a serious one. The column had marched a distance of 781 miles from Red River, and after the first eighteen had not seen a single human habitation beyond a few isolated Indian wigwams.

" It was now the middle of September," Colonel French notes, " and the appalling fact was ever pressing on my mind that on the 20th September of last year the whole country from the Cypress Hills to the Old Wives Lakes was covered with a foot of snow, several men and horses having been frozen to death. All over this country there is little wood, and snow would hide the buffalo chips, the only fuel available. I could not possibly reach this portion of the country till well into October ; however, the snowstorm we had experienced had been exceptionally early, and I hoped for the best, while determined to prepare for the worst."

The desire of the Commissioner now was to discover some place where good feed for the horses and cattle could be obtained. To this end the Force struck south to the

THE COMING OF THE POLICE

Trois Buttes, or Sweet Grass Hills. Meanwhile the Bow and Belly Rivers were explored, but without success. The only fact of importance elicited was that there were no whisky-trading posts in the vicinity. As this district, however, was one which had been favoured by the traders, and as they had signified their intention of returning after the Police had left the country, it was decided to allow a portion of the Force to be stationed there.

While this move was in progress, Colonel French and Colonel Macleod with a few guides proceeded to Fort Benton, Montana, to obtain fresh supplies of oats, moccasins, socks, and other necessaries. Here also were found telegrams from the authorities at Ottawa approving of the establishment of a Mounted Police post on the Belly River, and intimating that the headquarters of the Force in future would be the vicinity of Fort Pelly [1] instead of Fort Ellice. In accordance with his instructions Colonel French arranged with the Assistant-Commissioner, Colonel Macleod, to take a detachment to Fort Whoop Up,[2] on the Belly River, this old trading post to be the headquarters and main scene of operations in that part of the north-west.

Having left Colonel Macleod in his new quarters in the very heart of the Blackfeet country, and having further dispatched another detachment, under Inspector Walsh, northwards to Edmonton among the Assiniboines and Wood Crees, the Commissioner turned the main body in

---

[1] Near the Swan River, on the borders of Saskatchewan and Manitoba. An old Hudson's Bay Company post.

[2] The frequent use of the word " Fort " is explained by the fact that in the north-west any log hut where a trader made his headquarters was so designated. These posts were usually named after the trader who built them, as in the case of Fort Kipp, Fort Benton, and so on. Fort Whoop Up, by its name, would seem to have been a central meeting-place for traders.

the direction of home. The first, and most difficult, half of his task had been accomplished.

The return journey was made by way of the plains northward to Qu'Appelle, where the Hudson's Bay Company had an important post. Nothing eventful occurred during the march, save an occasional prairie fire and a consequent shortage in fodder for the horses and cattle. It was now much colder, the thermometer at times registering as low a temperature as 20 and 30 degrees below zero. With all this there was little or no grumbling. The men bore the discomforts of the trip bravely, and on their arrival at Dufferin early in November, gave the lie to the discreditable reports that had been circulated regarding the Force. It is a sad reflection on the Canadian press that several newspapers of that date grossly misrepresented the state of affairs, and, indeed, brought grave charges against those responsible for the organisation of the expedition. The officers were characterised as "incapable" and "inexperienced," while the men were said to be "careless" and "disheartened." How far removed were these rumours from the actual truth was speedily demonstrated.

The return of the Force to Dufferin, instead of to Fort Pelly, was due to the fact that their new headquarters were not yet ready for them. The delay caused, however, was insignificant. Colonel French had every reason to be satisfied with the results of the great march. In all, the Force had travelled 1959 miles, excluding the distances covered by detachments on special service, in four months, and this in a country the natural difficulties of which severely taxed the strength of both men and horses.

As the Commissioner stated in his report to the Govern-

THE COMING OF THE POLICE

ment, the Police troops on leaving Dufferin in July had started on an expedition which veteran soldiers might well have faltered at. " Tied down by no stringent rules or articles of war, but only by the silken cord of a civil contract, these men by their conduct gave little cause of complaint. Though naturally there were several officers and constables unaccustomed to command and having little experience or tact, yet such an event as striking a superior was unknown, and disobedience of orders was very rare. Day after day on the march, night after night on picquet or guard, and working at high pressure during four months from daylight until dark, and too frequently after dark, with little rest, not even on the day sacred to rest, the force ever pushed onward, delighted when occasionally a pure spring was met with. There was still no complaint when salt water or the refuse of a mud-hole was the only liquid available. And I have seen this whole force obliged to drink liquid, which when passed through a filter was still the colour of ink. The fact of horses and oxen failing and dying for want of food never disheartened or stopped them, but pushing on, on foot, with dogged determination, they carried through the service required of them, under difficulties which can only be appreciated by those who witnessed them."

Of such a march, truly one of the most extraordinary on record, all Canadians might well feel proud. The first blow had been struck in the far north-west against the elements of lawlessness and disorder, and momentous results were to follow therefrom.

CHAPTER III.

OUTPOSTS IN THE WILDERNESS.

Colonel Macleod's great task—Fort Macleod—The first blow at the liquor traffic—Dealings with the Indians—Chief Red Crow—Major-General Selby Smyth—Inspection of the Force—New posts established—Old Fort Walsh—The magic of the red coat—Important changes—Lieut.-Colonel Macleod, second Commissioner.

TO Colonel Macleod, the Assistant-Commissioner, at his lonely post in the north-west there now fell a most responsible task, the introduction of law and order into a country where hitherto no organised attempt at such had been made, and where a considerable amount of opposition might naturally be expected. For a long time past the region had been characterised by a spirit of lawlessness; it was the hunting-ground of desperadoes to whom as yet no check had been given. But over the temporary quarters of his detachment, little more than a hundred strong, now flew the British flag, to tell all and sundry that a new era had dawned for both white and red men. It was a notification to all that the Dominion had a law, and that henceforward that law was going to be carried into effect.

The first thing the Assistant-Commissioner set himself to do was to find a location suitable for his headquarters. A reconnaissance was made and a level strip of land chosen on the bank of the Old Man's River. This site held out the advantages of good wood and water, together with a

"F" DIVISION

OLD MAN'S RIVER

Quarters 23'	Kitchen 10'	Quarters 23'	Forge	Officers Latrine / B.DIV'N LATRINE

	18'			
	22' F	22' C	10' Mess Room 32'	32' B	11' Ord'ly Room / 11' Ass't Com'y

OFFICERS QUARTERS

GATE 18'

GUNS

Guard Room

Qu. 20'

MAGAZINE

15'

B. DIV'N. Latrine 40'

48'

N

OUTPOSTS IN THE WILDERNESS

fairly abundant crop of feed for the horses. The question of forage was of the utmost importance. Nearly all of the horses in his troop were run down, the best animals having been requisitioned by the Commissioner for his homeward march. Another advantage the place offered was the fact that it commanded the route most used by the American traders.

In due course a fort was erected here, and named after Colonel Macleod himself. It was in the approved form of a square, the buildings, which were of timber, including living quarters for officers and men, stables, workshops, stores, a hospital, forge, and magazine. Two 9-pounder field guns were mounted near the latter. There were two gates, one on the western and one on the southern side. The precise situation of its various features will be found on the accompanying map.

From the first, Colonel Macleod's position was no enviable one. He was many hundreds of miles away from the nearest reinforcements, and in a hostile country where, to use a colloquialism, he was sure to be " up against trouble." The whisky traders were not his only foes; the Indians—Blackfeet, Crees, Assiniboines, Bloods, and Piegans—had to be reckoned with as a possibly disturbing element, for their numbers and disposition towards the Police were unknown. But the right man had been selected for this onerous work. Colonel Macleod was not the man to let the grass grow under his feet or to show any sign of weakness in dealing with the difficult problem that confronted him.

Having established himself firmly in his new quarters, he proceeded to patrol the district and acquaint himself with the trading posts therein. The principal one of these,

THE RIDERS OF THE PLAINS

Fort Hamilton, a little to the south-east of Fort Macleod, and near to where the mining town of Lethbridge now stands, he occupied in October of the same year, 1874. This post, we are told, was " of the stockyard type, almost square, and with two bastions, or ' flankers ' as they were generally called on the frontier. The walls were loopholed, and there were two 3-pounder guns in the position. Outside the stockyard were two detached corrals and a hay-shed." Only a few hundred yards distant, it may be noted, were the ruins of old Fort Whoop Up, which had suffered almost complete destruction by fire.

It was characteristic of the Assistant-Commissioner's energy that by the end of October he was able to report a notable piece of work performed. "I am happy to inform you," he wrote to Colonel French, " that although we have all been very busy in the construction of our winter quarters, we have been able to carry on some Police duty as well, and have struck a first blow at the liquor traffic in this country."

The case in question was the capture and arrest of a coloured man named Bond and three other Americans, who had a trading post at a place called Pine Coulé, about 50 miles from Fort Macleod. Information as to this man and his dealings reached the Police through an Indian, " Three Bulls." The latter had bartered two of his horses for a couple of gallons of whisky. To avoid rousing suspicion in the traders' minds Colonel Macleod arranged for his interpreter, Jerry Potts, to meet " Three Bulls " at a certain point the next night and obtain more exact particulars. Mr. Crozier, of the Force, with ten mounted men, was to be ready to move out of camp when the moment for action came.

The scheme succeeded admirably. Guided by Potts, the Police troopers rode down upon Bond and his associates after a 40-miles' chase and arrested the entire party, five in number. They also captured two waggons, each of which contained cases of alcohol, some rifles, revolvers, and buffalo robes. These last were promptly confiscated, having been obviously traded for liquor by the Indians.

At the trial the Assistant-Commissioner and the inspectors who sat with him fined the two principals and Bond (their interpreter and guide) two hundred dollars each for having intoxicating liquors in their possession. The other two prisoners, who were less responsible, were fined fifty dollars apiece. On the following day a Benton trader named Weatherwax came in and paid all the fines with the exception of that of Bond. The coloured man was therefore detained on the other charge of trading liquor to "Three Bulls." As he was unable to pay his fine, Bond was sentenced to a term of imprisonment, but, later on, in December, he managed to break gaol and got clear away.

This salutary lesson, and others that followed, had the results that might have been expected. At the close of the year we find the Assistant-Commissioner "happy to be able to report" that the whisky trade had been completely stopped throughout the whole of that section of the country, and that the drunken riots, which in former years were of almost daily occurrence, were entirely at an end. A more peaceable community, he stated, with a very large number of Indians camped along the river, could not be found anywhere. The change that had come over the district was certainly remarkable. People left their doors unlocked at night without any fear of goods being stolen, whereas, before the arrival of the Police, gates and doors all had to be fastened securely after dark, and nothing could be left out of sight. So strong was the Indians' passion for whisky that locks and bars were ineffectual in keeping them out of the traders' houses. They had been known to climb up on the roofs and break a hole through the earth with which the buildings were covered, while in some instances they even slid down the chimneys.

Such a state of things was extremely gratifying to Colonel Macleod, and hardly less so to the Commissioner, who was now quartered at Fort Garry. To have performed so much in a few months augured well for Police work in the future. Next to the suppression of the whisky traffic the most important duty was the conciliation and protection of the Indians. In dealing with this side of his task the Assistant-Commissioner was signally successful. He held several interviews with the neighbouring chiefs, and impressed upon them the friendliness which the Government felt towards them. At the same time he did not hesitate to point out that the infringement of certain laws would entail punishment, and that the Police were there to see that these laws were enforced.

In this politic treatment one sees the striking contrast between the British and American methods. Recognising from the outset that the Indians possessed undoubted rights in the country, Colonel Macleod and others who later on entered into negotiations with the various tribes, showed themselves to be the true friends, protectors, and advisers of the red men. They were scrupulously honest in all transactions with them, and by this means so won their confidence and esteem that whenever a crisis arose the prestige of the Police carried them through it successfully.

It is interesting to note the expressions of the Indians themselves on this point at the subsequent treaty meetings —a time when, so Jerry Potts averred, they spoke their minds more freely than he had ever heard them do. Said Chief Crowfoot : " If the Police had not come to the country, where would we be all now ? Bad men and whisky were killing us so fast that very few, indeed, of us would have been left to-day. The Police have protected us as the feathers of the bird protect it from the frosts of winter. I wish them all good, and trust that all our hearts will increase in goodness from this time forward." And Red Crow : " Three years ago, when the Police first came to the country, I met and shook hands with Stamixotokon [1] (Colonel Macleod) at Pelly River. Since that time he made me many promises. He kept them all—not one of them was ever broken. Everything that the Police have done has been good. I entirely trust Stamixotokon, and will leave everything to him."

The same Crowfoot, Chief of the Blackfeet Indians, referred to above, had his first introduction to Colonel Macleod in December 1874. It was highly important that this tribe should be won over to the side of the Police, because of their large numbers and warlike nature. We have a glimpse of how these meetings were conducted in a report sent to the Commissioner about this date. Colonel Macleod writes :—

" The interviews with all the Indians are not carried on with the whole band, the chiefs and two or three of their chief warriors only being brought to me by my interpreter. Upon being introduced they all shake hands, and invariably

---

[1] The name given to Colonel Macleod by the Indians: literally " Bull's Head."

express their delight at meeting me. They then sit down, and my interpreter lights and hands the chief a pipe, which he smokes for a few seconds and then passes to the others, and all remain silent to hear what I have got to say. I then explain to them what the Government has sent this force into the country for, and endeavour to give them a general idea of the laws which will be enforced, telling them that not only the white men but Indians also will be punished for breaking them, and impressing upon them that they need not fear being punished for doing what they do not know is wrong. I then tell them also that we have not come to take their land from them (an intimation they all receive with great pleasure), but that when the Government want to speak to them about this matter their great men will be sent for the purpose, and that they will know the intentions of the Government before anything is done.

"The chief then stands up and shakes hands with every one, and makes a speech, expressing his great delight at our arrival; tells how they were being robbed and ruined by the whisky traders ; that their horses, robes, and women were taken from them ; that their young men were continually engaged in drunken riots, and numbers of them shot ; that their horses were gradually decreasing in numbers, and that before long they would not have enough to chase the buffalo, and would have no means of procuring food—that all this was now changed, and, as one old chief expressed it, suiting the action to his words, 'Before you came the Indian crept along, now he is not afraid to walk erect.' After the chief has finished, I make him and his warriors a few presents of clothing and tobacco, and a further quantity of tobacco in proportion to the number of his followers."

But it was not, of course, all plain sailing with the Indians, either then or in later years after the treaties had been concluded and the tribes were settled on their reservations. Witness this story of Red Crow, Chief of the Blood Indians.

The scene is again Fort Macleod. Two members of Red Crow's band were wanted on a serious charge of cattle-killing, " Prairie Chicken Old Man " being the picturesque name of one. Both men were known to be in the Indian camp in the vicinity of Fort Stand Off, and a sergeant and a constable were sent out to arrest them. With all promptitude they marched straight to the encampment. Having secured their prisoners, they were about to lead them away when their howls brought a number of squaws and young " braves " to the spot. There was a scuffle, and the Police found their captives forcibly wrested from them. In the excitement the youthful constable drew his revolver, and a worse riot would have been precipitated had not the sergeant immediately ordered him to replace the weapon.

Recognising that it was more discreet to retire for the time being, the Policemen returned to Fort Macleod to report to Superintendent Steele, then commandant. That officer approved of their action in the circumstances, but he had no intention of allowing the Indians to defy him. He accordingly ordered Inspector Wood, Dr. S. M. Fraser, and a non-commissioned officer with twenty troopers to proceed at once to the camp and demand the surrender of the two men. With them went that faithful ally, Jerry Potts, the half-breed interpreter.

THE RIDERS OF THE PLAINS

The little company marched out to within a mile or so of the camp, which lay on the other side of some low hills. Then Potts was sent forward to make known that Superintendent Steele required both the men previously arrested and those who had aided and abetted their release. In due time the interpreter returned to announce that Red Crow was smoking his pipe, and would think the matter over. The chief sent word also that his young " braves " were very excited ; a Sun Dance was being held, and they were getting out of hand. In a word, the old Indian game of " bluff " was tried. To this Inspector Wood replied curtly : " Tell Red Crow that we must have the two men wanted, and those who helped to rescue them, within one hour's time ; and Red Crow must bring them in in person. Otherwise, we shall ride in and take them. In which case," he added, " Red Crow will have to abide the consequences."

When the ultimatum was delivered by Potts there was a great uproar in the camp. The young men of the band were worked up to a high pitch of excitement by the dance, and were more in the mood for fighting than before. The situation was a critical one. The minutes slipped by, and the time limit fixed was nearly reached without any sign from the Indians. It was a tense moment for the Police as they waited ; there was no knowing that they were not in for a pretty stiff tussle. At last, the hour having expired, the Inspector gave the word to mount, and the troopers got ready to move, when suddenly a solitary Indian appeared on the brow of the hill. After him came another, then two more, followed by others in small parties, until quite a number were seen to be approaching. Among them was the chief, Red Crow, himself.

OUTPOSTS IN THE WILDERNESS

With the Police by their side the whole mob were marched into Fort Macleod, where Superintendent Steele was ready to sit in judgment upon them. Those who had helped in the recapture of the prisoners were dealt with first, and severely admonished for their behaviour. Then Red Crow was summoned to receive a sharp lecture on his conduct. After him " Prairie Chicken Old Man " was brought in, handcuffed, sentenced, and led out in full view of his friends to the guard-room. The second prisoner was similarly served, none of the other Indians daring to lift a finger in their defence.

This sharp lesson had its effect. Red Crow's band was duly impressed, and departed back to their camp with chastened hearts. In consideration of their final good behaviour, however, and of the fact that they had come some distance, the Superintendent made them a few presents of tea, tobacco, and other things before they left. It may be added that " Prairie Chicken Old Man " and his brother in crime subsequently each received a sentence of seven years' imprisonment.

Superintendent Steele, to whom reference has been made, and whose name will figure in several other exploits to be narrated, held the rank of Troop-Sergeant-Major in the earlier days of Fort Macleod. He formed one of the original party that made the memorable march into the north-west, and was left behind to help the Assistant-Commissioner in his work. In October 1874 he was detailed to accompany Inspector W. D. Jarvis to Edmonton. This expedition was a notable one, the long journey being accomplished with weak horses, little or no pasture, and for the last 500 miles without any grain. The latter part of the march was made over roads that were impassable until a number of men with axes went in advance to fell trees and make "corderoye" over mud-holes. Several bridges also had to be erected over rivers and creeks.

"Had it not been for the perfect conduct of the men," reported the Inspector, "and real hard work, much of the property (stores, etc.) must have been destroyed. I wish particularly to bring to your notice the names of Troop-Sergt.-Major Steele and Constable Labelle. Sergt.-Major Steele has been undeviating in his efforts to assist me, and he has also done the manual labour of at least two men. The attention paid by Constable Labelle to the horses has saved many of them."

The first winter passed by the Police in the north-west set at rest any doubts that may have existed as to their fitness for the great task entrusted to them. The whisky traders had been hit "well and good," and much had been done in winning the confidence of the Indians. All the next year (1875) the work went steadily forward, the area of operations being widely extended. New posts were established at different points, and patrols sent out to survey the country.[1]

In the summer of that year an important tour of military inspection was undertaken by Major-General E. Selby Smyth, the then commandant of the Canadian Militia. Starting from Fort Garry, in Manitoba, the general visited all the detachments of the Police in turn. He found them efficient in most respects, and reported

---

[1] At this period—during the winter of 1874–5—the disposition of the Police Force was as follows: A Division at Fort Ellice and Edmonton, under Inspector Jarvis; B, C, and F Divisions at Fort Macleod, under the Assistant-Commissioner; D Division at headquarters, Dufferin, Man.; and E Division at Fort Pelly and the Swan River post, under Inspector Carvell.

very favourably upon the work they had accomplished. It was satisfactory to note how, even at that early stage, the presence of the red-coated troopers caused a feeling of security in the minds of the settlers in the new territories.

On the question of the *personnel* of the force the General had some minor criticisms to make, as also upon the selection of horses. He advocated the recruiting of more men from the rural districts, especially sons of farmers, who were better fitted for the rough-and-ready open-air life than those from the towns. But on the whole, he was well satisfied with what he saw. " Of the constables and sub-constables," he said, " I can speak generally that they are an able body of men, of excellent material, and conspicuous for willingness, endurance, and, as far as I can learn, integrity of character. They are fairly disciplined, but there has hardly been an opportunity yet for maturing discipline to the extent desirable in bodies of armed men, and, dispersed as they are through the immensity of space without much communication with headquarters, a great deal must depend upon the individual intelligence, acquirements, and steadiness of the Inspectors in perfecting discipline, drill, interior economy, equitation, and care of horses, saddlery, and equipment, together with Police duties on which they might be occasionally required."

This passage in General Selby Smyth's report is interesting in touching upon the characteristic note of the Royal North-West Mounted Police. With such a small body controlling so wide an area, the call upon the individual intelligence of its members has been very great. A weight of responsibility has been thrown time after time upon

THE RIDERS OF THE PLAINS

the shoulders of both officers and men, and it is the boast of the force that very rarely indeed has the man been unequal to the occasion. When we come to examine the records we find abundant testimony to the ability, courage, and self-possession of the humblest trooper in circumstances which might well have daunted a more seasoned man. The following chapters contain several striking instances of this, selected from many, all of them exemplifying the remarkable *esprit de corps* that has grown up with the force.

Among the new Police posts inspected by General Selby Smyth on his tour, was that established on the Bow River at its junction with the Elbow River. At this spot there had been for some years a fur-trading station belonging to a well-known Montana firm. The site was an excellent one, and under the superintendence of Inspector Brisebois a Police fort was built. For a time this post was known as "Fort Brisebois," but finally the name of Calgarry was bestowed upon it by Colonel Macleod in honour of his birthplace in Scotland. The spelling of the name became modified in the course of years, one "r" being dropped, and thus we have the present form of Calgary (with the accent on the first syllable), which denominates the thriving town that has sprung up round the old fort.

Other posts that quickly came into existence were those at Fort Walsh, in the Cypress Hills; Fort Saskatchewan, in the Edmonton district; and at Battleford, Swan River, Shoal Lake, and Qu'Appelle. An encouraging feature of these stations was that settlements were beginning to spring up around them, as was soon the case at Calgary. In addition to their duties as guardians of law and order

OLD FORT MACLEOD.

THE RIDERS OF THE PLAINS

in the north-west, the Police acted literally as pioneers in the work of opening up the country for settlers. Once the illicit liquor traffic had been got under, they were enabled to turn their attention to the more peaceable but no less useful side of their mission.

Of old Fort Walsh we have a vivid picture presented to us in the several accounts of this post that have been given by old-timers. It was founded by Inspector Walsh of B Division in the spring of 1875, his instructions having been to proceed to the Cypress Hills with a view to choosing a location for a fort which should serve to keep in check the wandering bands of Crees, Salteaux, Assiniboines, Sioux, and other tribes near the International Boundary. These Indians, many of them belonging to the American States, were engaged in hunting the buffalo, and were subjected to many temptations on the part of traders who crossed the border.

The red hunters of the Cypress Hills must have gazed with considerable surprise at the long waggon train and string of uniformed riders toiling slowly over the plains from the south. But they were more surprised still to see the high, square stockade of the fort rear itself, with its bastions at the four corners, and its tall staff in the centre from which floated the British flag. Strategically considered, the new post was not in a very strong position, for it lay in a valley bordered by precipitous, bush-clad hills, which would have afforded vantage-ground to an enemy. The site was hastily chosen; winter was upon the heels of Inspector Walsh's little force, and they had to find shelter without delay.

In those old days when the painted Crees rode in on their wiry little ponies to treat with the commanding

SITE OF OLD FORT WALSH.
Now occupied by a ranch.

OUTPOSTS IN THE WILDERNESS

officer, many were the interesting scenes enacted at the historic old fort. Several times a tragedy was narrowly averted by the presence of mind and bold bearing of the Inspector and his officers. On one occasion a large number of Sioux, followers of the redoubtable chief, Sitting Bull, skulked in the underbrush of the hillside and were ready for any excuse to fire upon the troopers below. In this critical moment the commander of the little garrison went out bravely, tackled the old chief in person, and bluffed him so successfully that the band moved on without giving further trouble. On this occasion, by the way, Inspector Walsh literally carried his life in his hands. When he rode towards the Sioux camp he had on a short blue jacket with black braid, while his men were all wearing greatcoats. At the sight of the hated blue, the " American colour " to all Indians, the rifles of the " braves " went up instantly, covering the Inspector. Seeing his danger, one of the foremost troopers had the presence of mind to throw open his coat, revealing the scarlet tunic beneath, and in a moment the weapons dropped. These were the " Queen's soldiers " ; all was well.

More pleasing to the Police were the occasions when the Indians gathered in to the fort after a big buffalo hunt, and indulged in the amusements dear to them. Then there were trials of strength between the younger men, contests with bows and arrows, and dances of many kinds. Not least among the sports was that of horse-racing. The Indians were ever keen upon this, and the plains outside were the scene of wild enthusiasm when the races were held. There was never any lack of excitement. The dark-skinned competitors rode at full gallop from the start, and rode to win, quirting their ponies all

THE RIDERS OF THE PLAINS

the way, and making the place resound with their shrill cries.

In addition to the Indians, a considerable number of wandering bands of half-breeds were attracted to the post. These were in time collected together, so that in the winter of 1875–6 upwards of three hundred families were located in the vicinity, to be protected and helped through the long, dreary, cold months.

Old Fort Walsh is a thing of the past. It was abandoned in 1888, when the transcontinental railway crossed the prairies. Scarcely a vestige of it remains, and on its site in the fertile valley is now a large and prosperous ranch. And yet to the settler in the north-west its ruins might well have been as sacred as are those of old Fort Garry, the stones of which are so carefully preserved to this day in Winnipeg.

Following upon this development of the new western country came two important changes. From 1872 until 1875, what are now the extensive Provinces of Saskatchewan and Alberta had been under the control of the Lieutenant-Governor of Manitoba and a council appointed by the Dominion authorities. In the latter year a new bill was passed providing for the separate government of the North-West Territories, and in 1876 the Hon. David Laird, formerly Minister of the Interior, was appointed first Lieutenant-Governor.

The second change to be chronicled was the transference of control of the North-West Mounted Police from the Department of Justice to the Department of the Secretary of State. This came into force by an Order of Council dated 20th April 1876. In the following July Lieutenant-Colonel French resigned the Commissionership,

OUTPOSTS IN THE WILDERNESS

and was succeeded by Lieutenant-Colonel Macleod, with Lieutenant-Colonel A. G. Irvine as Assistant-Commissioner.[1]

On leaving the Police, Colonel French did not go into retirement. He returned to service in the Imperial army, and had a long and distinguished career, being particularly associated with the organisation of the Australian defensive forces. In 1877 he had been honoured with the C.M.G., in 1902 he became Major-General Sir George French, K.C.M.G., and in the same year retired from the service on full pay.

[1] At the end of 1876 the distribution of the North-West Mounted Police in the Territories was as follows:—

	Commissioner.	Assistant-Commissioner.	Surgeons.	Veterinary Surgeon.	Quartermaster.	Inspectors.	Sub-Inspectors.	Constables and Sub-Constables.	Horses.
Fort Macleod	1	1	1	...	...	1	5	103	105
Fort Walsh	...	...	1	...	1	1	4	95	90
Fort Calgary	...	...	...	...	...	1	1	35	37
Fort Saskatchewan	...	...	...	...	...	1	1	20	18
Battleford and Carlton	...	...	..	...	...	1	...	11	16
Swan River	...	...	1	1	...	1	1	29	10
Shoal Lake	...	...	...	...	...	...	1	7	4
Qu'Appelle	...	...	...	...	...	...	...	5	4
Beautiful Plains	...	...	...	...	...	...	...	4	3
Total	1	1	3	1	1	6	13	309	287

The expenditure during the fiscal year ending 30th June 1876, for the Mounted Police Service, was $369,518.39, this amount including $41,184.47 arrears of the fiscal years 1873–4 and 1874–5, also a charge of $19,762.95 for miscellaneous stores taken over from her Majesty's North American Boundary Commission in 1874–5.

CHAPTER IV.

INDIAN PROBLEMS.

The tribes in the north-west—Blackfeet and Crees—Savage warfare—Two sides of the shield—"The Moose that Walks"—Early Indian treaties — The Blackfeet Treaty — Indian oratory — A bloodless revolution.

AT this stage in our story of the Royal North-West Mounted Police it is necessary to say something about the numerous Indian tribes who occupied the north-west, and whose presence there caused the Government no little concern. Ever since 1869, when the first Riel Rebellion agitated the country, the maintenance of friendly relations with the red men was a problem that Canadian statesmen had to grapple with. The future of the western provinces depended on the proper treatment of this grave question.

Of the Canadian Indians the principal tribes living in the area between Lake Superior and the Rocky Mountains were the Ojibbeways (also known as Chippewas and Salteaux), Crees, Blackfeet, Assiniboines, and Sioux. The first-named favoured the Province of Manitoba and the district of Keewatin ("the land of the north wind"), having migrated thither in previous years after the settlement of Quebec and Ontario. The Crees, who were divided into Plain, Wood, and Swampy Crees, according to the localities in which they resided, spread very generally through the Territories. The Swampy Crees, however,

INDIAN PROBLEMS

mostly kept to Manitoba. Equally numerous and important were the Blackfeet, hereditary enemies of the Crees. This warlike tribe inhabited a district about 50,000 square miles in area, lying at the south-west angle of the territories, north of the boundary line, east of the Rocky Mountains, south of Red River, and west of the Cypress Hills.

What was known as the Blackfoot Confederacy included four clans, the Blackfeet, Bloods, Piegans, and Sarcees. The last-named were really a branch of the Peace River Indians, called Beavers. They were all highly intelligent, good hunters and fierce fighters. Moreover, they were extremely jealous of their country, and rarely allowed any white men, half-breeds, or other Indians to remain in it for any length of time.

The Assiniboines—a kindred race to the Sioux—took their name from the Assiniboine River (literally the "Stony River," whence the tribe are often referred to as the Stonies). A warlike people, like the Sioux, they were formerly much more powerful. War and other causes had reduced their numbers considerably.

Those "tigers of the Plains," as the Sioux were called in Western America, originally hailed from the Dakotas and the neighbouring country to the south-west. As the pioneer settlers pushed further and further into their lands many of the tribe became refugees, and fled northwards into Canadian territory. It was a pathetic feature of this invasion that they persisted in styling themselves British subjects, declaring that their fathers had always been loyal to the British flag since the days of the American Revolution. In evidence of this, they pointed proudly to many George III. medals which were heirlooms in their chiefs' families.

THE RIDERS OF THE PLAINS

A number of these Sioux settled in Manitoba, near Portage la Prairie, after the great massacre of the whites in Minnesota in 1862, and ten years later there were three camps of them, totalling about three hundred souls in all. Under Canadian rule they showed themselves to be quite tractable, and developed into good farmers. Their sinister reputation for blood-thirstiness is derived from the stern reprisals they made upon the "Long Knives," as they termed the Americans — reprisals marked by all the atrocities of savage warfare.

To the north of the tribes above mentioned were the Chippewayan or Athabascan Indians, and still further north, of course, the Eskimo. But with these the Mounted Police came into little contact, until their posts had moved so far into the interior.

By reason of their strength in numbers and their bellicose disposition, the Blackfeet and the Crees claim particular notice here. The conciliation of these tribes was of the utmost importance in the settlement of the newly opened territories.

From the earliest days these two tribes were always at variance. Their traditions cover a long record of bloody fights, from which first one and then the other emerged triumphant. Here is one instance of such a conflict. A party of Blackfeet, a hundred strong, went out on the warpath to raid a Cree camp among the hills. They accomplished their design, and entered a pass leading away from the stricken camp only to find a second and a third camp beyond it. Their presence was immediately discovered, and, as their sole chance of escape, the Blackfeet dashed straight on to fight their way through. But they now found themselves in a trap. They were hemmed in, in a

INDIAN PROBLEMS

deep hollow with precipitous slopes, the tops of which were deeply covered with snow. Within a few minutes the Crees had closed round them, and a terrible massacre began. After some seventy had been slain, the Crees, their bloodlust satisfied, perhaps, opened out and allowed the sorry remnant of their foes to escape.

Of the daring and strategy of the Blackfeet many stories are told. A large body of Crees on a hunting expedition were once camped by a lake in the open, when they observed a buffalo grazing quietly on the top of a hill some little way off. With natural suspicion at his apparent disregard of them, they waited for a time, until others emerged from the woods that lay between the hills. Then, urged on by hunger, the Crees crept stealthily up within striking distance. As they rose to their feet a volley of shots was poured into their midst. The buffalo became Blackfeet, and the would-be hunters found the tables turned upon them.

A favourite Blackfeet legend that is told in many a lodge to the younger members of the tribe relates to an old-time renowned chief, named "The Swan." One day he arrayed himself in all the barbaric finery of skins, beads, and feathers, mounted his swiftest horse, and rode at full gallop into a Cree camp near by. Before any could realise what was happening, he dashed into the centre of the camp where two noted "braves" sat gambling among a group of warriors, put his musket to the head of one, and blew out his brains. Then, like a flash, he was away again, pursued by a hail of bullets and arrows from the infuriated Crees. Thanks, however, to the fleetness of his steed he escaped without injury, and returned to his own tribe to tell the story of his successful raid.

That the North American Indian of the old days was

too often a merciless savage who took the most atrocious and inhuman revenges upon his enemies, cannot be gainsaid. Sir William Butler tells a story of an Ojibbeway "brave" who once set out alone to make war against the Sioux. In the woods he lost his way and wandered about for some days until he was nearly starving, in which condition he was found and befriended by a Sioux woman. He was taken to her lodge, where also was another woman with her children, given food, and bidden rest himself on a couch of skins. In the darkness of night this wretch rose up, tomahawked the helpless women and children, and disappeared with their scalps. In another case, an Ojibbeway band, who dared not risk a raid upon a strong Sioux camp, opened a newly made grave, dug up a squaw and scalped her, so that they might not return to their own people without a trophy.

This is one side of the shield, and it is certainly revolting enough. History records many and many an instance of such barbarous acts, and it cannot be wondered at that the Indian has gained an unenviable reputation for cruelty. But one must call to mind the old trite saying, "Other times, other manners." Savage days bred savage ways. The Indian expected no better treatment from his foe than that he himself meted out. And it must not be overlooked that the Indian mind was trained from infancy to regard torture and death with a stoicism of which white men are less capable. "Torture," as one writer says, "brought to the savage the opportunity for exhibiting the supreme virtue of his race—triumph over pain, and in death he went joyfully to the happy hunting-ground."

On the other hand, there were many qualities in the Indian character which undoubtedly call for our admiration

AN INDIAN ENCAMPMENT.

INDIAN PROBLEMS

and respect. The Blackfeet, Cree, Ojibbeway, and their blood brothers were not altogether so black as they have been painted. Those who dealt faithfully and honestly with them found that they in return met with the same fair treatment. And on many occasions have travellers in the Indians' country placed on record their tribute to the nobler traits of generosity and self-sacrifice of which they have had experience. As illustrating this better side of their nature, the following tale may be quoted, our authority again being Sir William Butler:[1]—

"The 'Moose that Walks' arrived at Hudson's Hope early in the spring. He was sorely in want of gunpowder and shot, for it was the season when the beaver leave their winter houses and when it is easy to shoot them. So he carried his thirty martens' skins to the fort, to barter them for shot, powder, and tobacco.

"There was no person at the Hope. The dwelling-house was closed, the store shut up, the man in charge had not yet come up from St. John's; now what was to be done? Inside that wooden house lay piles and piles of all that the 'Moose that Walks' most needed. There was a whole keg of powder; there were bags of shot and tobacco—there was as much as the 'Moose' could smoke in his whole life.

"Through a rent in the parchment window the 'Moose' looked at all these wonderful things, and at the red flannel shirts, and at the four flint guns, and the spotted cotton handkerchiefs, each worth a sable skin at one end of the fur trade, half a sixpence at the other. There was tea, too—tea, that magic medicine before which life's cares vanished like snow in spring sunshine.

"The 'Moose' sat down to think about all these things,

[1] *The Wild North Land.*

but thinking only made matters worse. He was short of ammunition, therefore he had no food, and to think of food when one is very hungry is an unsatisfactory business. It is true that the ' Moose that Walks ' had only to walk in through that parchment window and help himself until he was tired. But no, that would not do.

"'Ah,' my Christian friend will exclaim, 'Ah, yes, the poor Indian had known the good missionary, and had learnt the lesson of honesty and respect for his neighbour's property.'

" Yes ; he had learnt the lesson of honesty, but his teacher, my friend, had been other than human. The good missionary had never reached the Hope of Hudson, nor improved the morals of the ' Moose that Walks.'

" But let us go on. After waiting two days he determined to set off for St. John's, two full days' travel. He set out, but his heart failed him and he turned back again.

" At last, on the fourth day, he entered the parchment window, leaving outside his comrade, to whom he jealously denied admittance. Then he took from the cask of powder three skins' worth, from the tobacco four skins' worth, from the shot the same ; and, sticking the requisite number of martens' skins in the powder barrel and the shot bag and the tobacco case, he hung up his remaining skins on a nail to the credit of his account, and departed from this El Dorado, this Bank of England of the Red Man in the wilderness.

" And when it was all over he went his way, thinking he had done a very reprehensible act, and one by no means to be proud of."

So much for the inherent and somewhat inconsistent qualities of Indian nature. No apology need be offered for dwelling upon them at such length. It is essential that the character of the red man should be appreciated properly in

INDIAN PROBLEMS

considering his relations with the white settler in the northwest and with the Mounted Police in particular. We now come to the critical period when negotiations with the Indians had to be entered into with a view to ensuring their keeping the peace and allowing their lands to be more or less occupied by the white men.

The first treaties made date back to the early years of the nineteenth century. In 1817 the Indians of the Red River surrendered a wide tract of land to the Earl of Selkirk for occupation by his colonists, the consideration being the payment of "one hundred pounds of good merchantable tobacco to each nation annually." In 1850, after the discovery of minerals on the shores of Lakes Huron and Superior, the Government deputed the Hon. William B. Robinson to negotiate for the concession of the desired district. He accordingly carried out what are known as the Robinson Treaties, by which the Chippewas of the Lakes resigned their title to the lands in exchange for annuities, reserves for their own habitation, and the liberty to fish and hunt on the unconceded domain of the Crown. A feature of these treaties was the recognition of the claims of the half-breeds who then occupied the land side by side with the Indians.

Next in order came the Manitoulin Island Treaty of 1862, rendering this island in Lake Huron available for settlement ; and the Stone Fort and Manitoba Post Treaties Nos. 1 and 2 of 1871. By the latter, a tract of country three times as large as the Province of Manitoba was surrendered by the Indians to the Crown.

Of the more important treaties dating from the seventies, the first was that known as No. 3, or the North-West Angle Treaty. This was effected in 1873 by a com-

THE RIDERS OF THE PLAINS

mission comprising the Hon. Alexander Morris, then Lieutenant-Governor of Manitoba, and the North-West Territories, Lieutenant-Colonel Provencher, and Mr. S. J. Dawson, afterward M.P. for Algoma. The compact thus entered into was one of great importance, as it was the means of tranquillising a very large Indian population, and " securing the route known as ' the Dawson route ' for the passage of emigrants and the people of the Dominion generally." The route in question extended from Prince Arthur's Landing on Lake Superior to the north-west angle of the Lake of the Woods, and opened up for settlement a very valuable portion of territory.

As set out in the treaty, the boundaries of the land to be ceded began at the north-west angle eastward, " taking in all the Lake of the Woods, including White Fish Bay, Rat Portage, and north to White Dog in English River ; up English River to Lake Seul, and then south-east to Lake Nipigon ; westward to Rainy River, and down it to Lake of the Woods, and up nearly to Lac des Mille Lacs ; then beginning at the 49th Parallel, to White Mouth River, thence down it to the north, along the eastern boundary of the land ceded in 1871, embracing 55,000 square miles." [1] The number of Ojibbeway Indians thus affected was estimated at 14,000.

The North-West Angle Treaty served the purpose, further, of shaping the terms of the subsequent treaties, Nos. 4, 5, 6, and 7. No. 4, the Qu'Appelle Treaty, takes its name from the Qu'Appelle Lakes in Saskatchewan. It had the result of bringing into the hands of the Government about 75,000 square miles of very fertile land, formerly

[1] *The Treaties of Canada with the Indians*, by the Hon. Alexander Morris, P.C.

INDIAN PROBLEMS

held by the Crees, Chippewas, and Salteaux, and of securing permanently the goodwill of those tribes.

Treaty No. 5, the Winnipeg Treaty, embraced an area of approximately 100,000 square miles, including the land in the immediate vicinity of Lake Winnipeg and the Saskatchewan River. The western boundary was Cumberland House, on the Saskatchewan, and it extended as far north as Split Lake and the Nelson River. This region was occupied mostly by Chippewas and Swampy Crees. It was essential, reported the Minister of the Interior, that the Indian title to all the territory around the lake should be extinguished, so that settlers and traders might have undisturbed access to its waters, shores, islands, inlets, and tributary streams. The mouth of the Saskatchewan especially offered an eligible site for a future town.

At a final conference between the Commissioners (the Hon. Thomas Howard and Mr. J. Lestock Reid, Dominion Land Surveyor), and the Indians in 1876 this important treaty was brought to a successful conclusion, the several bands interested being allotted suitable reservations.

Following upon this, in the same year, came the treaties made at Forts Carlton and Pitt, by which a vast area of territory, 120,000 square miles in all, lying between the Saskatchewan and the Rocky Mountains, was taken over by the Government. This section of the north-west was the home of the Cree nation, and was partly populated by the Assiniboines. Both these tribes were at the time in a state of great unrest, the presence of railway surveying parties and others engaged in the construction of telegraph lines having led them to suppose that an attempt was about to be made to drive them from their lands. By diplomatic handling, however, they were persuaded of

THE RIDERS OF THE PLAINS

the good intentions of the Government towards them, and the negotiations had a successful issue.

Last, and by no means the least, in the series came the Blackfeet Treaty, No. 7. The need for making this treaty had become urgent, as will be seen from the following statement, which appears in the Annual Report of the Hon. David Mills, the Minister of the Interior, in 1877:—

"The conclusion, in 1876, of the treaty with the Crees, Assiniboines, and Salteaux Indians (being the sixth of the series of treaties up to that time negotiated with the Indians of the north-west), left but a small portion of the territory lying between the boundary line and the 54th parallel of latitude unsurrendered.

"The unsurrendered portion of the territory, including about fifty thousand square miles, lies at the south-west angle of the territories, north of the boundary line, east of the Rocky Mountains, south of Red River (Treaty No. 6), and west of the Cypress Hills, or Treaty No. 4. This portion of the north-west is occupied by the Blackfeet, Blood, Sarcee, and Piegan Indians, some of the most warlike and intelligent, but intractable bands of the north-west. These bands have for years past been anxiously expecting to be treated with, and have been much disappointed at the delay of negotiations.

"In last year's report I stated that his Honour Lieutenant-Governor Morris very strongly recommended that no further delay should take place in entering into negotiations with these Indians. His Honour reported in effect, 'that there was a general consent of opinion amongst the missionaries settled in that territory, and others who are acquainted with these Indians, as to the desirability of having such a treaty made at the earliest possible date,

INDIAN PROBLEMS

with a view to preserving the present friendly disposition of the tribes, which might easily give place to feelings of an unfriendly or hostile nature, should the treaty negotiations be much longer delayed.' "

Having these facts in view, and the increasing influx of white settlers into that part of the country, the Governor of Manitoba decided that these Indians should be treated with, and the Hon. David Laird and Lieut.-Colonel Macleod, C.M.G., the commandant of the North-West Mounted Police at Fort Macleod, were appointed Commissioners. The choice of the latter was undoubtedly wise. During his residence in the north-west Colonel Macleod had had a great deal to do with the Blackfeet, and had won their confidence and goodwill to a remarkable degree. It is on record that when the Sioux commenced their war against the United States they approached the Blackfeet to induce this tribe to take the war-path with them. Crowfoot, the leading chief of the Blackfeet, immediately went to Colonel Macleod for counsel, and, acting on his advice, refused the invitation.

The conference at which the treaty was concluded [1] was held at the Blackfoot Crossing on the Bow River, on 17th September 1877, and lasted five days. The total number of Indians whom it affected is put at 4392. In its terms the treaty was substantially the same as those completed at the North-West Angle and Qu'Appelle, the principal difference being that a provision was made to supply several of the bands with cattle instead of agricultural implements, they having avowed their intention to engage in pastoral pursuits.

In one respect the conclusion of this treaty with the

[1] The full text of this important treaty will be found in Appendix B.

THE RIDERS OF THE PLAINS

Blackfeet held more importance than can be attached to any previous treaty. The open war raging below the border between the Sioux and the American troops might very possibly have affected the tribes of this part of the Canadian territory, and have drawn them into the conflict. The pacific settlement of the country must then have been delayed inevitably for some years, if still more serious results had not followed.

In addressing the Indians at the great conference, Lieutenant-Governor Laird made quite clear to them the amiable intentions of the Government. His speech, which is given below, was delivered in front of the Council House, where were assembled nearly all the chiefs and minor chiefs of the Blackfeet, Blood, Piegan, Assiniboine, and Sarcee tribes. Beyond these, forming a semicircle of about one-third of a mile, were some 4000 men, women, and children, watching the proceedings with the keenest interest.

"The Great Spirit," said the Lieutenant-Governor, "has made all things—the sun, the moon, and the stars, the earth, the forests, and the swift-running rivers. It is by the Great Spirit that the Queen rules over this great country and other great countries. The Great Spirit has made the white men and the red men brothers, and we should take each other by the hand. The Great Mother loves all her children, white men and red men alike; she wishes to do them all good. The bad white men and the bad Indian she alone does not love, and them she punishes for their wickedness. The good Indian has nothing to fear from the Queen or her officers. You Indians know this to be true. When bad white men brought you whisky, robbed you, and made you poor, and, through whisky, quarrel amongst yourselves, she sent the Police to put an

THE FIRST FOUR COMMISSIONERS
with tenure of appointment.

LIEUT.-COL. G. A. FRENCH.
Now Major-Gen. Sir G. A. French, K.C.M.G.
1873–1876.

LIEUT.-COL. J. F. MACLEOD, C.M.G.
1876–1880.

LIEUT.-COL. A. G. IRVINE.
1880–1886.

LIEUT.-COL. L. W. HERCHMER.
1886–1900.

end to it. You know how they stopped this, and punished the offenders, and how much good this has done. I have to tell you how much pleased the Queen is that you have taken the Police by the hands and helped them, and obeyed her laws since the arrival of the Police. She hopes that you will continue to do so, and you will always find the Police on your side if you keep the Queen's laws. The Great Mother heard that the buffalo were being killed very fast, and to prevent them from being destroyed her Councillors have made a law to protect them. This law is for your good. It says that the calves are not to be killed, so that they may grow up and increase; that the cows are not to be killed in winter or spring, excepting by the Indians when they are in need of them as food. This will save the buffalo, and provide you with food for many years yet, and it shows you that the Queen and her Councillors wish you well.

" Many years ago our Great Mother made a treaty with the Indians far away by the great waters in the east. A few years ago she made a treaty with those beyond the Touchwood Hills and the Woody Mountains. Last year a treaty was made with the Crees along the Saskatchewan, and now the Queen has sent Colonel Macleod and myself to ask you to make a treaty. But in a very few years the buffalo will probably be all destroyed, and for this reason the Queen wishes to help you to live in the future in some other way. She wishes you to allow her white children to come and live on your land and raise cattle, and should you agree to this she will assist you to raise cattle and grain, and thus give you the means of living when the buffalo are no more. She will also pay you and your children money every year, which you can spend as you please.

THE RIDERS OF THE PLAINS

By being paid in money you cannot be cheated, as with it you can buy what you may think proper.

"The Queen wishes us to offer you the same as was accepted by the Crees. I do not mean exactly the same terms, but equivalent terms, that will cost the Queen the same amount of money. Some of the other Indians wanted farming implements, but these you do not require, as your lands are more adapted to raising cattle, and cattle perhaps would be better for you. The Commissioner will give you your choice, whether cattle or farming implements. I have already said we will give you money, I will now tell you how much. If you sign the treaty, every man, woman, and child will get twelve dollars each; the money will be paid to the head of each family, for himself, his women, and children; every year, for ever, you, your women, and your children will get five dollars each. This year Chiefs and Councillors will be paid a larger sum than this; Chiefs will get a suit of clothes, a silver medal,[1] and flag, and every third year will get another suit. A reserve of land will be set apart for yourselves and your cattle, upon which none others will be permitted to encroach; for every five persons one square mile will be allotted on this reserve, on which they can cut the trees and brush for firewood and other

[1] With regard to this practice of presenting Chiefs with medals, the Hon. Alexander Morris makes an interesting note in his valuable work on *The Treaties of Canada with the Indians of Manitoba and the North-West Territories.* He says: "These medals are given both in the United States and in Canada, in conformity with an ancient custom, and are much prized by the Chiefs and their families. Frequently the Indians have exhibited to me with pride old medals issued, with the likeness of the King before the American War of Independence, which have passed down as heirlooms. On one occasion a young Chief, who had come of age and aspired to be recognised as Chief, was decorated in my presence with the old King George medal by one of the band, to whom it had been entrusted for safe keeping by the young man's father, who was a Chief, with the charge that on the boy's coming of age it would be delivered over to him."

INDIAN PROBLEMS

purposes. The Queen's officers will permit no white man or half-breed to build or cut the timber on your reserves. If required, roads will be cut through them. Cattle will be given to you, and potatoes, the same as are grown at Fort Macleod. The Commissioners would strongly advise the Indians to take cattle, as you understand cattle better than you will farming for some time, at least so long as you continue to move about in lodges.

" Ammunition will be issued to you each year, and as soon as you sign the treaty one thousand five hundred dollars' worth will be distributed amongst the tribes, and as soon as you settle, teachers will be sent to you to instruct your children to read books like this one (the Bible), which is impossible so long as you continue to move from place to place. I have now spoken. I have made you acquainted with the principal terms contained in the treaty which you are asked to sign."

Some of the speeches made by the Indian chiefs in reply during the closing stages of the meeting may be quoted here, as showing their natural gift of oratory, and at the same time bearing evidence of their implicit faith in the Mounted Police, who had played so prominent a part in the negotiations.

Said " Button Chief " of the Blood tribe : " The Great Spirit sent the white man across the great waters to carry out His (the Great Spirit's) ends. The Great Spirit, and not the Great Mother (the Queen), gave us this land. The Great Mother sent Stamixotokon (Colonel Macleod) and the Police to put an end to the traffic in fire-water. I can sleep now safely. Before the arrival of the Police, when I laid my head down at night, every sound frightened me ; my sleep was broken ; now I can sleep sound, and am not

THE RIDERS OF THE PLAINS

afraid. The Great Mother sent you to this country, and we hope she will be good to us for many years. I hope and expect to get plenty; we think we will not get so much as the Indians receive from the Americans on the other side; they get large presents of flour, sugar, tea, and blankets. The Americans gave at first large bags of flour, sugar, and many blankets; the next year it was only half the quantity, and the following years it grew less and less, and now they give only a handful of flour." The chief then went on to outline the demands he wished to make on behalf of his people.

On the last day, when the terms of the treaty were accepted, Chief Crowfoot delivered himself thus :—

" While I speak be kind and patient. I have to speak for my people, who are numerous, and who rely upon me to follow that course which in the future will tend to their good. The plains are large and wide. We are the children of the plains, it is our home, and the buffalo has been our food always. I hope you look upon the Blackfeet, Bloods, and Sarcees as your children now, and that you will be indulgent and charitable to them. They all expect me to speak now for them, and I trust the Great Spirit will put into their breasts to be a good people—into the minds of the men, women, and children, and their future generations. The advice given me and my people has proved to be very good. If the Police had not come to the country, where would we be all now ? Bad men and whisky were killing us so fast that very few indeed of us would have been left to-day. The Police have protected us as the feathers of the bird protect it from the frosts of winter. I wish them all good, and trust that all our hearts will increase in goodness from this time forward. I am satisfied. I will sign the treaty."

INDIAN PROBLEMS

The remark let fall by Button Chief of the Bloods, to the effect that the coming of the Police had brought him ease and rest, may be taken as typical of the point of view held by the majority of the Indians in the Territories. One Ojibbeway expressed himself thus : " Before the Queen's Government sent the red-coated soldiers we were never safe, and now I can sleep in my tent anywhere, and have no fear. I can go to the Blackfeet and Cree camps, and they treat me as a friend." In a word, a stop had been put to the terrible internecine wars of the past. The days were over, or almost so, when parties of " braves " were to go out on the war-path and the fearful war-whoop was to resound in the woods. Among red men and white men alike there was to be peace.

The change was a welcome one to the Indians in general. Only in the minds of the ambitious younger men lingered any regret for the excitements and perils of former days ; when the settlement of the various tribes on their reserves became an accomplished fact, the pleasanter conditions of the new life made themselves apparent, and the Indians quickly slipped into the ways prepared for them. In the space of a few years, in fact, the north-west had witnessed a revolution take place within its borders, a bloodless revolution of a most remarkable kind. Over thirty thousand Indians, at war with one another and hostile to the white invasion, had been transformed into a peaceful community showing every disposition to remain contented and law-abiding.[1]

---

[1] It is interesting to note that at the present day there are over 100,000 acres under cultivation on the various Indian reserves in the Dominion. These yield annually many thousand bushels of grain, potatoes, and other vegetables, besides hay. Large numbers of cattle, horses, and sheep also are owned by the tribes, while from fish, furs, and other industries they derive an income of nearly $2,000,000.

CHAPTER V.

"SITTING BULL" AND THE SIOUX INVASION.

Early fugitives (1862)—Settling in the west—The Custer Massacre—First-fruits of Police policy—The Blackfeet stand firm—Negotiations with the Sioux—The Sitting Bull Commission—An anxious time—Sergeant M'Donald—The Bull Elk affair—Sitting Bull's surrender—A contrast in method.

THE years 1876 and 1877 are notable in the history of Canada and of the Royal North-West Mounted Police, for the critical situation brought about by the sudden irruption of American Sioux Indians into the North-West Territories. Under the leadership of a chief named "Sitting Bull," and several minor chiefs, fugitive bands of these Indians, who had come into conflict with the American troops, fled for refuge into Dominion territory. A large party, numbering well over 2000, under Chief Black Moon, crossed the border in December of 1876, to be followed in quick succession by others, until at length there were 700 lodges, or about 5600 souls, thus flinging themselves on the Government's clemency.

This tendency to claim sanctuary on Canadian soil was no new thing. The Dominion had had to reckon with it for more than a decade. As has been mentioned in the previous chapter, a portion of the Sioux tribe had settled in the Red River district as early as 1862. These undesirable immigrants had persisted in calling themselves

"SITTING BULL" AND THE SIOUX INVASION

British subjects, and though for some years strong efforts were made to induce them to return to their former country they refused to do so. In the end they were allowed to remain, and in the course of time the band distributed itself in Assiniboia and the adjacent territory.

It must be admitted that, except for occasional collisions with the Red Lake Salteaux, the Sioux behaved themselves well. They settled down quietly upon their chosen locations, engaged in farming, trapping, and other legitimate pursuits, and made themselves amenable to the authorities. Eventually, in 1874, a truce having been declared between them and the Salteaux, the Sioux were allotted reserves. Here they continued to reside in the same peaceful, orderly manner, and the only concern they gave the Government was their probable attitude towards the settlers who were then beginning to pour into the north-west.

Other sections of the Sioux tribe in Canada, besides that in Manitoba, were those in the Turtle Mountains (afterwards included in the Province), and in the country covered by the Qu'Appelle Treaty. To these also, in consideration of their good behaviour, reserves were given, it being made clear to them at the time that the act was one of grace, and that in reality they had no claim on the Queen's Government. Commenting on these Indians, an official report said : " Upon the whole, they appear to have made fair progress in cultivating the land, and their prospects for the future, had they the advice and assistance of some good farmers for a few years, would be encouraging. Indeed, the Sioux generally who are resident in Canada appear to be more intelligent, industrious, and self-reliant than the other Indian bands in the north-west."

The problem of dealing with the several portions of the

tribe in the circumstances presented few difficulties. The question, however, was complicated to a remarkable degree by the crisis reached after the memorable Custer Massacre in the summer of 1876. How this came about may be told briefly.

A few years prior to the beginning of actual hostilities the country round the Black Hills, by the Yellowstone River, where some of the Sioux had settled, was invaded by a small army of prospectors and miners. Gold and silver had been found there, and the usual " rush " thither took place. Immediately there was a conflict between the two races. On the Indians' part, representations were made to the authorities for protection from the miners who threatened to deprive them of their lands, or, failing this, for substantial compensation. The commission that was appointed to inquire into the matter declared that an armed force was necessary if the Indians were to be brought to terms, and steps were taken accordingly to meet this request. This becoming known to the Sioux, the majority of them answered to the call of the one who had been most prominent in resisting the demands of the Americans. The chief in question was Sitting Bull, who, in addition to his hereditary power, was high in the regard of his followers as a " medicine man."

The outcome of the situation was that Sitting Bull proclaimed war upon the United States Government, and in the spring of 1877 a considerable body of troops was dispatched against him. One of the three columns placed in the field was under the command of General Terry. Under this leader was General Custer, who had won distinction for himself in the late Civil War. Custer, moreover, was an Indian fighter of no mean reputation, and it was hardly to be expected that he, of all men, should court disaster. Yet

"SITTING BULL" AND THE SIOUX INVASION

such was the case. Making a march in advance of the main body, General Custer came unexpectedly upon the Sioux camp in the Valley of the Little Big Horn, and at a moment when he was scarcely in a position to attack.

With reckless contempt for his enemy, Custer moved directly upon the Indians. His force of about 1200 men was divided into three sections, one, under Major Reno, being ordered to make a frontal attack, while another, under himself, made a detour to the back of the position. The third section, comprising four companies, were detached a mile or so in the rear. In a little while Major Reno found himself compelled to draw off to a high bluff, so fierce was the fighting, but, disregarding this, Custer hurled himself into the thick of the battle. The result is a matter of history. The hapless General and every man of his command were slain; not a single one escaped the fury of the Sioux. For the rest, it is enough to say that Major Reno and the companies with him managed to hold their own until relief came.

That is the story of the Custer Massacre. Elated with their victory, but wishful to avoid further conflict, Sitting Bull and his warriors lost little time in pushing northwards, evading the American troops who were in hot pursuit. In May of 1877, the Canadian Government was apprised of the fact that the Sioux Chief had crossed the border and joined his compatriots who were already in the Territories.

This invasion in itself was alarming enough, but the danger was increased considerably when in due time other large bands of Sioux, fearing reprisals on the part of the United States authorities, trooped over the international line to throw in their lot with the rebels. To be thus suddenly burdened with the care of over five thousand hostile Indians was more than the Canadian Government had bargained for.

The immediate question that arose for the consideration of the Mounted Police was how this influx of Sioux would affect the Blackfeet and other tribes whom they had by this time got so well in hand. Fortunately, the answer was not left long in doubt. The humane and kindly treatment accorded to the Canadian Indians in the northwest now brought forth its fruits. Early in the breaking out of hostilities the Sioux had sent a message to the Blackfeet camp with a piece of tobacco. The latter was intended for them to smoke if they were in the mind to go over the line and join the Sioux in fighting the Americans. In return, the Sioux promised the Blackfeet horses and mules and other loot they had taken in the campaign. Furthermore, they promised to help the Blackfeet to exterminate the whites on the northern side of the boundary after they had settled with the Americans. To this the Blackfeet chiefs made answer: "We cannot smoke your tobacco on such terms; the whites are our friends, and we will not fight against them."

On receipt of this message, the Sioux leaders sent word back that they would go over the border in any case and show the Blackfeet that white soldiers were nothing before them, adding that after they had exterminated the latter and taken their forts they would attack the Blackfeet themselves. As has been noted earlier, Crowfoot, the head chief of the Blackfeet, went with some trepidation to Colonel Macleod to ask for advice. He received the answer that in the case of such an attack he might rely upon the support of the Mounted Police, who were bound to protect them as subjects of the country, and with this assurance the old chief was

"SITTING BULL" AND THE SIOUX INVASION

well content. He even offered the Commissioner to send out 2000 of his warriors against the invaders if help were needed.

The failure to secure the alliance of the Indian tribes in the north-west, however, did not lead to any active demonstration on the part of the Sioux. Sitting Bull pitched his principal camp in the vicinity of Fort Walsh, and sat down to await developments. There now ensued a long series of negotiations in which the Mounted Police were ever foremost, the purpose in view being to induce the rebels to return to the American side of the line and surrender themselves to the authorities there.

In May and June of 1877 Assistant-Commissioner Irvine had several interviews with the Sioux chief. " I was particularly struck with Sitting Bull," he says. " He is a man of somewhat short stature, but with a pleasant face, a mouth showing great determination, and a fine, high forehead. When he smiled, which he often did, his face brightened up wonderfully. I should say he is a man of about forty-five years of age. The warriors who came with him were all men of immense height and very muscular."

At these interviews Sitting Bull was confronted with some Americans delegated by the authorities at Washington to treat with the Indians. The chief was firm in repelling their advances, and in recapitulating his grievances and meeting their arguments showed himself to be possessed of much capability. The scene at the second conference at the Indian camp, as we have it described for us by Adjutant Dalrymple Clark[1] of the Force, was an effective one. The first proceeding was the lighting of the peace pipe. This was done by means of a buffalo chip, a match being considered to be deception. Then, taking his pipe,

[1] Died October 1880.

THE RIDERS OF THE PLAINS

Sitting Bull pointed it to the four quarters, and handed it to Colonel Irvine, holding the end himself and saying : " My grandfather,[1] have pity on me ; we are going to be raised with a new people." All the officers present smoked, and so did the others of the party, the smoking of the pipe being the strongest form of oath.

Sitting Bull now rose up and made a speech proclaiming how badly he had been treated by the Americans. In this he was supported by Sweet Bird and Spotted Eagle, members of his band, both of whom claimed the protection of the White Mother (the Queen), upon whose mercy they threw themselves. Later on, after one of the Americans, a priest, had pleaded with him, Sitting Bull spoke again in the following words :—

" O God, remember this is the land I was brought up on, me and a woman. That is the reason I came back ; I was brought up here. God brought up things from the ground for my children. I was brought where God made food for me. I sit on the ground and hold it strong now. When my grandfather lived I came back. Listen to me. Look into my eyes. Look straight at me. Do you know what you tell me is going to be so ? Do you know the cause of the war ? You ask me if I am going to return to your country. It is impossible for me to go back. God never told the Americans to come to the head of the Missouri. We were raised on this side of the sea. You were raised on the other side. The Great Spirit told me that at the same time He brought me up in a great blanket. On both sides of America there are only two blankets left to cover me. God made me big enough, I know, because

[1] In Indian oratory the term " Grandfather " sometimes signifies the spirit of the speaker's grandfather, and sometimes the Creator.

— 76 —

"SITTING BULL" AND THE SIOUX INVASION

His Great Mother covers me. My heart was made strong, but now really it is weak, and that is why the Americans want to lick my blood. Why do the Americans want to drive me ?—because they want only Americans to be there. God made me leader of the people, and that is why I am following the buffalo. God told me, if you do anything wrong your people will be destroyed, and that is why I came here. I was afraid. Look at me. See if anything wrong sticks to my body. I have nothing but my hand to fight the white men with. I told the Americans to keep off my land. You are waiting for my people to come to your land so that the 'Long Knives' may rush at them and kill them. If you want to make a treaty, give us back our horses. God made all Indians out of one Indian, and He came to smoke with the old Indians and make peace. Are you here to ask me if I am going to throw my land away ? I never thought of giving my land to the American people, and still you follow to bring something wrong to me. I came here to hear from my White Mother, and why, if I go back to the Americans, are they going to take all my stock away ? Did God tell you to come and make me poor ? I never tried to do anything wrong to the white men. My body is clean. I never saw the road " (the line) " before, but I came on till I got to this side of it. I only think of two people, the English and Spanish.[1] I am between them. The Americans tried to cut me up, and that is why I talk to the Chief (Colonel Irvine) there and to you. If you will use your influence with the President to send back the bad men to where they came from and leave the good men, there will be peace."

This speech, which is not without its pathetic touches,

[1] It had been Sitting Bull's intention to seek refuge in " the Spanish country " (probably Mexico) if not in Canada.

drew from Colonel Irvine an assurance that "the White Mother" would protect the Sioux while they remained in Canadian territory so long as they behaved themselves; but the Government had no intention of allowing the Indians to suppose that they would be granted permanent residence. In a dispatch to the Commissioner of the Mounted Police the Hon. R. W. Scott, the Secretary of State, wrote: "Important that Sitting Bull and other United States Indians should be induced to return to reservations. United States Government have sent Commissioners to treat with them. Co-operate with Commissioners, but do not unduly press Indians. Our action should be persuasive, not compulsory."

The American Commissioners were Generals M'Neill and Terry. A conference between them and the Sioux was arranged to take place at Fort Walsh, where Inspector Walsh, a man in whom the Indians placed great reliance, was in command. At the last moment it was doubtful whether Sitting Bull would leave his camp to meet the Commissioners, so great was his distrust of the Americans. The fact that about a hundred Nez Percés, men, women, and children, who had just escaped from the American troops under General Miles, had come into the Sioux camp wounded and bleeding, had a further disturbing effect upon the tribe. However, Inspector Walsh reassured them of their safety in the hands of the Police, and the Sioux proceeded to the Fort.

The Sitting Bull Commission arrived in Canada in October 1877, but only to fail completely in its attempt to secure the Indians' return. To General Terry's statement of terms, that the band should go back to their reservation and yield up their horses and arms, for which cattle would be given in exchange, Sitting Bull replied

"SITTING BULL" AND THE SIOUX INVASION

curtly that " he did not trust the ' Long Knives' ' word. He knew he was safe where he now was, and there he intended to remain. He distinctly and firmly refused to listen to any offer from the American President."

For the next four years the North-West Mounted Police had their hands full in looking after their Sioux charges. Constant watchfulness was needed to prevent open war breaking out between them and the Canadian Indians when matters went wrong—as they sometimes did— between the two peoples. And considerable diplomacy had to be exercised in controlling and regulating their movements. Suspicious of any attempt to induce him to place foot again on American territory, Sitting Bull resolutely turned a deaf ear to any overtures that were made. On their side the Police officers, acting on precise instructions from the authorities at Ottawa, spared no pains to alter his decision. The alarming diminution in the number of buffalo made it urgent that the Sioux should be sent over the border as quickly as possible, for each year saw the Indians of the north-west threatened more and more with famine. The consequent increase of the burden on the shoulders of the Mounted Police was very great, and called for serious consideration. That the Force itself, however, had complete confidence in its own strength is made evident by a report from the officer commanding the Wood Mountain post at that time. He recommended that " at least fifty men " should be stationed there, as there were about three thousand Sioux camped in the vicinity !

How the Police impressed Sitting Bull and his turbulent warriors is well illustrated by the affair in which Sergeant M'Donald figured. The scene is still Wood Mountain. One day the Police found half a dozen Salteaux Indians dead near their post, and not only dead but scalped. Another Salteaux who had witnessed the tragedy confirmed the belief that the perpetrators of the crime were Sioux, and if further proof were wanting it was afforded by Sitting Bull himself, who soon after appeared at the Police quarters and demanded the surrender of the surviving Salteaux. Sergeant M'Donald was a tough nut for the Sioux chief to attempt to crack. He was not a bit scared when Sitting Bull leaped from his pony and ran forward thrusting the muzzle of his gun into the other's stomach. The old soldier pushed the weapon to one side, and invited Sitting Bull and the four chiefs with him to enter the stockade and have a " pow-wow." The rest of the Indians—about five hundred in all—remained outside.

When Sergeant M'Donald conducted the chiefs into his quarters their arms were left stacked in the yard. This strategic move gave him the whip hand over them. First he commanded that the howling mob of " braves " without should be ordered to disperse. This was done ; then the sergeant explained the law to them, and announced that he was going to send to the Sioux camp to arrest the murderers of the dead Salteaux. Three constables went on this mission, and a lively time they had by all accounts, with the Sioux hustling them and trying to provoke a fight. But they got their men, whose names were known, and they brought the prisoners back. Sitting Bull received his first lesson in Police methods then ; the second came when the prisoners in question were tried for the murders and duly hanged.

A powerful factor on the side of the Police during this troublous period was the continuance of the good feeling existing between them and the Canadian Treaty Indians. The Sioux could not fail to observe these relations, and to

A DETACHMENT POST IN THE NORTH-WEST.

"SITTING BULL" AND THE SIOUX INVASION

note their effect upon the Indians themselves. In this way their confidence in Colonel Macleod and his officers was slowly established, and the way was paved for the subsequent successful negotiations. One incident that occurred at this juncture is worth chronicling here, as it well illustrates the respect in which the Indians held the Police.

"It is my pleasing duty," wrote the Commissioner to the Secretary of State, " to have to report a very creditable act of Mecasto (Red Crow), the head chief of the Bloods. One of his band, confined in our guard-room on a charge of theft, escaped across the line and some time afterwards returned to Mecasto's camp. The chief at once apprehended him, and, with a large number of his warriors, delivered him up at the Fort gate to the officer in command. Mecasto afterwards, at the payment, begged me to release him, but I told him I had no power to do so, as he must be tried for the offence with which he was charged. The prisoner pleaded guilty, and in consideration of all the circumstances I sentenced him to fourteen days' imprisonment only."

Only in extreme cases were there overt acts of rebellion on the part of the Indians, as in the trouble with Chief Little Child of the Salteaux tribe and Chief Crow's Dance of the Assiniboines. The conflict between these two was precipitated thus. The Salteaux had been camping with the Assiniboines and were desirous of moving away, but to this Crow's Dance would not agree, as he had formed a "war lodge" and given orders that no one should leave the camp without the permission of his warriors.[1] Little Child demurred at this, and, relying on Police protection in the event of hostilities, ordered his lodges to be pulled

---

[1] The "war" or "soldier" lodge constituted the governing power of the camp for the time being.

down. The Salteaux then began to move off, whereupon Crow's Dance and his angry followers fell upon them firing guns at random through the camp.

Inspector Walsh having been informed of what had taken place, that officer set out immediately for the Assiniboines' camp. He entered it, took the war lodge by surprise, and captured the defiant Crow's Dance, with nineteen of the latter's warriors. The prisoners were carried off to a butte some distance away, while the Inspector sent word to the other chiefs that he would meet them in an hour's time. In the end, Crow's Dance and those implicated with him were punished, and the Police had no further cases of parties being prevented from leaving the camp when they desired to do so.

Somewhat more serious was the affair of Bull Elk. This personage, a minor chief of the Blackfeet Indians, was wanted on a charge of attempting to shoot a white man employed on the reserve. Inspector Francis Dickens (a son of Charles Dickens the novelist), went with a sergeant and two constables to make the arrest. Seeing them coming, Bull Elk ran for it across the prairie, but he was cornered and captured. The sergeant and a constable then proceeded to march him off to the Police post at Blackfoot Crossing, on which about thirty young Indians came running up to protest.

"We managed by considerable exertion," says the sergeant, "to get him through the mob, but when we got on the ice, part of the Bow River which we had to cross, and which was frozen over, the mob increased here—old squaws with axes and knives, and young Indians with carbines. An Indian caught me by the right arm, another came behind me and tripped me up; the constable on the left was treated in the same manner. As soon as I fell, an

"SITTING BULL" AND THE SIOUX INVASION

old squaw ran at me and snatched the prisoner's gun out of my hand before I could recover myself. I still held on to the prisoner with my left hand, while Inspector Dickens kept the Indians back in rear with his revolver. I could hear the young Indians loading their carbines; one of them discharged his, and I heard the bullet whistle over my head. I then fired my revolver three times in the air, as I thought we had better get assistance, this being a pre-arranged signal for the men at our quarters to double down. Our strength was now, all told, thirteen in number, and we managed to get our prisoner up to our quarters all right."

Later on, the Blackfeet mustered in great strength at the Crossing, and clamoured for Bull Elk's release. The Indians took complete possession of the post, placing guards over the storeroom, stables, and other buildings. In the circumstances, as the Police were so outnumbered and the Blackfeet were in a highly dangerous condition, Inspector Dickens gave up his prisoner, but only on condition that Chief Crowfoot went bail for his appearance when Bull Elk was again wanted.

Some days later, Superintendent L. N. F. Crozier, of Fort Macleod, took the matter in hand. Going to the Indian camp he demanded the surrender of Bull Elk, and taking him to Blackfoot Crossing immediately sat to try the case in his capacity as magistrate. The Indians being still excited and defiant, the Police post was now placed in a state of defence, and the men stood to their arms. As was anticipated, Crowfoot's followers came itching for a fight, but happily the firm front presented by the Police held them in check. Eventually Crowfoot was persuaded by the Superintendent to pacify his people and bid them disperse, an order which they proceeded to obey with the worst possible grace.

THE RIDERS OF THE PLAINS

It had been a most tense time for the Police, for, as Superintendent Crozier pointed out, it was in such circumstances of strong feeling and excitement that the Indians were to be dreaded. Any enforcement of the law was distasteful to them, and when they were so worked up, or their superstitious feelings had been in some way wounded, they became entirely reckless of consequences. Bull Elk, it may be noted, was duly escorted to Fort Macleod, where he received a sentence of imprisonment.

In the meantime, Sitting Bull had been persuaded at last that the Canadian Government would not accept him and his followers as British subjects. Through pressure brought to bear upon him by the Police, he announced his intention of surrendering to the United States authorities, and by the end of December 1880 the Sioux had recrossed the frontier. In effecting this welcome departure Superintendent Crozier was largely responsible. By confining his attentions to the minor chiefs of the band, and dwelling on the possibilities of starvation and other hardships in the near future, he weakened Sitting Bull's influence in the council. The defection of Low Dog, Broad Trail, and other chiefs, who actually separated themselves from their head chief and started southwards for the States, turned the scale in the Bull's mind, and brought about the desired result.

The formal surrender was made at Fort Buford, U.S.A., in July of the following year, in the presence of Inspector Macdonell of the Mounted Police.

Apropos of the presence of hostile Indians in another territory than their own, and their subsequent deportation, an excellent story is told, for which there is good authority. Some time in the eighties, a band of Canadian Indians,

"SITTING BULL" AND THE SIOUX INVASION

mostly Crees, who feared punishment for their share in the half-breeds' rebellion, invited themselves to sojourn across the border where, on United States soil, they met with scanty welcome. "Uncle Sam," they were told, "had enough Indians of his own to keep him busy." As the party showed no inclination to leave their new home, the official wires were set in action, and much correspondence passed between Washington and Ottawa. The decision arrived at was that Canada would be responsible for her own Indians if America would kindly escort them to the border.

In due course 200 very dissatisfied and wild-eyed Crees, with 450 horses, were rounded up and started northwards, with a strong force of United States cavalry in attendance. They were met at the Boundary Line by three Mounted Policemen, one corporal and two troopers.

The American commanding officer looked at them with a surprised air.

" Where's your escort for these Indians ? " he asked.

" We're here," answered the corporal.

" Yes, yes, I see. But where is your regiment ? "

" I guess it's here all right," said the corporal. " The other fellow's looking after the breakfast things."

" But are there only *four* of you then ? "

" That's so, Colonel, but you see we wear the Queen's scarlet."

And the four red-coats proved sufficient. The corporal and his three men took over the Indians without any difficulty, and escorted the band 100 miles up into the north-west, where they would fret Uncle Sam no more.

Apart from the question of the cost incurred by the American and Canadian Governments respectively, the contrast in the methods employed is instructive.

CHAPTER VI.

CHANGES AND DEVELOPMENTS.

Lieut.-Colonel A. G. Irvine, third Commissioner (1880)—Fresh factors in the problem—Augmentation of the Force—New headquarters—Fort Regina—Long distance journeys—" Have done my best "—Notable reforms—Arms and equipment—Horse-stealing—Assisting the Indian Department—Railway pioneers.

BY the end of the year 1881, several important events had occurred directly affecting the North-West Mounted Police. The contract for the completion of the Canadian Pacific Railway, which was to link up the east and the west, had been signed ; Sir John Macdonald had again come into power as Premier, after the fall of the Mackenzie ministry, and had transferred the control of the Mounted Police from the Secretary of State's Department to that of the Interior, which came under his immediate direction ; lastly, the Force had a new Commissioner at its head. In November 1880, Lieut.-Colonel A. G. Irvine, formerly Assistant-Commissioner, succeeded Lieut.-Colonel Macleod, who, however, continued to represent the Government in the north-west as a stipendiary magistrate with residence at Fort Macleod.

The new Commissioner was a Canadian by birth, being the son of the late Lieut.-Colonel Irvine of Quebec, who was principal A.D.C. to the Governor-General of Canada. After serving in the Red River expedition of 1870, Colonel

CHANGES AND DEVELOPMENTS

(then Major) Irvine held a command in Manitoba, which he retained until being appointed to the Assistant-Commissionership of the Mounted Police. A slight man, with a keen, grey eye, and reddish beard closely trimmed, is the picture we have of him at this time.

In Colonel Irvine's first annual report, sent to the Government at the close of 1880, some important recommendations were made which were afterwards acted upon. In the first place, he urged the increase of the Force by 200 men. The reason for this, he explained, was that the new requirements of the country demanded it. Since the disappearance of the buffalo the Indian situation had assumed quite a different aspect. Previous to the decimation of the herds the Indian had been self-supporting, independent, and generally contented. Now he was in a very different position; his only means of support was virtually gone, and he was obliged to turn to the Government for assistance. The natural result was that Indians, more or less destitute, sought out the Police posts, Indian Agencies, and other settlements where they might obtain relief.

A very limited number of buffalo were still to be found south of the International Line, and this had been the means of keeping a certain portion of the Indians out of the north-west for a time, but this could not continue long. With their return the native population would be considerably increased, and in view of the hardships that must follow, the situation was one that would require power as well as care in handling.

There was, too, the Commissioner pointed out, the advancement of civilisation in the north-west. This was another great factor in the problem. New settlers, unaccustomed to Indian manners and habits, did not make sufficient allowances for the red men, and were lacking in tact and patience. "As an instance of this," notes the report, "during the last summer a settler within a few yards of Fort Walsh became annoyed at a Cree Indian whom he found leaning on his garden fence, and struck the Indian in the face with his fist. This so enraged the Indians of the tribe the assaulted man belonged to, that notwithstanding the fact that a fine was inflicted on the settler, they proceeded in a body to his garden, which they at once commenced to destroy, and, but for the timely arrival of the Police, much more serious consequences would have followed. Had this happened, it is hard to tell where it would have ended."

That is the bald official account of the affair. What remains to be told is that it was Colonel Irvine himself who, with his adjutant, Captain Cotton, appeared so opportunely on the scene. They were unarmed, but they rode straight into the midst of the infuriated mob, disregarding the rifles levelled at them with threatening glances, and by their coolness cowed the Indians into submission. Not every case of this kind finds its way into the reports. That they have occurred, however, time after time, every one knows who has talked much with the Mounted Policeman of long service. "It is all in the day's work," he says, simply, and leaves it at that. But he who listens can understand what any display of indecision or loss of temper would have meant in such circumstances, and his respect for the Force increases accordingly.

The recommendation made by the Commissioner had the desired effect. Early in 1882, the authorities sanctioned the augmentation of the Force by 200 men, and recruiting

CHANGES AND DEVELOPMENTS

was promptly commenced in Toronto and Winnipeg. The total strength was now brought up to 474 officers and men, an increase which soon proved most judicious, though even then it was scarcely adequate to the country's needs. The effect on the Indians throughout the Territory was to show them that the Government meant law and order to be kept, by white and red men alike, and that sufficient force would be forthcoming to accomplish this.

At this stage of the Force's development its distribution was as follows :—

Division.	Station.	Officers.	Non.-Com. Officers and Men.	Total.
A.	Fort Walsh	3	100	103
A.	On command	4	19	23
B.	Regina	1	55	56
B.	Qu'Appelle	2	15	17
B.	Wood Mountain	1	8	9
B.	On command	1	30	31
C.	Fort Macleod	2	84	86
D.	Battleford	2	56	58
D.	Prince Albert	–	3	3
D.	Fort Saskatchewan	1	15	16
E.	Fort Calgary	2	62	64
E.	On command	–	5	5
		19	452	471

With two officers away on leave and one on special duty, we have the full complement of 474. The men referred to in the above table as " On command " were stationed in small detachments at the following places : Shoal Lake, Broad View, Mosoomin, Troy, Moose Jaw, Rosetta's Crossing, Fort Pelly, End of C.P.R. track, Maple Creek, Ten-Mile Crossing, Crow's Nest Pass, Whoop Up, Stand Off, and along the Boundary Line.

THE RIDERS OF THE PLAINS

During the same year steps were taken to find a site suitable for new headquarters, the post at Fort Walsh, which had served as such hitherto, having been condemned. The Wascana ("Pile of Bones") Creek was at length chosen, and the construction of the necessary buildings begun. Substantial barracks with "all the modern improvements" were now the order of the day. The original Police quarters, built of cotton-wood, roofed with poles, and thatched with grass and earth, were being done away with. And such conveniences as recreation-rooms and canteens began to make their appearance, to the great satisfaction and comfort of the men. In December the headquarters of the Force were transferred to the new post, which was given the name of Fort Regina. In many respects the choice was an excellent one. From its central position on the Saskatchewan prairie, Regina was found to answer the purpose admirably, and it has since remained the chief dépôt of the Mounted Police.

In a later report of Colonel Irvine's we find an important note in regard to the age of enlistment in the Force. Up to this period young men from eighteen upwards had been recruited, and it was felt that the limit of age should be raised. Senior Surgeon Jukes emphasised this point strongly, averring that the efficiency of the corps would be increased, the sick reports materially diminished, and the number of men annually requiring to be invalided reduced to a minimum. He recommended the age limits for admission to be from twenty-three to forty. Eventually this suggestion was approved by the authorities, but the minimum age was fixed at twenty-two.

The standard of physique among the new recruits was, fortunately, fairly high. It was absolutely necessary that

CHANGES AND DEVELOPMENTS

this should be the case, as the duties thrown upon the Police were now very heavy. In addition to acting as Indian Agents and generally looking after the reserves, they had a great deal to do in checking horse thieves and illicit liquor traders, and rounding up stolen or strayed cattle. The revenue laws in the Territories were administered by them, and this often entailed long winter rides which taxed a man's strength to the utmost.

Distance, however, has never counted with the Mounted Police. In a country of such vast area and so sparsely settled, a few hundred miles are nothing. One New Year's Day a message reached the post at Saskatoon informing the officer there that a certain well-known horse thief, who had evaded capture for several weeks, had been located about 120 miles to the north-west. It was a meagre clue that was brought, but three men were detailed to follow it up, and in the face of a blinding snowstorm they mounted their horses and rode off. Two days later they ran their man to earth in a half-breed settlement. There were eighty of the breeds, and they were ready to show fight— long odds against three men. But the scarlet coats and the cool courage of the troopers carried the day, and they rode back across the prairie with their prisoner safely secured.

Note, too, this succinct but suggestive record of work done. There are many like it to be found in the files. "Constable J. A. W. O'Neill, on a patrol from Norway House into the interior of Keewatin for the purpose of arresting two Indians accused of murder. Time occupied, four months; distance travelled by dog train and canoes, 750 miles." And rarely, if ever, have the perils of a journey daunted the Policeman to whom a mission has been entrusted. Did not a sergeant and a constable each convoy

THE RIDERS OF THE PLAINS

a dangerous lunatic many hundreds of miles in midwinter through a wild and unknown country, as will be told later ? Witness, too, the pathetic story—it is not apocryphal—of the young constable who was sent out over the snow-covered prairie to hunt up some strayed horses at Pendant d'Oreille. Soon after he had left his post he was overtaken by a terrible blizzard, and man and horse wandered helplessly about in circles until they fell benumbed and exhausted. Several weeks later, when the snows had melted, a search party found the body of this Rider of the Plains. In his pocket was his notebook, on a leaf of which he had scribbled : " Lost. Horse dead. Am trying to push on. Have done my best." It is a fine thing for the Royal North-West Mounted Police that they have traditions such as these.

Recurring to the developments in the Force—accomplished or projected—at this period, it should be mentioned that the new Commissioner saw the need for the Territories to be divided into districts. Over each of these a Superintendent was to be placed in charge, with a suitable number of officers and men under him, " in accordance with the amount of Police work to be performed." Each Superintendent was to be responsible to the Commissioner for the discipline, peace, and order of his district, also for all district stores, etc.

Another noteworthy suggestion offered—to be carried into effect in due course—was that the new headquarters of the Force should be a dépôt of instruction, " at which place all officers and men joining the Force will be sent, where they will remain until thoroughly drilled and instructed in the various Police duties." That this could be accomplished by the aid of officers and non-commissioned officers then serving in the Force was quite possible, but

CHANGES AND DEVELOPMENTS

Colonel Irvine further recommended the engagement of at least three fully qualified non-commissioned officers from an Imperial cavalry regiment. "Instructors of this class," he added, "in addition to the knowledge they would impart to others, would serve as models for recruits, as regards soldier-like conduct and general bearing. The importance of the benefits the Force would thus derive cannot, in my opinion, be overrated."

Valuable advice such as this could not be lightly treated. Colonel Irvine had the satisfaction of seeing his proposed reforms brought into being, with the result that the organisation and all-round efficiency of the Force was much improved. To what a high pitch this instructional scheme was in time raised must be left for a later chapter to tell.

The arms and equipment which had been served out to the Police since 1874 were now the cause of no little discussion. The Snider carbine was still the principal weapon in use, but it was now considered to be obsolete. About a hundred Winchester repeating rifles, improved pattern, had been purchased and distributed among A and F Divisions, and it was a favourite arm with the western prairie men. The Winchester did not altogether commend itself as the ideal rifle for a Mounted Policeman, who in the course of his duty often subjected his weapon to a good deal of rough handling, but until some better arm was forthcoming, said the Commissioner, it would hold the field.

In the matter of saddlery—a very important item—the old "Universal" saddle was now being generally condemned in favour of other and improved types.

"I have myself," wrote the Commissioner, "ridden thousands of miles in the Californian and English saddles. Taking all things into consideration, I think the choice lies in favour of the English high-cantle dragoon saddle as being the most suitable and serviceable, but I would recommend some modifications." These were that the saddle should be reduced in weight, the "cantle" cut down a few inches, the crupper and breastplate done away with, and wooden stirrups used instead of iron ones. The reason advanced for this last alteration was that in winter the iron stirrups became so cold as to be almost unbearable. In summer, to a man whose boots were slippery from walking in the prairie grass, "it was a source of annoyance and discomfort, owing to the difficulty experienced in keeping the stirrup."

In addition to the need for more men in the Police Force there had been a similar call for more horses. The amount of work undergone by some of the latter is almost incredible, and speaks well for the hardy nature of the plains-bred animal. They frequently had to travel 50 miles a day for a week at a time. When the Marquess of Lorne, the Governor-General, made his tour through the north-west, his Police escort travelled 2072 miles at an average rate of 35 miles a day. One of his staff officers, belonging to a crack British cavalry corps, declared that a month of such work would break up his regiment. Here is a remarkable performance of a horse team. For seven months, from 1st April to 1st November 1880, its record was as follows:—

1 trip from Fort Walsh to Morleyville and return		640 miles.
2 trips ,, ,, ,, ,, Benton, U.S.A. ,,	.	640 ,,
2 ,, ,, ,, ,, ,, Fort Macleod ,,	.	720 ,,
1 trip ,, ,, ,, ,, Coal Bank, U.S.A. ,,	.	250 ,,
1 ,, ,, ,, ,, ,, Cow Island, U.S.A. ,,	.	400 ,,
1 ,, ,, ,, ,, ,, East End Post ,,	.	130 ,,
5 trips ,, ,, ,, ,, Maple Farm ,,	.	300 ,,
	Total	. 3080 miles.

CHANGES AND DEVELOPMENTS

A large number of fresh horses were accordingly drafted into the Force to relieve the pressure, and the suggestion of forming a " Police farm " near Fort Macleod, where many of the horses could be " wintered out," was adopted.

So much is necessary to follow the progress of the Mounted Police in the few years since 1876. What may be added is some account of the work entailed in the pursuit of horse and cattle thieves, and the recovery of stolen property. In these depredations both Americans and Indians were concerned. Just over the border in Montana was a rough white element to whom the temptation to raid the north-west was very strong. On the Canadian side of the line the Indians were rarely loth to take the opportunity to return the compliment, and swoop down upon some American settler's stock. All this business kept the Mounted Police, particularly those on the frontier, fully occupied, their duties being the heavier by reason of the fact that the law as to horse-stealing was almost a dead letter on the United States side. The Indians, as a matter of fact, called the International Boundary the " Medicine Line," assuming that in the absence of any agreement between the two Governments relative to this crime, they were perfectly safe on one side of the line with regard to what had been done on the other.

A typical instance of a horse-stealing raid by Canadian Indians is that in which Inspector Dickens figured as Nemesis. A bunch of horses had been " lifted " from the Yellowstone country in Montana, and certain members of the Blood tribe were known to be implicated. Sheriff John Healy, of Benton, U.S.A., laid information about this and other cases before the Police at Fort Macleod, and requested immediate investigation of the affair, with the return of the stolen animals.

From the tone of Sheriff Healy's letter one might gather that this raiding was a very one-sided affair, and the Police might well have countered by instancing the numerous occasions on which Canadian ranchmen and others had suffered at the hands of American white horsethieves. Once, be it noted, a large and valuable herd of horses was stolen from the Police Farm itself, and only recovered after a great deal of trouble and considerable expense in United States territory. However, the plain duty before the Police was the recapture of the Montana rancher's stock and the punishment of the thieves, and to this end they lost no time in taking action. We will let Inspector Dickens tell his own story of the affair.

"I have the honour to report," he wrote to Superintendent Crozier at Fort Macleod, "that, in obedience to your orders, I proceeded on the 1st instant (July 1, 1881) to the Blood Reservation to search for horses stolen from American citizens on the other side of the line. I was accompanied by Sergeant Spicer, Constable Callaghan, and the American citizens. On arriving at the reservation I had an interview with Red Crow, the chief, and explained to him that it would be better for his young men to give up the horses, so as to avoid further trouble, and he said he would do his best to have the horses returned; but he did not appear to have much control over the Indians, who were very loth to give up the stolen animals. Eventually, I recovered fourteen horses, which were identified by the Americans, and placed them in a corral. While we were waiting near the Agency for another horse which an Indian had promised to bring in, a minor chief, 'Many

A SEIZURE OF STOLEN HORSES.

CHANGES AND DEVELOPMENTS

Spotted Horses,' appeared and commenced a violent speech, calling upon the Indians not to give up the horses, and abused the party generally. I refused to talk with him, and he eventually retired. I went over to the Rev. Mr. Trivett's house for a few minutes, and on returning was told that an Indian who goes by the name of 'Joe Healy' had said that one of the Americans had stolen all 'Bull Back Fat's' horses last winter, and had set the camp on foot. This the American denied, but the Indians became violent and began to use threatening language. The Americans went up to the corral, and 'White Cap,' who had just come in, collected a body of Indians who commenced howling and yelling and started off to seize the Americans. It was impossible at the time to get a word in, so I started in front of the Indians towards the corral, and shouted to the party to mount their horses and to be ready to start in order to avoid disturbance. I mounted my horse and placed myself in the road between the party and the Indians, who began to hesitate. Sergeant Spicer, who was behind the crowd, called out that he wished to speak to them, and they turned back. The sergeant began to parley with them for a few minutes, and seeing all the party mounted, I rode back and met the sergeant coming out of the crowd of Indians, who became quieter, but who were still very sulky. No more horses being forthcoming, we collected the band and rode out of camp. I thought it best to get both men and horses as far away from the reservation as possible that night ; and after supping at Fred Wachter's ranch, we started for Fort Macleod, and although I heard a report that a war party had gone down the Kootenay River to intercept our passage, we forded the river safely, and reached the fort without being molested."

THE RIDERS OF THE PLAINS

For the Indian Department of the Government the Mounted Police continued to perform much valuable service. There were constantly parties of Crees, Assiniboines, and members of other tribes to be transported to their reservations, and for this work the Police waggons, with escorts, were requisitioned. Then, too, the payments of the treaty money had to be undertaken by the Force. That for the Fort Walsh and Macleod districts was conveyed by the Police from Qu'Appelle to Fort Walsh, a distance of 333 miles, where it was handed over to the Indian Department officials. At times it happened that this payment was accompanied with difficulties. A discreditable half-breed element, desirous of fomenting trouble, influenced the Indians to make exorbitant demands and otherwise conduct themselves in a disorderly manner. When this occurred, the presence of the Police officers alone prevented serious complications, a fact which the officials of the Department were not slow to acknowledge.

As showing the varied nature of Mounted Police work and the help afforded the Government generally, it is interesting to study the return giving the amount of Customs duties collected by the Force in one year, 1882:—

Port of Fort Walsh up to 8th December	$15,135.46
Port of Fort Macleod up to 30th October	33,525.76
Port of Wood Mountain up to 31st December	2,784.64
Port of Qu'Appelle up to 31st December	1,076.50
Total	$52,522.36

Value of articles imported, on which duty was collected :—

Port of Fort Walsh	$86,627.94
Port of Fort Macleod	224,522.50
Port of Wood Mountain	13,522.00
Total	$324,672.44

CHANGES AND DEVELOPMENTS

The construction of the Canadian Pacific Railway, which made great strides during the year 1882, was responsible for an additional amount of Police work of a peculiar kind. As is well known, the railway track was laid in two sections, one starting from the former eastern terminus to cross the prairies of Saskatchewan and Alberta, the other commencing at Vancouver, the western terminus, and traversing the passes of the Rocky Mountains, eventually to join that from the east.

For many years before, while the scheme for a transcontinental railway had been under consideration, survey parties had been busy all over the projected route. In the Rockies alone scores of engineers were exploring the gorges of the mountains in the endeavour to find the best and easiest road to follow. Twelve lines of survey pierced the Cascade Range alone. Like all great enterprises of this nature, the death-toll among this pioneer force was heavy. One party, seven in number, was surprised by a widespread forest fire on the northern shore of Lake Superior. The body of *one* of its members was found to tell the fate that had overtaken all. This was in 1871. In the succeeding years we read of others similarly stricken down, or drowned in flooded rivers, shipwrecked in the fierce storms that lash the inland lakes to demoniac fury, or waylaid and murdered by hostile Indians. It is all part of the romance of the north-west, their story; and the present generation will do well not to forget these soldiers of the " lost legion " whom Kipling had in mind when he wrote :—

" Follow after—we are waiting, by the trails that we lost,
For the sounds of many footsteps, for the tread of a host.
Follow after—follow after—for the harvest is sown :
By the bones about the wayside ye shall come to your own ! "[1]

---

[1] " A Song of the English."

When the huge task of actually laying the track was begun, an army of several thousands of workmen was employed. The Mounted Police now found themselves called upon to perform new and arduous duties which demanded considerable tact and firmness.

The railway camps were frequently the scenes of wild disorder. A number of the navvies were disreputable characters, and themselves a constant source of trouble. There was the utmost vigilance needed to prevent the wholesale supply of liqour to these men, who found themselves with money in their pockets and the usual outlets for it closed to them. There were, too, a host of undesirables always to be found in the vicinity, ready to prey upon the men and reap a golden harvest from them. Gamblers, thieves, loose women, and other scum—mostly from the western border States—flocked round the camps, and their supervision was no light task. Sometimes the Indians would interfere with the work, resenting this fresh invasion of their territory, and again the old Police work of pacifying these

> "Fluttered folk and wild—
> The new-caught, sullen peoples,
> Half-devil and half-child,"

had to be gone through patiently.

Not least among the troubles that arose were the strikes among the railway men themselves. On several occasions these threatened to assume serious dimensions, but in all the difficulties the Mounted Police kept the upper hand and maintained peace It was an achievement of the highest order, and we cannot grudge the pat on the back which the Commissioner gave himself in summing up the year's record. "I venture to state," he wrote to the Government,

CHANGES AND DEVELOPMENTS

" that it is unparalleled in the history of railway building in a western country that not a single serious crime has been committed along the line of work."

For their part the officials of the Canadian Pacific Railway were quick to recognise the important services thus rendered. The following is a copy of a letter received by Colonel Irvine from the Company's General Manager. It is dated January 1, 1883.

" DEAR SIR,—Our work of construction for the year of 1882 has just closed, and I cannot permit the occasion to pass without acknowledging the obligations of the Company to the North-West Mounted Police, whose zeal and industry in preventing traffic in liquor and preserving order along the line under construction have contributed so much to the successful prosecution of the work. Indeed, without the assistance of the officers and men of the splendid force under your command, it would have been impossible to have accomplished as much as we did. On no great work within my knowledge, where so many men have been employed, has such perfect order prevailed. On behalf of the Company, and of all the officers, I wish to return thanks, and to acknowledge particularly our obligations to yourself and Major Walsh.

(Signed) "W. C. VAN HORNE,
"General Manager."

CHAPTER VII.

RAILWAY PROGRESS : A NEW ERA.

The Canadian Pacific Railway—Indian disturbances—Chief Pie-a-pot—Railway strikes—Inspector Steele at Golden—A critical situation—Prohibition duties—A desperado from Idaho—Fort Walsh abandoned—New Fort Macleod—Changes in equipment—The Marquess of Lorne's tour.

BY January 1883, such progress had been made with the eastern portion of the Canadian Pacific Railway that the track had reached a point within twelve miles of the station now known as Maple Creek. Owing to the severity of the weather and the heavy fall of snow, work was suspended for the time, and the gangs of navvies, who wintered in the Cypress Hills, were employed in parties cutting and getting out timber. For a few months until spring came, they were condemned to camp life in the woods, with its varying delights and discomforts.

One discomfort which quickly made itself apparent to the men was the proximity of the Indians. To the railway employé every Indian seen was sure to be a hostile one. As a result, they were constantly experiencing scares which sent them flying to the Police for protection. The Indians were certainly much to blame in the matter. Emboldened by the men's timidity, they now and then attempted to interfere with the lumbering that was going on, hoping to be propitiated with presents of food and tobacco. One

RAILWAY PROGRESS: A NEW ERA

railway contractor thus approached sought refuge with his gang at the Police outpost at Maple Creek, where his fears were soon dispelled. A constable having been dispatched to summon the chief of the erring band, "Front Man" by name, the latter was severely lectured on his conduct, after which nothing more was heard from that quarter.

The Indians at this stage of the railway work were undoubtedly a source of much trouble. They stole the Company's horses whenever possible, and the Company's cattle which were intended to feed the host of employés. And they were often mischievous in placing obstructions on the track. One day it would be a tomahawk driven in between the ends of the rails, another day a piece of iron, called in railway parlance a "hanger," or a huge log sufficient to derail any engine. When these crimes were brought home to them, the penalties inflicted were usually severe.

At the same time, a certain amount of horse and cattle stealing imputed to the red men was really to be laid at the doors of some of the white desperadoes who came up from the border "bad lands." Whisky-smuggling and horse-thieving often went hand in hand, and their prevention occupied the attention of the Mounted Police very fully. Yet another source of anxiety was the frequency of prairie and forest fires. The checking of this scourge has always been an important feature of Police work. At this juncture especially, owing to the ignorance and carelessness of those working along the line, the number of fires was very large. In the mountains, where the spruce grew thick about the hillsides, a vast quantity of valuable timber was thus destroyed.

THE RIDERS OF THE PLAINS

It was in the early days of the C.P.R.'s progress across the prairies that the "Pie-a-pot" incident occurred. Readers of Mrs. Steel's stories may remember one which tells how a Hindu fanatic squatted in the permanent way of a new railway line in India, and resisted all efforts to dislodge him until at length he was run over and killed. The fanatic in question had a religious motive for his defiant attitude. So much could hardly be said of Pie-a-pot the Cree, who took it upon himself to play the same game. Pie-a-pot and his band had been giving no little trouble to the Police about this time. He and another chief named Long Lodge had left their reserve, and were wandering about the country at large. This proceeding was contrary to the law, and particularly so as their followers were all armed, and had the reputation of being a turbulent crowd.

What happened to bring Pie-a-pot into sudden collision with the Police was this. Fetching up with his band at last at a point some little distance ahead of the railway line, he encamped. His tepees were put up, the carts unloaded, the horses sent out on the prairie to feed, and there was every indication that the wanderers had found a choice spot from which they did not intend to move. By and by the railway track advanced closer towards them, and the contractors looked askance at the Indian settlement.

Pie-a-pot paid no attention to the oncoming army of white men. He was there first; it was his chosen location; let them shift him if they dared. The railway authorities sent emissaries demanding his evacuation of the spot, but Pie-a-pot laughed at them, while his "bucks" rode excitedly about on their ponies and fired off rifles at random, and shouted of what they would do to the whites if it came to a fight. Matters were at a deadlock. The railway men

STONY CREEK BRIDGE, BRITISH COLUMBIA.
Photo. Canadian Pacific Railway Co.]

could not go on so long as the Indian camp blocked the way.

Then the Lieutenant-Governor of the Territories was appealed to, and ere long there came a dispatch from the N.W.M.P. headquarters at Regina to the little post at Maple Creek much to this effect : " Please settle trouble ; move on Indians." On receipt of the message two men were at once detailed for the task. One was a sergeant, the other was a constable. With a written order to Chief Pie-a-pot, an official notice to quit, they rode out quietly to the camp and made known their instructions.

Their arrival was the signal for a fresh outburst on the part of the Indians. In their nomadic life the members of this band had not yet, to put it literally, run up against the law as personified by the North-West Mounted Police. They knew them by reputation to be firm, hard-dealing men whose hand was heavy upon the wrong-doer, but they had had no practical experience from which to learn caution. So they surrounded the two guardians of law and order, jeering at them, backing their ponies into the police horses, and otherwise trying to discompose them. The sergeant and the constable, in their scarlet tunics, with the smart-looking pill-box forage caps, set at an angle on their heads, meanwhile sat still, the former reading his order, which was that Pie-a-pot must break camp and take the northward trail.

To this command the chief insolently refused to listen.

The sergeant pulled out his watch. " I will give you fifteen minutes," he said calmly. " If by the end of that time you haven't begun to comply with the order we shall make you."

The quarter of an hour passed without any sign of a

move being made. Pie-a-pot sat in front of his tent and smoked. Round him and the policemen had gathered all the rest of the tribe, " bucks," squaws, and children, most of them yelling abuse and urging on the bolder spirits among them to still further exhibitions of defiance. The firing of rifles almost in the faces of the " red coats " was one form of sport indulged in, but it was of no avail.

" Time's up ! " said the sergeant, replacing his watch in his pocket. Then this amazing man dismounted, threw the reins of his horse to his companion, and walked over to Pie-a-pot's tepee. One kick of his foot at the key-pole and the painted buffalo-skin covering collapsed. Ignoring the shrieks of the discomfited squaws thereunder, and the threats of the men, the sergeant proceeded through the camp, kicking out key-pole after key-pole until all the tents had been overthrown.

" Now git ! " was what he said—or might have said, in the absence of any exact record of his utterance.

And it is some tribute to his sagacity that Pie-a-pot did so. He may have contemplated shooting the sergeant ; no doubt the thought flashed through his brain ; but— there were the consequences. Like many other Indian chiefs, Pie-a-pot was not without brains. In time, we may assume, he attained to some of that wholesome respect for the law which was instilled into the mind of Crowfoot of the Blackfeet nation.

On one of the first occasions that Crowfoot's followers got into trouble and were haled off by the Mounted Police to their court of law, the chief was greatly incensed. But he had the curiosity to follow and attend the hearing of the case, and at its conclusion—the proceedings having been interpreted to him—he said : " This is good medicine.

RAILWAY PROGRESS: A NEW ERA

There is no forked tongue here. When my people do wrong I will bring them here to be tried."

Next to the troubles with Indians the principal difficulty encountered by the railway contractors was the tendency to strike on the part of their employés. This was due largely to the fact that many of the men were working for small sub-contractors. The non-payment of wages and disputes raised under the " Masters' and Servants' Act " kept the several detachments of Mounted Police along the line as busy as a county court judge. But they were equal to the occasion, and many a time their rulings were the means of checking what might have been a serious disturbance.

More critical were the strikes which affected one or more sections of the workers as a whole. Such was the strike among the engineers and firemen, who refused to sign the articles of agreement proposed and submitted to them by the railway authorities, and demanded an increased rate of pay. It was at once apparent that the feeling between the Company and their employés was a bitter one, and it became evident soon that attempts would be made by the latter to destroy some valuable property. On warning of this intended move being received, a detachment of Police was furnished, under the command of Superintendent Herchmer, with the result that the malcontents were held in check, their nefarious designs frustrated, and order maintained until the dispute had been settled. Such service as this added very materially to the work of construction on the line, while it was not without its moral effect on the country generally.

A remarkable piece of Police work in this direction was performed at Golden City, a mining town in the Rockies,

THE RIDERS OF THE PLAINS

situated on the Columbia River. It was in the spring of 1885, when the western section of the track had been considerably advanced. At this period, it may be mentioned, there were Mounted Police posts in the following places among the mountains: Laggan, Third Siding, Golden City, First Crossing, Beaver Creek, Summit of the Selkirks, and Second Crossing. In all, however, only twenty-five officers and men were on duty. It may be noted, too, that the strength of the Force, owing to the exceptionally heavy increase of work in the Territories, was being raised gradually. By the end of the year it had reached a total of 1039. Five more divisions had been created, making ten in all, and these were distributed over twenty-four stations, with detachments "on command" and on special service.[1]

The British Columbian detachment in the Rockies was under the command of Inspector Steele, who had joined the Force at its inception and who is now a Colonel in the Canadian Military Forces. How the incident arose in which he played so prominent a part is narrated in the official report he sent to the Commissioner.

"About the first day of April," he writes, "owing to their wages being in arrears, 1200 of the workmen employed on the line struck, where the end of the track then was, and informed the manager of construction that unless paid up in full at once, and more regularly in future, they would do no more work. They also openly stated their intention of committing acts of violence upon the staff of the road

---

[1] The stations were as follows: Regina (headquarters), Maple Creek, Medicine Hat, Swift Current, Fort Qu'Appelle, Broadview, Moose Jaw, Moosomin, Moose Mountain, Shoal Lake, Whitewood, Fort Macleod, Stand Off, St. Mary's, Pincher Creek, Lethbridge, Piegan Reserve, Battleford, Calgary, Chief Mountain, Prince Albert, Edmonton, Fort Saskatchewan, and Old Fort Macleod.

and destroying property. I received a deputation of the ringleaders, and assured them that if they committed any act of violence, and were not orderly, in the strictest sense of the word, I would inflict upon the offenders the severest punishment the law would allow me. They saw the manager of construction, who promised to accede to their demands, so far as lay in his power, if they would return to their camps, their board not to cost them anything in the meantime. Some were satisfied with this, and several hundreds returned to their camps. The remainder stayed at the Beaver (where there was a population of 700 loose characters), ostensibly waiting for their money. They were apparently very quiet, but one morning word was brought to me that some of them were ordering the bricklayers to quit work, teamsters freighting supplies to leave their teams, and bridgemen to leave their work. I sent detachments of Police to the points threatened, leaving only two men to look after the prisoners at my post. I instructed the men in charge of the detachments to use the severest measures to prevent a cessation of the work of construction."

As will be seen from the above, all was done that was possible to prevent a breach of the peace. At Golden, however, the "tough" element among the would-be rioters was very strong. In addition to the railway men themselves the town possessed a large number of miners and well-known bad characters who had drifted to the spot in quest of plunder. These gentlemen, ready to promote any disorder, arranged themselves on the side of the strikers, and through their efforts what they called the "fun" began.

One afternoon Constable Kerr, one of Steele's two men,

had occasion to go into the town. While there he saw a certain contractor, a desperado of note and one known to be in sympathy with the disaffected employés, very drunk and disorderly. The constable attempted to arrest him, and was immediately attacked by a large crowd of strikers and "toughs," who maltreated him and rescued their comrade. Powerless in the face of such numbers, Constable Kerr returned to barracks to report the state of affairs to his officer.

Enters now upon the scene Sergeant Fury. "A determined, bull-dog little man" is the description we have of him, and that it fitted him well is borne out by his record in the Force. The sergeant came into the post with three men soon after Constable Kerr's return; he had been on duty at the end of the railway track. Acting on instructions from Inspector Steele, who was on a sick-bed at the time, he now took two constables and set off to apprehend the culprit. The latter was located in a saloon where he was in the midst of his gang, as rowdy and ugly-looking a crew as one could wish to meet. Without any ado the Policemen seized their man and hauled him out, but, like Constable Kerr, they found it no easy matter to get him away. There was a rush on the part of the crowd, the prisoner was set free a second time, and the strikers intimated that there would be shooting if any other attempt at arrest were made.

Sergeant Fury posted back to Inspector Steele to ask how far he should go in resorting to strong measures, and was told by that officer to return, seize the offender, and shoot any of the crowd who interfered. This order was carried out promptly and to the letter. The contractor was made prisoner a third time, while one of the ring-

RAILWAY PROGRESS: A NEW ERA

leaders was put out of action with a bullet in his shoulder. Then the Police started off for the barracks with their man well secured, and the mob of strikers followed at their heels growling and threatening what they would do.

On the road to the Police post was a bridge spanning a little stream. When this was reached the strikers began to gather courage anew. They outnumbered the Policemen ten times over, and they were determined to get their ally out of the law's clutches. So as the constables dragged their prisoner over the narrow wooden structure there was a shout of " Now, boys ! " and on came the crowd in a fierce rush. Knives and revolvers flashed out quickly in their hands ; it looked as if the Police were going to have trouble.

Sergeant Fury turned to cover his men, who were halfway across, and at this moment an unexpected reinforcement appeared. Down the road from the barracks, at full speed, came the Inspector himself, roused from his bed by the shouting. In a minute or two he was facing the angry mob, revolver in one hand, sword in the other.

" Now," he exclaimed, " the first man who sets foot on this bridge will be shot ! "

The crowd hesitated, and hung back before the grim figure confronting them. Sam Steele was a man of his word, and it meant certain death to him who dared to make the first move. And though plenty of " guns " were out not one was loosed, not a man among them had the nerve to fire a single shot.

The offending contractor and the ringleaders of the strikers, who were in turn arrested, were fined a hundred dollars each the next day, and the strike collapsed. There was no more trouble at Golden for a long time after.

THE RIDERS OF THE PLAINS

Of Sergeant Fury several good stories are related. One that may be called to mind here has for its scene this same town of Golden. At the time the railway camps were scattered through the mountains, the regulations with regard to whisky-selling were very strict, and through the vigilance of the Police very little found its way into the railway men's hands. Golden became almost a prohibition town, much to the disgust of the miners and railway workers alike. One day a daring spirit among them, "Bulldog Carney" by name, ordered in and duly received a whole carload of whisky. A host of friends and acquaintances were invited to sample the brand. When all were assembled, in strode Sergeant Fury and two constables. "My orders," said Fury, and he produced the written instructions, "are to destroy all whisky in Golden." There was no help for it. Every man of the crowd would gladly have seen the Policemen cut to pieces, but, though revolvers were out and threatening words were used, not a hand was laid upon them. And Sergeant Fury then and there tapped those kegs and spilled the whisky as per orders. Simple ? Yes ; but nerve-trying when one remembers what desperadoes those British Columbian mining towns harboured.

It is claimed by many people that all the exciting features of western life are now over, that "we don't do that sort of thing nowadays." A great deal of the romance and glamour that formerly attached to the "wild and woolly west," they add, has therewith disappeared, and so far as the Mounted Police are concerned their duties have been considerably lightened. In a sense this is true. The enforcement of the law has certainly brought about a wonderful change in the western Provinces ; cases of

COLONEL S. B. STEELE, C.B., M.V.O.,
CANADIAN MILITARY FORCES,
FORMERLY SUPERINTENDENT IN THE
R.N.W.M.P.

ASSISTANT-COMMISSIONER Z. T. WOOD,
COMMANDING R.N.W.M.P. FORCE
IN THE YUKON TERRITORY.

RAILWAY PROGRESS: A NEW ERA

extreme acts of violence are far less frequent than they were in those early days. But while the many instances of Police heroism, such as have been recorded here, stand out boldly by way of contrast, there are no grounds for the implication that the members of the Force at the present day would not conduct themselves just as bravely in similar circumstances. " Maintiens le droit " is no empty phrase. The tradition of the corps is as strong as ever, the sense of duty as firmly implanted in every man's breast.

It is only a few years ago that we had a striking illustration of what one Police constable can do in asserting his authority. The story has quite a flavour of the past. At Weyburn, a small town near the frontier, the citizens were one day disturbed by a visit from an Idaho desperado. He was a real " bad man," one of the " never-be-taken-alive-and-want-to-die-in-my-boots " class, and he paraded the streets taking pot shots at the hotel verandas. When any citizen put his head out of a window he was ordered to withdraw it if he didn't want to get hit. A prominent member of the community also had to suffer the indignity of holding up his hat in the middle of the street while this " terror " riddled it with bullets.

The same gentleman thus publicly ridiculed told the desperado that he had better keep quiet or he would be " run in."

" Thar ain't no Johnny Canuck kin arrest me," was the answer. " An' I'll bet you twenty-five dollars no descriptive North-West Mounted Policeman is goin' to hold up my show ! "

That was all very well, but it was a direct challenge. The local Justice of the Peace telegraphed hastily to

THE RIDERS OF THE PLAINS

Halbrite, the nearest Police post, and presently in rode Constable Lett. Finding out the retreat of the " wild and woolly one " from Idaho, he made the arrest. Insantly the other man's hand flew to his hip pocket, but the constable was too quick for him. There was a tussle on the floor, and Lett rose up with the ruffian's loaded revolver in his grip. Then the Policeman said curtly, " Hands up ! " The other obeyed. The bracelets were slipped upon his wrists, and he was haled off to gaol. It was all over in a very few minutes, but it earned Constable Lett well-merited commendation.

The increase of the Mounted Police's strength has already been commented upon. It is necessary to point out here that this augmentation was spread over the course of a whole year—1885—the same year that saw the outbreak of the Riel Rebellion, which is dealt with in the succeeding chapters. Among other changes in connection with the Force anterior to this date must be noted the abandonment of Fort Walsh. This post had outlived its usefulness. From a military point of view the site was an objectionable one, being commanded by hills on either side. Then there was the fact that it was some 30 miles south from the line of route followed by the Canadian Pacific Railway. Colonel Irvine, therefore, had the post demolished in May and June 1883. The serviceable portion of the lumber from which the old buildings had been constructed was conveyed to the Police camp at Maple Creek, to be used in the erection of a post there.

At about the same time a new fort was put into construction at Macleod. Old Fort Macleod had become untenable owing to sudden deviation in the course of the Old Man's River. At high water the stream followed two

RAILWAY PROGRESS: A NEW ERA

new channels, passing immediately in front and rear of the fort. In view of the fact that during the spring freshets some of the buildings might be carried away, it had been decided to remove the post to a new site. The location, at first recommended by the Commissioner was the Police Farm, about 30 miles south-west from where the old fort stood, but this position was abandoned later for another only $2\frac{1}{2}$ miles to the westward.

As giving an idea of what a Police post comprised, the following list of the buildings at the new Fort Macleod will not be amiss: 3 officers' quarters, with a kitchen 20 ft. square; 2 barrack-rooms, with wing extending back from centre, 28 ft. × 78 ft. × 14 ft.; 1 sergeants' mess; 1 sergeants' quarters; 1 recreation and billiard room; 1 guard-room, 10 cells; 1 artisans' building; 1 division office and orderly room building; 1 hospital, with wings 24 ft. square on either side, and one small detached building; 2 storehouses; 3 stables; 1 harness-room; 1 coal-house; 1 bakery; 1 blacksmith's shop; 1 waggon shed.

The arrangement of the buildings, which are painted grey, by the way, is in the form of a rectangle, 48 ft. long by 254 ft. wide, with the officers' quarters on the west side, the barrack-rooms facing them on the opposite side. The offices, guard-room, recreation-room, sergeants' mess, and quarters are at the north end, with the stables, storerooms, and harness-room at the south. The remaining buildings are outside the "square." As constructed in 1883 the underground magazine was covered with several inches of concrete and earth. Its capacity was for 150,000 rounds of Winchester ammunition, 25,000 rounds of revolver ammunition, and 10 kegs of (service) powder.

At the new fort the artillery branch of the Mounted

THE RIDERS OF THE PLAINS

Police was represented by two 9-pounder M.L.R. guns and two small mortars. The other large field pieces in the service were four bronze mountain guns, two of which were at Regina and two at Calgary.

The same year that saw the second Fort Macleod spring into existence marked a new departure for the North-West Mounted Police in the establishment of a recruiting dépôt at Winnipeg. One officer and ten men looked after this important base, which proved very serviceable.

In the matter of equipment not a few changes were being contemplated. The need for a more suitable head-gear, for one thing, was making itself felt, the old helmet which had been in use since the institution of the Force having been found somewhat cumbersome. " Future issues " (of the helmet), reported the Commissioner to the authorities, " should be of buff or brown leather. It would be better, also, if they were not so tall as the present pattern, which presents an unnecessary surface to the wind on the prairie, and is thereby rendered very uncomfortable to the wearer." The forage, or " pill-box," cap was more in favour, but this had the disadvantage of affording no shade to the head in the heat of summer. As yet, however, the now familiar cowboy " Stetson " hat had not found its way to recommendation.

The suitability of other parts of the Police dress had been a moot point for some time past. The red coat, from long association, had the confidence of the Indians, while it conduced to the smartness and soldierly appearance of the men. On the other hand, it was recognised that a red coat soon lost its colour amid the dust and dirt of prairie travel, and the suggestion was made that a working suit of some stout material should be provided. The red tunic, mean-

RAILWAY PROGRESS: A NEW ERA

while, which had superseded the loose-fitting Norfolk jacket, could be retained for full-dress parades and as a walking-out suit. That pipeclay, also, was superfluous was another point raised by the Commissioner. For this reason he urged the adoption of brown leather gauntlets, such as were worn by the mounted infantry of the Imperial Service, in place of the white ones with which the troopers were then equipped.

In a former report the English high-cantle dragoon saddle, with certain changes, had been recommended as a substitute for the obsolete " Universal " saddles. Experience, however, had decided in favour of the " Californian " type, and a further purchase of these was approved. Bits and bridoons of the " Whitman " make were also adopted. With regard to arms, the new pattern Winchester rifle had proved a most excellent weapon, and well adapted to the Police use. In place of the old " Adams " revolvers the " Enfield " were fast gaining approval, the type having stood the tests of service very satisfactorily.

The manner of carrying the Winchester carbines on horseback was another point that vexed the minds of the authorities. As a result of practical experience the conclusion arrived at was that two separate and distinct methods should be employed : (1) the use of a bucket attached to the saddle ; (2) the use of a sling, by means of which the carbine hung from the rider's body, the stock resting in a small leather open shoe attached to the saddle. The bucket could be used on long marches and on ordinary mounted (drill) parades ; the sling in cases when men might be called into action at any moment, or when they were sent out on detachment or patrolling duty.

Before closing this chapter of Police history, one important event has to be chronicled. In the summer of 1881 his Excellency the Governor-General of Canada, the Marquess of Lorne, made a memorable tour through the North-West Territories. On this occasion an escort of Mounted Police, under the command, in turn, of Superintendents Herchmer and Crozier, was provided. The contingent accompanied the Governor-General for thirty-five days' travel, making an average rate per day of 35 miles. In addition to covering this distance they had travelled, in the first place, from Fort Walsh to Fort Ellice, 443 miles; then again from Fort Shaw to Fort Macleod, and from Fort Macleod to Fort Walsh, 400 miles; the aggregate being 2072 miles.

It is characteristic of the high repute in which the Mounted Police were held even then that the whole responsibility of the trip rested on their shoulders. The westward route followed was by way of Fort Ellice, Qu'Appelle, Carlton, Battleford, Blackfoot Crossing, Calgary, High River, and Macleod; then south to Fort Shaw, in Montana, from which place his Excellency made the return journey through United States territory. During the tour several interviews with the Indians were held, notably with the Crees and Blackfeet.

How well the Police escort performed their onerous duties is well borne out by Superintendent Herchmer in his official report on the expedition, and by the Governor-General himself. Previous to taking farewell of the escort at Fort Shaw the latter had them paraded, and addressed the men as follows:—

"You have been subjected to the most severe criticism during the long march on which you have accompanied me, for I have on my personal staff experienced officers of the three branches of the service,—cavalry, artillery, and infantry,—and they one and all have expressed themselves astonished and delighted at the manner in which you have performed your arduous duties and at your great efficiency."

That his Excellency thoroughly appreciated the different kinds of service rendered by the Police of the Prairies is shown by these remarks : " Your Force is often spoken of in Canada as one of which Canada is justly proud. It is well that this pride is so fully justified, for your duties are most important and varied. Your work is not only that of military men, but you are called upon to perform the responsible duties which devolve upon you in your civil capacities, your officers in their capacity of magistrates, and other duties they are called upon to perform, even that of diplomacy. The perfect confidence in the maintenance of the authority of the law prevailing over these vast territories, a confidence most necessary with the settlement now proceeding, shows how thoroughly you have done your work."

CHAPTER VIII.

THE NORTH-WEST REBELLION.—I.

Completion of the Canadian Pacific Railway—Grievances of the half-breeds—The new land survey—Louis Riel—Signs of trouble—The Bill of Rights—The storm breaks—Fears for an Indian rising—Successful Police manœuvres—The affair at Duck Lake—Superintendent Crozier—At Prince Albert—Wild rumours—Militia troops from the east—General Middleton takes the field.

THE great task undertaken by the Canadian Pacific Railway Company was completed in November 1885. On the 7th of that month the rails from the east and the west were linked together, and Canada rejoiced in her first transcontinental line. What part the North-West Mounted Police played in assisting in its construction has been set forth in the preceding chapters. There now remains to be told how the same year (1885) saw them busily engaged in another capacity. The fires of insurrection, which had been smouldering for some time among the half-breed settlements, suddenly burst into flame during the wintry month of March, and the world was startled by the news of the Riel Rebellion.

It was not, of course, the first time that trouble with the *métis*, or French half-breeds, had been experienced by the Government. As long ago as 1869, when the great tract of country in the north-west ruled over by the Hudson's Bay Company was transferred to the Crown, the half-breeds—trappers, hunters, and *coureurs de bois*—rose in

THE NORTH-WEST REBELLION

revolt against what they believed to be an attempt to deprive them of their lands. Louis Riel was the leader of this rebellion; how this outbreak was short-lived, and how Riel became a fugitive in United States territory, has been referred to before. It need not be recapitulated here.

But though the incident itself was historically brief, the causes which gave rise to it did not die with Riel's expulsion. The half-breed population of the north-west, ignorant, superstitious, and resentful of the advance of civilisation, nursed their wrongs, though to outward seeming they were willing to accept the new conditions imposed upon them. By the introduction of the railway into the Territories the struggle to live was rendered keener than ever. In the old days the fur-trapping *métis* had thrived under the fur companies; now rail and steamboat transportation to the big cities in the south cut down their trade.

The most disturbing element in their life was the method of land settlement adopted by the Government. The opening up of the North-West Territories made room for both settlers and speculators in land by whom the country was parcelled out in square sections.[1] Previously the system of surveying had been based on the old French method of delimitation, under which they felt reasonably secure. Under the new system they feared having to change the location of their farms, and thus possibly suffer considerable

[1] Unlike the procedure followed in Eastern Canada, the system of survey in Manitoba and the North-West Territories blocks out the land in square sections and townships, which are numbered in regular order. Each township thus created is about 6 miles square, and is subdivided into 36 sections, each of which contains 1 square mile, or 640 acres. These sections, with the exception of a few retained for school buildings or other special purposes, are taken up by settlers.

loss. They not only dreaded the wiles of the land-grabbers, they distrusted the new Lieutenant-Governor of the Territories, the Hon. Edgar Dewdney. The latter they believed to be much in the hands of an unscrupulous clique.

With the possibility of being compelled to suffer wrongs against which they would have no redress, the French half-breeds began to stir among themselves. The spirit of unrest at last called for a leader, and the more active ones looked again to Louis Riel to help them in this crisis. His former determined stand against the Government, and the outstanding fact that no retribution had followed his armed rebellion, were remembered. There was, too, the recollection that the French vote in Eastern Canada had been largely in favour of Riel through all. In these circumstances none other was better fitted to head the popular agitation. Accordingly, in 1884, overtures were made to him at his home in America with a view to recalling him to the north-west.

Louis Riel cuts but a sorry figure on the stage of Canadian history. He was not a strong personality, nor a natural leader of men. Born of a white father and a half-breed mother, he came from a very mixed stock. Indian, half-breed, French, Irish, and Scandinavian blood ran in his veins, and produced a character that had both strong and weak points. He was a vain man, much susceptible to flattery. To be summoned again by his own people as their leader against oppression appealed to him as nothing else would. The Frenchman in him welcomed the opportunity for theatrical display.

Sir William Butler, who met the half-breed leader some years before this, thus describes him : " A short, stout man with a large head, a sallow, puffy face, a sharp, restless,

THE NORTH-WEST REBELLION

intelligent eye, a square-cut, massive forehead, overhung by a mass of long and thickly clustering hair, and marked with well-cut eyebrows—altogether, a remarkable-looking face, all the more so, perhaps, because it was to be seen in a land where such things are rare sights. This was M. Louis Riel, the head and front of the Red River Rebellion— the President, the little Napoleon, the Ogre, or whatever else he may be called. He was dressed in a curious mixture of clothing—a black frock-coat, vest, and trousers ; but the effect of this somewhat clerical costume was not a little marred by a pair of Indian moccasins, which nowhere look more out of place than on a carpeted floor."

To these details it may be added that he was physically above the average man in strength. Among the *métis* and the Indians he enjoyed the reputation of being a first-class shot and a buffalo hunter of great skill. It was by his prowess with the rifle that he mainly lived during his sojourn in the States, his experience of school-teaching in the west not being of long duration.

At the time his compatriots in the north-west approached him on the subject of their grievances, Riel was living quietly in Montana, where he had married a girl of his own race. In immediate response to their entreaties he crossed the border. The first official notice we have of his reappearance in Canadian territory is a report made by Superintendent Crozier of the Mounted Police, in July 1884, in which it is stated that Riel had held meetings at Prince Albert and Duck Lake. " At the latter place the audience was composed chiefly of French half-breeds and Indians, and Riel is said to have told the Indians that they had ' rights ' as well as the half-breeds, and that he wished to be the means of having them ' redressed.' "

THE RIDERS OF THE PLAINS

From this time on, the Mounted Police kept their eye upon the agitator. Wherever he went he was followed, and constant reports were sent to headquarters notifying the effect produced upon the people by his inflammatory speeches. In August, Sergeant Brooks, at Prince Albert, wired thus: " Returned from Duck Lake last night. Big Bear in council with ten other chiefs. Riel has held several private meetings at the South Branch, attended by leading half-breeds." And so on, until in December Superintendent Gagnon observed " that the half-breeds of St. Laurent and Batoche had held a public meeting to adopt a petition which had been duly forwarded to Ottawa, that the half-breeds were pressing Riel to settle among them, and had presented him with a house well furnished, and intended the next month to add thereto a purse." He continued : " As far as I can see, the chief grievance of the half-breeds is that they are afraid the Government will not sanction the way they, among themselves, have agreed to take their homesteads—10 chains frontage on the river by 2 miles back."

The petition referred to by Superintendent Gagnon was the Bill of Rights adopted by Riel and his followers at a large meeting held in the previous September. In effect its demands were : (1) the subdivision of the North-West Territories into Provinces ; (2) the extension to all half-breeds of land grants of 240 acres, and other advantages enjoyed by the Manitoba breeds ; (3) the issue of patents to all colonists then in possession ; (4) the sale of half a million acres of Dominion lands, the proceeds of which were to be expended upon building schools, hospitals, and similar institutions in the half-breed settlements, and in equipping the poorer classes with seed, grain, and agricultural implements ; (5) the reservation of a hundred townships, of swamp land, to be distributed among children of half-breeds during the next 120 years ; (6) money grants for certain religious institutions ; and (7) better provision for the Indians. A strong point made by Riel in dealing with the Indians was that their title to their lands in the north-west had never been properly extinguished. By holding out specious promises to the chiefs —promises of rich rewards for them in the future—he won over the allegiance of many.

The reception of this petition by the authorities at Ottawa was disappointing and humiliating to the halfbreeds. Little notice was taken of it ; the Government, indeed, treated the " Bill " with contempt, and affected to attach no importance to the rumours that discontent was widely spread in the Territories. In taking up this attitude we can see now that the Government was rashly impolitic. An examination of the questions raised would have shown that the half-breeds had undeniable claims to be respected ; that, for instance, they were justified in demanding patents for their farms. The tragedy of the situation was that the Government endeavoured to ride rough-shod over them, ignoring them as possessing any rights over the land. Had steps but been taken to reassure them of their security on their farms and their protection from the land-grabbing speculators, there would have been little or no cause for revolt.

Many of the North-West Mounted Police had a good word to say for the half-breeds as a class. In their dealings with them they found the *métis* inclined to be loyal and submissive, provided they were fairly treated and their future prospects not imperilled. Inspector Walsh was on good terms with them, and striking testimony of their friendship was afforded in the early days of the Sioux invasion. When Sitting Bull sounded the half-breeds to see how far he could rely on their support if he proclaimed war against the whites, they answered that wherever a dead red-coat was found there would be a dead half-breed beside him.

There is no doubt, nevertheless, that in Riel's brain there lurked one idea which more than all others impelled him to come to the front. With ambition fired by the flattery and adulation he received from his adherents, he conceived the notion of eventually founding an exclusively French province in the north-west. That he himself would be virtual dictator was obvious. This idea partly accounts for the political demands which were included in the Bill of Rights, and which were framed by Riel alone.

Through the winter of 1884-5 the half-breed agitators were busy formulating their plans. Meetings were held in many places—at St. Laurent, Batoche, Prince Albert, at Baptiste Boyer's house, at Nolin's house; emissaries went to and fro between the settlements and the Indian camps; and the people generally were worked up to a pitch of excitement. When a lull followed, and the cooler heads among them talked of temporising, a rumour was circulated to the effect that Riel was thinking of leaving the country, as the Government would not recognise him as a British subject. This served its purpose. At the end of February another meeting was held, Riel being present, and a resolution was carried expressing confidence in him, and begging that he would stay. Riel was pleased to stay, and the game went merrily on.

So we come to March of 1885. By this time the Mounted

THE NORTH-WEST REBELLION

Police were fully alive to the fact that a concerted rising was contemplated, and preparations were made to meet the movement. On the 13th, Superintendent Crozier was telegraphing to Regina : " Half-breed rebellion liable to break out any moment. Troops must be largely reinforced. If half-breeds rise Indians will join them." This message Colonel Irvine flashed to Ottawa, recommending that a hundred men had better be sent at once. Two days later the Commissioner telegraphed that the Lieutenant-Governor considered it advisable for him to go north with men immediately, and on the following day he did set out with a force of ninety.

These precautionary measures had a quieting effect for the moment, but it was only the lull before the storm. " No cause for alarm now," was Crozier's wire to headquarters on the 17th. On the 19th he changed his tone. The half-breeds had seized the stores at the South Branch, and made the Indian agent there a prisoner. The rebellion, in fact, had begun.[1] Only two days previously, Riel, speaking at the Catholic Church at Batoche, had declared that all peaceful and constitutional means had been tried without avail, and nothing was left but the arbitrament of arms.

When the storm broke, the Mounted Police were well distributed over the affected area. There was a detachment at Fort Carlton, a Hudson Bay Company's post, and others at Battleford, Fort Pitt, Calgary, and Prince Albert.

---

[1] The scene of the outbreak was the angle formed by the north and south branches of the Saskatchewan River. For about a hundred miles the two streams run nearly parallel. On the north branch (30 miles west of the Forks) is Prince Albert, and Fort Carlton is 50 miles further up. On the south branch, opposite Fort Carlton, is Batoche. Duck Lake, a small settlement, now a R.N.W.M.P. post, lies between the two.

THE RIDERS OF THE PLAINS

Few though they were in numbers, they felt themselves quite equal to stamping out the rising before it could become general. What had to be feared most was a widespread insurrection among the various Indian tribes. Crees and Assiniboines were known to have left their reserves, well armed, some weeks previous to the actual outbreak. The bands under Chiefs Beardy, One Arrow, Little Pine, and Big Bear, had joined forces with the rebels ; it remained to be seen how many others would swell the number.

The one Indian Chief whose attitude towards the halfbreeds was particularly observed was Poundmaker of the Crees. This personage was a fine specimen of his race, over six feet in height, of striking appearance, and as renowned in the council as in the fight. He it was who had brought about peace between the Crees and their old enemies the Blackfeet. Although only about a hundred and fifty were in his following, he was accepted as the most influential chief in the northern territories.

Big Bear, of the South Crees, had all along given the authorities trouble. He was the last to sign the treaty, the stumbling-block in the path being his objection to hanging as a penalty for murder. Under this chief were some 500 men. Little Pine was credited with the largest following of all, 450 warriors. Altogether, there were in the vicinity of Battleford 2000 or more Crees and about 300 Assiniboines, the majority of whom were of doubtful loyalty. The Blackfeet tribes, also well armed, were less a source of anxiety, but they were in close and tempting proximity to cattle and horse ranches, and it was just possible that the younger chiefs of the Bloods and Blackfeet might kick over the traces.

12-POUNDER GUNS IN POLICE CAMP AT EDMONTON.

THE NORTH-WEST REBELLION

The first act of the rebels was to form a provisional government of their own. A Council of twelve, with Riel at its head, came into being. By it captains were appointed to command various portions of the half-breed force, and guards placed at important points on the trail from Clark's Crossing to Batoche. The main objects of the half-breeds were to intercept supplies, and challenge the passage of Colonel Irvine's troop, which was on its way to Carlton and Superintendent Crozier. In the first of these they were successful; in the second they were outwitted. On his way to Prince Albert the Commissioner changed his plans, and instead of crossing the South Saskatchewan at Gabriel's Crossing he took the ford at another point, thus eluding the enemy. The half-breeds were greatly disappointed and furious at his having succeeded in crossing the river. Prince Albert was reached in the evening of the 24th, after a remarkable march of 291 miles, performed in seven days and in the severest wintry weather. Almost the whole of the section passed through was then in possession of the rebels.

At Prince Albert a thorough inspection of men, arms, and horses was ordered, and a body of volunteers from the town enrolled. " The services of these brave volunteers," notes the Commissioner, " were offered with a perfect knowledge of the dangers they might be called upon to face. Like the loyal and gallant citizens they proved themselves to be, they were ready for any service—in fact, all were anxious to be employed. I might mention that I accepted the services of these men with what I considered a most important object in view, and that was my desire, on arrival at Carlton, to be in a position to increase to a maximum the number of Police available for service outside the post. I hoped in this way, by a prompt and decided move, to quash the rebellion ere it had assumed more formidable proportions." The volunteers were intended principally as a garrison for Fort Carlton.

Colonel Irvine continued his march early in the morning of Thursday, March 26. When within 9 miles of Fort Carlton he received the following dispatch :—

"CARLTON, 26*th March.*

"Superintendent Crozier, with 100 men, started out on Duck Lake road to help one of our sergeants and small party in difficulty at Mitchell's store. I have 70 men, and can hold fort against odds. Do not expect Crozier to push on further than Duck Lake. Everything quiet here. S. GAGNON, Superintendent."

Before he had gone much further the Commissioner got a second dispatch from the Superintendent, briefly conveying the intelligence that Crozier had exchanged shots with the rebels, that six men were reported killed, and that the little force was retiring on Fort Carlton. This was discouraging and alarming news, but the full story of the reverse was soon to be learned.

From Crozier's account we gather that early in the morning of the same day he had sent a party, consisting of Sergeant Stewart and seventeen constables, with eight sleighs, and Mr. Thomas M'Kay, J.P., of Prince Albert, to secure a quantity of provisions and ammunition which was in the store of a trader named Mitchell, of Duck Lake. The latter place was situated $13\frac{1}{2}$ miles to the south-east of Fort Carlton. Mr. M'Kay rode in advance, and was

THE NORTH-WEST REBELLION

surprised on nearing the lake to see four Mounted Police scouts, who had been sent out, riding towards him with a large number of half-breeds and Indians in pursuit. Immediately Mr. M'Kay turned back to the sleighs, where he told the men to load their rifles and get ready. This done, he went ahead again to parley with the enemy.

The fact that the half-breeds did not at once open fire upon the party is explained by their being on the open prairie where no cover was available. But for this, a bloody fight must have ensued. To the demand for surrender the rebels returned a prompt refusal, whereupon Mr. M'Kay, speaking in the Cree tongue, said that if firing were commenced they would find that two could play the game. While he was thus talking, the excited rebels showed an inclination to push matters to an extremity. Two of them jumped into a sleigh and tried to possess themselves of it and the team, but the driver resolutely kept his seat. Gabriel Dumont, the famous buffalo-hunter, who was one of Riel's right-hand men, was at the head of the breeds, and he and others kept prodding loaded and cocked rifles into M'Kay's side, at the same time threatening to shoot him.

No actual assault, however, took place, and Mr. M'Kay's party beat a retreat to the fort to report the situation. Without any delay another and stronger body, led by Superintendent Crozier himself, now went out to secure the stores and ammunition, taking with them a 7-pounder mountain gun. Including several Prince Albert volunteers, the force totalled seventy-nine.

The Police encountered the rebels near to the spot where the previous party had been compelled to retire.

On the half-breeds' side there were fully 350 men, and the position occupied had been chosen in order to gain the cover of an adjacent wood. Throwing out some of his men to prevent being surrounded, Crozier formed the others under cover of the sleighs. The first move on the enemy's part was to send a man with a flag of truce, but this device was merely to cloak, if possible, an attempt to outflank the Police. It was discovered in time, and the engagement began.

"Had they accomplished their purpose," reported Superintendent Crozier, "we must have been annihilated. I consider that the line extended to our right prevented the rebels surrounding us. There we sustained the heaviest loss, because, concealed from view, to the right of the trail on which we approached, were two houses, in which were posted a large number of rebels, and whence they poured upon us a fierce fire. From this point they tried to gain, and were working upon our right rear. The deep, crusted snow, however, impeded their movements."

After thirty minutes' sharp fighting the half-breeds were driven back on the right flank. On the left flank, where the defence was weaker, the Police could do no more than hold their own. The order was at last given to retire, and Crozier and his gallant men, all of whom behaved superbly under a murderous fire, fell back upon the fort. They had suffered the loss of ten men killed, one Mounted Policemen and nine volunteers. Of the latter, one was Corporal William Napier, a nephew of General Sir Charles Napier, the victor of Meanee.

This was the affair at Duck Lake, the actual opening of hostilities. In reality the force of half-breeds and Indians was the advance guard of a much larger body,

THE NORTH-WEST REBELLION

with which Riel had intended to attack Fort Carlton.[1] Equally alive to the importance of securing the supplies and arms at Mitchell's store, the rebels had anticipated the Police and seized all they could find. What was even worse, they were now flushed with victory. They had met their foes in open fight, and had got the better of the contest. On the Indians especially this was bound to make a strong impression, and the situation took on a still more critical aspect.

The question that Colonel Irvine now had to decide was whether he should remain at Fort Carlton or make Prince Albert the base of his operations. At a council held in the Police quarters, many of the leading men from Prince Albert being present, it was resolved to concentrate upon the latter place. Prince Albert and the country immediately adjoining it practically represented the whole white settlement. Nearly all the district to the south was composed of half-breed settlements and farms. Another factor in determining this move was the desire of the town volunteers to return to protect their families.

Accordingly, on Saturday, 28th March, all the force from Fort Carlton marched out to Prince Albert. In the town itself their arrival was welcomed with the utmost relief. Wild rumours were in circulation, and the fear of an assault from half-breeds or Indians, particularly the latter, had driven the people almost panic-stricken.

---

[1] Shortly after the half-breeds had commenced to seize stores and ammunition, make prisoners of Government officials, and patrol the country in armed bands, Superintendent Crozier sought an interview with Riel to warn him of the consequences should a general rising take place. The answer returned by Riel, who would not meet the Police in person, was that Fort Carlton must be surrendered unconditionally. His words were: "We want blood! blood! If Carlton is not surrendered, it will be a war of extermination." (*From official reports.*)

As it was, no time was lost in putting the place in a strong position to withstand attack. The Presbyterian church and manse being the most suitable spots to form a central refuge, a stockade of wood 9 ft. in height was erected round them, this being loop-holed and lined with another pile of wood on which men could stand. All kinds of stores were hurried in, ice was cut from the river, and big supplies of arms and ammunition carried in to the improvised citadel. All the townspeople vacated their houses for the church and its precincts, and such buildings as commanded the square were pulled down.

It was an anxious time for the Mounted Police, with the whole of Prince Albert's population on their hands, together with a number of settlers and their families who had driven in from the outlying homesteads. The total number of refugees was about 1800. All kinds of reports were brought in. The half-breeds were marching direct upon the town, Big Bear and a hundred " braves " on snowshoes had crossed the prairie from Battleford and joined Riel, the Indians had committed terrible outrages, and a general rising among them was imminent. Nothing was too wild to be credited. But fortunately these rumours proved more alarming than true, and for the time Prince Albert was left undisturbed.

For his defensive force the Commissioner had the Mounted Police—225 non-commissioned officers and men, of whom eleven had been wounded in the Duck Lake fight—and four companies of volunteers, numbering just over 300. All of the latter, however, could not be adequately armed, as there was a paucity of guns. A band of scouts that was at once organised did good service in patrolling the district, and from their reports and a reconnaissance made in the direction of Batoche, the disposition of the rebel forces was ascertained.

In the meantime the authorities at Ottawa had taken further steps to suppress the rising. The 90th Rifles and a portion of the Winnipeg Field Battery had been hurried to the scene of the outbreak immediately on receipt of the news of the Duck Lake disaster. Other contingents were formed at Quebec, Montreal, Kingston, and Toronto—the whole of the troops being placed under the leadership of Major-General Middleton, the Commander-in-chief of the Canadian Militia. This well-known officer had had experience of Maori warfare in New Zealand, and had also seen service in the Santhal rebellion in India and in the great Mutiny.

Towards the end of March, Colonel Irvine received the following telegram from Mr. Frederick White, the Comptroller of the North-West Mounted Police at Ottawa: "Major-General Commanding Militia proceeds forthwith to Red River. On his arrival, in military operations when acting with militia, take orders from him." Subsequently Colonel Irvine was notified by General Middleton that the Police were under his orders and should report to him, directions which were literally followed. In the light of the imputations afterwards made reflecting upon the conduct of the Mounted Police during the campaign, it is important to bear in mind the precise nature of these instructions.

By the 9th of April the other troops from the east, C Company of regulars, the Royal Grenadiers, the Queen's Own Rifles, the Governor-General's Foot Guards and Body Guards, had arrived at Qu'Appelle, where they were awaited by the Winnipeg contingent. Qu'Appelle now became the

THE RIDERS OF THE PLAINS

base of militia operations. From it three columns were dispatched into the field : one, under General Strange, to advance against Big Bear in the district round Edmonton ; a second, under Colonel Otter, to relieve Battleford, which was threatened ; while the third, or main body, under General Middleton in person, had for its task the relief of Prince Albert and the crushing of the rebellion at its heart—Batoche. These three points above named, Edmonton, Battleford, and Prince Albert, all in the valley of the north branch of the Saskatchewan, were those most exposed to danger.

This, then, was the state of affairs in the north-west early in April. The militia forces, nearly two thousand strong, were moving upon the half-breeds' positions ; the Mounted Police held the posts at Prince Albert and Battleford, and at Fort Pitt, Fort Saskatchewan, and Edmonton in the north. The first act of the tragedy had been played, the second was about to commence.

CHAPTER IX.

THE NORTH-WEST REBELLION.—II.

The Frog Lake Massacre—Attack on Fort Pitt—Inspector Dickens' gallant defence—Indian raid at Battleford—The siege raised—Colonel Otter's column—Assault on Cut-Knife Hill—Chief Poundmaker—Battle of Batoche's Ferry—Enforced inactivity of the Police—Colonel Irvine's defence—Frenchman's Butte and Loon Lake—Inspector Perry's forced march—An exciting incident—Louis Riel captured—Big Bear—Execution of Riel.

THE Indian rising incited by Riel and his supporters had not been general, as has been explained in the preceding chapter. But the half-breeds were reinforced by a sufficient number of the most unruly chiefs to make the settlers in the north-west fear many atrocities. Their fears in some measure were realised. At Battleford a large party of Crees and Assiniboines fell upon the town, plundered and burnt some buildings, and held the Police garrison, with many refugees, in a state of siege. Some ranchers and other whites in outlying parts were foully murdered, and only the intervention of half-breeds prevented women and children from suffering a similar fate. But the worst deed was that witnessed at Frog Lake, where a cruel and treacherous massacre took place.

Frog Lake is near Fort Pitt, where at the time Inspector Dickens was stationed with twenty-two of the Police. In the vicinity were Long Lake and Onion Lake, around which had congregated several bands of Wood Crees whom Big Bear had won over to his side. At first the few white inhabitants of the district were much concerned for their safety, but the Indians were so loud in their professions of loyalty that suspicion was almost disarmed. The Indian sub-agent in charge at Frog Lake was himself doubtful as to the attitude of Big Bear and his chiefs. That he had good reason to be so was made clear quickly, and to some extent through his own rashness. Fearing that the presence of Police would exasperate the red-skins, he asked that the detachment on duty there should be withdrawn. This was done. Almost immediately after, the blow fell.

On 2nd April a band of Indians entered the village, and by their demeanour showed that trouble was to be apprehended. Going direct to the store belonging to the Hudson's Bay Company they demanded ammunition. The clerk in charge would have refused them, but in their excited condition this course might have been fatal to him. So much powder, ball, and caps as were in the place fell into their hands. It was only a small quantity, fortunately, most of the supply having been sent off earlier to Fort Pitt in anticipation of a raid.

After ransacking the store the Indians proceeded to take possession of the village. They invaded the church, in which a service was being held, their painted faces and warlike gear frightening the women and children present. Then, swaggering about the street, they laid hands upon Quinn, the Indian sub-agent, and several others, threatening to shoot them if they interfered in any way. Quinn himself was requested to accompany the Indians to Big Bear's camp, to be held as a prisoner there, no doubt, but he declined to go. With the rest of the people he intended to make for Fort Pitt and seek protection there. On his refusal, a minor chief named Travelling Spirit raised his

THE NORTH-WEST REBELLION

gun and without more ado shot the poor fellow through the head.

This act seemed to inflame the other Indians' lust for blood. In quick succession two French priests, Fathers Marchand and Fafard, were shot down, together with several settlers. A Mr. Gowanlock was killed while in company with his wife and another woman, all of whom were setting out for the Police barracks. He was struck in the back, as were most of those who fell. In all, eight men were massacred.[1] The women and other whites in the place had their lives spared through the humanity of the half-breeds, and were carried off to the Indian camp to spend some weeks of miserable confinement.

From Frog Lake Big Bear's band threw themselves upon Fort Pitt. The defence of this little post by Inspector Dickens and his handful of men is one of the most heroic in the annals of the Mounted Police. Situated on the north bank of the North Saskatchewan, and 98 miles north-west of Battleford, the fort had formerly been in a strong position. But the stockade that had enclosed it, with bastions on the corners, had been removed, and its log buildings arranged in a hollow square lay open to attack. Set in the midst of some cultivated fields its only attempt at protection was some common rail fences.

Fort Pitt held considerable supplies of food and ammunition. Apart from their desire to wipe out their old enemies the Police, the Indians were keenly anxious to lay hands upon these valuable stores. It was winter time, be it remembered, and there was much suffering among the Crees owing to the scarcity of provisions. Little Pine, one

[1] On July 10, 1909, the remains of the victims of this tragedy were removed to the new cemetery at Frog Lake, where they were reinterred. The grave is surrounded by an iron railing with iron crosses, on each of which the name and date of the massacre are engraved.

of the revolting chiefs, was the first to arrive on the scene. He was followed, a few days later, by Big Bear and a larger company. To the demand for surrender, Inspector Dickens made the reply that might have been expected; then, in the hope of persuading Big Bear to abandon his plans, he sent Mr. M'Lean, the Hudson's Bay Company factor, as ambassador to the Indian camp.

The hope proved vain. Mr. M'Lean was made prisoner. What was more, he was so impressed with the strength of the Indians that he wrote a note requesting his wife and family, who with several other civilians were shut up in the Police barracks, to join him at once. The effect of this communication was to induce every one in the fort, except the Police themselves, to abandon that refuge for the apparently more secure quarters of Big Bear's tepees. Dickens and his faithful twenty-two were deserted, and the scow which they had built as a means of taking the women and children down the river to Battleford after the ice had broken up seemed to mock their efforts. The clumsy-looking boat, however, was to serve a useful purpose yet.

In a reconnaissance outside the fort shortly afterwards, three of the Police constables came into touch with the Indian scouts. One, Cowan by name, was killed, the others escaped, but only just in time. Constable Loasby lost his horse and had to run for his life, being dragged into the fort with a bullet in his back. The point for the Inspector to consider now was whether he was justified or not in holding on to his practically untenable position. He had been sent thither to protect the white settlers: the latter had voluntarily chosen to place themselves at Big Bear's mercy. His next duty was, of course, to prevent the supplies of arms and ammunition from falling into the Indians' hands. This done, there would be no reason for him to keep the flag flying at the fort, while the detachment at Battleford might well be glad to be reinforced by him. In the circumstances, he came to the conclusion that he must retire.

As the ice on the river was giving, he resolved to trust himself and his twenty-one men to the scow, which was at once prepared for the journey. One night, while a heavy snowstorm obscured the air, the little party set out to cross the river. All the arms and ammunition that were not wanted for their own use had been destroyed, so that the Indians would find the fort bare on invading it. The overloaded, patched-up old tub filled as soon as she was pushed off into the water, and it looked as if she was useless, but Constable Rutledge pluckily jumped on board and volunteered to pilot her across. So, "by hand-baling and skilful management," the perilous trip to the other bank was successfully accomplished. The Police spent the hours of darkness in an improvised camp, making themselves as comfortable as wet blankets and a bitter wind would allow. Early the next morning they pushed off once more in the scow, and without further adventure reached Battleford.

At Battleford the commanding officer of the Mounted Police was Inspector W. S. Morris. With his detachment of 200 men and 300 of the inhabitants he had entrenched himself in the " new town." The " old town," as the lower part was called, was where the Indians had run riot at their first attack. All the telegraph wires had been cut, so that communication with Fort Pitt was completely cut off. The Police barracks, indeed, as has been stated, were in a state of siege.

What the scene was like after the Indian raiders had ransacked the houses, only those can imagine who have passed through a similar experience. Everything portable had been thrown out into the streets, which were littered with bedsteads, furniture, crockery, and all kinds of odds and ends. Broken pictures, fragments of window sashes, the contents of valises and wardrobes lay about the sidewalks or hung disreputably from open windows. What the Indians could not use or did not wish to appropriate they wreaked their spite upon. Feather beds, after being ripped open, were saturated with coal oil and set alight. Viewing the " old town " afterwards one man said : " It was just like taking a lady's trunk, packed ready for Saratoga, and pulling both ends two miles apart, with all between them."

Where Government stores had been discovered, the same wanton destruction went on. Bags of flour were emptied ; bread and other eatables flung into the roadway ; pigs and chickens killed, and their carcases thrown aside. In the midst of the disorder were to be seen the incongruous figures of Indian squaws strutting about in the feminine finery which they had found within the houses.

Meanwhile, help was on its way to the beleaguered garrison. Superintendent Herchmer had been ordered by General Middleton to proceed to Battleford by way of Swift Current. Unfortunately the ice in the river had given way, making it impassable, whereupon the Superintendent moved towards Medicine Hat, where the steamer *Northcote* was being prepared to come down the river for the purpose of conveying troops to the north. A party of Crees were camped here ready for any mischief, but the arrival of the Police sent them flying.

From Medicine Hat the Superintendent was hastily recalled to Swift Current to oppose a large number of mounted and armed Indians who had suddenly appeared there, and at this place he received a dispatch from

Inspector Morris. That officer reported that the Stonies (Assiniboines) were "up" and were concentrating on Poundmaker's reserve. "They have killed two white men, Mr. Payne and Mr. Applegarth ; also one Mr. Fremont, a rancher." From the bearer of the message, Constable Storer, Superintendent Herchmer learnt that Battleford had provisions sufficient to last three months. Storer, by the way, had an exciting ride from his post to Swift Current. For nearly 60 miles he was hard chased by the enemy.

On 12th April Colonel Otter, in command of the second column of the militia forces, arrived at Swift Current. As the Mounted Police had orders to join this body, the Superintendent forthwith marched his men with it to Battleford, meeting with no resistance from the Indians on the way. Although there were many signs of the savages' handiwork —burning farmhouses, and much wreckage of implements and household gear—no Indians were to be seen. Before the approach of the column, nearly 600 strong, they fell back upon their reserve. The people of Battleford had nothing more to fear from them.

The relief of the town was achieved about the 29th of the month. Two days later Colonel Otter deemed it desirable to make a movement upon Poundmaker, whose reserve was so near. It must be admitted that this Cree chief had given really little cause for anxiety in the minds of the whites, but as his loyalty was in question the militia leader thought it safest to take the bull by the horns and make his own terms. On the 30th of April a half-breed named Denison was brought into camp by Major Short of B Battery, R.C.A. He stated that he had that morning escaped from Poundmaker's camp, and that about twenty families of half-breeds had been captured by the chief and were held as prisoners.

The next day Colonel Otter formed a flying column consisting of 75 Mounted Police, under Superintendent Neale, 80 B Battery, R.C.A., with two 7-pounder guns and one Gatling, 45 C Company, I.S.C., 20 of the Governor-General's Foot Guards, 50 Queen's Own Rifles, and 50 Battleford Rifles. Forty-eight waggons accompanied the force. As usual, the Mounted Police acted as the advance guard. They were in this position early in the morning of the 2nd, when the scouts, on ascending a slope, signalled " Enemy in sight." By this time the column had entered the deep ravine through which flows the Cut-Knife Creek. The stream caused some little delay, and when the troops began the ascent of the opposite hill the Indians had secured a strong position in the bushes.

Firing opened immediately, the front ranks of the Police suffering severely. The first man to fall, shot through the mouth, was Corporal B. Sleigh. Shortly after Corporal Lowry and Trumpeter Burke fell mortally wounded, while several others were more or less badly hit. The heavy casualties among the Mounted Police are explained by the fact that they occupied the most forward positions and bore the brunt of the battle throughout. Eighteen of them had the distinction of being "mentioned in dispatches" when Superintendent Herchmer came to write his report of the action, but, as he said, it was difficult to individualise where all had behaved with such dash and bravery.

The assault on Cut-Knife Hill does not reflect especial glory upon the attacking force. The gallantry of the Mounted Police and Poundmaker's magnanimity at the close of the action are its distinguishing features. In all, the fighting lasted seven hours, the honours remaining with the Indians, whose cover gave them an overwhelming

R.N.W.M.P. HEADQUARTERS POST AT REGINA, FROM THE PRAIRIE.

advantage over their foes. Poundmaker, who had only two hundred and fifty poorly armed warriors, showed his generalship in the skilful disposition of his men, and that he succeeded in saving his wigwams from destruction against so superior a body must be placed to his credit. After the last shot had been fired and Colonel Otter had given the signal to retire, Poundmaker made no attempt to follow up his victory. His " braves " rested on their rifles, and through the thick screen of bushes watched the soldiers fall back across the creek. Had any spirit of revenge actuated the old chief there is little doubt but that his warriors might have cut the flying column to pieces, and the inglorious retreat would have been turned into a terrible disaster.

While these events were taking place, General Middleton with the main body of the militia forces was advancing against the half-breeds down both banks of the South Saskatchewan, in order to preclude the possibility of their escaping should they refuse to show fight. For this purpose the column was divided into two sections. The advance was slow, but in the main successful. On the 26th of April the General came into contact with the half-breeds' army at Fish Creek, and after a stubborn fight drove the rebels back, inflicting heavy loss. On the 11th of May occurred the battle of Batoche's Ferry, in which the issue of the war was decided. At this memorable engagement the half-breeds were dispersed, and their leader, Louis Riel, became again a fugitive.

During these decisive operations Colonel Irvine was forced to remain inactive at Prince Albert. Communication with the outside world had been cut off, and very little, if any, news of what was transpiring in the actual theatre of war trickled through. The Commissioner at the first had suggested the advisability of combining forces with the militia, either by the Mounted Police joining the latter or by General Middleton bringing his troops to Prince Albert. This suggestion was not accepted. Colonel Irvine was instructed to remain where he was—to "sit tight," in fact, and guard that important post. This he did, having been placed directly under the General's orders and having no option to act otherwise. Not until 16th April did any message from the front reach Prince Albert.

All that could be done in the interim to assist the main column was to thoroughly scout the adjacent country. In this respect the Mounted Police performed notable service. "The importance of their work," states the Commissioner in his subsequent explanatory report, " could not, I think, have been surpassed. These men, all perfectly familiar with the country, were kept constantly employed from the outset, under the direction of a man (Mr. Thomas M'Kay) well qualified for such work. The scouts at all times laboured incessantly, cheerfully, and efficiently. By the employment of these scouts I was enabled not only to keep myself posted as to the movements of General Middleton's column, but also by holding scouts well to the front, in close proximity to the rebel camp, to force the enemy to keep a strong portion of their force on the west side of the river (at Batoche). Perhaps the most important part of the work done by my scouts was the driving back of the men employed on similar duty by Riel, who on various occasions tried to scout right into Prince Albert.

" The entrenchments made by the rebels on the west side of the river, quite as strong as those on the opposite side, were thrown up owing to the fact that the constant presence of my scouts was known to Riel. The whole country round Prince Albert was thoroughly scouted, and I feel satisfied that it cannot but be clearly and perfectly understood that the nature of the service performed by my force, in and about Prince Albert, was as important as it was successful. Prince Albert and the settlements around it were not pillaged. There is no Indian massacre to record. In saying this, I consider that there can be no prouder testimony in support of my statement, unless, indeed, it is considered that it was my duty to have disobeyed the orders of the general officer under whom I was ordered to serve, by attacking with less than 200 men and endeavouring to defeat the rebels in entrenched positions at Batoche, where the resistance made against something like 1200 men, with four 9-pounder M.L.R. guns and one Gatling, is a matter of history."

It should be added here that Colonel Irvine on his own responsibility placed guards on the Hudson's Bay Crossing of the Saskatchewan and at other important points, while he ordered the steamer *Marquis*, with an escort of Mounted Police under Inspector White Fraser, to proceed to Batoche. This steamer was afterwards of considerable use to the field force under General Middleton.

For his inactivity throughout those anxious weeks the Commissioner was severely handled by the press of the country. "What are the Mounted Police doing?" was the question bandied about by the newspapers, who could not understand the reason for shutting up some 200 efficient men at Prince Albert. It must be borne in mind that all the militia troops had with them newspaper correspondents, from whom came regularly information respecting the movements in the field ; there was no press representative on the Police side. Not until many months had elapsed after the close of the campaign was Colonel

Irvine's position made clear, and the reputation of the North-West Mounted Police re-established in the minds of those who had been biased by newspaper misrepresentation.

When the Commissioner's statement was received and properly appreciated, it was understood that the presence of his force undoubtedly saved Prince Albert from falling into the hands of the rebels. Had such a catastrophe as this come about, Riel would have held the key of the whole position, and the rebellion would have lasted much longer. Besides this, there was a large number of Sioux Indians in the vicinity, who, but for the Police garrison, might have swooped down upon the town with all the horrors of a savage raid. That this was more than probable was borne out by the strongest testimony.

An unfortunate feature of the situation was the fact that lack of communication with headquarters prevented Colonel Irvine from knowing the extent of General Middleton's force. He understood that the latter had only 350 troops with him; it was some weeks before the news of contingents having been dispatched from the eastern provinces reached his ears. Then there were the constant changes in the General's plans, necessitated by the difficulties of a winter campaign. Orders and counter-orders followed each other in rapid and bewildering succession.

The main charge brought against the Commissioner was his failure to attack the half-breeds on the north side of Batoche at the same time that the main column of the militia troops was attacking on the opposite side. To this Colonel Irvine rendered a complete answer. Messrs. M'Dowall and Bedson, the bearers of a dispatch from the General, in which he announced his intention of engaging the enemy at Batoche on 18th April, saw the importance

THE NORTH-WEST REBELLION

of the main body of the Police force remaining at Prince Albert, and said they would inform the General accordingly. They asserted that the orders were for Colonel Irvine not to attack, but to look out for flying half-breeds. Furthermore, the dispatch itself was vague as to the actual date of the assault. Circumstances, it explained, might delay or expedite the advance. On 19th April (a Sunday) Colonel Irvine made a reconnaissance in force towards Batoche for a distance of 12 miles. Failing to gain any information as to an attack by the main body, and gathering that delay had occurred, he returned to Prince Albert.

So much explanation is necessary if we are to understand the part played by the Mounted Police in the short but eventful Riel Rebellion. Those who had perforce to remain at their commands rendered no less valuable service in the campaign than did their comrades who were at the front. Superintendent Cotton, at Macleod, kept the Blackfeet quiescent and patrolled his district in a way that stifled any attempt at insurrection; Superintendent M'Illree (the present Assistant-Commissioner), at Maple Creek, scouted the difficult country of the Cypress Hills; and Inspector Griesbach, at Fort Saskatchewan, further north, kept his extensive district well in hand prior to the arrival of the militia column under General Strange. Such work as this did not loom big in the public eye, but its value must not be overlooked. What remains now to be told is the history of the other Mounted Police detachments on service which took part in the operations following upon the half-breeds' signal defeat.[1]

In addition to the force under the command first of

[1] The N.W.M.P. troops employed in the field during the rebellion comprised the following: A Division, 47; B Division, 132; C Division, 73; D Division, 199; E Division, 111; total (officers and men), 562. For list of casualties, see Appendix C.

THE RIDERS OF THE PLAINS

Superintendent Herchmer and later of Superintendent Neale, there were two other detachments, in charge of which were Inspector S. B. Steele and Inspector A. Bowen Perry, the present Commissioner. Both these commands served with the Alberta Field Force, the western column before referred to as being led by Major-General Strange. The base of this body was Calgary. Inspector Steele was summoned from the Rocky Mountains, where he was policing the railway camps. He raised a troop of scouts, and these, with his own Mounted Policemen, performed notable work in the northern districts around Edmonton. They fought at Frenchman's Butte and at Loon Lake, both of them hot engagements with members of Big Bear's band, and covered themselves with distinction before returning to Calgary in July to be disbanded.

The detachment of which Inspector Perry was in command was sent from Fort Macleod, where Superintendent Cotton was the chief officer. It comprised twenty non-commissioned officers and men, three teamsters (civil), and a 9-pounder M.L.R. gun. Starting on 18th April it marched to Calgary, covering 105 miles in three and a half days, and at this post the Inspector found new orders awaiting him. General Strange had proceeded to Edmonton. Major Perry (he had just been promoted to that rank in the Canadian Militia) was to follow with the second column, of which he was to take command.

Owing to the severe storms of rain and snow, the march northwards from Calgary was rendered extremely difficult. At Red Deer River it was marked by an exciting incident. When reached on 28th April, the river was found to be impassable, having risen rapidly since General Strange's force had crossed it. It was fully 250 yards wide, with a current flowing at the rate of five miles per hour, and the

THE NORTH-WEST REBELLION

only means of transport in view was a small skiff. The old ferry-boat formerly employed at this point had been broken up by the ice.

In this dilemma Major Perry determined to construct a swinging raft. An advance guard was thrown over the river by means of the skiff, while others of the party went in search of lumber. Portions of the old ferry-boat were found, and at once impressed into service. In two hours' time a very strong raft, capable of carrying six tons, was ready, and on it the gun, gun-carriage, ammunition, and harness were placed. Meanwhile, a rope, some 1200 feet long, was carried across, this having been made by tying together the picketing ropes of the horses. When all preparations were complete the word was given, and the raft, with Major Perry and the gun detachment on board, swung out into the stream.

All went well until the north bank was approached, then the slender rope snapped, and the raft began to drift down stream. "Aided by Constable Diamond, N.W.M.P.," says Major Perry, "I succeeded in landing a rope and attaching it to a tree." This modest statement leaves much to the imagination. What actually happened was that the Major and Diamond threw themselves into the rush of water, and at the risk of their lives fought their way to shore. However, the raft was going along too quickly to be checked; the rope again broke, and it went careering down the river for three miles before being driven into the bank on the south side. Then it was secured, and gun-carriage and men were hauled up the steep 30-ft. bank.

After this narrow escape from disaster the party had to make a detour of several miles round a swamp, cutting a new road over a mile in length through a heavy wood. But it was all done, and when the "crossing" was once more gained waggons and carts were taken to pieces and ferried over in part to carry ammunition, while the horses crossed by swimming. Later on, during the night, as war parties of Indians were reported to be in the immediate neighbourhood, a whole regiment (the 65th) was transferred over the river to the north bank by the little skiff, not an accident occurring in any one of its trips.

Even before the construction of the raft Major Perry had seen the necessity for rebuilding the ferry-boat, and this work was hastily pushed forward. In a day or two it was ready for use, and the column crossed in safety. Edmonton was reached on the thirteenth day from the start, which made a pretty good record, seeing that four and a half days were lost in crossing Red Deer River. From now on, the column was busily employed in scouting the country in the direction of Frog Lake and Fort Pitt, and in hunting down Big Bear and his band. All the settlements between Calgary and Edmonton, and Edmonton and Fort Pitt, had been raided by the Indians after the massacre at Frog Lake. The advance of the Alberta Field Force had the effect of overaweing the Indians and preventing them joining the rebels. At the fight at Frenchman's Butte the Police gun proved invaluable, being mainly instrumental in demoralising the enemy. Altogether this detachment acquitted itself with the greatest credit, and won high encomiums from General Strange.

It was while Major Perry was thus engaged in the pursuit of Big Bear that he learned of the capture of Riel and the surrender of Poundmaker. The half-breed leader did not enjoy many days' freedom after his reverse at Batoche's Ferry. A party of scouts under Colonel Boulton spread across the country to intercept his flight, but it fell to the lot of two Mounted Policemen to effect the capture.

THE NORTH-WEST REBELLION

Constables Armstrong and Diehl were bearing dispatches from Colonel Irvine to General Middleton when, in company with a third scout, Howie by name, they came upon four men standing near a fence. One of the quartette, coatless and bareheaded, was easily recognised as Riel. His three companions carried rifles, he himself was unarmed.

The scouts rode up. "You are Louis Riel?" asked Armstrong. "Yes, I am," was the answer; "I want to give myself up." Then he produced a slip of paper from his pocket. It was a note which General Middleton had sent him saying that if he would surrender he would be given a fair trial. A horse having been obtained for him, Riel was escorted to the camp at Battleford, whence on 23rd May he was conveyed to Regina.

Poundmaker's submission was made on the 26th of the same month, he and several minor chiefs under his authority coming in to Battleford to place themselves in General Middleton's hands. In view of his good behaviour during the rebellion, the Cree chief was not visited with any severe penalty, but two Indians who had sought refuge on his reserve, and who admitted the murders of the two white settlers, Payne and Fremont, were arrested and in due course hung.

The capture of the notorious Big Bear had little of the dramatic about it. There was no "last stand," no "wolf at bay" touch in this final scene of the drama. The hunt for him had gone on throughout June with no success, though reports were still firm in the belief that he was lurking on the north side of the Saskatchewan. Then one morning early in July, while patrols were riding north and south, east and west, for miles around, the picquet at the Police camp on the river crossing near Fort Carlton learned that "a few of Big Bear's Indians" were hiding close by.

THE RIDERS OF THE PLAINS

A settler had passed them on the trail. Sergeant Smart and three constables were promptly detailed to follow up this clue, and they crossed the stream to the other bank. They had not gone far along the path through the wood to Battleford when they discovered their quarry. Round a camp fire lay three Indians—Big Bear, his youngest son, and one of his councillors, known by the strange name of " All-and-a-half."

Big Bear was arrested and taken back to the camp. A few hours later he was sent on to Prince Albert, where he was consigned to a strong and well-guarded cell. Corporal Donkin of the N.W.M.P., who was in the town at the time, saw the old Cree chief in prison. " Big Bear," he say, " was in a pitiable condition of filth and hunger. He was given a good scrubbing in a tub at the barracks, though this was anything but pleasing to him. A new blanket and a pair of trousers were procured for him from the Hudson's Bay store. His arms consisted of a Winchester, and he stated that his only food for eleven days had been what he was enabled to secure in the woods. A little, shrivelled-up looking piece of humanity he was, his cunning face seamed and wrinkled like crumpled parchment."

Louis Riel suffered the penalty of his rebellion on 16th November, when he was executed at the Mounted Police barracks at Regina. The same fate met Big Bear and seven other Indians who had figured in the Frog Lake massacre. After the long series of trials had been concluded a large number of Indians and half-breeds inculpated in the rising were sentenced to varying terms of penal servitude.

CHAPTER X.

TEN YEARS' WORK, 1885-1895.

After the war—Lawlessness among the Indians—Liquor law difficulties—Cattle-killing—A rush of immigrants—Visit of the Marquess of Lansdowne—Lawrence W. Herchmer, Esq., fourth Commissioner—The *personnel* of the Force—A high standard of efficiency—Lord Stanley—Patrolling the border—Prairie fires—Death of Sir John Macdonald—Reduction in strength—Indian progress—A wider sphere of operations—The Earl of Aberdeen, Governor-General—Off to the Yukon.

ALTHOUGH the North-West Rebellion had been quashed, and both half-breeds and Indians taught a severe lesson, the Mounted Police had still much work before them ere the Territories could be said to have regained any aspect of tranquillity. The half-breeds to some extent were pacified by concessions from the Government. Patents for their farms were granted them, and other steps taken to reassure them as to their security of tenure. But the very nature of their mixed descent was bound to manifest itself in a spirit of unrest, and in a reluctance to adapt themselves to the new life forced upon them.

In the old days, before their country had been invaded from the east, existence had been easy and pleasant. Buffalo-hunting, trapping, and trading with the Indians enabled them to live well and often luxuriously. Then with the disappearance of the buffalo they took to freighting, and throve wonderfully well upon it. But this occupation was doomed as soon as the railway pushed itself across the plains. The old routes over which the pack-trains of horses and sleighs had passed for years were abandoned one by one.[1] Not only were goods sent by rail, but an active competition entered into the freighting market, and the half-breeds found their means of living fast narrowing. As a set-off to this, it was hoped that they would take more generally to farming. In this expectation, however, the authorities were disappointed. All that the *métis* seemed inclined to do was to undertake the cultivation of small fields, and raise just sufficient crops for their own use. Not for a long time would they bestir themselves to greater efforts and endeavour to meet the competition of the more experienced white settlers whose homesteads sprang up around them.

But it was the Indians who continued to give the greatest trouble. Their pacification was no easy matter, the influence of the revolting tribes having made itself felt more widely than was anticipated. The hereditary instincts of the savage had been aroused. There had been war—red war, with its opportunities for fighting, for revenge, and for the many other outlets of energy so dear to the primitive mind. These instincts are hard to eradicate. The red man does not take kindly to civilisation; he is not naturally willing to earn his living by the sweat of his brow. If he is fed by the Government and otherwise well looked after he will be content, but will do next to nothing for himself. If, on the other hand, rations are cut down and an attempt is made to force him to work, then he becomes shiftless and vagrant, and he and his family struggle on in a state of semi-starvation.

This is the problem with which the Indian Department of the Dominion Government has always had to cope. In

---

[1] Freight which was hauled from Winnipeg in 1880 was sent *via* Brandon in 1881, and *via* Qu'Appelle in a year later. In 1883 the freight route to and from Battleford and Edmonton ceased to exist at all.

the years immediately following the half-breeds' insurrection the duties of the Mounted Police in this respect were perhaps harder than they had ever been before or have been since. The lawless spirit engendered in the Indians by the rising displayed itself in divers ways. Several murders of whites occurred, and there was an increase in the number of thefts of horses, cattle, and other property of the settlers. But for the presence of the Mounted Police in the Territories this defiant and aggressive attitude on the part of the Indians must have led to far more serious consequences.

Horse-stealing and drunkenness were the two crimes which brought the red man most frequently into the Police guard-room. In the enforcement of the liquor law great difficulty was experienced. The "permit" system, by which citizens were allowed to have up to five gallons of liquor—usually whisky—in their possession, admitted of considerable abuse, and much illicit spirit was "run" into the country. It came in in every conceivable manner, in barrels of sugar, salt, and imitation eggs, in tins of tomatoes, in cases of thick—(very thick) soled boots, in ginger ale, and even in dummy Bibles and prayer-books. As it was possible for a saloon-keeper with a circle of friends who also held permits to keep a good stock of smuggled liquor on his premises, the Police were often hoodwinked. And the temptations offered to the lower-class inhabitants of the townships and to the Indians were consequently many.

Few Indians were proof against the wiles of the illicit whisky traders. One of these worthies had only to take a keg of spirit into a camp to be sure of making a profitable deal. Running Deer's pony or Wild Cat's shot-gun soon changed hands at the sight of the precious "fire-water," and ere long there was a "bad Indian" making trouble

THE RIDERS OF THE PLAINS

somewhere—trouble for his neighbours and trouble for himself. Well might the Police bless the elasticity of the law which enabled much smuggled liquor to pass in under their very noses.

In the matter of stealing horses some of the more aggressive tribes were notorious. The Blackfeet, Bloods, and Crees were adepts at the game, and they cared little whether they stole from each other or from the whites. Whole parties set out on thieving expeditions, sometimes venturing very far afield into United States territory. The frequent success that attended these forays had the natural result. As Superintendent Cotton pointed out, " if one man succeeded in evading arrest the others were prompted to copy him, and so doing was considered a signal sign of personal bravery that invariably met with universal approbation." In crossing the Boundary Line to the south, the Bloods and other members of the Blackfeet tribes received willing aid from their near relations, the South Piegans. The latter did not venture to steal American horses themselves, but they were " accessories to the deed " both before and after.

One great cause of discontent among the Indians of the north-west in respect to horse-stealing was the Canadian law which prohibits stolen property being brought into the Dominion. They did not mind so much being punished for appropriating horses on their own side of the border, but they felt it unjust to be punished for similar thefts from Americans—the more so as there was no reciprocal provision south of the line.

In addition to horse-stealing, no little vigilance was necessary to prevent the wholesale killing of cattle belonging to settlers. It was a serious offence for any Indian to be found with " fresh-killed meat " in his possession unless he could give a satisfactory explanation. On such occasions when the Mounted Police happened upon a criminal *in flagrante delicto* there was often a scene. Here is a case in point, noted by Superintendent Steele while in command of the Macleod district :—

" On the 19th of October (1891) a party of Police under Staff-Sergeant Hilliard left the Stand Off detachment soon after dark to intercept a band of whisky smugglers that our scouts had located about 10 miles up the river. Soon after the party started they separated, (Constables) Alexander and Ryan being instructed to scout down the river and cross at the Cochrane crossing ; if they did not meet the rest of the party they were to go up to the Eight Mile Rock and await them. Alexander and Ryan carried out their orders and crossed the river at Cochrane's crossing, ascending on to the high land on the other side, all the time on the alert to catch a glimpse of the smugglers. Soon after reaching the high ground Alexander caught sight of something moving in the distance, which on a nearer approach proved to be horsemen with two pack animals. The constables immediately gave chase at full gallop, and on coming up with them discovered them to be Indians with fresh-killed meat.

" As they galloped up to make the arrest one of the Indians threw his rifle into the hollow of his arm, pointing it at Alexander, and as the constable dashed in to seize him fired point-blank at his head, the bullet taking effect on the neck of the constable, who was only about three feet from the muzzle of the rifle. Constable Ryan, seeing Alexander reel in his saddle and imagining him to be seriously wounded, if not killed, drew his revolver and opened fire on the Indian, who returned it, one bullet passing very close to Ryan's head, while one of the latter's shots struck the Indian in the back, passing through his lungs and coming out at his left breast. Alexander then rode into the detachment for a waggon to convey the wounded Indian in, Ryan staying with him till assistance arrived. In trying to put the wounded Indian, who is named 'Steals Fire,' on his own horse, the savage tried to draw his knife. He was too weak to do anything, and Ryan took the knife away. As the man's cries had attracted a small party of Indians who took cover in the brush close to where Ryan was, he got on his horse and galloped for help to remove the Indian, who, however, was carried away by other Indians before he returned. Dr. Aylen, the Police surgeon, was at once sent out to render assistance, but the Indian refused all such offers, placing his faith in a medicine man to whom he paid ten ponies to ensure his recovery, and, strange to say, in a fortnight's time he was riding round. Alexander's wound proved very slight."

Another case of killing cattle, in which one " Medicine White Horse " figured, is interesting, as it brings into prominence a new feature of the Mounted Police system, the employment of full-blooded Indian scouts. These useful members of the Force were introduced in 1887. The scouts were attached to the patrols and were invaluable as trailers, being able and willing to trail excessive distances in an almost incredible space of time. By their engagement it was hoped also to strengthen the good understanding between the Indians and the Police. At the present time there are many such scouts on the roll, but as a rule they are short-service men. When they have accumulated some pay they apply for discharge, and return home to live a life of luxury until forced to again seek employment.

THE BARRACKS AT REGINA
A party of men leaving by waggon on transfer.

TEN YEARS' WORK, 1885-1895

It was two of these Indian "trailers," Owl Child and Black Eagle by name, who came across Medicine White Horse, who had been wanted for over a year for cattle-killing. They arrested him and were taking him off to the Stand Off detachment when he was rescued by an Indian named Good Young Man, assisted by his squaw, and the prisoner succeeded in effecting his escape. Good Young Man and his spouse were promptly secured, and some constables were sent in pursuit of Medicine White Horse, who eventually surrendered himself to Iron Shield, another Indian scout. For the crime of cattle-killing he was sentenced to two years in the penitentiary, but he was expert enough to break prison by sawing a hole in the wall of the corridor in the guard-room, and eventually he got clear.

The increase in the force of Mounted Police, which took place in 1885, has already been referred to. That this addition of over 500 men was justified, irrespective of the extra duty entailed by the half-breeds' rebellion, is shown by the result of a few years' work. The rush of fresh immigrants into the north-west following upon the end of the war necessitated a much wider and more exhaustive control of the Territories. Settlers flocked in to the rich ranching country of Southern Alberta and the wheat-growing plains further to the east. Prince Albert, originally a half-breed settlement, and Battleford, offered many inducements to Canadians to forsake the more populated Provinces of Ontario and Quebec, particularly now that the railway was beginning to branch out in several directions. To the Police, therefore, fell the responsibility of looking after the numerous townships and villages that sprang up as if by magic, and of rigidly enforcing the law of the land.

A new impetus to immigration was given in the autumn of the same year by the visit to the Territories of Lord Lansdowne, who succeeded the Marquess of Lorne as Governor-General of Canada in 1883. His Excellency began his tour at Indian Head, proceeding hence to Fort Qu'Appelle, Regina, Dunmore, Lethbridge, Fort Kipp, Fort Macleod, and Calgary. During the journey he was escorted by various detachments of Mounted Police, whose smartness and efficiency called forth high praise.

In April of the following year an important change in the Force occurred. Commissioner Irvine retired, and Mr. Lawrence W. Herchmer, a brother of Superintendent W. M. Herchmer, was appointed to the vacant post. The new chief had had no little experience of the north-west, having acted as a commissariat officer on the staff of the International Boundary Commission. In June Superintendent Crozier, who had been promoted to the Assistant-Commissionership, also retired, and Superintendent Herchmer took over his duties as Inspecting Superintendent until formally gazetted as Assistant-Commissioner.

The year 1886 was further marked by the issue of new Standing Orders for the Force, and of a new concise drill-book, which explained to every constable his manifold duties and included the elementary rules of veterinary practice. At Regina the regular drilling of recruits went on, both as regards Police work and riding, but the constant drafting of new men to the several divisions made the course of instruction all too short.

Of the general physique of the Force at this period the new Commissioner was pleased to report that it was " of a very high standard." There were very few men, he said, who were not in the prime of life, well set up, and fit for the arduous work they were liable at any time to be called upon

TEN YEARS' WORK, 1885-1895

to perform. The *personnel* of the Police, both as regards officers and the rank and file, was varied and interesting in its character. The life of a Rider of the Plains had attracted men of all conditions and ranks, offering as it did a career of active service under somewhat romantic conditions. Mr. John G. Donkin, who served as Constable and Corporal in the Force in the eighties, gives us a vivid glimpse of the kind of man who then donned the scarlet tunic.[1] He says :—

" After having been about two months in the corps, I was able to form some idea of the class of comrades among whom my lot was cast. I discovered that there were truly ' all sorts and conditions of men.' Many I found, in various troops, were related to English families in good position. There were three men at Regina who had held commissions in the British service. There was also an ex-officer of militia, and one of volunteers. There was an ex-midshipman, son of the Governor of one of our small Colonial dependencies. A son of a major-general, an ex-cadet of the Canadian Royal Military College at Kingston, a medical student from Dublin, two ex-troopers of the Scots Greys, a son of a captain in the line, an Oxford B.A., and several of the ubiquitous natives of Scotland, comprised the mixture. In addition, there were many Canadians belonging to families of influence, as well as several from the backwoods who had never seen the light till their fathers had hewed a way through the bush to a concession road. They were none the worse fellows on that account, though. Several of our men sported medals won in South Africa, Egypt, and Afghanistan. There was one, brother of a Yorkshire baronet, formerly an officer of a certain regiment of foot, who as a contortionist and lion-comique

[1] *Trooper and Redskin in the Far North-West*, by John G. Donkin, 1889.

was the best amateur I ever knew. There was only an ex-circus clown from Dublin who could beat him. These two would give gratuitous performances nightly, using the barrack-room furniture as acrobatic ' properties.' "

A further illustration of the composite character of the Mounted Police was afforded during the Earl of Aberdeen's term of office as Governor-General. While on a visit to the north-west his Lordship stopped at Fort Macleod, and the Police trooper who was sent down from the barracks with his mail proved to be his own nephew. But these surprises are characteristic of Canada. The " younger son " of many an historic English house has found his way out to the farms, ranches, and other settlements of Manitoba, the North-West Territories, and British Columbia. Side by side with cowboys and miners these bearers of distinguished names have borne their full share of pioneer work, sometimes sinking their identity in an assumed name, sometimes frankly proclaiming it to the world. That the Mounted Police should enrol several of these soldiers of fortune was only to be expected. At the present day the altered conditions of the north-west do not attract so many of this class to the ranks, but there are still among the troopers some who in Europe would be the social superiors of many of their officers. Is there not at Regina a corporal who bears one of the most famous names belonging to the ancient Danish nobility ?

With regard to the efficiency of the Force a high standard of excellence was being reached in target practice. The Enfield revolvers with which the men were now all armed proved to be well adapted for the work. The Winchester carbine, however, was not giving such general satisfaction. For a military weapon the trajectory was much too high. The Winchester had the further drawbacks of easily getting out of order, and of being liable to break off at the stock. As a consequence of the unfavourable report made on this rifle the new Lee-Metford carbine was soon after introduced, with satisfactory results. At a test match between the best shots at Macleod the Lee-Metfords showed their superiority over the older type.

In all the divisions there was constant practice with both rifle and revolver at the targets, and when possible competitions were held between the crack teams of the various Police posts. Encouragement was also given to the men to take part in the several Dominion and North-West Rifle League matches which were held annually. That a great number of the men developed into expert shots is borne out by their records in the prize-lists, the Police always making a good show at these contests.

How quick and sure some were with the rifle is testified to by Superintendent Deane, now in command at Calgary. While stationed at Lethbridge in 1894 he had in his detachment a Corporal Dickson, who was "*facile princeps* with either weapon." One day Dickson was out with a shooting party and broke the trigger of his rifle. An antelope got up, and two or three shots were fired at it which took no effect. Seeing this, the corporal said, "Well, I suppose I'll have to kill it," and drawing back the hammer with his finger, he fired and brought the antelope down.

The most notable events of the ten years under record were the vice-regal and other important official visits to the Territories, and the extension of Mounted Police work further north into the Athabasca, Peace River, and Yukon districts. The Governor-General in succession to Lord Lansdowne was Lord Stanley of Preston (afterwards the Earl of Derby). In 1889 the new Viceroy made an extended tour in the north-west, during which he was attended by escorts and patrols of the Mounted Police.

In the same year the Hon. Mackenzie Bowell, the Canadian Minister of Customs, was able to see for himself the invaluable work performed for his Department by the Force. Driving in a Police transport he passed through the whole line of patrols extending along the boundary from the Red River to the foot of the Rocky Mountains. The distance covered was close on 800 miles. All the main trails of the north-west were well guarded at this period, and the strict watch that was kept upon the smuggling traders had a beneficial effect upon the country at large. As an example of the patrols undertaken, we may quote from a report made by Superintendent Norman of B Division :—

"The main work to be done during the summer consisted in keeping a strict quarantine on all animals coming into the district from the United States ; to see that no smuggling or illicit traffic of any kind took place along the border ; and to have a good look out for all criminals either coming into our country or endeavouring to evade capture by ' clearing out ' to the other side.

"Taking Wood Mountain post as a centre, our western patrol extended to a distance of 65 miles due west to a point on the Snake Creek where we made connection on every Wednesday with a similar patrol from A Division. This patrol then proceeded south along the White Mud River to the Boundary Line, and returned along the border by Rock Creek, Cart Coulée, and the Hinsdale Trail to the post, having covered a distance of about 160 miles. As this patrol covered the most important part of the district for our work, I found it necessary to station a permanent camp during the latter part of the summer at a point where the Hinsdale Trail crosses the Boundary Line. The presence of large herds of United States cattle made this absolutely essential. After a few days' absence of our patrol these cattle would drift many miles north of the boundary, and have to be driven south on the return of the next patrol. The stationing of a permanent camp had the desired effect of keeping these cattle within bounds, but owing to the very broken-up nature of this portion of the district this was no easy work, and it will be seen from the various reports I sent in during the season how very satisfactorily the work was carried out by our men.

" The patrol to the south went out from the post once a week and covered a distance of 100 miles, passing along the boundary and crossing the country lying between the Cart Coulée and where the trail to Fort Buford cuts the boundary. This patrol had also supervision over the Glasgow, Wolf Point, and Poplar River Trails leading from the United States into our country. Very few American cattle were seen in this district, most of it being unfit for grazing purposes and bad land.

" A weekly patrol was kept up to the east between the post and Willow Bunch Station, covering a distance of about 100 miles. Its chief work was to keep in touch with the settlers located to the north of the mountain—to learn if they had any complaints to make, and to keep a sharp look out for any individuals starting prairie fires.

" Two patrols were carried on from the Willow Bunch Station. An easterly one proceeded by the Moose Pond, Alkali Springs, Big Butte, and Long Creek, as far as the Buffalo Head, and there made connection with our patrol from Estevan (fortnightly), the distance covered being about 150 miles. Nothing of importance occurred on this line of patrol during the summer. The patrol south from Willow Bunch went along the Big Muddy Creek as far as the border, returning to the station by different routes, having traversed about 100 miles. Very few American cattle were seen in this district, and the country is very broken up and difficult to travel over. The fortnightly mail from Regina was carried to Wood Mountain post by a Willow Bunch patrol. The half-breed settlement at Willow Bunch, containing over three hundred souls, was constantly patrolled by our men."

Mention of prairie fires in Superintendent Norman's report brings to our notice one of the most important duties of the Mounted Police in the Territories. From the earliest days the prevalence of this scourge had called for great vigilance, but of late, owing to the number of new settlers in the country, the efforts of the Police had to be redoubled in the attempt to check the conflagrations. Carelessness was too often the cause of disaster. Take one case : Sergeant Higinbotham, when riding in from the Milk River on special duty saw the smoke of a fire in the river valley. He found that a man had not properly extinguished his camp fire, and it had got beyond his control, setting blaze to the grass around it for a considerable distance. Again : " A fire swept down from the Sweet Grass Hills and burnt over about a township on the south side of Milk River on our side of the line, before it was extinguished by the men at Writing-on-Stone. This fire is supposed to have been started by sheepmen in the hills, so as to drive cattle away from their neighbourhood."

The area covered by a prairie fire when once started is sometimes immense, and the consequent damage very heavy. Here is what happened in the autumn of 1895 in the Lethbridge district, as reported by Superintendent Deane :—

TEN YEARS' WORK, 1885-1895

" A large fire loomed up to the south of us on the afternoon of the 16th October at a great distance from town, and Sergeant Higinbotham was sent out. He returned late on the night of the 18th with one Robert Farrar, who admitted that he had made his camp fire at a short distance from his hay-stack in the Ridge, and had picqueted his horse close by. He said the horse scattered the fire—the probabilities are that he dragged his picquet rope over it. An alarming fire in the hay country was the result. At daylight on the 19th Sergeant-Major Macdonell with nine constables and eleven horses started for the scene. They reached the fire after about 20 miles travel, and by dint of hard work put out about 30 miles of fire, returning to barracks at 4.20 next morning. Farrar was fined $100. The fire was caused by rank carelessness. It is estimated that nine townships were completely, and eight others partly, burnt over by this fire, and these represent a large area of good feed and hay, lying to the west of the A. R. & C. Co. Railway to Montana."

To show how a fire will jump under favourable conditions it is only necessary to mention an instance recorded by Commissioner Herchmer. A prairie fire that had been running some distance actually crossed the Saskatchewan, near Limestone Lake, where the river is 900 ft. wide. A rotten tree having caught fire, some of the lighted bark or punk was blown across the water by the strong southerly wind. The imposition of fines, and the insistence on proper fire-guards—the ploughing up of the prairie around homesteads and other similar precautions—on the part of settlers, were measures which to some extent checked the ravages for which fires were responsible, but the vigilance of Police fire-patrols was never relaxed, nor, indeed, has it ever been down to the present day.

THE RIDERS OF THE PLAINS

The year 1891 is memorable in the history of the Mounted Police for the death of their loyal friend, Sir John Macdonald. As has been seen, in all his administrations the Premier kept the control of the Force in his own hands; it was, in a sense, his own pet scheme, and he saw to it that both in its military and civil capacities the corps maintained its efficiency and smartness in the highest degree. Thanks to his guidance the North-West Mounted Police passed through their early stormy years to a place in the country's regard which few were found to cavil at.

Three years later the Force was reduced from its strength of 1000 non-commissioned officers and constables to 750.[1] When one remembers the vast extent of territory to be supervised, and the varied nature of the duties falling to the lot of the Police, this seems a daring step to have taken. But the bulk of the work had been done; Indians, half-breeds, and whites were all settling down fairly comfortably to the routine of life in the north-west; there was no prospect of any fresh revolt against the Government; and the Mounted Police had won such respect for themselves

---

[1] The following was the state of distribution of the Mounted Police in November 1895, according to divisions and stations: "A," Maple Creek, East End, Ten Mile, Medicine Lodge, Josefsburg, Medicine Hat, Farwell, Swift Current; "C," Battleford, Onion Lake, Jack Fish, Macfarlane's, Henrietta; "D," Macleod, Pincher Creek, Big Bend, Kootenai, Stand Off, St. Mary's, Lee's Creek, Boundary Creek, Kipp, Leavings, Mosquito Creek, Porcupines, Piegan; "E," Calgary, Banff, Gleichen, High River, Morley, Olds, Ings, Dewdney, Waites; "F," Prince Albert, Duck Lake, Batoche, Saskatoon, Snake Plains; "G," Fort Saskatchewan, Edmonton, South Edmonton, Lac St. Anne, Red Deer, Innisfail, St. Albert, Wetaskiwin, Lewisville, Lammerton; "K," Lethbridge, Milk River Ridge, Coutts, Writing-on-Stone, Pendant d'Oreille, St. Mary's, Little Bow, Macleod; "Dépôt," Regina, Moosomin, Cannington, Fort Qu'Appelle, Grenfell, Indian Head, Qu'Appelle, Whitewood, Wolseley, Moose Jaw, Estevan, North Portal, Carnduff, Gainsboro', Oxbow, Roche Percée, Percy, Wood End, Saltcoats, Fort Pelly, Quill Plains, Yorkton, Kutawa, Nut Lake, Wood Mountain, Willow Bunch, Yukon, Ottawa. Total of officers and men, including scouts and supernumeraries, 774. Total of horses, ponies, and mules, 792.

TEN YEARS' WORK, 1885-1895

throughout the country, that where before a detachment of some size had been needed to keep law and order it was now felt that a mere handful of men was equal to the task. No greater tribute to the Force could have been paid. From that time on, the record of Police work in the Territories has been largely individual in its character; at a divisional post, thirty or forty men; at another, from ten to twenty. Here and there, scattered along the trails, north and south and east and west, in settled localities or in the veritable wilderness, two, three, four, and five men stationed as the guardians of the Pax Britannica. Truly a wonderful thing this, and a splendid realisation of Sir John Macdonald's ambition.[1]

It is interesting at this point to contrast the Indian situation in 1895 with that of ten years back. By this time all the tribes, except the Bloods, Piegans, Sarcees, and Blackfeet, had set themselves to acquire large herds of cattle, and numbers of steers were sold by them annually to the drovers. Mowers, rakes, and waggons for haymaking were now to be found on most reserves. "At Regina," states the Commissioner, "the Indians have furnished the Police with a very large proportion of the hay required, drawing it 30 miles and stacking it to the admiration of every one." Considerable freighting, too, was being done

---

[1] Speaking in the Canadian Senate in the session of 1894, the Hon. W. B. Ives, then President of the Privy Council, said: "The State of Montana is immeasurably smaller in extent than the territory over which our North-West Mounted Police have jurisdiction. There are about the same number of Indians in Montana and Dakota as in the Canadian North-West; and whereas we use a force of under 800 men, who have been successful to a degree in preserving order in that country, the smallest number of troops the United States have found sufficient for a much smaller territory, and with about the same number of Indians, belonging to the same tribes, is some 3500 to 4000 men. Any one familiar with the state of things in their country and ours must admit that our force, though only a small fraction of theirs, has succeeded admirably."

by them. In 1895 the Bloods secured, in the open market, the contract for a good deal of the coal used by the Police at Macleod, purchasing it from the coal company and delivering it with their own four-horse teams at the barracks and outposts. At the Onion Lake N.W.M.P. outpost, where the agent had contracted to build a house, stables, storehouse, etc., all the material was sawn and all the buildings were erected by Indians.

In their own buildings the Indians had made great progress. The old skin lodges were fast disappearing, to give place to neatly constructed log houses, whitewashed and comfortably furnished ; on some reserves brick residences were even to be seen. Red Crow, Chief of the Bloods, had his house well carpeted throughout, and could boast of up-to-date bedsteads and washstands. These improvements were due to a judicious expenditure of the treaty money paid at regular intervals by the Government. On all reserves, too, schools were being established, at which the youthful Indians were compelled to attend.

The wider extension of the sphere of operations before alluded to dates from the year 1892. Far up to the northeast of Prince Albert was a Hudson's Bay Company post known as Cumberland House, situated on the Saskatchewan River. Here were many Indians, and owing to their exposure to the machinations of liquor traders it was decided to send a small force of Police to supervise the district. The step was a wise and necessary one ; Cumberland House became a permanent post, exercising surveillance over a large section of country not previously patrolled.

In the following year, which saw a new Governor-General in the person of the Earl of Aberdeen, detachments were pushed northwards into Athabasca. The chief care

TEN YEARS' WORK, 1885-1895

of the Police was the enforcement of the liquor laws, especially under the new " permit " system, but the increasing settlement of the fertile valleys of the Peace River demanded their presence in any case.

Then, in 1894, came the first rush of miners and prospectors to the Yukon territory, where gold had been discovered. By the next year the stream of fortune-hunters pouring into the country was so great and comprised so many mixed elements that the call came for Government supervision. At once the authorities turned to the Mounted Police; none other could undertake the work so well and so economically. And thus on 5th June we find Inspector Constantine leading a detachment into the Yukon, to establish himself at a post some hundreds of miles up country.

The story of Police work in the Yukon demands a chapter to itself. But before we come to consider this an historic and sensational episode has to be narrated. In 1895 occurred the tragedy of " Almighty Voice."

CHAPTER XI.

"ALMIGHTY VOICE," BAD INDIAN.

Sergeant Colebrook shot—Hunt for the murderer—On the trail—Inspector Allan—In a death-trap—Shelling the bluff—The end of the drama—The "Charcoal" case—A long pursuit—Indian aid—Death of Interpreter Jerry Potts.

WHEN the Cree Indian Ka-kee-man-i-tou-wayo (which, being interpreted, is "Almighty Voice") killed a cow that was not his own property, he little dreamed of what a coil of trouble would arise from his act. He was in great want of fresh meat, the cow offered a tempting mark, and the moment seemed propitious; so he brought his gun to his shoulder, fired, and became a criminal. How the truth leaked out is not explained. Almighty Voice may have talked too much, or some enemy may have given him away. What is certain is that on the 22nd of October 1895, Regimental No. 605, Sergeant C. C. Colebrook went to One Arrow's reserve, on which the offender was located, and arrested Almighty Voice upon a warrant for killing cattle.

From the reserve, near Batoche, Almighty Voice was taken to Duck Lake to appear before the Indian agent, Mr. M'Kenzie, who was a justice of the peace. He was sentenced to a month's imprisonment, but during the night he managed to escape. Thereafter, for a few days, he hung about the reserve, where attempts to recapture

"ALMIGHTY VOICE," BAD INDIAN

him proved unavailing. On the 27th, finding the hunt becoming too hot, he called his squaw to him and started off to seek a safe hiding-place. But if he thought by this means to shake off the Police from his heels he was mistaken. The very next day Sergeant Colebrook took up the trail and pressed the pursuit so hard that he came up with the fugitives on the morning of the 29th. They were on the open prairie, where they had just killed a chicken.

With the sergeant was a half-breed guide, Dumont by name. When the two came within hearing Almighty Voice unslung his gun, a double-barrelled muzzle-loader, and warned the guide to advise the Policeman to go away. "If he does not," he said, " I shall shoot." Colebrook had his orders, whch were to arrest Almighty Voice, escaped prisoner, and he had no option but to go forward. So, bidding the guide tell the Indian to surrender, he rode slowly on, holding up his right hand as a sign of peace. His left was gripping his revolver in his overcoat pocket, ready for action if need be.

A second warning came from the Cree's lips. Then, seeing the other still advancing upon him, Almighty Voice got desperate. Levelling his gun at the sergeant, he pulled the trigger while the ill-fated Policeman was only a few yards away and shot him through the neck. Colebrook dropped from his horse and expired a moment or two later. The half-breed, in no mind to face the gleaming barrels, turned and rode off for help.

Almighty Voice was now a criminal twice over, and with the worst of crimes to his account. He promptly took to his heels once more, and by the time the hue and cry was up had put some distance between him and his pursuers. Constable Tennent, who was the first on the scene, having been stationed on prairie fire duty in the adjacent settlement, tried to take up the trail, but neither he nor others who followed could run the murderer to earth.

For several months Almighty Voice lay low, and the Mounted Police scoured the country round for hundreds of miles in vain. No trace of his whereabouts was obtainable. A price was set upon his head, a hundred dollars were offered for his recapture, but none came to claim the reward. In the March following his reckless deed, the horse which he had with him when the sergeant was shot was found about forty miles south of Batoche. This led to the supposition that he was in the vicinity, and a search party was at once sent out. The clue was a false one; the trackers were obliged to return baffled. A little later the disappearance of the snow rendered the hunt more difficult, and it began to look as if the Cree had broken through the cordon of patrols and got clear away.

All the summer a keen watch was kept in the neighbourhood of the Indian reserves at La Corne and Crooked Lake, and at that near Duck Lake where One Arrow ruled. It was hoped that the release of the fugitive's father, John Sounding Sky, who had been in prison, might lead to something, but this hope, too, proved vain. Almighty Voice never showed himself near his own people, nor did he apparently hold any communication with them. The natural difficulties in the way of his capture were very great. He had a large area of country over which to roam. It was practically limitless, and was uninhabited except by roving bands of Indians who might be expected to befriend him. A very large portion of the district, too, was hilly and densely wooded, offering numerous safe retreats.

Summer gave way to winter and winter again to spring without the Police meeting with success. Then chance

R.N.W.M.P. POST AT WHITE HORSE, YUKON TERRITORY.

"ALMIGHTY VOICE," BAD INDIAN

brought tidings of the missing man. One evening in May of 1897 a half-breed scout named Napoleon Venne came riding in hot haste to an outpost near Duck Lake to pour an exciting tale into the ears of the sergeant in charge. He had been after a horse-thief, had caught him and was bringing the rascal back, when in passing through a copse the latter suddenly vanished. In his place appeared an Indian, Almighty Voice. The moment he saw the Cree's evil face and the gun-barrel pointing at him, the scout wheeled his horse and fled. He was not lucky enough, however, to escape scot-free. As he galloped, leaning low upon his horse's neck, a bullet from the Indian's muzzle-loader struck him in the back, while another ripped through his broad-brimmed hat.

On receipt of the news at Prince Albert, where F Division was stationed, a detachment of Mounted Police was immediately sent out. Inspector Allan was in command. They rode through the night without a stop—eighty miles in all, heading for the Minnichinas Hills, wherein Venne had seen the murderer. In the morning, soon after dawn, they were rewarded by the sight of three dark figures stealing into a bluff. "Our men!" said Inspector Allan, shortly. And he was right. Almighty Voice, with two companions whom he had persuaded to join him, was cornered at last. But though the Indians were seemingly in a trap the end was not yet. There was to be some hot work before Sergeant Colebrook's death was to be avenged.

Ever the first to lead when duty called, the Inspector rode towards a clump of poplars on the bluff, while his men opened out on either side to prevent escape. He had not gone far when a shot rang out, and a bullet crashed into his right shoulder. Almighty Voice had winged him, but the Indian himself had a broken ankle to his score. Allan's revolver had spat out in quick answer. Crawling away through the thick grass the wounded officer was brought up suddenly by a few sharp words in Cree. He looked up to find himself in a terrible position. The Indian had him covered. "Stay right where you are," was the stern command he heard from the dusky face behind the rifle barrel, "and throw me your cartridge-belt. If you don't, I will kill you!"

Allan made no answer. He realised the situation. Almighty Voice was short of ammunition; every cartridge he had left was precious if he meant to hold his own. Would he risk a shot now, even though his enemy lay at his mercy? That was the question.

"Throw me your cartridge-belt, or I'll kill you," repeated the Indian, who dared not leave his shelter to secure the much-needed ammunition.

Then Allan spoke. "Never!" he said. He expected to be shot instantly, but as by a miracle he escaped. One of his comrades, sighting Almighty Voice's face through the bushes at that moment, fired, and the Indian dropped back out of view.

Another Policeman had been wounded at this juncture —Sergeant Raven. He and the Inspector were carefully tended to prevent their bleeding to death, and then the others proceeded to renew the attack. A fire was started round the bluff, but the green bushes and trees refused to catch alight. This move having failed, three plucky Policemen—Corporal Hocking and two constables—discovered some openings in the bushes, and pushed their way in stealthily among the thick undergrowth in the hope of surprising their quarry. It was a desperate attempt, and how was each one of the three to know that he was crawling into a death-trap ? Yet such was the case. Not one of them was seen alive again.

With diabolical ingenuity the Indians had contrived to make one or two " runways " into the heart of their lair, each of these paths through the bushes leading right up to a rifle pit dug in the ground. In this pit Almighty Voice and his companions crouched ready to deal out death the moment an enemy showed himself.

In his graphic account of this incident, Mr. W. A. Fraser, the Canadian writer, tells how two other Policemen, Cook and O'Kelly, went in to do what three had failed to accomplish. He says : " The two constables avoided the paths and kept to the thick growth. Suddenly O'Kelly became aware of a pair of khaki-coloured legs in front of him. Thinking it was one of his dead comrades, he reached out to pull the body back. As he did so the feet were wrenched violently from his grasp, and disappeared over the embankment into the pit. The rifles belched forth in his very face, and an Indian sprang upon the embankment to get a better shot at him. A bullet from O'Kelly's rifle went crashing through the redskin's brain. The constable flattened his body out, and hugged his mother earth as though he loved her. A shot from Almighty Voice tore a spur from off his heel.

" Ten feet away Cook was lying flat and motionless behind the dead limb of a fallen tree. He saw the smoke of the rifle from the Indians' pit, but he did not see the pair of lynx-like eyes, motionless as the rock of Gibraltar, that watched steadily the limb that covered his face. Cautiously he raised his head a few inches. There was a sharp crack, a puff of smoke, and bark and chips were driven into his eyes with terrific force. Luckily the aim had been a little low. The bullet had glanced.

"They recovered the body of one of their companions (Corporal Hocking) a little later, and inch by inch worked their way backward, dragging him between them. All that night they guarded the bluff. Once Almighty Voice tried to creep out, but was driven back. In the morning a little trail, and a crutch dropped from the blood-stained hands of the Indian, showed where he had tried to escape. About midnight Almighty Voice called to the Police: 'Brothers, we've had a good fight to-day. I've worked hard, and am hungry. You've plenty of grub; send me in some. To-morrow we'll finish the fight.'"

The best that can be said for Almighty Voice is that he died game. During that long night, while a strong force of Mounted Police surrounded his stronghold, he must have realised that the end was near. Yet he never made a sign of surrender. And all the next day he and his two allies held their own. By the evening a reinforcement from Regina had arrived. A party of men under the command of Superintendent (now Assistant-Commissioner) M'Illree, with a 9-pounder field gun, had been sent to finish the business.

The final scene of the drama was a striking one. A large crowd of Indians, half-breeds, and settlers had gathered to watch the fight, and among them was Almighty Voice's wrinkled old mother, who sat upon a low hill near by, wrapped in a gaudy blanket, and chanted her son's death-song. It was a dirge which recounted his former prowess in battle, his skill in hunting, and other great deeds, and it called on him to die like the Indian "brave" that he was.

Assistant-Commissioner M'Illree, to whom the writer is indebted for many of the above particulars, now gave the order for the bluff to be shelled. The 9-pounder and a 7-pounder that had been sent from Prince Albert were

"ALMIGHTY VOICE," BAD INDIAN

brought into action. When the smoke had cleared away M'Illree and some of his constables " rushed " the place, and found their task at an end. In the rifle pit lay two dead Indians, Almighty Voice and another, identified as Little Salteaux. The third of the trio had been killed by a rifle bullet.

The effect produced in the Saskatchewan district by this exceptional act of outlawry was somewhat marked. Writing of it some time later, Superintendent Cotton said : " The trouble over ' Almighty Voice ' has been much talked of among the Indians, treaty and non-treaty. The result has not as far as known made itself apparent in any overt act on the part of the Indians : as I have said, all is quiet ; still, the way the Indians talk over this matter (Indian fashion, of course) comes to my ears and the ears of the Indian Department officials also. It is quite evident that the spirit of unrest, though apparently dormant, is by no means dead among the younger men. It is not to be wondered at ; the habits of a lifetime are not easy to unlearn. While the chiefs and the older men are adverse to, and even fear, any trouble arising, the young men are not all of the same mind. They not only realise what an amount of mischief a few Indians can do before being punished, but they have an enormously exaggerated idea of their own power. This, added to the love of notoriety, largely developed in Indian character, points them out as an element requiring careful Police supervision at all times.

" Another point, the Indians in the district are not as well off as they have been in the past. As to non-treaty Indians, the hunting and fishing have been poor. The treaty Indians find it hard, they say next to impossible, to earn money by working for, or making sales of wood to, white men ; in other words, the Indians' power to earn something over and above what they receive as aid (in

THE RIDERS OF THE PLAINS

the shape of rations) from the Government has in the past been overrated. A hungry Indian, like a hungry white, is not so docile or as contented as he is found to be under more favourable circumstances. In talking among themselves as well as to their half-breed and white friends, the Indians maintain that the daily ration received is too small to live on, and that their power of supplementing such ration by their own labour has become minimised. In addition to this, though strictly speaking not relating to Indians, the poorer class of half-breeds are in bad circumstances, some utterly destitute; of these some are really Indians by birth though they do not take treaty. These people (who I might note have had much consideration and aid from the Government) are related to the Indians, speaking the same language. They exercise a certain influence, which I fear is not in the majority of cases likely to be a favourable one, even if comparatively passive. Then again, there are always those white men who should know better, who, when occasion offers, as it must from time to time, are not too glad to sympathise with Indian statements, and conclusions drawn therefrom, to an extent that establishes a belief in a grievance."

That Almighty Voice was not without followers who yearned to emulate his example was shown not many months after his outbreak. In October of 1896 occurred the case of Charcoal, *alias* Bad Young Man, who gave the Police nearly as bad a time as his notorious predecessor. Briefly stated, the story of this Indian's downfall was as follows: On 13th October the body of another Blood Indian, named Medicine Pipe Stem, was found in a cattle shed. There was no clue to the murderer until, a week or two later, one Little Pine, also a Blood, admitted that Charcoal had been to his lodge and confessed having killed Medicine Pipe Stem. It had been his intention, added Charcoal, to further kill the Indian agent, Mr. Wilson, and Chief Red Crow. Little Pine stated that he wanted to arrest Charcoal then and there, but could not do so without assistance. He went out, therefore, to assemble some of his friends for the purpose, but on his return Charcoal had disappeared, taking with him his family of four squaws and two children.

Acting on this information, Inspector Jarvis of the Big Bend N.W.M.P. post, in the Macleod district, set off in pursuit with Police and scouts. After searching vainly for some days it was concluded that the fugitives had made towards the Rockies, and a party proceeded along the Belly River. At this juncture the first tidings of Charcoal were received. A settler reported having had his coat stolen by an Indian while he was loading timber. The description of the thief so tallied with that of the missing man that Inspector Jarvis felt sure that he was on the right track at last. Upon reaching the timber where the theft had taken place, the Police removed their hats and boots so as to enable them to move noiselessly, and in this manner proceeded for a distance of five miles. Then the murderer's tepee was located in a valley below. It was situated in a thick wood consisting of about 500 acres of dense pine, and was surrounded by mountains.

Despite the utmost caution being observed, Charcoal detected the approach of the Police. Running out of his tent he fired several shots, one of which almost hit the Inspector. The camping-place was at once rushed, but the Indian himself eluded capture, taking to the wood with two squaws and one child.

This was the beginning of a stern chase which lasted many weeks. From the shelter of the woods Charcoal escaped on a stolen horse, and was next heard of on the

Piegan Reserve. Thence he fled to the Porcupine Hills with Mounted Police, Indian trailers, and numerous volunteers in hot pursuit. Inspectors Cuthbert and Sanders had now joined in the search, and the vigilance of their patrols narrowed Charcoal's chances of freedom considerably. He was now heard of frequently. Corporal Armer at Cardston was fired at one night by the fugitive. A settler's wife alone in her house had a visit from him, as a raided larder proved the next morning. Then word was brought that he was camping on Beaver Creek near the Piegan Agency, and from this spot his trail was taken up in the direction of the Blood Reserve.

Sergeant Wilde, in charge at Pincher Creek, now organised a party including himself, Constable Ambrose, Scout Holloway, and two Indian scouts. In the thick snow they pushed their horses as fast as was possible, and sighted Charcoal near a ranch on the north fork of the Kootenai River. When the murderer was first seen he was riding a pony barebacked, leading another which was saddled and laden with provisions. All the horses of the Police party, with the exception of that ridden by the sergeant, were used up, so that when the latter pressed on ahead the others were compelled to follow on foot.

Sergeant Wilde, like Colebrook, was not to be daunted by any Indian, however desperate. He probably knew that he carried his life in his hands, but the knowledge did not deter him from doing his duty, and like Colebrook he paid the penalty of his bravery. When quite close to the Indian he placed his carbine in front of his body across the saddle, and reached over to take hold of Charcoal, who swerved round in his seat and fired. The bullet entered Wilde's right side, coming out at a point opposite on the left side, and was found in the poor fellow's left gauntlet which was

THE BRITISH FLAG IN THE YUKON.

Camp of Stikine River Detachment, showing where Inspector Primrose, Assistant-Surgeon Fraser, and Twenty Non-Coms. and men settled in March 1898, during the stampede.

"ALMIGHTY VOICE," BAD INDIAN

on his hand. The Indian then rode on a few yards, turned, rode back to where the sergeant had fallen off his horse, and fired a second time, the shot taking effect in the abdomen. His own horse being a poor one, he now exchanged it for Wilde's, taking also the latter's carbine as he made off.

In solitary pursuit of Charcoal went the Indian scout, Many-tail-feathers-round-his-neck, who jumped on the murderer's horse. All the night the scout hung on to his man until he had tracked him to the mountains at the head of one of the branches of the north fork of the Kootenai. Others—mostly civilian volunteers—joined in the hunt at this point, but the roughness of the country and the thickness of the brush on the hills afforded Charcoal facilities for eluding them. All that could be done, and was done, was to drive him from his refuge.

Later on, Inspector Sanders and his party learned that an Indian had been seen cooking food in the dry fork of the Kootenai. They moved in that direction, and *en route* were strengthened by the arrival of Inspector Jarvis and the volunteers who had come to the help of Many-tail-feathers-round-his-neck. The result of their united " drive " was to force the runaway to seek refuge at the house of his brother, Left Hand, on the Blood Reservation.

Charcoal had now sealed his own death-warrant. Both Left Hand and another brother, with the picturesque name of Bear's Back Bone, had promised their assistance to the Police. Having admitted the murderer into the house, they disarmed him and sent word of the capture to the nearest outpost. In a very little time Charcoal was safely bestowed in a cell, chained to the floor, and under a guard of five men, pending his removal for trial and eventual execution.

THE RIDERS OF THE PLAINS

One of the most notable features of this case was the readiness displayed by the Indians in lending their valuable aid to the Police. No fewer than thirty native scouts were under arms and engaged in the pursuit at one time. After a week of hard work some would become tired out, fatigued from loss of sleep, their moccasins worn through, clothing torn, or horses used up, in which case they would turn in their arms and give up their places to others. But several remained keen on the chase and kept on it to the end.

That the Indians recognised even more than the Police did how tough a nut they had to crack and what the fugitive was capable of doing, there is no doubt whatever. They were all very much frightened, and generally desired to have the criminal captured.

" As examples of the Indians' fears," says Inspector (now Superintendent) G. E. Sanders, " I might say that ' Red Crow ' during the whole of the pursuit slept on the floor of his house ; he was afraid to sleep in his bed, the position of which ' Charcoal ' knew, for fear of a pot shot through the window. ' Red Crow ' was also afraid the fugitive might go to the High River school and kill his son. ' White Calf ' (another tracker) used to sleep in the loft over his house and pull the ladder by which he ascended up after him when he retired for the night.

" The Indians we had employed did excellent work, and everything that Indian ingenuity could suggest they did. Their power of tracking and picking up signs were, in some instances, simply marvellous, and in this connection I would mention ' Green Grass,' ' Many-tail-feathers-round-his-neck,' and ' Calf Tail,' who are regularly employed scouts. There was not much to choose, however, between any of them ; they were all apparently willing to go any-

"ALMIGHTY VOICE," BAD INDIAN

where and take any chances. All, I think, who have been connected with this pursuit, have come away with a much higher idea of the Indian character than they had before."

This alliance had been brought about by careful management, by kind and just treatment coupled with firmness, and the result was not without its effect on the community. Both settlers and Indians had had presented to them the unusual spectacle of white men and red men working together under Police officers in as determined a pursuit of a criminal as they had ever witnessed.

With the capture of Almighty Voice and Charcoal, the story of Police work in 1896 may come to an end. But no record of the year would be complete without mention of the death of a valued servant of the Mounted Police, which occurred in July. On the 14th of that month Interpreter Jerry Potts died of consumption, after twenty-two years of continuous service. He had joined the Force in 1874, at Fort Benton, and it was he who had guided Colonel Macleod's little command from the Sweet Grass Hills to where the first Police post in the north-west was established. As a guide Jerry Potts had no equal, and many were the expeditions led by him over the vast plains in summer and winter alike. Owing to his knowledge of the Indians, and his reputation with them for fair and honest dealing, he was of the utmost assistance to the Police in their dealings with the tribes. On not a few occasions, it is safe to say, the presence of Jerry Potts with the Police troops was alone the means of averting serious bloodshed.

CHAPTER XII.

IN THE YUKON.—I.

Police protection called for—Inspector Constantine—Rush to the gold-fields—Skagway—" Soapy Smith "—A miners' meeting—Lynch law—A gruesome ride—Police posts on the summits—Relief work—Customs officers—Mail-carrying and other duties—A claim-jumping story—" Old man D——."

IN the summer of 1895, as has been noted already, a small body of Mounted Police under Inspector Constantine was sent up into the Yukon Territory. This was in response to representations made to the Canadian Government pointing out that all that part of the Dominion lying north of British Columbia and west of the Mackenzie district was in need of Police protection. The discovery of gold in the Territory was then attracting large numbers of miners and prospectors, most of whom came up from the Western American States. From that date onwards the rush to the new El Dorado continued, until in the winter of 1897–8 it assumed sensational proportions.

It is to the lasting credit of the North-West Mounted Police that through all this trying time they kept a firm control over the country within their jurisdiction. All the worst elements of mining camps such as had given Western America an evil reputation in past years—the desperadoes, gamblers, bullies, and other male and female parasites—were represented in the Yukon or Klondike region. With the genuine miners and prospectors there drifted up all the

IN THE YUKON

scum of Oregon, Washington, and Nevada; yet such was the power of the law, personified by a mere handful of Police scattered along the passes and among the camps, that there was little lawlessness and disorder. Scenes of violence there were at times—it was hardly to be expected that it would be otherwise where men were not all lambs; but in general the newcomer in the Yukon felt the protecting influence of the British flag, and knew that his rights would be respected. It came to be characteristic of Skagway, where the long journey into the gold country really commenced, that after leaving that city one packed one's revolver away; there was little likelihood that it would be wanted on the road.

The duties of the Police at this period were varied indeed. They had to enforce the laws of the country to begin with, to keep order; they acted as Customs officers at points in all the passes; they took charge of the mail, even running a dog-team mail service from the Yukon into the interior; they were mining recorders and arbitrators; and they played the rôle of guide, philosopher, and friend to every struggling "packer," whatsoever his nationality, who claimed their help.

"When we got to the Yukon," says Inspector Constantine, "the thermometer marked 77 degrees below. We had only four hours' daylight, and at that time candles were a dollar apiece—one hundred and twenty dollars, or £24, a box. I was Chief-Magistrate, Commander-in-Chief, Home and Foreign Secretary. I had three tables in my room, and a different kind of work on each. I walked from one to the other to rest. I arrived there with twenty men on July 26 (1895), and by 8th November we had built nine houses, one of them 75 ft. long. We cut and carried and squared all the timber ourselves. Yes, our shoulders were raw." These barracks constituted Fort Constantine,

THE RIDERS OF THE PLAINS

the first N.W.M.P. post in the Yukon. It was situated nearly 40 miles north of Dawson City, at the junction of Forty-Mile River with the Yukon River.

Practically everything that happened in the Territory had to be taken cognizance of by the Police. Cases of cabins broken into, caches rifled, claims jumped, and all kinds of disputes were brought before them for settlement. Then there was constant vigilance needed to prevent the smuggling of liquor into the country. That old acquaintance of theirs, the illicit whisky trader, was quickly on the scene with his goods, and the tricks he resorted to were legion. So every steamer that passed down the river after the ice had broken, and every camp outfit along the trail, had to be carefully examined. There was an astounding amount of work to be got through, and a great weight of responsibility to be borne.

After Inspector Constantine left the Dawson district, having carried out all he was commissioned to do, he was succeeded by Inspector Cortlandt Starnes. The latter held command until relieved by Superintendent Steele, who, in January 1898, was appointed to the supreme control of the North-West Mounted Police in the Yukon Territory.[1] The great rush over the passes, far surpassing any of previous years, had now begun. From Skagway, " a city of tents " which had sprung up in a few weeks, to the Summit of the Chilkoot Pass, the principal line of route followed, extended a never-ending stream of pack-trains, heading for the new rich gold-fields just

---

[1] The Yukon was declared a " judicial district " by the Governor-General's proclamation in 1897. In the following year it was constituted a Territory by Act of the Dominion Parliament. A Commissioner (Major Walsh) was appointed, a Council of six members assisting him in the government. Superintendent S. B. Steele served on this Council on taking up the command of the Yukon N.W.M.P. detachments.

IN THE YUKON

opened on the Klondike. And over the three other routes available toiled thousands more.

Superintendent Steele's report of that year is eloquent of the condition of affairs. At the end of 1897, be it noted, the Police in the Yukon totalled eight officers and eighty-eight men, including dog-drivers. Not a large number this, but those composing it were picked men, selected from a force which had been made purposely very difficult to enter and very easy to get out of. Within the next twelve months the strength of the detachments was increased to two Superintendents, eight inspectors, two assistant-surgeons, and 254 non-commissioned officers and men. The officers in question, in addition to Superintendent Steele, were as follows: Superintendent Z. T. Wood at Tagish ; Inspector Primrose at Bennett ; Inspector Starnes at Dawson City, acting as quartermaster and paymaster ; Inspector Harper at Dawson, acting as sheriff ; Inspectors Scarth and Belcher, also at Dawson ; Inspectors Strickland and Jarvis at Tagish ; Inspector Cartwright at White Pass Post ; Assistant-Surgeon Fraser at the Dalton Trail Post ; and Assistant-Surgeon Thompson at Dawson. Between all the posts, widely scattered though they were, lines of patrols were constantly kept up.

"From the date of my arrival in Skagway," says Superintendent Steele, "until the 27th of March, many important events took place. The officers in charge of the summits (of the several passes) displayed much ability, using great firmness and tact, and were loyally supported by the non-commissioned officers and constables under their command, who in circumstances of the most trying character displayed the greatest fortitude and endurance amidst the terrific snowstorms which raged

THE RIDERS OF THE PLAINS

round their respective camps. Large numbers of people were packing and hauling their supplies in relays over the passes. The rush to the Yukon being at its height, the office at Skagway was besieged at all hours of the day and night by people seeking information.

"The town of Skagway at this time, and for some months later, was little better than a hell upon earth. The desperado commonly called ' Soapy Smith ' and a numerous gang of ruffians ran the town. Murder and robbery were daily occurrences, hundreds came there with plenty of money and the next morning had not sufficient to buy a meal, having been robbed or cheated out of their cash. Men were seen frequently exchanging shots in the streets. On one occasion half a dozen, in the vicinity and around the North-West Mounted Police Offices, were firing upon one another, bullets passing through the buildings. There was a United States deputy-marshal at Skagway at this time for the purpose of maintaining law and order, but no protection was expected from him.

" An American expedition with supplies for the relief of American citizens, supposed to be starving in the Yukon Territory and Alaska, arrived at Dyea a few days before the posts were established on the summits ; they had reindeer and several hundreds of tons of provisions. Pack animals and snow locomotives were to be used for transport purposes, and there was to be a small army of United States troops, packers, guides, etc. The arrival of one of the snow locomotives afforded endless amusement to the people of Skagway and Dyea. It could hardly move on the level streets, much less ascend the slightest elevation."

This expedition, it may be remarked, proved utterly futile. It could make very little progress northwards, and the reindeer never reached their destination. The

CANADIAN CUSTOMS-HOUSE ON THE SUMMIT OF CHILKOOT PASS, 1898.
R.N.W.M.P. detachment in charge.

IN THE YUKON

moss eaten by the animals was not to be found as expected, and, not having their customary diet, they died like flies !

"At this time," continues the Superintendent, "there were many thousands of people living at a place called 'Sheep Camp,' some distance from the Summit. Most were engaged in packing their supplies to the Summit : all were apparently anxious to get through. Chiefly owing to the fact that neither law nor order prevailed in that section, murder, robbery, and petty theft were of common occurrence ; the 'shell game' could be seen at every turn of the trail, operations being pushed with the utmost vigour, so as not to lose the golden opportunity which they would be unable to find or take advantage of on the other side of the line in British territory."

"Soapy Smith," who has been alluded to, was an American, and the most notorious personage in the Yukon. His quaint nickname he derived from his ability to sell for ten dollars apiece small cakes of soap round which were wrapped one-dollar bills. This was while he was in Denver City some years before. On pushing north with the gold-seekers he soon made himself the " boss " of Skagway, enlisting all the " toughs " and " crooks " of the place under his rule, and so terrorising the authorities that for a long time no one dared to dispute his word. After some atrocious murders had been committed by members of Smith's gang, a vigilance committee was organised to purge Skagway of their presence. To this " Soapy Smith " replied by calling his followers round him, and there was every prospect of a bitter fight when the tension was relieved by the sudden death of Smith himself. He was killed in the open street in a pistol duel with one of the reform party. With the loss of their leader the rest of the gang dispersed, the chief among them being given twelve hours in which to leave the town.

As was to be expected, it was in Skagway and between that place and the Summit of the Chilkoot Pass that the Mounted Police encountered the roughest part of their work. So long as "Soapy Smith" and his associates ran the town, with the American authorities under their thumb, it was highly difficult to preserve any semblance of order. What control the Police could exercise was never relaxed, and their firmness as a rule won the day. But sometimes the *cheechacos*, as the incomers were styled, would take the law into their own hands, call a "miners' meeting," and execute summary justice on an offender.

One of the worst crimes possible for a man to commit on the Yukon trail was to break into another's "cache." By this term is signified a store of provisions left at some spot by a number of prospectors as a safeguard for themselves on a return journey or for the assistance of others in the same party. Often a cache would contain other valuable property, such as rifles and ammunition. When any one was discovered to have robbed one of these storeplaces it was usually a case for Judge Lynch to settle. The sacredness of a cache was recognised far and wide, for on its security many lives might depend.

This is well illustrated by an instance recorded by Inspector J. D. Moodie. "When the cache on the Ospica River was robbed," he says, "all the ammunition with exception of a few rounds 45–75 was taken. In consequence, I purchased two rifles here (Ottawa). 45–75 cartridges cannot be obtained in that country. This cache was the means of saving the life of one man in the spring. Two men tried to go through from Fort St. John on our trail in May, and got to within 6 miles of Fort Graham, when they

IN THE YUKON

branched off on a fresh track. Some Indians found them and took them in. They then started to go back to Summit of the Mountains, and in some way one man got astray, and coming to the cache, stayed there until found. He repaid all he took."

In those early days before 1898 not a few cache-thieves were strung up on trees by the trail. If the crime had any mitigating circumstances the culprit might escape with a flogging or some other punishment.

There is one Mounted Police official, high up in the service, who carries a vivid recollection of one of these scenes when a thief was arraigned before a miners' meeting. This is his story, as narrated to the writer:—

" I had been up on the Chilkoot Summit, where a Police post was being established, and was on my way back to Skagway. At the foot of the Summit was Sheep Camp, a large dépôt of traders and their goods. I should say there were from two to three thousand people in it then, mostly men. Into this camp I descended in an unusual manner, shooting straight down the precipice to the bottom on a snowslide. Thanks to the heavy rough furs I was wearing, I was none the worse for the adventure. When I thus landed among the crowd it was to find that a miners' meeting was being held. Two thieves had been caught in the act of robbing caches, and feeling ran so high in the camp that lynch law was demanded. I endeavoured to remonstrate, but I was only one Police officer, and, moreover, it was not British territory. The miners brushed my objections away, and started off up the trail with their victims.

" A big spruce overhanging the cliff was to be the scene of the execution. But on the way, while my back was turned, I heard a loud report, and turning round saw that one of the thieves had drawn a revolver (evidently he had not been searched). While I looked he was shot down, his body being literally riddled with bullets. There was general excitement at this incident, and the crowd seemed to feel something of the horror of the tragedy. As a result of fresh expostulation, to which I added my voice, we all turned back to the camp to hold another meeting.

" The verdict now given was that the second thief should not be hung. Instead, it was decided to do what had been done to a previous rascal, that is, send him back to the coast. So the poor devil had his hands tied securely behind his back, while round his neck was slung a board inscribed : ' This is a thief. Pass him along ! ' What happened to him I don't know. Perhaps he eventually got to the coast, perhaps he didn't. I remember hearing of one man served in this fashion whose dead body was found on the trail. It was explained that he had accidentally shot himself in the head while firing at his pursuers ! "

This same officer had a gruesome experience following on the Sheep Camp tragedy. The United States sheriff at Skagway learned of the "shooting scrape," and sent a message for the dead body of the cache-thief to be consigned to him. As the N.W.M.P. officer was going down the trail with the next team it was arranged that the buckboard should also carry the body. So the latter was disinterred from the snow in which it had been buried, placed in a rough box, and deposited under the seat. The driver—an Irishman—had a rude sense of humour. Passing at night through a black cañon which itself exhaled an atmosphere of gloom, he took the opportunity to lean towards his fellow-passenger on the seat beside him and whisper : "Sa-ay, didn't you feel him *kick* ? " The Police officer is not above admitting that he jumped.

IN THE YUKON

In the stampede for the gold regions four routes were followed. The first of these was by way of the Stikine River, the mouth of which is near Wrangel. It was not long before this was abandoned for that of the White Pass, *via* Skagway, the journey to the latter place being made direct by steamer. From White Pass one took the trail to Bennett, near the lake of that name, and, crossing the water to where Carcross now stands, joined the main trail leading up to Lake Labarge. The third route was along the Chilkoot Pass, for which one started from Dyea on the opposite side of the inlet to Skagway. The fourth was that of the Dalton Trail, the jumping-off place being Haines Mission, by Pyramid Harbour.

Early in February of 1898 Superintendent Perry established a Police post in the White Pass, while Inspector Belcher similarly took command at the Summit of the Chilkoot Pass. On the Dalton Trail, in the vicinity of the Chilkat Pass, was Inspector Jarvis with a small detachment. This post was taken over some months later by Assistant-Surgeon S. M. Fraser.

The great problem now before the Police was the security of supplies. In Dawson famine prices were obtaining, so great was the demand for provisions of all kinds and for hay and oats. Very many of the gold-seekers were forced to turn back before they had gone far, through their stock of food giving out or by reason of some other mischance having overtaken them. Thus, in addition to the care of those northward-bound, the Police had constantly to face the demands of the famishing wretches who turned back to civilisation, overwhelmed by the difficulties and perils of the ice-bound passes. Hundreds there were who abandoned the attempt as hopeless, or who perished miserably in the snow along the trail. For this is the law of the Yukon,

> "and ever she makes it plain :
> Send not your foolish and feeble ; send me your strong and your sane,
> Strong for the red rage of battle ; sane, for I harry them sore ;
> Send me men girt for the combat, men who are grit to the core ;
> Swift as the panther in triumph, fierce as the bear in defeat,
> Sired of a bulldog parent, steeled in the furnace heat.
>
> . . . .
>
> Them will I gild with my treasure, them will I glut with my meat ;
> But the others—the misfits, the failures—I trample under my feet.' "[1]

To such an extent was this Police protection afforded that there was great danger of undue advantage being taken of it. In the newspapers published at Dawson and in many Canadian and American ones reports were circulated to the effect that people travelling in and out over the ice during the winter would be furnished " with accommodation, blankets, and even dog teams " at the various Police detachments *en route*. Writing from Tagish, on the Upper Yukon, Superintendent Wood had this to say on the subject :—

"We were put to so much trouble and annoyance last winter through people coming out from Dawson, buying or begging food from our detachments, that, in absence of any orders to the contrary, I have directed non-commissioned officers and constables in charge of the various posts, not to sell provisions under any circumstances ; there are now stopping-places where travellers can purchase supplies if they need them, and if no stores are sold by our men they cannot be accused, as they were last winter, of disposing of Government property and pocketing the proceeds. Furthermore, I have given instructions that no provisions are to be given away unless a man is absolutely destitute

[1] "Songs of a Sourdough," by Robert W. Service.

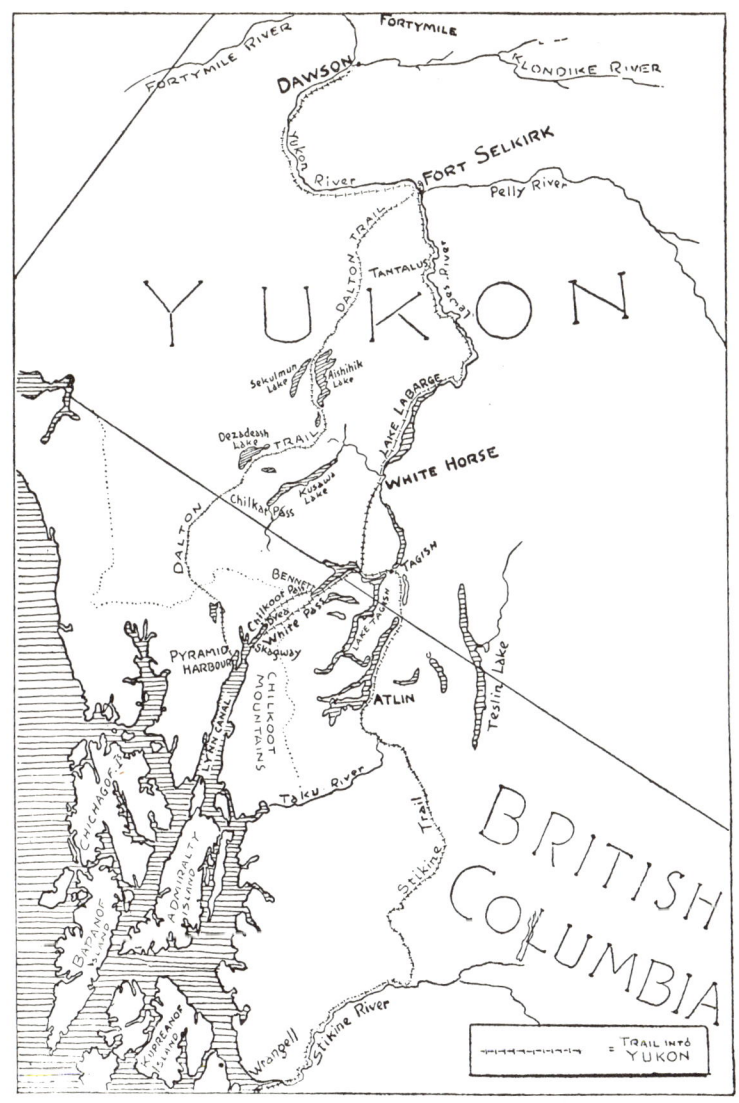

SKETCH MAP SHOWING TRAILS LEADING INTO THE YUKON TERRITORY.

and in such health that he cannot work. As long as he can perform any manual labour, he must do enough work to earn his meals and sufficient food to carry him to the next detachment. Many persons on arriving in Skagway last year from the interior boasted that they had lived on the Police on the way out. Some claimed that they had paid for their meals, others that they had beaten their way out, though they had lots of money.

" A case in point occurred here only the other day. Five able-bodied men arrived here from Dawson in a small boat, and walked in to the orderly room about 10 a.m. and demanded food. They had come by steamer as far as White Horse, and paid their way until they reached here. I told them to go to the stopping-places, but they said they had no money, and Mr. Campbell would not give meals for nothing. Taking them to the wood-pile, I told them that they could not get food here for nothing either, but they could have dinner after an hour's work sawing wood. Not a bit of it, however; they were not going to work, and they demanded food. They said they were told before they left Dawson that the Police had to see them through and provide anything they required. They were so insolent that I ordered them out of the barracks. They went back to the stopping-place, where they produced money, and not only paid for their meals but expended $48 before they left. When the crowd is coming out similar occurrences will happen every day."

Hardly less in importance was the work of the Police as Customs officers. Very early in the rush it became necessary to define the limits of American and Canadian territory as laid out by the terms of the Alaska Treaty. It was with this in view that Superintendent Perry hastened to place a Police post, with Inspector D'Arcy Strickland in

IN THE YUKON

charge on the White Pass, on the road to Lake Bennett. As a matter of fact, he found the Americans in camp at the lake waiting for the ice to break, and ready to hoist the Stars and Stripes there as sign that they claimed it. The Government was at once notified of the contention, and after some negotiations the Canadian claims were upheld. On all the summits of the passes, which were taken as marking the boundary line, the British flag flew, and there in quick succession the Police took their stand to collect Customs duties.[1]

The carrying out of this work was accomplished in the face of enormous difficulties. All through the winter months thousands of people were streaming over the summits, and most of the time the weather was at its worst. Fierce snowstorms raged, the snow on one occasion falling six feet on the level within twenty-four hours. It was estimated that no fewer than three thousand horses lay dead on the side of the trail between Lake Bennett and Skagway. Such inclement weather forced the Police to hurry the people forward on their journey as fast as was possible in order to prevent them being caught in the storms which would have been fatal to so many.

[1] " For some time after we occupied the Summits, the United States Customs officials did not recognise our presence there, and ordered convoys to accompany goods to Bennett, 20 miles on our side of the line. The idea of an American convoy escorting Canadian goods through British territory was too much for the Police at the Summits, and convoys were politely but firmly impressed with the necessity of returning to Skagway or Dyea as soon as they reached our camps. The convoy system was kept up, in spite of many protests, until the 15th May, when a United States Customs official was placed at each Summit to cancel bonds of goods in transit through the United States territory." (*Report of Superintendent Z. T. Wood*, 1898.)

The Mounted Police continued to perform the duties of Customs officers at the White Pass and Chilkoot Summits until the end of June 1898. They were then relieved by officials sent up by the Customs Department, who moved the Customs-houses to the White Pass Post (Log Cabin) and Lindeman. The first Customs post in the Territory was that established at Tagish in September 1897.

The examination of the goods was as careful as circumstances would permit. It was impossible, of course, to be strict in overhauling the outfits. Large quantities of the goods might have perished, or a jam have been caused on the summits, thereby entailing great suffering. " Rush 'em through ! " was the order, and the Police found the majority of the " packers " so anxious to get on that they gave very little trouble, and as a result very few were found to have underpaid their duty when the goods were re-inspected at Tagish.

What the scene in the passes was like at this time is vividly described for us by Superintendent Steele in one of his reports. He says : " From the head of Lake Lindeman to Tagish, people were to be seen whip-sawing lumber and building boats, and the picture presented was one of the most remarkable ever witnessed. People hurrying through in thousands, using every means of transport, some packing loads on their backs, some hauling sleds, others using dog trains, men and dogs hitched up together, and hundreds of sleds propelled over the ice by means of sails. The animals used for freighting were horses, mules, oxen, and dogs. The majority of people were new to this kind of work, and belonged to every race except Chinamen. The Mounted Police were in request in every direction. The whole demeanour of the people changed the moment they crossed the Summit. The desperado, if there, had changed his ways ; no one feared him. The Commissioner of the Yukon early in the year issued an order that no one would be permitted into the Yukon Territory without having a year's provisions ; this was strictly enforced—notices had been posted in Skagway, Dyea, and other important points. The regulation, I think, although only an order from the Commissioner, enforced by the North-West Mounted

IN THE YUKON

Police, was a wise one, and has saved the country much expense and has prevented a great deal of suffering in the Yukon this winter, there being thousands of people here now, who, if that order had not been enforced, would either starve or be fed by public subscription or at Government expense, for they have no money or means to purchase food. From the time I arrived in Bennett until I left on the 1st September, from 9 o'clock in the morning to nearly midnight, I was busy with thousands of people who desired information on all points. Every individual in the Police Force was considered a bureau of information, was questioned about everything imaginable, and gave general satisfaction. The demeanour of all ranks was so soldier-like and obliging that they became universal favourites, particularly with American citizens."

The rush by boat from Bennett and other points down commenced on the 29th May, and remarkable as was the spectacle the previous winter of hundreds of people crossing into Canadian territory over the stormy mountain passes, hauling sleds, packing enormous loads, driving goats, mules, dogs, and horses, it was completely eclipsed by the tremendous fleet of boats that started down the river. From one point on Lake Bennett Superintendent Steele counted, on an 8-mile stretch of water, over eight hundred boats under full sail; and for 45 miles at no point were the boats more than 200 yards apart. At Tagish, Inspector Strickland and his men were kept busy night and day, inspecting the boats, taking the names and addresses of people, and examining goods for intoxicants. Just before the opening of navigation the names and addresses of every one passing through this post were obtained; the boats were numbered, and these particulars kept in a register, so that in the event of boats being cast

THE RIDERS OF THE PLAINS

away or smashed up in the rapids or other places and the occupants not found, the Police were in a position to give some information of the fate of these people.

Onerous and exacting as were all these duties, the Police yet found time to attend to such matters as the recording of mining claims and the distribution of the heavy mail that came in periodically. Up to the middle of 1898 all the mails between Skagway and Dawson, from one end of the Yukon to the other, were handled exclusively by the North-West Mounted Police. In the summer they were forwarded by horse patrols; in the winter by dog-trains. This latter service was often attended by great risk. Here is Corporal Richardson's experience. He started out from Dawson City at the end of November with orders to change dogs at every post, and made good time down the river until he reached the 8-mile cabin near Hootalinqua Post. Then, as he was about to go ashore with his outfit, the ice in the river began to move. It quickly broke up into pieces, and swept the corporal and his dog-driver down the stream. The two men narrowly escaped with their lives by hanging on to the projecting limb of a tree, but, though every effort was made, the mail could not be recovered.

From five hundred to seven hundred pounds of mail was dispatched twice a month each way under Police supervision, and the regularity and rapidity with which the service was conducted was highly appreciated. Only for three months in the year was the transportation of mail *via* the Yukon River rendered impossible. After the close of navigation it took two months to make the ice fit to travel upon, and for one month before the river and lakes again opened the rotting ice was fraught with terrible dangers.

IN THE YUKON

Most of the Inspectors stationed at the principal posts in the Territory might have been thought to have had their time fully occupied with ordinary Police duties. Every commissioned officer in the Force serving in the Yukon had the powers of two Justices of the Peace, and was called upon to sit on the magisterial bench. In addition, he frequently had a good deal of inspecting to do with regard to licences, both those of miners and saloon-keepers. But, as the Americans have it, the Police officers are " hogs for work." In the Yukon they not only issued miners' licences, they recorded claims and generally acted as a bureau of information on everything concerning mining.

It was a strenuous life, without a doubt. With men of all nationalities (we have Superintendent Steele's word for it that only Chinese were wanting) the adjustment of difficulties demanded the utmost tact and diplomacy. Dr. S. M. Fraser, who took over the recording duties (and every other duty) at the Dalton Trail Post, was probably one of the busiest men in the Territory for several months. Apart from others there were plenty of sick people to be attended, particularly sufferers from frost-bite. Up at Tagish Inspector Strickland was recorder, until relieved by Superintendent Wood, while Corporal Green did similar duty for the Stewart River district; and another non-commissioned officer, at Fort Constantine, took charge of Forty-Mile.

In the hurried selection of claims mistakes were constantly being made. Prospectors blundered upon one another's claims, causing endless disputes. As a rule, the arbitration of the Police was accepted without demur—it was recognised as being always honest and fair. But in a mob of miners greedy for the best locations, with tempers roughened by the hardships of the journey north, and embarrassed by speaking several tongues, one could not avoid occasional scenes of violence.

It was at a mining settlement by the Dalton Trail that a very cold-blooded shooting affair arising out of a dispute took place. Miner No. 1 had staked out a claim, and duly recorded it, when Miner No. 2, not observing the little stakes, repegged out the ground as his own. An altercation followed, then reference to the recorder, explanations, and full apologies from the innocent claim-jumper. The quarrel was considered to have been amicably settled. But it was not so. Miner No. 1, nursing his grievance and fearful of yet being robbed of his claim, proceeded later to the shack of Miner No. 2, found the latter sprawled on his bunk asleep, and emptied his Winchester into him. A miners' jury did not return a verdict of murder,—the circumstances were deemed mitigating, and eventually the accused was sentenced to five years' imprisonment.

There is quite a touch of the good old days about this story. It reminds one of "Old man D——," one of the pioneers of the Yukon country. A shrewd and keen man of business, he had made a "pile" out of the Chilkat Indians and others. The Chilkats traded with the Sticks, who in turn traded with the natives of the Coppermine River in the interior. One day D—— learned that another trader at the coast was trying to oust him from the field. This man had incited the Chilkats to break with D——, and even go the length of pilfering his caches. D—— was a man of few words but quick action. Taking a party of the Indians with him back to the coast, he got them to point out the cause of the trouble. Then he shot his rival on sight, and was duly acquitted.

CHAPTER XIII.

IN THE YUKON.—II.

New routes to the Territory—Inspector Routledge's patrol—Inspector Moodie's patrol—Down the Pelly River—Disasters of the trail—Winter travel—Dog sleds—Superintendent Perry in command—Strength of the Force—Dawson City—" Good Samaritans "—Winter clothing—Crime in the Yukon—A case of witchcraft—" Murder Island " mystery—Labelle and Fournier—Smart Police work—Assistant-Commissioner Wood.

AT the same time that there were four main routes by which to enter the Yukon Territory, many detached parties were seeking a way thither on the eastern side. Some hit the trail from Edmonton, working north and north-west through Athabasca to the mountain passes; others followed the great Mackenzie River almost to its mouth, and thence gained the upper reaches of the several streams running into the Yukon River. With a view to finding the most practicable route to the gold-fields through the North-West Territories, Commissioner Herchmer in September and December 1897 sent out two patrols, under the command of Inspectors J. D. Moodie and W. H. Routledge respectively.

Inspector Routledge's trip was made from Fort Saskatchewan, his party consisting of himself, three men, three sleds, and thirteen dogs. The objective was Fort Simpson, about 200 miles to the north-west of Great Slave Lake. This old post, which is situated on an island at the junction of the Liard and Mackenzie Rivers, is the Hudson's Bay Company's headquarters for that district, and has a history extending back over a hundred years. On the journey the patrol overtook several Yukon-bound parties lying over for the winter at Fort Resolution and elsewhere, and was warmly welcomed, as it brought letters from friends and relatives in the east. It also afforded opportunity for a good deal of mail matter to be sent back in return. In all, this useful trip covered a distance of 1086 miles each way, and was the means of acquiring much valuable information.

A far longer and more arduous patrol was that undertaken by Inspector Moodie, who left Edmonton somewhat earlier. His destination was Fort Selkirk, at the junction of the Pelly and Yukon Rivers, in the heart of the Territory. From the starting-place this was a distance of over 1600 miles, and fourteen months were occupied in accomplishing the journey.

On leaving Edmonton the Inspector with his party got across the mountains by an easy pass in the vicinity of the head-waters of Half-Way River, but the necessity of having to kill his horses in order to feed his dogs delayed him in the spring. Fresh horses were difficult to procure. However, the Pelly Banks were reached after no little hardship, and the rest of the trip was made by canoe. The patrol established the fact that the cheapest and easiest way into the north-eastern portion of British Columbia is *via* Edmonton and the pass through the mountains to Fort Graham. With regard to its usefulness as a route to the Yukon, the Inspector was not sanguine. He did not expect it to be preferred to the quicker and simpler one *via* Skagway and the White Pass.

Inspector Moodie's diary of his adventurous journey

PLEASANT CAMP POST, ON THE KLEEHINE RIVER, NEAR DALTON TRAIL, YUKON TERRITORY.

IN THE YUKON

makes interesting reading. The passages telling of the voyage down the Pelly River are eloquent of the perils experienced from ice-jams and rapids. One or two extracts may serve to show the nature of the difficulties encountered on such a winter patrol :—

"*Tuesday, 4th October* (1898). — River thick with floating ice ; loaded canoe and started down river and ran through ice for one and a half hours ; river very shallow, struck frequently, and had to land at noon to repair canoe, six patches required. Made a raft for two men and some supplies in order to lighten canoe. Cut a pack cover in strips and sewed them to cover of canoe, and lashed this lightly over her as a protection against ice and rocks. Started at 4 p.m., raft capsized, fortunately in shallow water. Took the two men on canoe again and went down 1 mile and camped.

"*Wednesday, 5th October.* — Made another long and wide raft with large dry logs — this carried three men well and steered well—and sent her ahead of canoe so that we could run down to her assistance quickly in case of need. All went well for about two hours, when raft ran into a channel in ice which was only open for a short distance. Ice closed in behind it and she was completely blocked. I threw the men lines and an axe, and they cut her out whilst we pulled it into shore. Ice was slush to the bottom, about ten feet, and would not bear. Had a three-quarter mile portage in consequence ; camped.

"*Thursday, 6th October.*—Had fair run down to above Hoole River. Pelly very shallow ; had frequently to get out and lift canoe off and over bars ; cold work in running ice. River nearly blocked in some places. Portaged outfit over rapids at mouth of Hoole River, about half a mile. Dropped empty canoe down these with ropes, and ran on about 5 miles, when canoe taking water we had to camp and repair her.

"*Friday, 7th October.*—Ran with many shallows to rapid about 1 mile above Hoole cañon. Here three men got out to lighten canoe, and walked down to cañon. Canoe stuck badly in rapids, and canvas badly cut. On account of low water, had to portage from about $\frac{1}{4}$ mile above cañon, and it took us until midnight to get outfit to top of first rocks above, about 50 ft."

Cold work this in running ice, as the Inspector notes, and trying to the temper, as any one can bear witness to who has handled a Peterboro' canoe in such broken water. But the jams and other danger-points were passed in safety, though at one place the voyagers "got to shore only just in time, as the canoes would have been swept under the ice 150 yards lower down." Later on, the ice-blocks piled up in real business-like fashion, and boats and all other property were stacked on the beach under canvas, while the party set out on a two-days' tramp to the Police barracks at Fort Selkirk.

The dangers that this route held for inexperienced travellers attempting to make their way into the Yukon were illustrated at the time by one or two notable disasters. Sir Arthur Curtis, a young English baronet, who joined a party heading for Klondike *via* Athabasca, got lost in the wilds and was never heard of again. Four other men, from Ontario, were induced by a glowing newspaper account of the route along the Peel and Porcupine Rivers to set out somewhat light-heartedly on this long and arduous journey. From Edmonton the party took the trail to the Great Slave Lake and the Mackenzie River, thence travelling up the Peel and across the Rockies from Fort Macpherson to La Pierre House and Bell River. From there they went

IN THE YUKON

down the Bell to the Porcupine, and up the latter to Sheep, or Tatondu, River. At this point one of the party, Mr. J. A. Ritchie, with another man, went forward to the head waters of the Porcupine, killing two caribou *en route*, and packing the meat to the portage across the Tatondu, where it was cached. He then returned for the rest of his companions, and all started for the Tatondu.

On the second day one of the five (they had picked up another man on the road) froze his feet badly. They had now only a few days' provisions. It was arranged that the sick man and two more should make their way back to a salmon pool on the river, while Ritchie and his companion, M'Phee, went ahead for food. So they parted company, and when some weeks later Ritchie went back 200 miles in search of the missing ones it was to discover a brief note saying that they had run short of food, had killed a dog, and gone down the Porcupine in the hope of reaching La Pierre House and some friendly Indians. Being out of food himself, it was impossible for Ritchie to follow, and he reluctantly retraced his steps. The impression is, concludes the report of this ill-starred expedition, that the party that started for La Pierre House must have perished as there were few moose or caribou to be seen.

Similar cases might be cited, almost without number. Hundreds of gold-seekers lured into making the perilous journey were totally unfitted for the life of the trail, and as a rule burdened themselves with a quantity of stuff for which they had no use. Want of care in nursing their provisions, the lack of capable guides and of knowledge as to where to camp and how to guard against disaster, were the causes of many being posted "missing." Their subsequent fate is one of the secrets which the "great lone land" still has in its keeping.

On all like journeys, and on Police patrols such as those undertaken by Inspectors Routledge and Moodie, a great part of the route followed must necessarily be covered by means of dog trains. As this mode of transport plays an important part in the life of those whose duties take them into the more remote regions of the north-west, a few particulars may be given. The dog sled is generally made of thin oak or birch-wood boards about 9 ft. long, nailed, or lashed together with deer-skin thongs. It is turned up in front like a Norwegian snowshoe. The traces are of leather. In the Police dog trains the animals are harnessed in tandem fashion, four or six at a time, with about 2 ft. distance between each. They are attached to the traces by collars slipped over the head and ears and lying close to the swell of the neck. In most dog trains these collars buckle to the traces on each side, which are kept from touching the ground by a backband of leather fastened under the dogs' ribs or stomachs.

The harnessing of sled dogs varies in many parts of the north-west. The Eskimo run theirs abreast; the natives of Labrador and the shores of Hudson's Bay attach theirs by separate lines in a kind of pack. In the Saskatchewan country, however, the tandem fashion will be found to prevail.

The dogs themselves are almost entirely of the "husky" breed—hardy, thick-coated animals with a strong wolf strain in them. For Police purposes many Labrador dogs have been bought, these averaging over seventy pounds in weight when in condition. This weight is as heavy as dogs are required to be for ordinary travelling, and such dogs on fair loads can do 30 miles a day as against 20 by

IN THE YUKON

heavier ones.[1] The rate of progress, of course, depends on the state of the snow and trails. On a soft track from 20 to 25 miles a day will be good running. For food, supplies of biscuit and fish are carried, these being supplemented by fresh meat and fish when procurable.

The dog train as a mail-carrier has always been a feature of the North-West Territories. In olden days in the winter a sled team used to leave Fort Garry in Manitoba and proceed along the Red River to Lake Winnipeg. Crossing the lake to the north shore it reached the Norway House post, and thence, with its mail packet lightened, travelled for twenty days up the Great Saskatchewan to Carlton House. Here the Saskatchewan and Lesser Slave Lake letters were left for further distribution, and the train continued its long journey across the snow plains to the Upper Yukon. It was in all a trip of about 3000 miles, necessitating the use of a score of dog teams.

During the rush to the Yukon several dog trains carrying and bringing back mail were dispatched from Mounted Police posts in the Territories. In addition to those under Inspectors Routledge and Moodie, was one led by Inspector Snyder. On December 11, 1897, this officer left Fort Saskatchewan for St. John's, on the Peace River, proceeding by way of Old Fort Assiniboine and Lesser Slave Lake. Reaching the lake on the 26th, he remained there until the 30th, in order to rest his dogs, of which he had three trains of four dogs each, with one spare dog. The journey to St. John's was completed on 12th January, the distance thus covered being about 540 miles. On

---

[1] In April 1899, Inspector A. M. Jarvis was driven in a sled drawn by Labrador dogs from Tagish to Atlin and back, and the distance, some 47 miles each way, was covered between sunrise and sunset both times. This is a wonderful record when the conditions of the trail at that early period of the year are taken into consideration.

the road Inspector Snyder distributed letters among numerous parties of Klondikers, receiving from them a quantity of mail to take back.

In the Yukon itself in 1898 there were on the strength well over a hundred dogs, these being distributed at Dawson, Tagish, Tantalus, and the other posts between those points and Lindeman. Their usefulness in mail and other transport work was well evidenced. Long before and after horses could be employed in hauling sleds on the ice it was safe enough for dog teams to travel along the edge of the lakes and rivers.

In September 1899 an important change took place in connection with the force of Mounted Police in the Territory. On the 26th of that month Superintendent A. Bowen Perry relieved Superintendent Steele of the supreme command, the latter officer being recalled to duty in the North-West Territories. Other changes in the staff followed, and by the end of November the other officers serving in the Yukon were :—

H DIVISION, TAGISH.

Superintendent Z. T. Wood, commanding division; Inspectors D'Arcy Strickland, W. H. Routledge, A. M. Jarvis ; Assistant - Surgeons S. M. Fraser, L. A. Paré, J. Madore.

B DIVISION, DAWSON.

Superintendent P. C. H. Primrose, commanding division; Inspectors C. Starnes, W. H. Scarth, F. L. Cartwright ; Assistant-Surgeon W. E. Thompson.

At this period the total strength of the force was 258, the men being distributed at two division headquarters and thirty detachments, ranging 800 miles from the Stikine River to Forty-Mile.

IN THE YUKON

Within the year great strides had been made in the Territory. A railway had been constructed over the White Pass to Lake Bennett, the headquarters of navigation of the Yukon River. This solved the problem of quick communication with the gold-fields during the season that the river was open. An extension of the railway to the foot of the White Horse Rapids was being undertaken, and with the completion of this line transportation into the Territory would be greatly facilitated. On the river several steamboat companies had placed some large craft which had been of much service, but these could only be relied upon between White Horse and Dawson for about four months. The rest of the year the only communication with the outside was by trail on the river and a part of the way inland. Progress, however, was rendered easier by the formation of new and better land-trails, most of which gave access to the important gold-bearing creeks and considerably lessened the cost of transporting supplies to the mines. There was, further, a Government telegraph line in course of construction between Bennett and Dawson, so that the vast country of the Yukon could no longer be regarded as beyond the confines of civilisation.

Perhaps the most marked sign of development was afforded by Dawson. Little more than a year had seen its mushroom growth into a flourishing city. " At the end of 1897," says Dr. J. W. Good, the health officer of Dawson, "we found it practically one vast swamp which was usually navigable in the early spring. It was still in almost a primitive condition, or even worse—cesspools and filth of all kinds occupying irregular positions, typhoid fever and scurvy rife in the land." The Board of Health, on which Superintendent Steele served, went to work promptly to " put their house in order," and by inaugurating a proper system of drainage, purifying the water, and effecting other reforms the city was given a fresh start

In 1898 Dawson was well on the road to success. Superintendent Perry's report contrasts vividly with the picture presented by Dr. Good. He says : " Dawson is the centre of the business and social life of the district. I am told that the improvement during the past year has been remarkable. I was astonished to find so many substantial buildings and enormous warehouses. Some of the shops would be a credit to any city, and the articles exposed for sale are of the costliest and handsomest description. Its hospitals and churches reveal the charitable and philanthropic character of the people. The Yukon Council have provided side-walks, bridges, graded and drained streets, fire brigades, electric street-lighting, and many conveniences not now enjoyed by older towns of greater population."

With regard to the maintenance of law and order, an equally favourable report was returned. Crimes of violence were remarkably few, and we find the significant statement made that " a man carrying a six-shooter exposed on his person would be as great a curiosity in Dawson as in Ottawa." Petty thieving and assaults, such as were common to all communities, were the principal offences occupying the attention of the authorities. For this satisfactory state of affairs the North-West Mounted Police were responsible. From the start the work had been performed thoroughly under the most efficient organisation ; moreover, it had been done without ostentation. To talk little, but to think and act quickly and to hit hard has ever been the way of the Police.

In the Yukon even more than in the North-West Territories, owing to the peculiar conditions of the service demanded, the individuality of the Force was strongly emphasised. There was hardly a constable whose work did not leave its impress. This is a point which deserves to be borne in mind when reckoning up the sum of those notable years. "Regimental No. —" never knew what he might be called upon to do at any moment. He had to be a handy man in very truth, grappling with any new situation that arose. One day he might be building a log shack, a temporary barracks, or Customs house; another day, escorting a gold train from the mines; on another, running a canoe full of mail bags through the broken ice of a river, or perhaps fighting a bush fire; on yet another, acting as doctor and nurse to some poor wretch whom he found exhausted by the snow-covered track.

How often were the Police called upon to play the Good Samaritan! On all the trails during the worst of the wintry weather there was a great deal of suffering; not a few of those who passed northward over the summits, hopefully dragging their sled-packs behind them, turned back eventually, disheartened by hardship and privation or rendered well-nigh destitute by some unforeseen calamity. These instances of Police benevolence speak for themselves: "Five boats were supplied by this post (Telegraph Creek) for the conveying of the sick and destitute from Glenora to Wrangel; of the outfit that passed Glenora, four had their feet frozen, and sixteen were down with scurvy."—"A party, consisting of ten men, having lost everything by the upsetting of their boat on the Stikine River, about 50 miles above the Stikine Post, were given assistance, in the way of provisions, by the Police."—"One Fred J—— was picked up by the Police dog train from Lower Labarge, suffering from varicose veins. He was in hospital fifteen days during the month of March 1899."—"John G——, destitute, brought by

Police dog train from Lower Labarge, suffering from pneumonia, was admitted to the Police hospital, Tagish, on 7th April 1899 ; died the same night, and was buried on the west shore of the Six-Mile River by the Police."

But the records do not chronicle all the personal devotion and self-sacrifice that characterised the work of officers and men alike in that wild region. One learns of these by word of mouth from those benefited. And there is many a Klondiker of the present day who has reason to remember the North-West Mounted Police with feelings of sincere affection and gratitude.

And for what, it may be asked, was all this service performed ?[1] Here is the scale of additional pay *per diem* then allowed to the N.W.M.P. Force in the Yukon: Officers, $1.25 (5s.) ; staff-sergeants and sergeants, 75 cents (3s.) ; corporals and constables, 50 cents (2s.). At the most a constable would receive $1.25, that is, 5s. *per diem*, or about one-fourth of the pay of a labourer or artisan. In the mines the ruling rate of wages for labourers was $5 (£1) *per diem*, with board, or 80 cents (3s. 4d.) per hour, without board. Artisans were paid $1.00 to $1.25 per hour. The Police remuneration was not really adequate. The extra $1.25 allowed an officer by no means covered the additional expenses entailed by life in the Yukon. Besides having to pay high prices for such common luxuries as eggs (at

---

[1] As representing only one phase of Police work in the Yukon the following note from Supt. Perry's report for 1899 is illuminating : " At the request of the Honourable the Postmaster-General the duty of carrying the mail during last winter was undertaken by the Police, and a very satisfactory service was given. In performing this service the men employed travelled 64,012 miles with dog teams. I recently recommended that the sum of $9,601.80 be distributed among them as extra pay for service ; the distribution to be made according to the number of miles travelled by each man. This duty entailed a great deal of work and often much hardship, and could scarcely have been contemplated under the terms of their original engagement as members of the North-West Mounted Police."

IN THE YUKON

$3 per dozen) and tomatoes (at $1.50 per tin), he had to provide himself with a large outfit of Yukon fur caps, parkas, winter boots, and other necessaries of clothing which the rigour of the climate rendered imperative.

The question of a suitable winter clothing for the Police in the Yukon was a difficult one to settle. The "Klondike uniform" supplied did not give general satisfaction, as it was not sufficiently distinctive. In material, colour, and cut it too closely resembled the clothes worn by nine out of every ten persons who came into the country. It was unfitted, too, for many of the duties that the men had to perform. Serge tunics, riding-breeches, and top-boots did not lend themselves well to work in canoes, boats, and scows. The regimental fur cap, worn in place of the forage cap or helmet, were reported upon as giving little protection against the severe cold, and eventually a more improved pattern was provided. Fur-lined coats, rough pea-jackets, and long black sheep-skin coats, with a supply of fur mitts and moccasins, thick woollen socks, and stockings, helped to complete the constable's outfit.

It is interesting to note that at this period (1898–9) the now well-known "Stetson" or "cowboy" hat was being introduced into the Force. Many prominent officers had been urging for some time the adoption of some such headgear for summer wear, and the authorities at last had been persuaded of its usefulness. In Superintendent Wood's recommendations to the Commissioner we find him suggesting that a uniform pattern of this hat "should be issued free, and not, as heretofore, on repayment."

Recurring to the statement that crimes of violence in the Yukon Territory were remarkably few, it may be noted that in the few years following upon the great "gold rush" there was only one grave case of outstanding importance. This was the murder of three French Canadian prospectors in 1902. Shooting affrays had not been infrequent, and murders of an unsensational character had been committed by Indians and whites. There had been, also, some stage " hold-ups," on the American pattern, in which masked robbers had made rich hauls of cash and gold-dust from the passengers. But the vigilance of the Police, and the early provision made that every one passing into the Yukon over the summits should have at least a year's supplies with him, were instrumental in keeping out a dangerous " tough " element. Many desperate characters who were recognised were turned back in time or subsequently deported. By these means, coupled with the strict supervision of saloons and dance-halls and other resorts, the Territory escaped being branded with the worst of reputations.

The Yukon Indians in general gave little trouble to the authorities. They lived mostly in small roving bands, and were thus more easy to handle. Drunkenness, the pilfering of caches and cabins, and other petty thefts for which the carelessness of miners was partly to blame, were the offences that caused them to figure occasionally on the charge-sheet. Very rarely was a murder or other serious crime committed. Those tribes which resided nearest to the coast, and came most frequently into contact with white men, naturally developed faster than their brethren of the interior. The Chilkats, with their opportunities for freighting, soon became an industrious tribe, but with all their prosperity and thrift they remained savages at heart. The crudest superstitions prevailed among them, and at times these found vent in extraordinary ways. Here is an instance which came under the notice of Inspector M'Donell.

IN THE YUKON

One February evening the N.W.M.P. detachment at Wells, on the Chilkat River, received a visit from Mr. Sellon, the missionary at Kluk-wan, the headquarters of the Indians some three miles away. He wanted assistance, he said, to release an Indian boy named Kodik, who was accused of witchcraft and was being tortured by another Indian, Yekesha. As the Chilkat village was situated on the American side of the line, Constable Leeson, in charge of the Wells detachment, explained that officially he could not do anything. He offered, however, to go down with Mr. Sellon to see what could be done in the matter, and with him went, as volunteers, Constables Brown and Simpson. All three put on civilian clothes, taking their private revolvers as well as a pick, shovel, and axe.

"On arriving at Kluk-wan," says Leeson, "we surprised the house and entered without resistance, having drawn pistols as a precaution. On searching we found the boy, Kodik, in a hole below the boards of an outer house, with large blocks of firewood piled on the boards to keep them down. He was not bound, and had on his clothes and one blanket, but as no firewood was kept in this outhouse, he was nearly frozen as well as being half starved. He could hardly walk or speak when we took him out of the hole, so we carried him to Mr. Sellon's house and brought him round with restoratives and food.

"At my request Constables Brown and Simpson then went back to the detachment, as all trouble seemed to be over, while I remained to act as guard in case of any attempt at recapturing Kodik. The boy stated that he had had no food for five days. We saw the following marks of ill-usage on him: (1) large bumps on the head where he had been kicked; (2) wrists badly cut with thin rope; (3) cuts and scratches on the back done by some pointed instrument ; (4) scalds in the hollows at back of knees."

Poor Kodik accounted for his cut wrists by saying that his hands had been tied tightly behind his back, drawn up and tied to the front lock of his hair, and that he had been left for hours in this torturing position. The cuts and scratches down his back had been done with a stick, while the scalds came from boiling water. All these cruelties had been practised upon him because Yekesha was ill in bed, and Kodik was believed to have cast spells on the sick man. If Kodik could have held out for ten days he would have proved himself a wizard of the first grade, and Yekesha would have been given up for dead ; if, on the other hand, the boy had been forced to renounce witchcraft before that time (presumably by dying), then Yekesha would have been expected to recover.

The discovery that Kodik was released from confinement quickly brought a crowd of excited and angry Chilkats round the missionary's house. But the firm attitude of Constable Leeson and Mr. Sellon held them at bay, even though Chief Yiltcock himself was loud in his assertions that witchcraft (and Kodik) were responsible for the deaths of many people in the village. After some opposition the boy was safely smuggled up the river to the Police quarters at Wells, which he never left until arrangements had been made for him to be sent to the Industrial School at Sitka. And there the matter ended. Through Mr. Sellon's intervention there was no prosecution of the Indians implicated, and probably nothing would have been known of it at all had not Constable Leeson's weekly report briefly noted the fact of Kodik's release.

The grave case of crime before referred to is that which is associated with the little island known as " Murder

IN THE YUKON

Island," in the Yukon River, just below the Police post at Stewart's Crossing and about 70 miles south of Dawson. Apart from its sensational details this tragedy of the bleak north land is remarkable for the most able manner in which the Police, working on the slenderest of clues, unravelled what appeared to be an impenetrable mystery.

On 16th July 1902, a body of a man was discovered near Indian River. He had evidently been shot, and the jury brought in a verdict that deceased had come to his death by bullet wounds " at the hands of some person, or persons, unknown." No mark of identification was found on the body. The only thing that could point to his name—if the inference were correct—was a small key-ring containing three keys and a tag. The latter was inscribed: " Bouthillette, E. Broughton, Beauce, P.Q." Telegrams were at once sent to Beauce, in the Province of Quebec, and the information was elicited that Bouthillette had left that town early in June for the Yukon. It was also stated that he had written to a friend from Vancouver on the 11th of the month announcing his departure for Dawson with two French Canadians, Constantin and Guy Beaudoin.

With these facts in their possession, the Police began to follow up the progress of Bouthillette and his companions. They soon brought to light the fact that the party arrived at White Horse on or about 15th June, and left for Dawson in a " small double-ender boat " on the next day. At White Horse Bouthillette picked up two more men, also French Canadians, their names being given as Ladoceur and La Forest. The importance of the Police regulation as to the numbering of every boat that passed down the river was now made evident. The "double-ender" was numbered at White Horse, 3744. Inquiries at Dawson failed to prove its arrival there, although Nos. 3743, 3745, and 3746 were all accounted for, and a close search was instituted to trace its whereabouts. Finally, it was discovered in Klondike City and added to the few " exhibits " of the case.

The next development was the finding of another body—presumably that of a murdered man—in the river not far from Selkirk. From particulars in the possession of the Police the body was identified as being that of Guy Beaudoin. An open verdict was returned in his case, and the Police bent all their energies to the task of tracing the dead men's missing three companions. To this end three detectives were sent out, one, Detective Welsh, being dispatched to work in White Horse, Skagway, Seattle, and Portland, on the possibility of one of these places yielding some information. " We were at our wits' end as to what to do next," says Inspector Routledge of the Dawson post ; " all the clues were exhausted and followed out to their end with the greatest possible care."

While the detectives were thus employed, a constable of the Dawson detachment, Burns by name, had been detailed on the case. Burns was proficient in French, and, attiring himself in plain clothes, he frequented all the quarters where French was spoken. It was not long before his efforts were rewarded. He learned from various people that two men, named Fournier and Labelle, had gone down the river from Dawson early in June and had changed their names. Other scraps of information were pieced together, until Constable Burns knew that these two men were at White Horse about the time of arrival of a train from Skagway containing a party of Frenchmen. This was good enough to go upon. The sharp-witted constable located the man Fournier in Dawson and " shadowed " him successfully. Later on, a Mr. Cleveland of White Horse, who had sold the boat No. 3744 to the Frenchmen, arrived

A POLICE DOG TEAM AND SLED.
Party under Dr. S. M. Fraser (on the right) returned from a patrol. Dalton Trail Post, 1898.

IN THE YUKON

at Dawson and identified Fournier as one of the purchasers. The latter was now arrested, and charged with the murders of Bouthillette and Beaudoin.

The next step was to find Fournier's partner, Labelle. To do this Detective Welsh, who picked up a clue in Seattle, had to search through six different States of America, but in the end he was successful. The missing man was run to earth at Wadsworth, in Nevada. On being arrested, Labelle made a partial confession, in which he endeavoured to throw all the onus of the crime on to Fournier's shoulders. His story was that he and Fournier had gone to White Horse with the deliberate intention of meeting some men with money, striking up an acquaintance with them, and then murdering them while on the road to Dawson. He revealed the fact that a third man, Constantin, had been killed at the same time on Murder Island, where they had camped for the night. From the three victims the sum total of the plunder amounted to no more than one hundred and forty dollars (£28)!

The murder was now out. A host of witnesses had been secured who testified to Fournier, and whose evidence enabled the Police to follow all his movements since first leaving Dawson. Both men were held for trial, and in October of the same year were found guilty and sentenced to be hanged. So ended a mystery which in its solution reflected the greatest credit upon the Police. Constable Burns and Detective Welsh, in particular, came in for commendation, and were duly rewarded for their smart work.

The whole of this case occupied the attention of the Yukon Police no longer than seven weeks, a remarkably short time when one remembers how bare were the initial facts before them. In several other instances where evidence was far stronger as many months had elapsed before justice was finally done. The story is on record of how Inspector Constantine, whose name figures in early Yukon history, hunted a criminal for six months over North America until he caught him at Loredo in Mexico. To avoid extradition formalities the fugitive was taken to the Gulf of Mexico to be placed on board a British vessel. As it happened, the only British craft in the harbour was bound for Jamaica. There was no help for it. Officer and criminal embarked, sailed to the West Indies, and re-shipped there for Halifax, where the law at last had its way.

By November 30, 1902, the total of the N.W.M.P. Force serving in the Yukon was 290 officers and men, including scouts, interpreters, and special constables. At that date the officers comprised the following:—

Assistant-Commissioner Z. T. Wood, commanding the Territory.[1]

H Division.

Superintendent A. E. Snyder, commanding division; Inspectors F. P. Horrigan, A. E. C. M'Donell (commanding Dalton Trail), S. Crosthwaite, E. A. Pelletier; and Assistant-Surgeons L. A. Paré and S. M. Fraser.

B Division.

Superintendent A. R. Cuthbert, commanding division; Inspectors W. H. Routledge, D. M. Howard, A. M. Jarvis, C.M.G., T. A. Wroughton, F. L. Cosby, J. Taylor; and Assistant-Surgeons W. E. Thompson and G. A. Madore.

In summing up the condition of affairs in the Territory, the Assistant-Commissioner details "a few" of the numer-

---

[1] Superintendent Wood relieved Superintendent Perry of the command in the Yukon on April 18, 1900; he was given the rank of Assistant-Commissioner in 1902. Superintendent Perry was recalled to duty in the North-West Territories.

IN THE YUKON

ous duties then undertaken by the members of the Force. Their variety is interesting. The Police were called upon to inspect road houses, ascertaining if they had proper accommodation and were duly licensed; serve notices *re* changes in Ordinances; render assistance to tax-collectors and fire-inspectors; act as deputy-sheriffs and deputy-clerks of the court; perform all the duties of postmasters at several posts (for which services they were remunerated by a commission of 40 per cent. of the amount of stamps sold, or about three cents per day); and, as before, help the Customs Department to a great extent. In addition, they assisted in timber inspection and the repairing of telegraph lines, furnished orderlies for all law and police courts, served jury summons, subpœnas, and writs, etc., were appointed receivers of claims, and supplied guards for some of the banks.

From all of which it may be gathered that, while the unquestionable abilities of the Police were appreciated, there was a too-evident disposition on the part of more than one department to call upon their services when the work to be done should have fallen to its own employés. But the fact remains that the North-West Mounted Police did it all—and more, for they never neglected their primary duties in the Territory. And the result was that out of seeming chaos emerged order. As an old-timer, a real " sour-dough," put it to the writer : " Those Police fellers got a cinch on the country from the word go, an' they never let up. They just ran the place, sir, like an all-fired day and night school. An' it wasn't no picnic, neither ! "

THE RIDERS OF THE PLAINS

Statement showing Routes over which the Yukon Mails were carried by R.N.W.M. Police Patrols, 1905.

From	To	Miles One Way.	Service.	With Horses or Dogs.	Remuneration.	Remarks.
Dawson	Glacier	60	Fortnightly	Horses	$10 per month	During summer months only. Mail limited to 1st class matter.
Forty-Mile	Glacier	56	Fortnightly	Dogs	$10 per month	During winter months only. 1st and 2nd class matter carried.
Dawson	Stewart River P.O.	50	Weekly	Dogs	None	Number of miles from Stewart Crossing from which point mail is received from mail stages. It is distributed from Stewart P.O. to Thistle, Henderson, and other creeks and points on Yukon River by police patrols.
Dominion	Mayo Landing	118	Fortnightly	Dogs	$25 per trip	This patrol carries mail to Duncan, M'Questen, Mayo, and all points on Stewart River. Service commenced under present arrangements with P.O. Department on 1st November 1904, viz.: Police to be paid $25 per round trip.
Hunker	All Gold Creek	18	Fortnightly	Horses, dogs, and snowshoes	None	Discontinued 15th of December, for winter.
Grand Forks	Eureka	28	Fortnightly	Horses	None.	
Selkirk	Pelly Crossing	4	Tri-weekly	Horses	$1 per trip	This patrol carries the mail between the Pelly P.O. and the stage post at Pelly Crossing, during winter months.
Dawson	White Horse	332	Weekly	Horses	$2,000 for season	This service will commence 1st December, 1905, and will carry 625 lb. 2nd class matter per week from White Horse to Dawson.
Dawson	Fort Macpherson	475	Annual	Dogs	None	First patrol from Dawson left on 27th December 1904, and travelled via Sixteen-Mile River, the Seela Pass, Blackstone, Hart, Little Wind, Wind and Peel Rivers. This year the route will be via Mayo detachment, Beaver, Wind, and Peel rivers.
White Horse	Kluahne	152	Fortnightly	Horses and dogs	$20 per trip	This patrol supplies the miners on Ruby, Fourth July, and other creeks in Kluahne district with mail.
White Horse	Livingstone Creek	75	Fortnightly	Horses and dogs	None.	

CHAPTER XIV.

BACK TO THE TERRITORIES.

Foreign immigrants—Doukhobors—Adamites—Dreamers—Mormon settlements—Drains on the Force—Lieut.-Colonel A. Bowen Perry, fifth Commissioner—Increase of strength authorised—A 1300 miles trip—Indian " Sun Dance "—Medicine Pipe Society—The Great Bond Robbery —An arrest in the Rockies—A Royal visit.

THE foregoing account of Police work in the Yukon has carried us several years forward. It is now time to again take up the tale of the North-West Territories, and see what progress has been made there in the meanwhile.

The opening up of Athabasca has been briefly alluded to. One of the most striking features in the settlement of this northern district was the influx of foreign immigrants. Russians, Swedes, Finns, Galicians, Germans, Hungarians, and representatives of other nations were quick to see in the Canadian North-West a promised land offering them a happy and comfortable home with freedom from restrictions such as they might not enjoy under any other flag. On the whole, these new settlers made themselves acceptable to their neighbours. The majority, after some acquaintance with the conditions of the country, proved themselves thrifty and law-abiding citizens. Only here and there, where certain peculiar religious tenets held ground, was that fanaticism encountered which sooner or later led to trouble.

Among the earliest comers were the Galicians. These settled in the vicinity of Fort Saskatchewan, Fish Creek, and Yorkton. Essentially agriculturists, their little communities prospered slowly if surely. The capital they brought into the country was never large, and at first the pinch of poverty made itself felt to a degree, but, under the careful guidance of the Police, the newcomers weathered the bad seasons until they were at last able to stand alone.

With the Galicians came some Doukhobors, who were followed soon after by larger parties. In May 1899, Prince Hilkoff headed a deputation which sought to find a spot whereon to found a Doukhobor colony. Suitable locations were allotted near the North Saskatchewan, and three villages sprang into being. These immigrants were provided with horses, oxen, and agricultural implements, so that the work of breaking the prairie began forthwith, and within a few months an excellent start had been made. Reporting upon them, Corporal Lindsay of the Henrietta detachment said :—

" Owing to the lack of an interpreter, it is very difficult to gain any information as to their financial standing, whether they are satisfied with their location, or their future prospects, but I have made the following observations as to their manners and customs. They appear to be a patient, industrious, and self-supporting race, the women equalling the men in endurance and skill at all kinds of manual labour ; in fact, the women do one-half of the ordinary work, besides attending to their household duties. The houses are built of sods, and in some cases of logs, and most of them have a stable attached. The floors are of pounded earth. Both houses and stables have a coat of mud inside and out. The houses are warm and

BACK TO THE TERRITORIES

clean, but very dark. A large oven, built of home-made, sun-dried bricks, is the chief feature in the interior of each house. Each oven has a flat roof, and there the younger members of the family sleep.

"Since their arrival here, their principal diet has consisted of dry bread, potatoes, different kinds of fungi, and berries, and on that simple diet they have got through quite a lot of hard work; they are gradually departing from their vegetarian principles, and some of them already eat meat whenever they can get it. They are very slow in learning English, and, living in their communistic way, it will be a long time before they forsake their own language and customs."

This estimation of the Doukhobors was justified in the main as the years went by. While engaged in living peaceably on their farms they worked hard and were able to show good results for their labour. The one drawback to their presence—and it was no light one—was their tendency to break out in a burst of religious frenzy. This generally took the form of a pilgrimage, in which those who joined were expected to denude themselves of all clothing. Under the command of some one of their band, a procession of a hundred or more men, women, and children would thus march upon some adjoining settlement or town, to the great consternation of its inhabitants. One well-known leader of the Doukhobors went by the name of John the Apostle. A black-bearded giant of 6 ft. 3 in. or more, his strength was prodigious. The late Inspector Frank Church, himself a man of splendid physique, had more than one tussle with him, and used to tell an amusing story of how the refractory "Apostle" was once subdued.

With the Doukhobors, in a way, are allied the

Adamites. This sect first came to the notice of the Police in July 1908, when the Commissioner of Immigration at Winnipeg wired to the headquarters at Regina to say that a band of people was entering Canada from the United States armed with rifles, contrary to the Immigration Act: "Leader says he is Christ going to the Doukhobors. Five or six men with six women and children. Please instruct officers to arrest and eject these people." On investigation the party proved to consist of five men, two women, and five children, with a covered waggon and a single horse. The leader, Sharpe by name, called himself Christ, the one whom the fanatical Doukhobors were making pilgrimages to find, while his wife went by the name of the Virgin Mary. All the adults were armed, and but one person at a time was allowed to approach the camp, even then only at the muzzle of a rifle.

As it was evident that the progress of Sharpe and his followers could only be stayed by bloodshed, he was allowed to pass from Manitoba into Saskatchewan. It was hoped to effect an arrest by a ruse, but this plan failed through some sympathisers having given the fanatics warning. Meanwhile, the Police had reason to believe that the difficulty would solve itself in a natural and easy manner. Sharpe had written to the head of the sect a letter, couched in Scriptural phraseology, in which he stated his intention to return to the States if the Doukhobors did not accept him as their leader. No notice was taken of this epistle, and eventually, towards the end of August, the Adamites concluded that "the people of God," *i.e.* the Doukhobors, did not want them, and they retraced their steps southward. To everybody's relief, they were seen safely over the line under Police supervision, and headed for their former home.

BACK TO THE TERRITORIES

Even more troublesome have been the fanatics known as the " Dreamers." Originally from Russia, they found their way into Canada from the United States. This sect startled the other settlers in the neighbourhood of Medicine Hat, Alberta, by proceeding to burn the latters' houses, an outrage which quickly brought the Police on their track. To Inspector Parker, in charge of the station at "The Hat," was given the task of restoring quietude, and after several arrests had been effected there was a cessation of the annoyance. A result of these outbreaks on the part of Doukhobors and other communities with strongly pronounced religious opinions is that a detachment of Police has to be constantly on the watch to check any sign of such disorderly occurrences. In a district where the R.N.W.M.P. post is a small one, this duty is a severe tax upon the heavily worked men.

A prominent sect that has established itself on Canadian soil is that of the Mormons. Their northward trek from the States was of a peculiar character. Certain "brethren" of the flock conceived that they had a call to migrate, and a movement was set on foot. Many of the Mormons selected to go on the pilgrimage were very comfortably settled where they were, but, acknowledging that the interests of the Church must be served, they "pulled up stakes" and set out to start life afresh. The bulk of them had little to say in the choice of destination. Some were ordered to build up and occupy what is now the thriving settlement of Stirling, near Lethbridge; others were located at Magrath, and so on, and the work of colonisation went forward briskly.

With the Mormons, as with most other American settlers, the Police have no quarrel. They quickly adapt themselves to the new life, and develop into excellent members of the community. It is the newly arrived foreign element—often primitive in its habits—that gives the Police extra work to do. The difficulty is to make these uncouth immigrants understand what the law is and how literally it must be obeyed. This is harder work than actually enforcing the law, but experience has shown that it is easier to do in the long-run than waiting until ignorance brings about a serious breach of the peace.

In most other respects the policing of the Territories had proceeded much as usual, although the number of men required for service in the Yukon had considerably depleted the Force.[1] As a matter of fact, the bulk of the collar work had now been done; far and wide through the immense tract of country the influence of the Mounted Police was recognised, and the scattered population, white and Indian and half-breed, had settled down in harmony. By this time some of the larger towns were provided with police forces of their own; the smaller centres of inhabited districts were content to rely on the N.W.M.P.

Something like a hundred and a half officers and men were constantly employed on detached duty, being placed, two or three at a time, on various outposts many miles apart. Taking the " organised " portion of the Territories only, to quote from a report of the Commissioner, there was an average of one constable to every 500 square miles, and to 350 of the population. In ten years from 1880 the number of people in the north-west had practically doubled, while the strength of the Police had been reduced by one-half. With the increase of population

---

[1] On November 30, 1899, the distribution of the Force by divisions was as follows: Regina District (officers and men), 155; Maple Creek District, 36; Battleford and Prince Albert District, 63; Macleod-Lethbridge District, 136; Calgary District, 52; Saskatchewan District, 59. Total in North-West Territories, 501. Total in Yukon Territory, 254. Grand total, 755.

BACK TO THE TERRITORIES

had arisen the continuous need for fresh detachments, and the number of these had jumped from 49 to 79.

In 1900 a further drain on the Force was caused by the South African War, when no fewer than 178 officers and men volunteered for the front. This chapter of Police history will receive attention in due course. The same year saw the retirement of Commissioner L. W. Herchmer and the gazetting of Superintendent A. Bowen Perry as his successor. The new Commissioner's successful administration in the Yukon had marked him out for promotion, and his appointment was received with universal approbation. A graduate of the Royal Military College, Kingston, Ontario, Commissioner Perry served for some years in the Royal Engineers before joining the N.W.M.P. Early in the present year the distinction of C.M.G. was conferred upon him.

Soon after entering upon his new duties the Commissioner set himself to bring the Force to a state of efficiency even higher than that it had already reached. In submitting to Sir Wilfrid Laurier, the President of the Privy Council, the view that it was desirable to maintain a high standard of military as well as police efficiency, he urged that the Force should be kept at its full strength at all times, with a sufficient number of men undergoing training to meet the constant waste. The yearly waste amounted to at least 10 per cent. The authorised strength of the N.W.M.P. was therefore to stand at 800 in future.

The reasons for taking this step were cogent ones. As the Commissioner pointed out, the men on detached duty were in responsible positions; they had to act on their own initiative, often on matters of much public concern; their advice was sought by new settlers. To satisfactorily carry out their important duties it was imperative that they should be well trained, experienced, and of good character. It was unwise, therefore, to send on such duty men who had not the proper qualifications, necessary experience, and who had not established a character for reliability and sobriety. He recommended that only trained, proved men should be drafted from the dépôt, and to meet this 50 above strength should be under training.

To recapitulate the history of the growth of the Force: it had been launched in 1873 with a strength of some 300 men. In 1882, when the railway inaugurated a new era of settlement, the strength was increased to 500; three years later the half-breeds' rebellion caused it to swell to 1000, a figure at which it stood for ten years. Then, owing to the peaceful state of the Territories, the submission of the Indians, and the rapid means of communication afforded by the railway, it was reduced to 750. In the North-West Territories in 1898 the actual number of officers and men available for duty was 500, the gold rush to the Yukon having necessitated the drafting of 250 men thither. A few years later a further reduction was made, decreasing the strength in the Territories by 50 in order to increase the Force in the Yukon by that number.

What particularly called for an immediate augmentation of the Force was the rapid development of the Athabasca district, "a country of enormous extent, with no facilities for travel." When members of the Police were sent out on special duty from any of the outlying posts in this newly opened portion of the north-west, the distances to be covered were often very great. Corporal Field one winter made a remarkable trip. While stationed at Fort Chipewyan, on Lake Athabasca, he was informed that a man had gone violently insane at Hay River, 350

BACK TO THE TERRITORIES

miles away. This was a case to be attended to without delay, so the corporal, with one companion, an interpreter, started out for Hay River by dog train. Having taken charge of the maniac, he brought him back to Fort Chipewyan, and thence took him to Fort Saskatchewan, travelling a total distance of 1300 miles with dogs, and occupying forty-four days on the journey.

This is not an isolated instance. Nearly every North-West Mounted Policeman who has been on duty in the more northern parts of the Territories has had similar experiences. Inspector Parker of Medicine Hat can call to mind " a devil of a trip " in a dog sled to Fort Churchill, on the far-off shores of Hudson's Bay, nearly 600 miles from his post at Prince Albert. It was all to investigate a charge of murder brought against an old squaw who was suspected of having done away with her son. After toiling over the heavy snow and soft ice of the rivers, the Inspector sat in judgment on the accused, and found her more sinned against than sinning. The charge could not be upheld, and back again to Prince Albert went the officer, the last hundred miles of the return journey having to be made on foot, as the dog team broke down!

So far as the Indians were concerned, there was little friction with the authorities. It had been found necessary to put an interdict upon certain dances held among the tribes, particularly the " Ghost Dance " and the " Sun Dance." Both of these celebrations had the effect of working up the " braves " to a pitch of frenzy that contained elements of danger. The " Sun Dance " in itself was a cruel, barbarous ordeal which a young Indian who had " made his medicine " was compelled to undergo before he could aspire to be a " brave." It meant his standing almost naked, but with his war-gear of shield and

— 237 —

weapons on, while his breast was lacerated with wooden splints attached by cords to the top of a long pole. In the presence of a number of the warriors of his tribe, who assembled to mark his demeanour and to encourage him, the young aspirant threw himself back from the cords and with his face to the sun followed its course in a circle round the pole. If he passed the test successfully, he was admitted into the circle of the chosen ones.

A variant of the ordeal was for the would-be " brave " to submit to his skin being cut just under the shoulder blades. The flesh and muscles were then raised, and tied round with thongs to the ends of which were attached buffalo skulls. The thongs were made long enough to allow the skulls to dangle below the knees. Thus encumbered, the youth proceeded to dance round the circle, to the accompaniment of drums and the chanting of the spectators, until the weight of the skulls tore their fastenings from his flesh. If the thongs were obdurate and would not release themselves, a favourite method was to tie them to a lariat and compel the sufferer to be dragged round the ring by a pony. A young Indian might be strong enough to endure even this for a time, but he would fall exhausted at last, when the pony would be backed up, a slack taken on the lariat, and the animal started off suddenly with a jerk that never failed to end the business.

The Police found it by no means easy to stop this historic " dance " among some of the tribes, but wise counsels prevailed in the end, and the leading chiefs acquiesced in its suppression. In place of it some other " dance," such as that known as " the Medicine," was held when the interdict went forth. The latter festival was a general gathering at which the " Medicine Men " instructed

BACK TO THE TERRITORIES

the others in certain of their so-called arts, but it included nothing of a cruel or inflammatory nature.

Sometimes it happened that peculiar circumstances arose in connection with an Indian " dance," and the Police officers appealed to had to exercise the utmost tact and discretion in dealing with the matter. Take this occasion, noted by Superintendent Deane while he was in command of the Macleod district in 1898. The Indians in question belonged to the Blood Reserve.

" A picturesque bevy of both sexes paid me a visit on the 29th June. It seemed that some one had inadvisedly coupled the word ' arrest ' with ' Red Crow's ' name, and the old chief keenly resented the connection. He and his following came to ask me what he was to be arrested for. As a matter of fact I did not know, and it took me the whole of a long hot afternoon, with the aid of the best interpreter in the country, to get at the facts and to pour oil on the troubled waters.

" There is, it appears, an eminent secret society among the Indians, known as the Medicine Pipe Society, entrance to which entails due formalities of election and contribution. Women are as eligible as men. This society holds certain superstitions of a religious character. The wife of an Indian, named ' Heavy Shield,' at one time on her deathbed, as she thought, vowed that she would purchase a certain Medicine Pipe in the event of her recovery, and so become a member of the society. In course of time she regained her health, and desired to fulfil her vow. There is but a limited number of Medicine Pipes (15) among the Bloods, and that which she was eager to acquire was in possession of a squaw of ' Red Crow's,' who was equally anxious to part with it upon receiving its value in kind (viz. 15 horses), according to the custom of the tribe.

"'Red Crow,' as president, felt bound to call the members of the society together to consider the election of the new applicant, the prescribed formalities extending over some eleven days, there being four distinct dances. He convened the meeting at a time, unfortunately, when the Indians should have been setting about their haymaking operations and this naturally displeased the agent, who pointed to the clause in the Indian Act forbidding 'giving away' dances. Any one who knows anything of an Indian agent's difficulties must know that he is at times exasperated almost beyond endurance at the intractability of his wards, but it is an aphorism to say that in the last resort the application of a statute must perforce be referable to the courts of law, and it is a measure of common prudence to anticipate the verdict of a jury if possible. Whether this particular transaction on the part of the woman be looked upon in the light of a thank-offering, from an Indian's religious point of view, or whether it be considered analogous to the initiatory fee payable on joining a secret society, the fact remains that there are the Indians' superstitions which cannot be eradicated in one generation. How are they to be dealt with ?

"'Red Crow' said, *inter alia*, that he was too old to give up his own prayers, and would not do so. He desired the prayers of the sisterhood for his wife. He liked the Christians' prayers, but he liked the Indians' prayers too. It seemed clear to me that if the Indians were honest in their promises that there should be no dedication or exchange of property beyond that directly required for the acquisition of the Medicine Pipe, no court would hold that the Indian Act had been infringed. They promised unreservedly all I asked, and agreed to give up agitating about a 'Sun Dance' this year (which was in the minds of

A SQUAD OF RECRUITS, REGINA BARRACKS.

BACK TO THE TERRITORIES

some of them), and I agreed to ask the Indian agent to allow the Medicine Pipe to pass on this one occasion, out of consideration for ' Red Crow ' and his advanced age.

"I made inquiries afterwards and was informed that they had strictly kept their promises, and, after the eleven days' formalities were completed, had returned to their homes."

An important and smart piece of Police work that occurred in the following year was the arrest of one of two men wanted in connection with a large bond robbery in England. The credit for this was largely due to Staff-Sergeant (now Inspector) Heffernan. As many will remember who read the newspapers at the time, a young clerk named Christie, while in the employ of Sigmund Neumann & Co., of London, stole a number of Buenos Ayres bonds to the value of over £10,000. In this theft he was abetted by a man named Crick, the latter being, in fact, the arch-conspirator. The securities were kept in boxes at a bank, and were brought thence to Neumann & Co.'s office periodically for the coupons to be cut off. In May 1899, two months before the date when a batch of coupons was due, Christie was absent from the office on a plea of ill-health. Before July came he had resigned his position and was on his way to Klondike, *via* British Columbia, with his accomplice.

In August Christie returned to England, having injured a leg while in the mountains. The loss of the bonds now having been discovered, the Canadian police were notified that Crick was somewhere in the Dominion, and Inspector Abbott, of New Scotland Yard, was sent out to get on the trail of the missing man. Meanwhile, Sergeant Heffernan was detailed from the North-West Mounted Police to assist in the search. He proceeded to Qu'Appelle, where a brother of Christie lived, and from that source gained much important information. Both Crick and Christie had been there, had spent money freely, and with an outfit of men and pack-horses had gone prospecting to the Tete Jeune Cache, some 200 miles to the north-west of Donald, in British Columbia.

Off to Donald, therefore, went Sergeant Heffernan to lie in wait for Crick, whose companion was known to have left him. The arrest was made successfully and in somewhat dramatic circumstances, which are worth relating. As the story belongs to Heffernan, he may tell it in his own way.

"When I got to Donald," he says, "I learned that Crick and his party were coming through the mountains and might be expected any day. I was only waiting for a man who was being sent to help me in the arrest. The latter arrived in due course, but he was not the 'sleuth' I had expected, so I decided to do without him rather than risk a capture with an incompetent ally. In this dilemma I looked round for some one more capable, and I found one in the most unexpected fashion.

" In one of the saloons in the town, when I happened in one evening, was a bunch of men playing cards. Among them was a man known to the others as the 'Deacon.' He wore a semi-clerical rig, and was presumably an ex-clergyman who had fallen on evil times. He looked a hard case. As I watched him it dawned on me that here was the man for the job. His appearance had nothing of the Police about it. At the first opportunity I took him aside, and told him some of the facts of the case.

" ' Now, Deacon,' I said, ' I want you to stand in with me. What do you say ? '

" The Deacon considered the proposition, and announced

BACK TO THE TERRITORIES

that he was 'on.' 'I'll do it,' he said, 'for five dollars a day.' It was a good price, but he was worth it, I was sure, so the deal was concluded and I swore him in.

"The next day the Deacon and I (he in his clerical rig and I in rough miner's clothes) started out on our trip. We were both armed with revolvers. At the mouth of a certain pass the prospecting party, all of whom were mounted (and a very innocent outfit they looked), hove in sight.

"'That's the bunch we want, Deacon,' I said, and we waited until they approached. Then we whipped out our guns, and I cried: 'Hands up!'

"Crick was properly astonished, as were his companions, who probably were as innocent as they appeared. When I called on him to surrender himself, he tried to laugh it off as a mistake. 'I'm Philip Somers,' he explained, this being the name he had assumed on leaving England.

"'You're William George Oaks Crick,' I replied, and I detailed the charge down in the warrant. He still protested, and threatened me with dire penalties if I interfered with him, but I knew I had my man all right. So he was arrested, and the Deacon and I returned triumphantly to Donald."

There had been no mistake. Crick, *alias* Somers, was duly taken back to London to stand his trial with Christie, who had been caught in the meantime, and both were sentenced to several years' penal servitude.

In the year 1901, an event of exceptional interest to the North-West Mounted Police was the visit to the Territories of the Prince and Princess of Wales, then Duke and Duchess of Cornwall and York. Their Royal Highnesses were then completing their tour round the world. On 27th September the Royal party arrived at Regina, where a captain's escort of thirty-three men, commanded by Superintendent Morris, was in attendance. Guards of honour were provided at Government House, where a reception was held, and at the railway station when the Duke and Duchess left *en route* for Calgary. At this post the Mounted Police were inspected, and several decorations and medals were presented to those who had served in South Africa. Among the recipients was Inspector Belcher, upon whom had been conferred the Companionship of the Order of St. Michael and St. George.

From Calgary the royal party proceeded through the mountains to Vancouver and Victoria, the Police still providing escorts, and also supplying the carriages and saddle-horses used by the distinguished travellers. The return journey was made *via* Banff, the health resort in the Rockies. As an appreciation of the way in which the Police undertook the entire charge of the Royal cortège during this trip, Commissioner Perry received the following letter from Sir Arthur Bigge, the Duke's Private Secretary:—

"DEAR COLONEL PERRY,—The Duke of Cornwall and York directs me to express to you his gratification at the very smart appearance of that portion of your Force which he had the pleasure to inspect at Calgary.

"His Royal Highness also wishes to thank you, and all under your command, for the admirable manner in which the escort and other duties were performed during his stay in Western Canada.—Yours very truly,

(Signed) "ARTHUR BIGGE."

The following two communications appeared later in the General Orders :—

"The Commissioner has much pleasure in publishing

BACK TO THE TERRITORIES

for the information of the Force the following letter received from the Comptroller :—

"'SIR,—I am directed by the Right Honourable Sir Wilfrid Laurier to convey to you his appreciation of the manner in which the escort and other duties of the North-West Mounted Police in connection with the recent visit of Their Royal Highnesses the Duke and Duchess of Cornwall and York to the North-West Territories and British Columbia were performed ; and further to say that, as Minister of the Crown, having the control and management of the Force, he was greatly pleased with the efficiency and general bearing of the various detachments, which came under his personal observation.'"

"The Commissioner has much pleasure in publishing the following extract from a letter from the Duke of Cornwall and York to His Excellency the Governor-General, published in the *Canada Gazette* of October 26, 1901 :—

"'I am especially anxious to record my appreciation of that splendid force, the North-West Mounted Police. I had the pleasure of inspecting a portion of the corps at Calgary, and was much struck with the smart appearance of both men and horses, and with their general steadiness on parade. They furnished escorts throughout our stay in Western Canada, frequently horses for our carriages, and found the transport, all of which duties were performed with ready willingness and in a highly creditable manner.'"

CHAPTER XV.

AT THE FRONT IN SOUTH AFRICA.

The 1st C.M.R.—N.W.M.P. contributions to the war—Strathcona's Horse—South African Constabulary—Notable performances—Major Sanders' heroism—Lieutenant Chalmers' sad fate—A V.C. exploit—Scouting—An exhibition of riding—Distribution of honours—The death-roll.

WHEN the war in South Africa broke out in 1899, it was not to be expected that Canada would be backward in helping the mother-country. Nor was it to be expected that such a fine body of men as the North-West Mounted Police would be behind others in sending out their best to the front. To the first Canadian contingent, which sailed in October 1899, the Police were not called upon to contribute any officers or men, but they were nevertheless represented. A goodly number of ex-non-commissioned officers and constables volunteered their services and were enrolled.

When, some months later, a second contingent was asked for, the recruiting for this corps was placed in the hands of the Mounted Police. And thus came into being the 2nd (afterwards called the " 1st ") Battalion Canadian Mounted Rifles. The original contingent, raised in Eastern Canada, became known as the Royal Canadian Dragoons, in order to connect them with the permanent cavalry which bear that name. In addition to the 1st C.M.R., the Police also supplied men to Strathcona's Horse, the 2nd C.M.R., the South African Constabulary, and the 5th

AT THE FRONT IN SOUTH AFRICA

C.M.R. It is a great pity that in so doing the N.W.M.P. lost their identity as a Force while in South Africa. Two hundred and ninety officers and men in all thus went to the front, and were merged with other volunteers in the different Canadian contingents.[1] No other permanent corps in the Dominion could boast of such a representation, and this fact alone speaks volumes for the splendid spirit which animated the members of the Force. " With but few exceptions," says the Commissioner, " all ranks were willing to volunteer. It was not a question of who would go, but who must stay at home."

In recruiting for the 1st C.M.R., for which the North-West Mounted Police were to be responsible, it was obviously impossible that the corps could be composed entirely of men then on the active list. About one-third of the Force were on special duty in the Yukon Territory, leaving some five hundred from which to choose. The Commissioner was therefore instructed to enrol as many non-commissioned officers and men as he could spare, and to make up the required strength with such others whom he and his officers considered suitable. Every N.W.M.P. post in the Territories now became a recruiting station, printed notices being displayed calling for volunteers. The pay offered was fixed to be the same as that obtaining in the Force.

The officers who joined this contingent on its formation in December 1899, and received commissions in the militia,

---

[1] The contributions of the N.W.M.P. to the war were :—

	Officers.	Men.	Horses.
1st C.M.R.	11	134	155
Strathcona's Horse	7	26	—
2nd C.M.R.	4	31	—
S.A. Constabulary	4	38	—
5th C.M.R.	4	31	—
Total	30	260	155

THE RIDERS OF THE PLAINS

were : Lieut.-Col. L. W. Herchmer, the then Commissioner of the Police, who assumed command of the battalion; Superintendent J. Howe (in command), Inspector A. C. Macdonell (afterwards in command of the 5th C.M.R.), Inspector J. D. Moodie, Inspector J. V. Bégin, Inspector T. A. Wroughton, who were attached to C Squadron; Superintendent G. E. Sanders (in command), Inspector A. E. R. Cuthbert, Inspector H. J. A. Davidson, Inspector F. L. Cosby, Inspector M. Baker, Inspector J. B. Allan, who were attached to D Squadron.

In Strathcona's Horse the N.W.M.P. officers serving were : Superintendent S. B. Steele (in command, with the rank of Lieut.-Colonel), and Inspectors R. Belcher, A. E. Snyder, A. M. Jarvis, D. M. Howard, F. L. Cartwright, and F. Harper. Included in this corps were ex-Inspector M. H. White-Fraser, Sergeant-Major W. Parker, and Staff-Sergeant H. D. B. Ketchen. The two last-named were afterwards granted commissions in the Army and Colonial Forces. The commissions of the officers of this corps were all in the Imperial Service.

On the formation of the South African Constabulary, Superintendent Steele was appointed its Colonel, while Inspector Scarth, who was granted leave to serve, took rank as Captain. Constables C. P. Ermatinger and J. G. French were later given commissions as Lieutenants. Other members of the Force who similarly gained commissions through serving in the 2nd and 5th C.M.R. were : Inspector J. Taylor, Inspector Demers, Sergeant-Major J. Richards, Sergeant-Major F. Church, Sergeant E. Hilliam, Sergeant H. R. Skirving, and Constables A. N. Bredin and J. A. Ballantine.

What the Canadians did in the Boer War of 1899–1901 is a matter of public history. What part in it the North-

AT THE FRONT IN SOUTH AFRICA

West Mounted Police played is not so generally known and appreciated. To particularise where all were distinguished is by no means easy, but it must be admitted that the work performed by the 1st C.M.R. has never received its proper recognition at the hands of the public. Perhaps the prominence given to Strathcona's Horse may account for this. This splendid corps, which rendered such useful service to the army in South Africa, was accorded more attention from the newspapers than any other Canadian contingent. The fault—if fault it is—lies with the correspondents at the front, who without doubt underestimated the merits of the several battalions of the Canadian Mounted Rifles.

In the 1st C.M.R. the Empire had placed at its service an almost unique body of men, trained to a very high pitch of efficiency, and eminently fitted for such a campaign as that on the veldt. Hard riders, keen shots, and men for the most part enured to all conditions of open-air life by their varied duties in the North-West Territories, the Police volunteers proved themselves among the best scouts and sharpshooters on the British side. Well might General Hutton, General Lord Methuen, and the Commander-in-Chief himself, pass upon them the high encomiums that they did. In the operations in the Orange Free State, and later during the march on to Pretoria under Lord Roberts, the Canadian Mounted Rifles nearly always formed the advance guard, a striking testimony to their ability for scouting and patrol work.

One notable performance of the 1st Battalion was the spirited fight against a superior force of Boers in the neighbourhood of Middleburg. This was on 5th September 1900. A detachment of 125 men, under the command of Major Sanders, was guarding the railway between the towns of Pan and Wonderfontein, when it was attacked by the enemy, who brought two field pieces and a pom-pom into action. Before a reinforcement arrived on the scene the Mounted Rifles had beaten off the Boers. In this sharp fight Major Sanders and Lieutenant Moodie were wounded.

Major Sanders, one of the most popular officers in the N.W.M.P., figured in another exciting incident a month or two later. The 1st C.M.R. had been moving southwards from Pretoria whilst the 2nd C.M.R. was on its way north from its posts in the Orange River Colony. After joining forces, they did duty together along the line of the Natal-Transvaal Railway in the south-east, and followed the main advance towards Koomati Poort. In this task of guarding the railway there were frequent brushes with the enemy. On 1st November a column under General Smith-Dorrien, who commanded the 19th Brigade, was marching south from Belfast in the direction of the Koomati valley. On the following day Major Sanders was sent forward with sixty men of his squadron to form an advance guard. Some time after leaving the column the Major's guide made a false turn, and when the little company of Mounted Rifles came in touch with the enemy the main body was nearly two miles away.

The position was a highly dangerous one, but the Rifles determined to hold it at all costs. Reinforcements could not be long in coming. Meanwhile, the Boers were raining in a deadly fire upon the Canadians, and particularly upon Lieutenant Chalmers (a former N.W.M.P. Inspector) and the few men with him in the extreme advance. News of their predicament soon reached the General Officer Commanding, and word was sent to the party ordering them to retire. Chalmers now fell back upon his supports,

AT THE FRONT IN SOUTH AFRICA

and the retirement was being successfully carried out when the horse ridden by Corporal Schell was shot under him, its rider being injured by its fall. Seeing this, Sergeant Tryon gave up his own horse to his comrade, and continued his retreat on foot. But Major Sanders had no intention of leaving the brave fellow in the lurch, and, riding to his assistance, he endeavoured to mount the sergeant in front of him. The gallant effort failed. As he struggled to pick up Tryon his saddle slipped, and both men were thrown to the ground.

On getting to his feet, Major Sanders, who was dazed by his fall, called to the sergeant to make for cover, and was doing the same himself when a Boer bullet struck him down. In a moment Lieutenant Chalmers wheeled his horse and came galloping towards his superior officer to lend a hand, but he was unable to move him alone, so returned to the firing line for help. As he rode back another bullet found its mark, and he dropped from his horse mortally shot through the body. Both the Major and the sergeant by good fortune were rescued in time.

The highest distinction that can be gained on the field of battle—the Victoria Cross—was won, on 5th July 1900, by Sergeant A. H. L. Richardson, a North-West Mounted Policeman of C Division, Battleford, who had joined Strathcona's Horse. His deed of valour was performed in the following circumstances: During the fighting round Standerton in the South Transvaal a company of Strathcona's Horse, thirty-eight strong, came to close quarters with a force of Boers which outnumbered them by more than two to one. The scene of the engagement was the village of Wolvespruit. When the enemy's fire became too hot for the little party to stand, the order was given to retire. In executing this movement a dismounted man was

THE RIDERS OF THE PLAINS

left behind on the field, being himself wounded in two places, and he would have fallen into the Boers' hands had not Sergeant Richardson seen his predicament. Turning back, the latter rode to his comrade's assistance and safely brought him in, despite a fierce cross fire at a range of only 300 yds., and despite, too, the fact that his horse was wounded and was able to make but slow progress. Sergeant Richardson enjoyed the distinction of being the first Colonial to be gazetted during the war.

This exploit reminds one vividly of that plucky rescue in the Riel Rebellion which has enshrined the name of Inspector Jack French (a brother of the first N.W.M.P. Commissioner, by the way) in the memories of his comrades. It was at Batoche, the last stand made by the half-breeds, and French was fighting in the front ranks of the Police when he saw Constable Cook fall. The wounded man lay out in the open, but French took the risk of being "potted," and running up to the prostrate figure he lifted Cook in his arms to carry him back to safety. To the honour of the half-breeds and their Indian allies be it said that one and all ceased firing for the moment, and French reached the lines unscathed. It is sad to have to record that not long after his heroic rescue the brave fellow was killed by a half-breed bullet.

In the ranks of the Canadian contingents, as has been said, were many ex-Policemen who answered the call to arms. Many an old comrade was recognised on the veldt, and excellent soldiers did they prove themselves to be. Ross's Scouts, who did such dashing work during the latter half of the war, took their name from Charlie Ross, ex-constable of the N.W.M.P. Ross made his mark as a scout during the half-breeds' rebellion in 1885, when he served with the Battleford column under Superintendent Herchmer.

AT THE FRONT IN SOUTH AFRICA

On the outbreak of the Boer War he promptly volunteered for the front, obtained a lieutenancy in Roberts' Horse and eventually was placed in command of a body of scouts. Lord Roberts has paid high tribute to the valuable help afforded by these corps, who were literally the eyes and ears of the army.

Military men who came into contact with these and other Western Canadian troops in South Africa are always ready to admit that they were as fine a body as any in the country. They could shoot well and they could ride well, and they were no whit behind the Boers in " slimness " and mobility. The men who at home were constantly in the saddle, for days and weeks at an end, often covering extraordinary distances in the course of duty, were " to the manner born " on the veldt. What they could not assimilate was the dull routine of garrison life at the base, where red tape was rampant and a host of petty, vexatious restrictions hampered their movements.

" Keep 'em on the trot, with plenty of work ahead of 'em," said one officer, an old Horse Guards man, " and you couldn't want better fellows to lead. But you can't expect men bred to the free life of the prairies—we had a lot of one-time cowboys in our troops—to sit down easily to the tame business of duty at Cape Town. That was where we had trouble with 'em. Fortunately, the general officers saw what was wrong, and sent 'em up to the front as quickly as possible."

This was the case with the C.M.R. regiments. They had come out to see active service, and they saw that they got it. In riding, they were the admiration of the regulars. The story is told of how a well-known Imperial officer on one occasion was treated to an exhibition of "broncho busting" such as he had never before witnessed, and was not likely to witness again outside North America.

A line regiment under General Hutton's command in the Bloemfontein district was boasting one evening of a horse, an Australian waler, which none of their men could mount. The horse was a big, powerful, black brute, full of devil, and the consensus of opinion was that he had better be shot or sent to the Remount Department to be broken in. He was of no use for present service. An officer of the C.M.R. happened to hear this, and ventured to dissent.

"I'll bet you fellows," he said, "that I've a man in my troop who'll ride him."

The challenge was taken up, and the following morning fixed upon for the contest. The C.M.R. officer went to his men and said: "The —th over there have a horse they can't manage. Now I want one of you to show 'em how to ride it." At this pretty well all the troop stepped forward, but it was explained to them that they couldn't all get on the waler's back, and that *one* man alone was needed.

"You can settle it among yourselves," said their officer, "I just want the best man, that's all."

The troop decided the question by selecting Billy H——, an ex-cow-puncher of wide reputation as a "buster." The horse wasn't born, he declared, that could beat him. So in the morning Billy, dressed in cowboy style, shirt and "shaps," and wide-brimmed hat, and armed with a stout quirt, strolled down to the appointed place where the —th were waiting to see the fun.

Walking leisurely up to the Imperial officer, who was resplendent in all his glory of gold lace and plumes, Billy prodded him in the chest with his quirt.

AT THE FRONT IN SOUTH AFRICA

"Whar's this son-of-a-gun you say you kain't ride?" he asked.

For a moment or two the officer had no breath to make a reply with, but, on recovering himself, he ordered the waler to be brought out. Then Billy H—— took the matter in hand. The big black horse having been turned loose was skilfully "roped" by Billy's friends, and the ex-cow-puncher's own saddle was placed upon it. When the animal struggled to its feet Billy was in his seat, ready for action.

The waler was something of a terror; there was no gainsaying the fact. He bucked and corkscrewed and twisted and bit, and indulged in all the devilments that an outlaw horse could possibly devise. But through it all Billy H—— sat tight, as if he were part of the animal itself. To his comrades' loud cries of "Stay with him, Billy! Stay with him!" he spurred and quirted the waler to a pitch of madness, until the frenzied brute tore wildly across the veldt. It came back to give vent to more bucking, but not for long. The cowboy proved the master, and when he threw himself off at last he had succeeded in making the horse do just what he ordered. The buck-jumper was tamed.

The Imperial officer had watched the exhibition with amazement, nor was he alone in this. Very few of those present had seen a better display of riding.

"Wonderful!" he exclaimed; "wonderful, by Jove! I should never have believed it possible!"

Billy H——, with his saddle on his arm and his quirt trailing on the ground, spat some of the dust out of his mouth.

"Wa'al," he said, "I dunno. I guess in my country we'd jest call that hoss *a goldarned cayuse!*"

In the distribution of rewards at the close of the Boer War the North-West Mounted Police came in for their share. In addition to the Cross for Valour, the following honours gained by members of the Force while on active service were announced in the General Orders :—

To be a Companion of the Order of the Bath.

Superintendent S. B. Steele, Lieut.-Colonel Commanding Lord Strathcona's Horse.

To be Companions of the Order of St. Michael and St. George.

Inspector R. Belcher, Major, 2nd in command, Lord Strathcona's Horse.

Inspector A. M. Jarvis, Major, Lord Strathcona's Horse.

To be Companions of the Distinguished Service Order.

Superintendent G. E. Sanders, Major, 2nd in command, Canadian Mounted Rifles.

Inspector A. C. Macdonell, Captain, Canadian Mounted Rifles.

Inspector F. L. Cartwright, Captain, Lord Strathcona's Horse.

To be a Member of the Victorian Order (4th Class).

Superintendent S. B. Steele, Lieut.-Colonel Commanding Lord Strathcona's Horse (*London Gazette*, 8–3–01).

Awarded the Distinguished Conduct Medal.

Reg. No. 995, Sergeant J. Hynes, Regt. Sergt.-Major, Lord Strathcona's Horse.

THE RIDING SCHOOL, REGINA BARRACKS.

AT THE FRONT IN SOUTH AFRICA

Reg. No. 895, Sergt.-Major Richards, Sqd.-Sergt.-Major, Lord Strathcona's Horse.

Reg. No. 3263, Constable A. S. Waite, Private, Canadian Mounted Rifles.

Promotions, etc., gained by members of the North-West Mounted Police while on service in South Africa and in recognition of their services there :—

N.W.M.P. Rank.	Name.	Corps.	Rank.	Remarks.
Commissioner	L. W. Herchmer	Canadian Mounted Rifles.	Lt.-Colonel.	Hon. Colonel on retired list from May 17, '01.
Superintendent	J. Howe	,,	Major, 2nd in command.	March 7, '00, seconded May 20, '00. Major on reserve of officers, active militia, 29-12-'99.
,,	G. E. Sanders	,,	Major, 2nd in command C.M.R.	2nd in command, May 20, '00. Lt.-Col. on reserve of officers, active militia, 1-8-'01.
Inspector	A. R. Cuthbert	,,	Capt.-Major	Promoted 7-3-'00. Major on reserve of officers, active militia, 7-3-'00.
,,	J. D. Moodie	,,	Lt.-Captain	Promoted 20-5-'01. Major on reserve of officers, active militia, 20-5-'00.
,,	J. V. Bégin	,,	,,	Promoted 3-11-'00. Capt. on reserve of officers, active militia, 3-11-'00.
,,	H. J. A. Davidson	,,	Lieutenant	Lieut. on reserve of officers, active militia, 15-5-'02.
,,	M. Baker	,,	Captain	Capt. on reserve of officers, active militia, 15-5-'02.
,,	A. C. Macdonell	,,	Capt.-Major	Promoted 20-5-'00. Lt.-Col. on reserve of officers, active militia.
,,	T. A. Wroughton	,,	Lieutenant	Lieut. on reserve of officers, active militia, 1-3-'98.
,,	J. L. Cosby	,,	,,	Lieut. on reserve of officers, active militia, 29-10-'99.
,,	E. A. Pelletier	2nd S. S. Battalion R.C.I.	,,	Lieut. on reserve of officers, active militia, 27-10-'99.
,,	J. Taylor	Canadian Mounted Rifles.	,,	Capt. on reserve of officers, active militia, 2-8-'01.
Superintendent	S. B. Steele	Lord Strathcona's Horse.	Lt.-Colonel	Brevet Col., 17-5-'01. Hon. Lt.-Col. Imperial Army, (LondonGazette,20-9-'01).
Inspector	A. E. Snyder	,,	Major	Hon. Major Imperial Army (London Gazette,20-9-'01).
,,	A. M. Jarvis	,,	,,	,, ,, ,,
,,	F. Harper	,,	Lieutenant	Hon. Lt. Imperial Army (LondonGazette,20-9-'01).
,,	D. M. Howard	,,	Capt.-Major	Hon. Major Imperial Army (LondonGazette,20-9-'01).
,,	R. Belcher	,,	Major 2nd in command.	,, ,, ,,
,,	F. L. Cartwright	,,	Captain	Hon. Capt. Imperial Army (LondonGazette,20-9-'01).
Sergt.-Major	W. Parker	,,	Lieutenant	Temporary Lt. Imperial Army (London Gazette, 20-9-'01).

THE RIDERS OF THE PLAINS

The death-roll of the Force in the campaign was, fortunately, not a long one. Seven men, whose names are given below, died in action or in hospital.

Reg. No.	Rank.	Name.	Corps.	Cause.
3165	Const.	Lewis, Z. R. E.	R.C.R.	Killed in action.
3337	[1] ,,	Davidson, F.	Howard's Scouts	,, ,,
2431	Corpl.	Taylor, J. R.	C.M.R.	,, ,,
3188	[1]Sergt.	Skirving, H. R.	Imperial Army	,, ,,
3051	Corpl.	O'Kelly, G. M.	C.M.R.	Enteric fever.
3369	Const.	Lett, R.	,,	,, ,,
3380	,,	Clements, H. H.	,,	,, ,,

[1] Were not members of the North-West Mounted Police at the time of their death.

CHAPTER XVI.

PUSHING NORTHWARD.

In Athabasca—Detachment at Fort Macpherson—In the Arctic Circle—Herschell Island—Eskimo—Inspector Howard—Police posts at Hudson's Bay—"The-place-where-ghosts-chase-women"—Fort Churchill—"On Special Duty"—King Murder Case—Title of "Royal" conferred on the Force—Earl of Minto, Honorary Commissioner—Earl Grey, new Governor-General—Provinces of Alberta and Saskatchewan created—Increase of pay.

"IN my last annual report I called your attention to the largely increased demands on the Force, and the difficulty I find in meeting them. This year these difficulties have been emphasised. The continued development of the country, the increase of population, the settlement of remote districts, many new towns that have sprung up, and the construction of new railways, have greatly added to our work. In the train of the immigration has come a number of the criminal class, which, though not large, will probably increase.

"The new settlers are principally from foreign countries, a great number being from the United States. The American settler is much impressed by the fair and impartial administration of justice. He finds a constabulary force such as he has not been accustomed to, but the advantages of which he is quick to acknowledge, and a country free from all lawlessness and enjoying liberty without licence. The European sees no novelty, but he quickly learns that there is no oppression, and that his

THE RIDERS OF THE PLAINS

best friends and advisers are the constables of the Force. I cannot well exaggerate the admirable work done by the members of the Force among these immigrants who, speaking a foreign language, of an alien race, and unaccustomed to our laws, require timely advice and careful guidance."

This comment, made by Commissioner Perry in his report for the year 1902, draws our attention once more to the extension of Police duties in the north-west. The settlement of the Athabasca district had been progressing steadily, and the little communities that had established themselves were well satisfied with their prospects. But in the footsteps of these pioneers of the northern country more were expected to follow, particularly as there was a project to build a railway through the fertile Peace River valley. There would be need, therefore, for a new Police district to be formed with headquarters at, say, Fort Chipewyan.

Beyond this country, into which outposts had been flung, stretched a still vaster expanse of land reaching to the very edge of the Arctic Ocean. The need for Police supervision to be extended even to this Ultima Thule was now beginning to make itself felt. The northern trade was steadily growing in volume, and it was urged that detachments should be placed on the Mackenzie River. There was, moreover, the fact that many American whalers wintered annually on the Arctic coast in Canadian territory. The crews of these vessels, if rumour was to be relied upon, had gained an evil reputation, by reason of their treatment of the Eskimo Indians and their general lawlessness. It was time that the North-West Mounted Police assumed definite control of this region.

Early in 1903 steps were taken to comply with this demand. About the date that a small detachment under Inspector Moodie accompanied a Hudson's Bay expedition,

PUSHING NORTHWARD

another party set off for the shores of the Arctic Ocean. This latter detachment consisted similarly of five men, of whom Superintendent Constantine was in charge. In July it reached Fort Macpherson, on the Pelly River, over 1800 miles from Athabasca Landing, and here Sergeant (now Inspector) F. J. Fitzgerald was placed in command while the Superintendent returned to Fort Saskatchewan. This post on the Pelly was northerly indeed, but Fitzgerald had instructions to push on even further. In the following month he had the satisfaction of reaching Herschell Island, in the Arctic Ocean itself, and about 80 miles north-west of the mouth of the Mackenzie.

The establishment of these posts, as the Commissioner pointed out, was of far-reaching importance. They stood for law and good order, and they showed that, no matter what the cost, nor how remote the region, the laws of Canada would be enforced and the native population protected.

Sergeant Fitzgerald's report of his remarkable trip is worthy of more than passing notice. He describes Herschell Island as being 12 miles long by from 2 to 4 miles wide. " It is very barren, no trees or scrub on it; all fuel has to be brought from the mainland during the winter by dogs, and during the summer by the Mission steamboat. There are six large buildings on the island, four owned by the Pacific Steam Whaling Company. One of these is loaned to the Mission and used as a dwelling-house, three are storehouses of the Company; the other two are storehouses owned by the Mission and Captain McKenna, whaler. Besides these there are fifteen huts, made of any old boards or packing-cases, and very heavily covered with sods; they are very warm. These are owned by the P.S.W. Co., and are used in the winter by the officers of the whalers."

There were eight or nine vessels touching at the island while the sergeant was there, but little trading was done as the natives had nothing to sell. Having no tariff as to Customs duties he was unable to collect any dues, and had to content himself with warning all captains against supplying liquor to the natives. One Eskimo who got hold of liquor with disastrous results our sergeant sentenced to a few days' imprisonment, " to make an effect upon the others." The only way to take any active measures *in re* Customs and liquor, he concluded, was by having a revenue cutter patrolling that part of the coast. However, he was ready to make a shift with the huts for two years, until suitable buildings could be put up.

There is something that appeals to the imagination in the picture of Sergeant Fitzgerald with two companions (Constable Sutherland and Interpreter Thompson) squatting on this lonely, bare, moss-covered rock of an island as the representatives of British justice. It was, perhaps, the least-inviting post in the whole of the Dominion. In those latitudes for two whole months—from the middle of November to the middle of January—the sun does not come above the horizon, and in the shortest days there is only between one and two hours' daylight. There being no fresh water on the island, blocks of ice have to be cut from a small lake in October to supply drinking water throughout the year. In the summer months the lake is unfit for use, owing to the amount of sediment and green weed in it. For Police barracks the little detachment had to put up with houses made from land staves and any drift-wood that could be found. The frame was covered with sod and the walls were lined with canvas, ventilation being obtained by the simple process of making a hole in the roof. Most of the whalers provided comfortable quarters for

PUSHING NORTHWARD

themselves by bringing with them roofs all ready to place over the ships.

By May 1905 our sergeant was in a position to make a fuller report. He had collected no Customs, one reason being that the ships' captains did most of their trading on their way into and out of Herschell Island; but he had acquired a great deal of useful information respecting the natives. We find him writing learnedly and picturesquely about Eskimo called Kogmollycks, and others called Nunatalmutes, or Deermen, with much interesting detail as to their habits and pursuits.

The two tribes of the Kogmollycks, the Co-pucks and the Herschell Island natives, he says, average about 5 feet 3 or 4 inches in height. "All the older men have their lower lips pierced for labrets, and the women have their chins tattooed; of late years they have stopped this, and men and women of twenty years of age have no marks. There are about 250 Kogmollycks, who are very dirty in their habits, never washing. The Nunatalmutes, or Deermen, are inland Eskimos. Their hunting starts from about 40 miles from Herschell Island and runs west of Point Barrow. They are a strongly built people, the men averaging about 5 feet 7 or 8 inches in height. The older natives have the labrets and tattooing the same as the Kogmollycks. There are about 100 of these natives around this district. There are also a few families of Eskimos from the Behring Straits; they call themselves Masinkers, but almost all are from different tribes.

"Mostly all of the Kogmollycks stay along the coast the whole year, some at the island, some at Co-puck, and the rest at Baillie Island. They fish and seal all summer. Small fish they catch in twine nets, which they set from the shore, the fish being small herring. White whale fishing is done in kyaks. Four or five natives hunt together ; the first throws a spear, with a string and float attached ; the fish dives, but the float stays on top of the water ; the natives follow the float, and when the fish rises throw another spear, and so on until there are four or five spears in the fish, when it is easy to kill. (The white whale is like a large porpoise.) They eat the meat raw, use the skins for boats and boot-soles, and get a lot of oil out of the blubber.

" Seals are caught in the summer, by shooting and with large nets made from seal skin. One native caught 28 seals, in one net, in one day at Herschell Island. In the winter, seals are shot in open spaces of water. The skin is made into boots, clothing, and sled lines ; the fat used as oil for their stone lamps—the meat as a rule is eaten raw. Travelling in the winter, the Kogmollycks camp on any place on the ice, make a snow house, and with their stone lamps soon have it nice and warm. The Nunatalmutes all go inland. Most of them go up the different branches of the Mackenzie river in the fall, and hunt and trap all the winter, returning to the island about July 1 ; some stay with the few Masinkers and hunt deer for the ships. They are a smarter native than the Kogmollycks ; I should think that this was because they came in contact with the whalers long before the Kogmollycks. They are good hunters and trappers, getting more fur than the Indians. They bring their fur first to Fort Macpherson to trade, but, unlike the Indians, they will not trade unless there is something there that they want. They have been known to keep some of their fur over until the next year, which is a thing an Indian will not do.

" All these natives are very handy with tools ; most of them get working tools from the ships at the present time,

IN THE FAR NORTH: AFLOAT IN A KAYAK.

PUSHING NORTHWARD

but they still have a number of tools that they have made in past years; they are experts in working wood, bone, ivory, and horn. The women make all the clothing, and are very handy at it. The boots are made out of deer skin, for winter wear, and out of seal skin and white whale skin, for summer wear. These are waterproof. The shirts are made from squirrel and rat skins, and the coats and pants from deer and seal skins.

" There are always a few ' medicine men ' in each tribe, and they have a dance for almost everything. If anything is about to happen, the medicine man has a dance and tells the tribe what it is. If a native is sick, this man is called in to drive the devil out of him, but if they can get a doctor they will always have him, so it would seem as if they did not put much faith in the medicine man."

Like all other Indians, the sergeant adds, the Eskimo will do anything to obtain liquor. The task of preventing such illicit trading taxed all the energies of the detachment, but very few cases of drunkenness occurred.

Speaking of the Eskimo of this region and of their simple trust in the white man's medicine, Inspector Jarvis, who had later experience of Arctic Police work, tells an amusing story. A Dr. Howe, an American physician, spent a winter among the natives. He was very much in request. " His medical supplies at last running low, Dr. Howe experimented along faith-cure lines with one old Eskimo woman, who was supposed to be suffering with some internal complaint. Giving her a pill, the effect of which he knew was to be the turning yellow of the sclerotic coat of her eye, he solemnly told her that if her eye did not present a yellow appearance next day she would surely die; otherwise, her cure would be absolute, complete, and final. She was to report next day. The following morning the patient presented herself bright and early at the doctor's door, yellow-eyed, radiant, and completely cured. With Caucasian and Eskimo alike, great is the power of faith!"

In July 1905, Inspector D. M. Howard, commanding the Macpherson district, paid a visit to Herschell Island, and in the main was able to refute the stories that had been circulated concerning the American whalers and their ill-treatment of the natives. During August and November the Inspector was again at the island, the round trip from the Mackenzie post being 520 miles. "There is no shelter in this distance," he notes, "and those going must sleep in the snow every night. It is fairly sheltered in the river, but the journey from the mouth of the river to the island along the Arctic coast is a very cold and bleak one." Such trips as these, however, made by dog sleds, were the only means of keeping a check upon the whaling vessels, until proper accommodation for the Police was provided.

For travelling in these regions in the summer the Police have to rely on the native-made boats. These are of two kinds: the kyak, a light, hunting boat, and the umiak, a larger, travelling craft. The kyak is a light skin boat of about 15 ft. in length, and 2 ft. 6 in. wide. It is made of small strips of wood running lengthwise and lashed firmly together at either end by raw hide cords. These are connected by curved ribs. The upper rail, also of wood, is a little heavier, and in this the upper ends of the ribs are inserted and similarly lashed. The occupant of the kyak sits or kneels in a circular opening in the middle. The deck frame is covered by seal skin which has been tanned with the hair off, and sewn together with sinew. After having been tightly stretched and allowed

PUSHING NORTHWARD

to dry, it contracts and becomes as tight as the parchment of a drum. A novice paddling in this craft finds that he has much to learn, for it is easily capsizable, but once the art of propelling it has been acquired it is a pleasant boat to travel in.

The umiak, which is a more open craft, only partially covered, is similarly constructed of wood and skin. It will carry five or six passengers, and is useful for the purpose of transporting freight.

In winter travelling must be done by means of dogs and sleds. The latter are after the model of those used in the Yukon, being about 9 ft. long, and of heavy frame. From seven to nine dogs are needed for the larger sleds, a load usually consisting of between three and four hundred pounds.

In the meantime, while the British flag was thus being carried into the Arctic Circle, Inspector Moodie, with Inspector Pelletier and nine non-commissioned officers and constables, had proceeded a second time to Hudson's Bay by the steamer *Arctic*, and spent the winter of 1904 at Cape Fullerton. At this place a Police post had been established in the previous winter. The following summer was devoted to patrols in the Bay, and the collection of Customs duties from the whalers and traders at various stations.

It was Inspector Moodie's intention to establish the headquarters of the newly created M Division, to be stationed in the Hudson's Bay district, in the vicinity of Cape Wolstenholme. In July 1905, a suitable site was selected here. But it was at Fort Churchill, at the mouth of the Churchill River, on the west side of the Bay, that the Police were finally to settle. To this point a regular patrol from inland was eventually dispatched, the need

THE RIDERS OF THE PLAINS

for a detachment elsewhere on the shores of the Bay having disappeared.

From Inspector Moodie's report we get a glimpse of what a Police patrol in the waters of Hudson's Bay is like. Soon after arriving at Cape Wolstenholme, the *Arctic* was obliged to return home to repair her machinery, and the detachment was transferred to another steamer, the *Neptune*. In this boat they passed through Hudson's Strait, meeting a great many icebergs on the way. "At 7 p.m. on the 5th (October)," says the Inspector, "we rounded north end of Mansfield and set course for Churchill. On the 6th the sun was only visible for about five minutes and no sights were obtained. At 4.15 a.m. on the 7th, position by dead reckoning being lat. 60·20 N.,long. 86·50 W. (almost in the centre of Hudson's Bay), we struck heavily on reefs, pounding over them for fifteen minutes. The morning was pitch dark with snow squalls. After apparently getting inside the reef, vessel again struck three times. The captain kept her as nearly as possible in position until dawn, when the seas could be seen breaking on the reefs all around us. He then took her through the only visible channel, with barely water to take us through. Wind increased to strong, from S.E. by E. true, with heavy short seas. Weather thick, with frequent squalls of snow and sleet.

"Morning of 8th was fairly clear, course S.W. by S., engines going slow. Just before noon the sun appeared for a short time, and a sight was obtained giving us the latitude of Marble Island, which was sighted at 5.30 p.m. After consulting with Captain Bartlett I decided to go to Fullerton, from which we were distant only about 90 miles, before proceeding to Churchill; by doing so time would be saved. The vessel was making water, our compasses were

PUSHING NORTHWARD

totally unreliable, and it was not considered advisable to get out of sight of land until they could be adjusted. The 9th was comparatively fine and clear. Ran along coast until evening, but on account of mirage no landmarks could be made out—the whole coast appeared to be lifted up like high perpendicular cliffs. Towards night it came on to blow a gale with very heavy sea. Soundings were taken every fifteen minutes during the night, the Police on board being told off into watches for this purpose—one seaman and two of the Police being in each watch of two hours. Lay-to, going slow and half-speed as required to keep the vessel head on; frequent heavy squalls of snow and sleet.

The 10th was a repetition of the previous night, the gale veering from N.N.E. to N.N.W. with tremendous sea, pumps going all the time. This continued, with wind and sea getting worse, all the 11th. At 4 p.m. on this day a heavy sea struck forward end of bridge on port side. It curled over chart-room and falling on main deck smashed to splinters the two whale-boats swinging inboard from davits. The stern of starboard boat was cut off and left hanging from davit. Main boom broken from gooseneck, both poop ladders torn from the bolts, and with two harness casks, lashed on deck, swept overboard. The lumber, etc., on port side of poop was torn from its lashings and washing about, and the rest loosened up. The cattle pens forward were smashed. Sea and wind increasing, it was decided to jettison the rest of the deck load, and so relieve the vessel from the heavy straining. The danger was that if the deck load broke loose it would carry away the cabin skylight and flood the vessel. The morning of the 12th the wind began to moderate and the sea quickly went down. This day was fine, with sun shining through scattered clouds.

Shortly before 9 a.m. made out beacons at Fullerton, and ran in on rising tide, anchoring in harbour at 11.30 a.m."

Nor was this the last squall encountered. It was ugly weather nearly all the way to Churchill, snowstorms and heavy gales of wind battering the vessel terribly. But the voyage was accomplished successfully without any serious disaster.

In the winter of 1905-6 two noteworthy patrols were made by men of Inspector Moodie's detachment. One, led by Corporal Rowley, went to the head of Chesterfield Inlet, a trip of 350 miles; the other, under Constable Seller, to Lyon's Inlet, this being a 955-miles' trip. Seller's instructions were to find a Scottish vessel, the *Ernest William*, which was supposed to be wintering in Repulse Bay, about 20 miles north of the place where Parry, the Arctic explorer, wintered in 1821 with the *Fury* and *Hecla*. On arriving there, however, it was discovered that the ship had left, the natives declaring that she had gone to Melachuseetuck ("The-place-where-ghosts-chase-women"). This meant a three-days' journey, but the constable decided to enlarge his orders, and with a native guide proceeded thither to find the ship in its winter quarters. The *Ernest William* had a stock of trading goods on board, hardware, rifles, and ammunition, clothing, and a variety of miscellaneous articles, such as matches, thimbles, combs, mirrors, knives, and pencils, all of which were duly invoiced for import duty, and reported to the Collector of Customs at Port Fullerton.

Constable Seller's notes on this trip are instructive. He left the detachment with 150 lb. meat, in addition to which he purchased 1160 lb. from natives. For the ten sled dogs 30 lb. pemmican and 500 lb. fresh deer meat were needed, giving an average of 3 lb. per dog per day.

PUSHING NORTHWARD

The Constable, Interpreter Ford, and Special Constable (native) Tupearlock consumed their rations in little more than a third of the time for which they were intended, and were forced to rely on deer until provisions could be obtained from the ship. One small alcohol lamp was carried by the party, and when the spirit was exhausted the food had to be eaten frozen and raw, unless any pieces of wood could be got together to make a fire. Such is travelling on Police duty in the far north of Canada!

In September 1906 Inspector Moodie was again at Fort Churchill, choosing a site for the N.W.M.P. post which it had been decided to build there. To establish connection with this new station two detachments of three men each were placed at Norway House and Split Lake. It was arranged, also, that a patrol should leave Regina with mail and dispatches for Fort Churchill in the following December. This trip, being 1500 miles, took three months to complete, travelling with dogs.

Fort Churchill and Herschell Island are still outposts of the North-West Mounted Police. On the Arctic island the detachment reports annually on the whaling industry, the condition of the natives, and any other points of interest to the Government. Of the Eskimo, it is satisfactory to note, the best accounts are given. There have been no " Indian troubles " to record in this remote quarter of Canada. So law-abiding and honest have they showed themselves, indeed, carrying religion into their everyday lives, that one Police Inspector has said : " After my experiences of this world, I could almost wish I had been born an Eskimo ! "

Norway House, which is referred to above, was an old Hudson's Bay Company post, and was a place of call for the dog train carrying mail from Fort Garry to the trading

THE RIDERS OF THE PLAINS

posts in the Athabasca and Great Slave Lake country. When it became a N.W.M.P. post as well, a sergeant and two constables were stationed here. The area under their control was an immense one; a case calling for investigation might occur many hundreds of miles away in the north, but it had to be looked into and reported upon in due course. One finds these instances of "special duty" tucked away in the files, summed up with official brevity which almost—but not quite—conceals the romance to be read between the lines.

Word was brought down to Norway House one day that a horrible murder had been committed in a far-off Indian encampment. Justice had to be done, so the sergeant detailed his two constables, Cashman and O'Neill, on the case. He himself remained to do the regular guard and patrol duty alone. The two Policemen, well wrapped in furs, set off by dog sled for the scene of the murder, and to the great astonishment of the Indians, to whom it was ever a mystery that the white men should take so much trouble about their affairs, they came in time to the camp, investigated the crime, arrested four of those implicated, and started back along the trail with their prisoners. One of the Indians was sentenced to death; another committed suicide before he could be brought to trial; the other two received varying sentences.[1] And the daily round of duty at Norway House went on again, as if nothing particular had happened to disturb it.

It was in the wild Athabasca region that some years ago a case of crime occurred which occupies an historic place in Police annals. This was the "Wilderness Murder." In the unravelling of the mystery the Police had the assistance of the Indians, and but for them, it must be

[1] See page 309 for further particulars of this case.

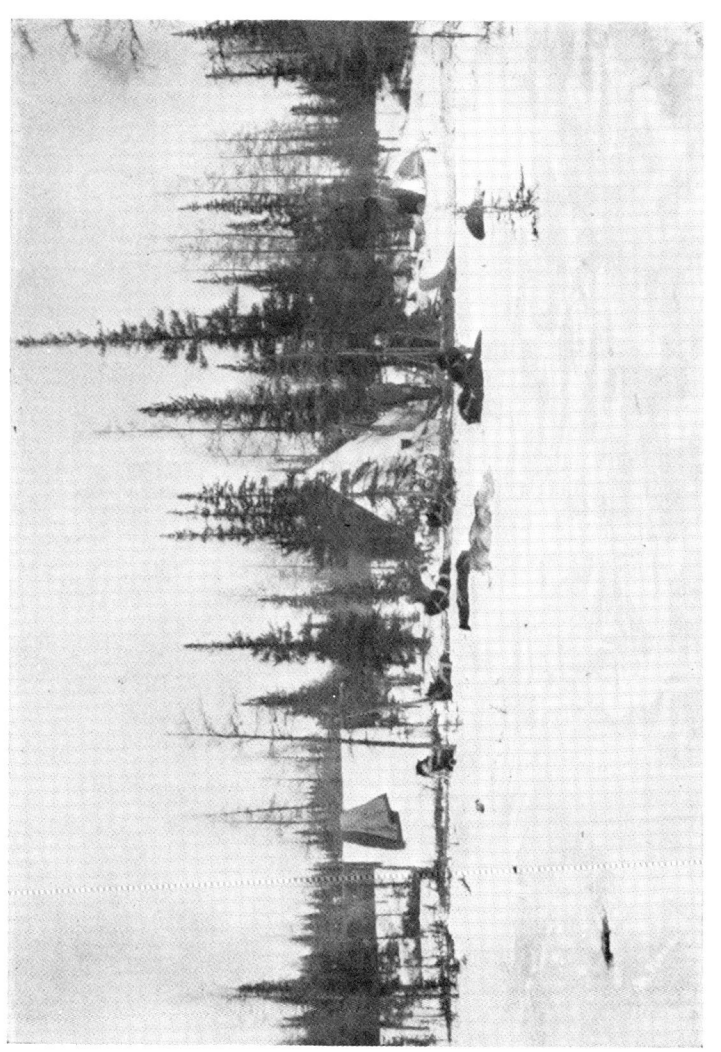

A POLICE WOOD CAMP ON CHURCHILL RIVER.

PUSHING NORTHWARD

admitted, the foul deed which King expiated on the scaffold would probably never have been brought to light.

The opening scene of the story was the Moostoos Indian Reserve, close to Sucker Creek, in the vicinity of Lesser Slave Lake. Into the reserve, one day in October 1904, rode Charles King, with three pack-horses and a dog. He was taking the trail northward. He might have gone on a day or two later, but for a strange circumstance. An Indian boy noticed that the white man's dog would not follow him, and remarked on it to his elders. It was certainly a curious fact, an even suspicious fact to the Indian mind. Chief Moostoos pondered it, and when Joseph Kisanis, "The Little Old Man," came in with a tale of having seen *two* men in camp at Swan Hill, near his tepee, the chief began to put two and two together. Kisanis had this to say further, that on the third night the men had stayed there he had heard a gunshot, and in the morning had seen one man only (King) riding on the trail.

In the circumstances Chief Moostoos thought his friends the Mounted Police should be informed of this strange happening. So a messenger was sent to the nearest detachment, and Staff-Sergeant Anderson with Constable M'Donald took the matter in hand. The first thing to be done was to search the camp on Swan Hill at which the two men had been seen. "I dug in the ashes of the fire with my hands," says the sergeant, "and found some pieces of bone, and about a foot down, in a hole evidently made only a short time previously, I found a heart and some pieces of flesh which I thought at the time were those of a human being." There were other traces also, sufficient to point to foul play.

Chief Moostoos had accompanied the sergeant on

this tour of investigation. The two now proceeded to a slough near by, such a spot offering strong temptation to a criminal who sought to get rid of damning evidence. In the swamp was discovered a camp kettle with a piece of stove-pipe wire attached to it. This article was subsequently identified as that used by King and his companion. On being questioned, King averred that his partner, Lyman by name, had taken the trail to Sturgeon Lake. This was possible, if not probable, but Indian trackers who were sent out failed to find any traces of the missing man. The natural assumption was that King had lied. Pending further inquiry Sergeant Anderson now arrested him.

The next development was the finding of other relics in the slough. Chief Moostoos and two or three more Indians waded into the muddy water and shuffled their bare feet about, until at length they came upon a pair of boots in which were a gold nugget and a small bundle stuffed with various articles that later formed important links in the chain of evidence. Among the things thus found was a broken needle which exactly fitted another piece that had been sifted from the dead fire.

On the strength of this circumstantial evidence, King was removed under escort to Edmonton. The question now to be answered was, who was the missing man ? After some time, inquiry revealed the fact that he was one Edward Hayward, an Englishman, in whose company King had been seen at Edmonton. A number of witnesses came forward to identify King and also various articles that were the property of Hayward. The case was now complete. In March 1905 King was tried at Edmonton, and found guilty of murder. Some months later he was hung at the Police barracks at Fort Saskatchewan.

A remarkable feature of this case was the intelligent

PUSHING NORTHWARD

aid afforded the Police by the Sucker Creek Indians. From the very first, when the boy observed that "the white man's dog would not follow him," to the final discoveries in the slough, they worked with unremitting keenness, displaying to the full their abilities as trackers. But the most extraordinary thing of all was the experience that fell to Henry Hayward, a brother of the murdered man. On the night of September 18 (the day of the crime), while at his home in England, he had a dream in which was revealed to him the whole of the awful tragedy. He saw his brother shot and the remains burnt in a fire. Every detail of the crime was clear to him, even to the features of the man who was the assassin. This vision Mr. Hayward related to his sister and others long before any message was received from the North-West Mounted Police, and thus vouched for it must ever remain as a wonderful instance of mental telepathy.

Before concluding this chapter, one or two notable events in Police history must be chronicled. As a result of recommendations in high quarters, a Bill was passed by the Dominion Parliament which provided for the pensions of officers of the Mounted Police. Those who have risen from the ranks benefit largely by the generous provisions made, as service is reckoned from the time of entry into the Force.

In 1904 a signal honour was bestowed upon the Police by the King, as announced in the *Canada Gazette* of June 24, as follows: "His Majesty the King has been graciously pleased to confer the title of 'Royal' upon the North-West Mounted Police." This mark of distinction and recognition of the magnificent work performed by the Force for so many years, was in some part due to the Earl of Minto, the then Governor-General of Canada. Lord Minto was on the point of relinquishing his office, and with Lady Minto he paid a farewell visit to the North-West Territories in the autumn. As is usual on such occasions, ceremonial escorts were provided by the Police at all posts touched by the vice-regal party, together with all saddle-horses, carriages, camp equipment, and transport that was required.

In the same year, for the first time in the history of the Force, the post of Honorary Commissioner was created and offered to the Earl of Minto, who signified his acceptance in the following letter to Earl Grey, his successor as Governor-General :—

" MY LORD,—I have the honour to acknowledge the receipt of your Lordship's dispatch of December 29, 1904, enclosing an extract from a report of a committee of the Privy Council, informing me that I have been appointed, on the recommendation of the President of the Council, Honorary Commissioner of the Royal North-West Mounted Police.

" I would be much obliged if you would express to Sir Wilfrid Laurier my sincere appreciation of the honour that has been conferred upon me.

" I have the honour to be, my Lord, your obedient servant, (Signed) MINTO."

The following year, 1905, saw the formation of the two new provinces of Alberta and Saskatchewan, which started on their career, from a Police point of view, in a most satisfactory condition. These provinces embraced the original territory placed within the sphere of the Force, and their inauguration was a matter of great gratification and pride to the Royal North-West Mounted Police, who had played so prominent a part in their development. The capitals of Alberta and Saskatchewan were placed respectively at Edmonton and Regina, and at both these towns large detachments of the Police shared in the celebrations and were reviewed by the Governor-General.

The northerly patrol led by Superintendent Constantine to Fort Macpherson has been dealt with in the present chapter. It remains to add that, as a result of this expedition, a new Police district, known as "Athabasca," was created, and a division, designated "N," was organised for duty in that part of the country.[1] Temporary headquarters were established at Lesser Slave Lake. Of this division Superintendent Constantine was in command, and one of his earliest duties was the opening up of a pack trail from Fort St. John, B.C., to Teslin Lake, in the Yukon Territory, across the mountains of British Columbia. As a special side of Police work, and as illustrating one of its most useful features, the precise nature of this duty may be detailed here. Superintendent Constantine's instructions were as follows :—

"The trail to be constructed is to be one suitable for

[1] By November 30, 1905, the distribution of the Force, by Divisions, was as follows :—

		Commissioner.	Assistant-Commissioner.	Superintendents.	Inspectors.	Surgeons and Asst.-Surgeons.	Veterinary Surgeons.	Staff-Sergeants.	Sergeants.	Corporals.	Constables.	Supernumerary Constables.	Total.	Horses.	Dogs.
Dépôt	Regina	1	1	1	10	1	1	17	12	15	133	19	211	127	..
A	Maple Creek	..	..	1	2	..	..	4	3	4	23	3	40	51	..
C	Battleford	..	..	1	1	..	..	4	2	2	18	4	32	28	..
D	Macleod	..	..	1	4	..	..	4	6	4	48	15	82	83	..
E	Calgary	..	..	1	1	..	..	4	4	5	26	7	48	41	..
F	Prince Albert	..	..	..	1	..	..	2	2	3	14	4	26	27	..
G	Fort Saskatchewan	..	..	..	3	..	..	4	2	7	25	5	46	42	..
K	Lethbridge	..	..	1	1	..	..	4	6	2	19	6	39	44	..
N	Peace-Yukon Trail	..	..	1	2	..	..	1	6	4	24	6	44	70	..
M	Hudson's Bay	..	..	1	1	..	..	2	..	3	10	..	17	..	..
B	Dawson	..	1	1	5	2	..	5	6	12	74	27	133	37	58
H	White Horse	..	..	1	4	2	..	4	7	8	56	13	95	56	38
	Grand total	1	2	10	35	5	1	55	56	69	470	109	813	606	96

THE RIDERS OF THE PLAINS

pack animals. In selecting the location, you should bear in mind the fact that at some future time it may be made into a waggon trail. You should therefore select your grades and ground with this in view. Through timber the trail should be 8 ft. wide. All boggy and soft places should be brushed, and, where possible, small streams should be bridged. The trail is to be clearly marked, so that it can be followed by any traveller without a guide. In open country large posts should be planted at intervals of 2 miles. These posts should be marked with the distances in miles, from Fort St. John. The numbers should be burnt in so that they can not easily be erased. Through timber, trees are to be blazed at frequent intervals. The distances should be marked every 2 miles on trees conspicuously placed. Rest-houses are to be built every 30 miles, or at such distances as are most convenient for camping, where wood and water are easily obtainable. The rest-houses should be simple in construction, 10 or 12 ft. square, and with mud roofs."

The detachment to which was assigned this important work carried it through successfully in the face of no little difficulty. At the same time, another patrol was engaged on special service in the neighbourhood of Lake Winnipeg, where the Indians were being demoralised by the liquor traffic. Finding themselves barred from openly selling whisky and other spirits to the natives, some traders had tried to evade the law by putting up the liquor in the shape of essences and patent medicines. The trade in these articles went up by leaps and bounds, until it compelled the attention of the authorities, and the North-West Mounted Police were directed to check it forthwith. This was done in an effective manner, a steamer, the *Redwing*, being commissioned for the patrol of the Lake and rivers, and

PUSHING NORTHWARD

from that date the officers commanding the posts in the district were able to report a great decrease in drunkenness among the Indian and half-breed population.

A matter of great importance to the Force was the augmentation in pay of all ranks which was voted by the Dominion Parliament in the 1905 session. For several years this question had been raised and urged by the Commissioner of the Police, the additional duties thrown upon officers and men, through the extension of area under supervision and the constant increase of population, making some such recognition imperative. The Prime Minister, Sir Wilfrid Laurier, himself the supreme head of the Mounted Police, introduced the measure providing for a new scale of payment, and the Bill was passed without dissent.

The increases made per annum were: Commissioner, from $2600 to $3000; Assistant-Commissioners, from $1600 to $2000; Superintendents, Surgeons, and Assistant-Surgeons, from $1400 to $1800; Veterinary Surgeons, from $1000 to $1400. Per day, the increases were: Staff-Sergeants, from $1.50 to $1.75; non-commissioned officers from $1 to $1.25; constables, from 60 cents to $1. For special constables and scouts the rate of pay was to be $1.50 a day; for buglers (under eighteen years of age), 50 cents; and for working artisans, 75 cents.

In all, this increase was estimated at $50,000 per annum, but few could be found to say that it was not well earned. Thirty years of strenuous work in the Territories had brought about results that can only be termed wonderful. The record was one of which the Mounted Police had every reason to be proud. The thirty years, too, had gained for them a reputation that was not only second to none in the Dominion, but was known far and wide throughout the Empire.

CHAPTER XVII.

A BATCH OF STORIES.

Corporal Smith at Norway House—"Cowboy Jack's" arrest—Fighting a prairie fire—Sergeant Field's trip—Constable Pedley—In charge of a madman—Sergeant Field again—A tragedy of the far north—1788 miles by land and water.

THE Royal North-West Mounted Police have no Roll of Honour, nor have they any decoration of their own for distinguished service "in the field." It is characteristic of them that this is so. They do not boast of what they have done, they do not court publicity. It is all in the day's work, so to speak. But there are many deeds to their credit which deserve a better fate than the oblivion of Blue Books, and which might well be gathered into a Livre d'Or worthy to rank with the best. In such a volume one would include the names of gallant Jack French, who died at Batoche, as has been told; of Lieutenant Chalmers and Major Sanders, the one killed and the other wounded in the attempt to save life under fire; and of humbler heroes such as Corporal Smith and Constables Pedley and Conradi.

It was all in the day's work to Corporal Smith—D. B. Smith of Dépôt Division—when he found himself face to face with a grave situation at the Norway House post on the north corner of Lake Winnipeg. Diphtheria and scarlet fever had broken out in virulent form in the district, and Indians and half-breeds were dying by scores. But

A BATCH OF STORIES

the Corporal did not flinch from his duty. He was "untiring in his efforts to aid the unfortunate people." Was there food required, or medicine, or was there a house to be disinfected ? Corporal Smith was ever present to supply the need. And day by day while the epidemic raged and ran its course he tended the sick, and was doctor, nurse, and lawyer in turn as he passed from one bedside to another. At the end, when the dread disease claimed its victim, it was he who dug the grave and buried the dead. For this simple act of devotion—simple, but splendid in its way—the Corporal was promoted to the rank of Sergeant.

Sick-room duty is an extra office any member of the Force may be compelled to take. In one of Superintendent Macdonell's reports we read that he had "one really bad case of a man suffering from delirium tremens, opthalmia, and erysipelas, all at the same time. Constable Darby took entire charge of him, and nursed him night and day." You will find record of this and other instances in the Police Blue Books, a brief note as a rule, saying little but suggesting much.

To any one who knows the Mounted Police at all intimately, the official reports sent in by non-commissioned officers and constables on duty have their amusing side. There is so much that is left unsaid, as if the writer had definite instructions to give no more than the barest facts, or as if he feared the imputation of a desire to show off. Here is a model of brevity in this respect. The author is Corporal Hogg, who at the time was stationed at North Portal, near the Boundary Line.

" On the 17th inst., I, Corporal Hogg, was called to the hotel to quiet a disturbance. I found the room full of cowboys, and one Monaghan, or ' Cowboy Jack,' was carrying a gun and pointed it at me, against sections 105 and 109 of the Criminal Code. We struggled. Finally I got him handcuffed behind and put him inside. His head being in bad shape I had to engage the services of a doctor, who dressed his wound and pronounced it as nothing serious. To the doctor Monaghan said that if I hadn't grabbed his gun there'd be another death in Canadian history. All of which I have the honour to report.

     (Signed) "C. Hogg, Corporal."

To this statement the Corporal's superior officer adds: "During the arrest of Monaghan the following Government property was damaged: Door broken, screen smashed up, chair broken, field-jacket belonging to Corporal Hogg spoiled by being covered with blood, wall bespattered with blood." In the light of which, there is reason to assume that a good deal happened between "We struggled" and "Finally."

The fighting of a prairie fire is a duty which falls very frequently to the lot of Policemen in some districts. It is a duty, too, demanding a terrible amount of hard work and involving much danger. To get caught by one of these scourges and be swept up in a wall of flame means certain death. Whole townships have thus been razed to the ground, only heaps of blackened ashes being left to show that houses and human beings had once been there. But a fire, however far it has run, must be fought and got under before more dread consequences result. There must be no wavering, no half-hearted measures; the fire-fiend must be stayed in his course or his path diverted to where he can do little or no damage.

It was a prairie fire which brought Constable Conradi of C Division, Battleford, the opportunity to show of

A BATCH OF STORIES

what right good stuff he was made. The day was the 5th of October 1905. At noon he was sitting at dinner with a rancher named O'Neill, when a tremendous fire was seen sweeping across the country from the south-east. It had been running for a long distance, having come from Red Deer. Jumping up from the table, Conradi asked: " Are there any settlers in danger ? " Mr. O'Neill answered that Mr. Young's homestead was in the path of the fire. " He has a wife and ten children," he added, " but I wouldn't try to make his place, the fire is coming up at such a pace." " Is he fire-guarded ? " was the next question. " No," said the rancher.

" Then I must see what I can do," said the constable, and in another minute he was galloping towards the doomed homestead. From this point Mr. Young may take up the story :—

" When Mr. Conradi arrived he promptly helped me with the plough, and we finished the furrow. He, thinking the guard was large enough, got the horses inside. Mr. Conradi then thought it was time for us to get ready to fight the fire ; we got pails and baths of water, soaking blankets and sacks for fighting fire. Mr. Conradi then set a back-fire going, he taking the south-east corner, I taking the south-west, and everything seemed to be going on satisfactorily. My wife and family were all helping. Suddenly the fire appeared on some hills to the south-east, rushing down with hurricane force, and jumping the back-fire Mr. Conradi had made, he fighting it all the time with most heroic pluck, not giving in till hope had gone. The fire he fought was of extraordinary fierceness, the grass being very long and dry, and the wind blowing a gale. His pluck and endurance I cannot praise too highly. He was fighting till he was nearly suffocated, his hat burned off his head, hair singed, and vest on fire. When all hope had gone, he rushed to me and told me to get my wife and family and follow him to the outhouses. We could not see them, the smoke and flames were so thick—we could only see a few yards. Mr. Conradi ran through the fire, and eventually found my wife and children standing in the middle of a slough. He rushed in and took the two youngest in his arms and brought all safely through, and not too soon, for they were nearly suffocated with smoke, and almost immediately fire surrounded the slough. They must have either been suffocated or badly burned had he not rescued them. We then turned our attention to the horses, and found them terribly burnt; Mr. Conradi's was badly burned about the head and hind-quarters; we cut them loose and led them to a place of safety. The next morning I looked at the horses, and found Mr. Conradi's in a terrible state; its eyes were burnt so badly it could not see, and its mouth burnt to such an extent that it could not eat or drink, and it was in most dreadful agony. He mercifully shot it on his return. It could not possibly have lived, and eventually must have starved to death. My wife and family owe their lives to Mr. Conradi, and I feel with them we shall never be able to repay him for his brave conduct."

It was a plucky piece of work, without doubt, and the constable well deserved the immediate promotion he obtained.

Another unpleasant duty that a Mounted Policeman may be called upon at any time to perform is the escort of a lunatic from an outlying settlement, where no provision is made for such cases, to some town where he may receive proper attention. It is a sad feature of life in the unsettled parts of the north-west that some would-be

A BATCH OF STORIES

homesteaders there are unable to stand the strain of the continuous heavy work, and endure the awful loneliness of their situation. In the summer, life may be easier to bear; it is in the winter, when all the prairie is one vast white sheet of snow for months on end, and communication with the outside world is more or less cut off, that the mind falls to brooding and comes near to breaking-point if it does not actually give way. It is a case too often of the man being in the wrong hole. To wrest a living from the soil while condemned to practical isolation for a great part of the year, needs a strong man; not every one can make the sudden change from the life of the town to that of the wilds and be adamant against failing crops, business worries of all kinds, and, not least, the oppression of solitude.

True it is that men and women in the back-blocks sometimes break down under the stress of adverse circumstances and go mad. Then the Mounted Police are called in to take charge, and as a rule, owing to the small strength of the detachments, it becomes a one-man job. But it is not always the lonely homesteader who thus is thrown upon their hands. It may be an Indian or a stranger from "down east" whose mind has become affected. One of Sergeant Field's hardest trips was made with an Indian lunatic from Fort M'Kay on the Athabasca River. Early in February 1007, he received a letter (at Fort Chipewyan) informing him that an Indian, the son of one Joseph Bouchier, living at Fort M'Kay, was violently insane and beyond control. The sergeant had just returned from a northern patrol, and his dogs were not in a condition to make another long journey, so he asked Bouchier to try and wait until the summer, but the man replied that his son was becoming more violent and dangerous daily.

In the face of this, the sergeant had no option but to inspect the case for himself. He hired a team of dogs, fought his way through heavy snowstorms to Fort M'Kay, and set off southwards with the lunatic. It was bad going all the way. A good part of the journey across country there was no trail; and in addition to the strain on the dogs there was the fact that the Indian was constantly troublesome. He had to be strapped to the sled frequently, otherwise he fought and bit like a mad dog. But Sergeant Field worried through, and came at last to Fort Saskatchewan, where he handed over his charge to the provost in the guard-room. This was a 500-mile trip, taking seventeen days in all.

More arduous still was the duty that fell to Constable A. Pedley, stationed at Fort Chipewyan, in December 1904. This Police outpost, which has been mentioned frequently in these pages, was formerly an important centre of the fur trade, and served also as the starting-point of many notable exploratory parties to the northern coast. From it Mackenzie set out to follow to its mouth the great river that bears his name, and Simpson started to trace the coast-line of the Arctic Ocean. It was, further, a resting-place for the expeditions under Franklin, Back, Richardson, and Rae.

A lonely spot at all seasons of the year, it is at its worst in the winter, when lake and river are ice-bound, and all the country, as far as the eye can reach, is covered with deep snow. Travelling is almost impossible without a competent guide and a strong team of dogs, and few besides trappers are to be met on the trail. In the winter of 1904, however, a Presbyterian minister named Mr. B—— found his way into this wild region. He was an evangelist, engaged on a missionary tour in the north-west, and during

A BATCH OF STORIES

the summer had been visiting the far north where only Indians and half-breeds wander. Later on he went over the cañon trail of the Peace River into the gold country of British Columbia. Thence he returned to the Hudson's Bay dépôt at Peace Station to make this his quarters for the winter.

The " dépôt " is described as having been a " long, low, log cabin " in the sole charge of a half-breed. It was many miles from any other post or settlement, and was only occasionally visited by Indian traders bringing in furs and supplies. Here the missionary elected to pitch his camp, and here he abode for some months, shut up in a dark, smoky hut, half buried in snow, with the half-breed for sole companion. Their food consisted of bacon and corn meal, varied by a jack rabbit whenever the weather was mild enough to allow the breed to go " gunning."

Such an existence would have been depressing enough in any circumstances. It was rendered doubly so by the fact that conversation between the two men was next to impossible. The half-breed, Anton Ribeaux by name, had no English, and the missionary only a few words of the other's *patois*. It is scarcely to be wondered at that this solitary life told upon the less-hardened nerves of the evangelist. When one day a squad of Royal North-West Mounted Police, on a patrol eastward, rode by the log hut they found Ribeaux much concerned about his guest's state. He begged that the other might be removed, as there was little doubt he was becoming insane.

Proceeding on their way, the patrol reported the case to the detachment of three men at Fort Chipewyan. The sergeant in charge of this Police post promised to look into the matter, and Constable Pedley was detailed to make the trip to Peace Station. Pedley set off with his dog team,

THE RIDERS OF THE PLAINS

in due course reached the hut, found the missionary by this time a raving madman, and carried him back to the post. The next thing to be done was to get the madman down to the nearest settlement for medical treatment—down to Fort Saskatchewan, in fact, immediately to the north of Edmonton. For this task Constable Pedley was eminently the man, as the stronger and more experienced of the two constables. Only one could be spared for the journey; the sergeant and the remaining constable had to stand by their post.

It was now the second week in December. The weather was bitterly cold, but the real rigour of the Arctic winter had not yet been felt. When Pedley started out with his insane charge the grimmest and most daunting part of the season lay before him. According to instructions, he was to follow the course of the Athabasca River so far as was possible, the distance from Fort Chipewyan to Fort Saskatchewan being, as the crow flies, nearly 400 miles. By trail it was well over 500. For the journey a team of the best dogs available was provided, and a strong, light-running sled. The latter was loaded with provisions and clothing, a small tent, and some blankets.

On leaving Fort Chipewyan the mad missionary was wrapped in thick furs, with his feet, which were frost-bitten, encased in large moccasins. He was put into an Eskimo sleeping bag and fastened by straps to the sled. For most of the journey Pedley himself travelled on foot, running with the dogs and helping them at times to pull the sled over bad places. Soon after starting, the party encountered heavy, blinding snowstorms, which made it very difficult to keep to the trail. The Athabasca is a winding river, fringed for scores of miles by thick timber, but in places broad and clear. When frozen over, these

GROUP OF ESKIMO NATIVES, FORT CHURCHILL, HUDSON'S BAY.

wide reaches of water make travelling easier than on the snow-packed trail.

In his report of the trip Constable Pedley dwells on the great depth of snow encountered and the severity of the storms. The temperature, he notes, was from 20 to 50 degrees below zero, being at its lowest in the long hours of the dawn. Every day at 4 p.m. he made his camp, to dine on cold meat, tinned beans, and tea, if a fire could be got going. The madman would eat little at first, and later refused to touch any food at all. Pedley therefore had to force him to eat, fearing that he might succumb to exposure and exhaustion before reaching their destination. It was all pretty lonely and horrible, this daily routine of trudging through the snow, facing a bitter east wind, and with never a pause except when a rabbit or a bird crossed their path and gave the constable a chance for a shot. As the missionary could not be kept fastened to the sled all the time, he was released now and then to walk, and on these occasions careful watch had to be kept to see that he did not try to escape.

On the fourth day out the madman did make an attempt. Bursting his bonds with a superhuman effort, he leapt from the sled and ran for some woods not far off. Pedley gave chase instantly, and after a desperate struggle succeeded in mastering him. It was only a few days after this episode that they were held prisoners by the most terrible snowstorm of the whole journey. For forty-eight hours a perfect gale raged, and for protection Pedley lashed himself and the madman, in their fur bags, to a tree, the dogs having been entrenched in the snow, with the upturned sled as a wind-shield. The portable tent was of no use in such conditions; it would have been blown to bits in no time.

As the more wooded country below Fort M'Kay was approached game became more plentiful. There was sometimes a caribou to be shot, yielding a welcome meal of fresh meat. But with the deer were wolves, first the smaller variety, and later the larger timber wolves, for whom at night it was necessary to light great fires, lest their hunger should embolden them to attack the camp. Thanks to these precautions, and the constable's vigilance, there was no disaster. And so at length the little party of two men reached Fort M'Murray, where they crossed to the eastern side of the great river.

"I knew now," says Pedley, "that one half of our long journey was completed. During the summer perhaps half a dozen persons live at Fort M'Murray, but we found only a single individual there, a half-breed Indian. He did his best to make us comfortable, and after a rest of two days we took the trail again, and, much refreshed, journeyed on down the river. Fresh troubles were at hand, however. The missionary grew sullen again and refused to eat. When food could no longer be forced down his throat I became alarmed, and concluded to once more loosen his fastenings to give him exercise, hoping thus to restore his appetite. While I was gathering fuel for a fire he became violent, picked up a stick, and attacked the dogs. Then, seeing me with my arms full of kindling wood, he made a dash for the open prairie. With all his fasting and confinement he gained speed, and soon outdistanced me. But I kept on running, and found that he was too weak to go far. In the end I overtook him, and fastened his legs and arms so that he could not do any injury to himself and me.

"I am a pretty strong man," adds Pedley, "but in the wind and numbing cold it was really a difficult job to carry him a quarter of a mile to camp. However, I got him

A BATCH OF STORIES

there and was well rewarded, for he began eating again, and from that time his appetite grew better."

At Big Weechume Lake a guide was requisitioned, there being no trail over this part of the country. Thence they travelled to Lac La Biche, where a team of horses was found, and these were taken in place of the dogs. And so, without further adventure, Constable Pedley duly arrived at Fort Saskatchewan, the date being 7th January. The unfortunate missionary was here turned over to the guard-room to be examined by the Assistant-Surgeon. The doctor pronounced it a most remarkable case.

"He (the madman) was badly frozen about the feet, and the exposure to the cold had caused paralysis of the tongue for several days. Every care and attention was given him at the hospital (to which he was transferred), with the result that he was discharged on 23rd February, with the loss only of the first joint of a big toe. His mind and speech were as good as ever. His life was saved."

So much for the Rev. Mr. B———. The plucky constable, who had brought him hundreds of miles down to civilisation in the depth of winter, fared the worse of the two. His mission accomplished, Pedley commenced his return trip to Fort Chipewyan, to report himself to his sergeant. He faced the terrors of the lonely trail again with a brave heart, but, though none guessed it at Fort Saskatchewan, the strain of that fearful journey, alone with a madman, had been too much for him. At Lac La Biche the poor fellow broke down and became violently insane. From this point he was immediately brought back to Fort Saskatchewan, to be ordered away to the asylum at Brandon. In this institution the constable remained for six months, at the end of which time he was discharged "cured."

THE RIDERS OF THE PLAINS

Pedley returned to headquarters, and in consideration of his remarkable service was granted three months' leave. He came back to his home in England—he is an East-Anglian—but if any effort was made to induce him to stay here permanently he stoutly resisted it. The expiration of his leave saw him again at Regina, ready to resume his duty and, eventually, to re-engage for a further term of service. You may see Constable Pedley at the headquarters barracks still, but you will not find him quite the same man. That one experience has left its mark upon him, and it is likely to remain.

Another great feat of a somewhat similar character was performed by Sergeant Field (the hero of several long-distance journeys) in the same year, 1904. This was the arrest of an Indian near Lake Athabasca, who was wanted on a charge of deserting his adopted children in the bush, some time in the previous September. The sergeant's statement of the case, as given in the Commissioner's Report, ran as follows:—

"This Indian, Paul Izo Azie, was camped on an island in Black Lake (about 250 miles east of Fort Chipewyan), where he intended fishing and hunting during the fall and winter. One day he sighted four or five canoes, with a number of men on board, coming towards his camp. He fired two shots in the air, as is customary amongst Indians as a sign of friendliness. They did not reply or take any notice of his shooting, but paddled off in another direction, and landed on the main shore of the lake. This man being very superstitious, as most Indians are, concluded that these were bad people, and intended killing him and all his family. He got very frightened, so he put his wife, sister, and the two little children and himself into his canoe and paddled ashore, leaving his camping outfit and all his belongings behind him. When he landed on shore he started off on foot for Fond-du-Lac, followed by his wife and sister, leaving the two children behind unprotected, one a little boy, and the other a little girl, aged two and three years respectively.

" It being an eight days' trip, or about 130 or 140 miles from his camp to Fond-du-Lac, his sister, a young girl about fifteen years old, got fatigued after the first or second day's travel. He left her behind on the road also, without food or protection. This poor girl wandered about the woods for several days in a dreadful state of starvation, until she was picked up by some Indians who were camped in that direction. She told them her story, how her brother had deserted the two little ones on the lake shore. Some of these Indians started back to search for the children. When they got to the camp they found it just as the Indian had left it, nothing taken or stolen. They tracked the children along the shore, and where they went into the bush. They followed their tracks up into the woods, fired two or three shots, and then called out as loud as they could, but got no reply. Then they went on a little further, and there they found a little dress, all blood-stained and torn, and wolf tracks all around where the little girl had evidently been eaten by wolves. They could find no trace of the other child anywhere. There is no doubt that the little boy was devoured by wolves also.

" These Indians who found the little dress, and also this man's sister, being the principal witnesses in the case, were not at Fond-du-Lac at the time Constable Pedley was out there, so he did not arrest this Paul Izo Azie, as he could not get the witnesses. They will all be at Fond-du-Lac next summer for treaty payments. I will then go myself and arrest this Indian, and get the witnesses and all

THE RIDERS OF THE PLAINS

necessary evidence on the case, and take them out for trial."

Sergeant Field's dispatch was dated December 1903. It was June in the following summer when, as he expected, the Indian was found at Fond-du-Lac. The arrest was made and the witnesses secured. The next stage in the proceedings was the escort of every one concerned to Edmonton, a thousand miles away. A long journey this, in very truth, and not without its difficulties, but justice demanded full retribution for that bloodstained and torn little frock which told such a tragic story, and without any delay the party set off.

For 667 miles the sergeant and his manacled prisoner travelled down the river in a canoe, the others following in similar fashion. On leaving the stream the trail was taken for 90 miles, after which the rest of the trip was accomplished by train. The total distance thus traversed was 1788 miles ! At Edmonton the Indian murderer (one can call him by no other name) was tried and sentenced to two years' imprisonment.

The punishment was none too heavy, but the mere bringing of the criminal all those hundreds of miles by land and water, at some considerable expense to the Government, was in itself a valuable object lesson to the Indians. It made known in the "outlands" that no place was too remote, no crime too insignificant, for the arm of the law to stretch out and lay its hand upon the guilty party. All honour, then, to the Royal North-West Mounted Police for that, even in the loneliest, most inaccessible quarter of the vast Dominion, the law of the land is a living thing which no man, white or red, can set at naught.

CHAPTER XVIII.

HORSE THIEVES AND "CATTLE RUSTLERS."

A prevalent crime—Swift retribution—An American apology—"Mavericks"—Sergeant Egan—Trapping a thief—"Rustler" methods—Need for vigilance—Exposure of hides—A lost foal—Detecting brands—Patrols on the boundary.

HORSE and cattle thieves have been a thorn in the flesh to the Mounted Police from the earliest days, and though much of the evil has been abated, they still remain a source of constant trouble. On the American border more particularly the vigilance of the boundary riders must never be relaxed. The temptation to "run" a bunch of stolen horses or cattle over the frontier is great, the profits on the venture, if successful, are large, and there are plenty of men ready to take the chance that offers and put their fortune to the hazard.

Something has been said already in earlier chapters with regard to the prevalence of horse-thieving. In this respect the honours have been fairly well divided between white and red men. In the Montana "bad lands" there has always existed a class of desperado to whom the game of horse-stealing is most alluring. On both sides of the border the Indians and half-breeds have been even more susceptible to the fascination. It must be admitted, however, on their behalf, that such depredations on their neighbours have all the weighty sanction of tradition behind. In Indian warfare, among tribes between whom an hereditary enmity existed, the raiding of each other's horses was a recognised form of reprisal. Blackfeet and Crees waged such a war among themselves from time immemorial, and their young men were brought up to learn the game of horse-lifting as an essential part of their education.

It was the advent of the Royal North-West Mounted Police in the Territories that put a damper on this raiding. But it took many long and patient years to effect a change, to bring about any real diminution in the evil. The Indian mind was slow to grasp the new doctrine preached, the more so, as has been pointed out before, because the law below the border was lax, and the red man failed to reconcile the *laisser-aller* spirit of the one side with the relentless severity of the other.

The policy of the Police was to hit hard and quickly. Where retribution followed swiftly upon the execution of the deed, the moral of the lesson was increased tenfold in value. Such an instance as the following, we may be sure, had its beneficial effect in its own area. Three men came in to the Maple Creek N.W.M.P. post to announce that a war party of Crees had stolen thirty-four head of horses from J. G. Baker & Co.'s ranch in Montana. On discovering their loss they had at once followed up the Indians' trail, and arrived at Fort Walsh a little in advance of the raiders. The latter, on reaching the Cypress Hills (a favourite hiding-place), divided into three parties, each of which took a separate trail to their camp, situated about thirty miles from the Fort.

In less than half an hour from the time the information was lodged Sergeant Paterson, with ten troopers, was on the track of the thieves. When ten miles out he intercepted seven Indians with seventeen head of horses. These were

IN WINTER DRESS.
Walking out order, without bandoliers.

HORSE THIEVES AND "CATTLE RUSTLERS"

arrested and sent to Fort Walsh. Further on other Indians with stolen horses were caught up and similarly dealt with, and at the camp the balance was duly recovered. Within twelve hours after their bringing in the tidings of the theft, J. G. Baker's men were on their way back to Montana with their thirty-four horses, and eleven crestfallen Crees were under lock and key in the Police guardroom. The Indians were sentenced later to two years' imprisonment each in the Manitoba Penitentiary.

As a rule the American authorities co-operate willingly with the North-West Mounted Police once the machinery of the law has been set in motion. But the different conditions of life on the southern side of the frontier have created at times unforeseen difficulties. A case in point was afforded some years ago, and it is worth recording as illustrating also the cheapness of life in the wilder parts of the West.

One, Stowell, had stolen seven horses from a stockman of Montana, and carried them off into Canadian territory. The Mounted Police having been notified, quickly got on the man's trail, with the result that he was traced to Regina, where it was found that he had disposed of his booty for a hundred and fifty dollars. From Regina he had gone by train to St. Paul, U.S.A. Superintendent Howe, then commanding the Dépôt Division, wired this information to the Chief of Police at St. Paul, and also to the Stock Inspector at Glasgow, Montana. Some time later he received the following letter from the latter gentleman :—

" DEAR SIR,—I have just arrested Stowell at Pleasant Town, Iowa, and much regret not having replied to your telegram. I must apologise to you for not doing so. I have to look after a country 160 miles in length by 109 wide, and they only give me one deputy. Now, on the afternoon of the 4th (August), I handed to him a reply to your telegram, and told him to send it off to you at once. He went out to send it and was shot dead, and this morning the coroner handed the telegram to me. It had never been sent, so you will see that I am not altogether to blame.

"Trusting that you will pardon me for not replying at once, I remain, yours respectively,

(Signed) "———, Inspector."

The lack of comment on the unfortunate cause of the delay is significant.

Apart from the stealing of horses that have been sent out on the ranges, and "lifted" thence by night, or that have been actually taken out of the corrals, a profitable form of theft was the seizure of "mavericks," or young unbranded animals. These having been driven off, were eventually marked with a new brand, which rendered identification very difficult. Many stock-owners in Canada —principally in Alberta—suffered heavy losses in this direction. In one district a gang of skilful thieves worked the game successfully for a long time, and it was only through the smartness of a N.W.M.P. officer that a stop was put to their practices.

It had been suspected that the thieves were working in conjunction with some unscrupulous rancher. Their raids were so timed that it was clear they received special information as to the various stock-owners' "round-ups," the movements of the Police, and so on. In order to get at the root of the mystery Sergeant Egan, who had done good detective work of a similar kind before, was detailed to make investigations. Attired in plain clothes, he watched

HORSE THIEVES AND "CATTLE RUSTLERS"

the country closely until his suspicions fell upon a certain ranchman. It was a slight clue, but it might lead to something, so he determined to follow it up.

One day he appeared at the ranch in question, looking very much like the scores of other "hobos" who drifted about more or less seeking employment.

"Got a job for me?" he inquired.

The rancher looked him over, and presumably was impressed in his favour.

"What can you do?" he asked. "Broncho busting?"

"No, I ain't great shakes on bronchos. Not my line. I can cook a bit, and do odd chores."

"Well, sling your bunk in that shed," said the other. "As it happens, I want a feller for light work just now."

So Egan was taken on. He stopped at the ranch for four or five months, making himself generally useful through the winter, and establishing himself in his employer's confidence.

One morning in the early spring the rancher asked him, "Do you think you can ride a bit now?"

Egan replied that he thought by that time he had had enough practice to be able to stick on pretty well.

"Very good, then," said the rancher. "Come along with me; I've got a job for you."

A little later the two men were riding out to the hills and the sergeant felt that there was a surprise in store for him. There was. In a corral, nicely sheltered from observation by a circle of low bluffs, was a bunch of "mavericks," a very taking lot altogether, and certainly some one else's property, for the sergeant knew the extent of the stock on the ranch. He asked no questions, however, but proceeded to follow his employer's instructions, and assist in the branding of the animals. One by one they were roped, thrown, and stamped with the rancher's brand. After this had been accomplished the horses were herded together, and they started back homewards.

At a certain point the trail divided, one fork leading on to the ranch, while the other led south to a place near which was a Police post. When they came to this fork Egan steered the horses into the southern road.

"See here, what are you doing ? " cried the rancher. "Swing 'em round, you fool; that ain't our way ! "

"I guess it is," was the answer.

"Not it ! That's the road to Twenty-Mile. This other's our trail."

The sergeant turned in his saddle. "I know what I'm doing," he said quietly. "We're going to Twenty-Mile. I guess it's about time you knew who I am. I'm a Mounted Policeman. You're the fellow we've been looking for, an' I reckon we've got you all right."

He drew out his revolver, and the rancher saw that the game was up. Egan sent him on ahead, and in due course arrived with his man at the post. It was a true bill. The gang with which his prisoner was operating was broken up; some were caught, and at the subsequent trial exemplary sentences were inflicted. And for a time that part of Alberta enjoyed a rest from the attentions of horse thieves.

"Cattle rustling," the seizure of young unbranded steers and heifers, offers similar attractions to the unscrupulous. As in the case of the rancher who was brought to justice, the "rustler" takes fewer chances than the common thief who relies on getting beyond pursuit with his booty. In company with others he rides the ranges with a running iron strapped to his saddle, and picks up calves which have arrived at the age when they can be easily weaned from their mothers. To rope a calf and drive it to some place where it may be held till it would not be claimed by its mother or recognised by its owner is a comparatively simple matter. It was recommended as a precaution against this dishonest practice that the use of running irons should be prohibited, but such a restriction would be unjust to others, by whom a legitimate use of the irons would be made. In a round-up of a rancher's cattle some distance from their range the new calves are branded by his own men, who carry the straight iron or running brand for the purpose.

The unlawful making of "mavericks" at a round-up is a question that has occupied the attention of the courts more than once. Some stock associations hold that an unbranded animal on the range is an incentive to theft, and consider that they have a perfect right to brand and sell the same for their own benefit, and without infringing any law. This is a point that might be conceded, were it not for the ease with which "mavericks" may be made. One Police official puts the case in a nutshell :—

"I will assume," he says, " that the rounding-up has been completed, and the cattle are gathered at the rendezvous in readiness for the cutting out. The first class of animals to be cut out are the cows with calves. That is an operation that requires great care, and in a properly conducted round-up only the most capable and knowledgable and best mounted men are allowed to enter the herd. Two men apply themselves to each cow and calf, riding on each side and a little behind the animals, which are quietly conducted out of the day-herd (as it is called), and headed towards the 'cut' which they are intended to join. There are mounted men in charge of each 'cut,' and others all around the day-herd, whose duty it is to see that unauthorised animals do not break out or in. A very little harrying of a cow and calf in the day-herd will result in the calf being separated from its dam. This may be done unintentionally, and when it has happened the only recourse is to let the cow stay in the herd until she shall have reclaimed her calf. But suppose, for the sake of example, that the herd has been harried a good deal, and that some cows and calves have been separated : it is a mere matter of detail to cut out the cows and leave the calves until the close, when there will then appear so many unbranded calves (or ' mavericks'), which become the property of the association and are sold accordingly. I should explain that at this stage the calf of which I speak has not yet been branded, and if it becomes separated from its branded mother there is no way of telling who its owner is.

" A prominent stock-owner has spoken of cows having been driven across a river while their calves remained on the other side. That is a ready way of making ' mavericks.' A calfless cow with a distended bag is no unusual sight on the range, and we know that all the calves have not been killed by coyotes and wolves. It is to be noted that a round-up does not necessarily confine its attentions to cattle that are the property of members of the association which it represents, as ought to be the case, unless it can show express authority to the contrary. There is no greater autocrat on the continent than the captain of a round-up ; but if owners suffer from unauthorised handling of their cattle, it is not because there is any ambiguity in the law. The Stray Animals' Ordinance provides that any person who (1) takes, rides, or drives off any horse or head of cattle belonging to another ; or (2), when taking his own animals from pasture, takes or drives off the

HORSE THIEVES AND "CATTLE RUSTLERS"

animal of any other person grazing with his own, without the owner's consent, is liable to a penalty not exceeding one hundred dollars."

Thanks to the persistence of the Mounted Police, a legal decision was obtained on this much-debated point. It was ruled that people have a right to allow their cattle to range on the prairie unbranded if they please to do so, and that a round-up has no justification for gathering cattle that are not the property of members of the association, without the consent of their owners.

This, however, is but a phase of the subject. What more particularly concerns us in this chapter is the open theft of "mavericks" by "rustlers." To the Police stationed in the ranching districts the need for vigilance in this respect is continuous. A part of the duty that falls to a patrol is a house to house visitation among all the farmers and settlers. If a carcase is found without a hide exposed on the fence, or a satisfactory explanation being offered, a prosecution may follow. Although this, as an offence, is not so serious in itself as actual cattle stealing, a case of this nature not infrequently elicits evidence of an animal having been stolen. Every man who kills an ox, cow, or calf is required by law to have the hide punched by an official inspector, and to expose it in some conspicuous place for a specified time. The Police are, of course, familiar with all the brands in their own districts, and can tell at once whether things are in order or not.

A difficulty with which the Police have to cope in connection with horse and cattle thieves is the reluctance on the part of some ranchers to give evidence. Many of those who suffer loss, and are certain that their stock has been stolen, are fearful of laying information, lest even worse consequences should befall them. Particularly is this the case in portions of Southern Alberta and South-Western Saskatchewan, where homesteaders have flocked into the ranching country. Not a few of the new settlers are of an undesirable class, and prone to the temptations offered by horses and cattle roaming at will on the ranges.

A typical example of the prairie species that preys upon his neighbours, taking a colt here, a calf there, and so on, was unmasked in the Maple Creek district a few years ago. A rancher near Medicine Lodge had a foal born to a mare of his, and kept the pair on view for over a week, and then found that the bunch of horses to which the mare belonged had disappeared. When they were discovered the foal was missing.

A corporal of the Medicine Lodge detachment in the meantime had been riding round that post on a tour of inspection. He visited a ranch, whose owner did not bear the best of reputations, and, as he wanted supper and a night's lodging, received permission to stop. While waiting for the ranch owner's return, he took the opportunity to look round the premises, paying special attention to the corral. In the latter he noticed a mare and a colt, and noticed, moreover, that although the youngster was only some days old, the mare would not allow it to suck. When the rancher came in shortly after with a load of hay, the corporal remarked casually on the colt, and was informed that it was a "maverick," whose owner was unknown. The Policeman next volunteered to help in the unloading of the hay, and made another interesting discovery. In the hay-rack was the newly slaughtered carcase of a sheep.

"Bought it from a herder," said the rancher curtly, on being questioned about this.

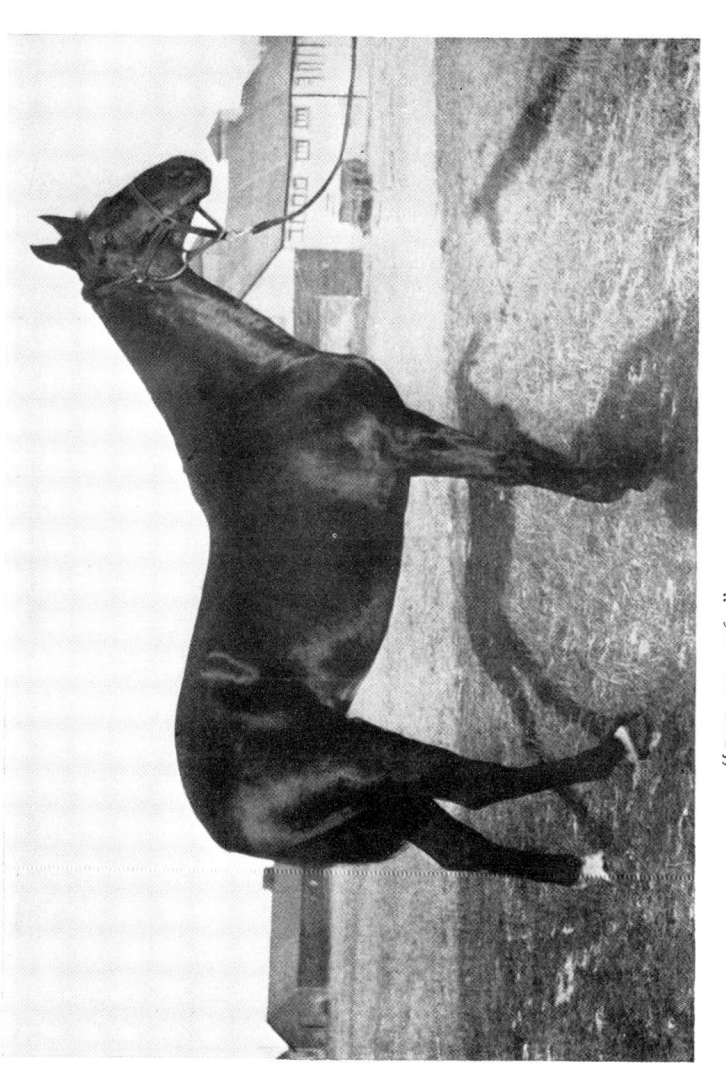

"REG. NO. 2561." A POLICE TROOP HORSE.
Purchased from an Albertan Ranch.

HORSE THIEVES AND "CATTLE RUSTLERS"

In the words of an American poet, the corporal said to himself, "Well, it may hev been so; I dunno. Jest so, it might 'a been. But then agin!" Anyway, there was no harm done in making inquiry; so the next day he rode round the neighbourhood and could find no one who had sold or given a sheep to his late host. Nor did any one admit having lost a colt, until, one day later, the owner of the mare referred to reported that the foal was missing.

"Come to So-and-so's ranch," said the corporal; and Rancher No. 1, with several witnesses who could identify the "maverick," accepted the invitation. A number of horses, including the mare, were driven into the corral, and the mare and foal claimed one another instantly. Rancher No. 2 was able to boast that he had been arrested previously on eight different occasions and had escaped scot-free. This time Nemesis overtook him. Two years in the penitentiary was the punishment meted out to him.

Another not uncommon method of robbery is for the thief to obliterate the brand on a horse or cow, and claim the animal as his own. In one case the accused was proved to have heated a waggon rod, and with it almost entirely to have burnt out the old mark. By shaving and photographing the part of the skin thus treated, the first brand was faintly revealed. The Police have adopted an even surer way of thus showing up brands that have been removed. They kill the animal, skin the part and soak the skin, when the brands are seen to show clearly on the underside.

That organised bands of horse and cattle "rustlers" are still operating on the frontier is an undoubted fact. The "line riders," whether Mounted Policemen or special men engaged by stock-owners for this service, have plenty

THE RIDERS OF THE PLAINS

to do in frustrating their wiles. How desperate some of these characters are is shown by a case which came under the notice of the American authorities some time back. A trio of Montana " rustlers " visited the house of a settler and carried him off into the district known as the " bad lands," where he was kept prisoner for twelve days. After having relieved him of his horses, arms, and money, and subjected him to cruel treatment, they blindfolded their victim and turned him loose. The reason for this audacious act was their desire to prevent the settler appearing as a witness against another of their party who was being tried on some criminal charge.

In their supervision of the 700 miles of frontier the Mounted Policemen are day and night on the *qui vive* for these gentry. The patrols are purposely made irregular, so that no " rustler " can say where at any moment a Rider of the Plains is to be expected. By this means some check is maintained upon their movements.

CHAPTER XIX.

ON A PATROL.

Varieties of patrol work—Nature of reports—A typical instance—Inspector Pelletier's journey—Norway House to Sandy Lake—Cranes and Sucker Indians—A nine months' patrol—Far north—The rough side of Arctic travelling.

REFERENCE has been made so frequently in these pages to Police Patrols that this subject may well be dealt with at greater length. Patrols are of many kinds. There is the regular house-to-house visitation on the prairie between certain definite points, to enable the officer in charge of a district to assure himself of the well-being of outlying settlers and others ; there is the incessant patrol of the southern border line, from Red River to the foothills of the Rockies ; and there is the patrol which is sent out with some special object in view. This last one may have for its purpose the investigation of a crime some distance away from a Police post, or the compiling of a report on a new piece of country through which it is proposed to drive a trail. It may, further, be a mail-carrying patrol, or a six-monthly, or annual, visit paid by an Inspector or other officer to a post situated far out in the wilds and only brought into touch with headquarters by this means.

In many cases, therefore, patrols of a special nature have to travel over great distances. We have had instances under our notice already, such as the long trips made by

THE RIDERS OF THE PLAINS

Inspectors Moodie and Routledge at the time of the Yukon rush. Other notable patrols have been made by Inspector A. M. Jarvis in the Mackenzie River district, thus obtaining much valuable information concerning the Arctic coast; by Superintendent Routledge in the Athabasca district, to report upon the wild buffalo which the Indians and half-breeds were said to be ruthlessly slaughtering; by the late Inspector M'Ginnis in the Cat Lake district, far up in Keewatin where no white man had before penetrated; and by Inspector Genereux, who travelled 1750 miles by canoe and dog train into the far north to inquire into a case of alleged murder.

In all such patrols very exhaustive reports have to be made, as often a part of the Territories is traversed that has not before been known. The officer in charge is instructed to note down details with regard to the country passed through, its natural features and inhabitants, the conditions of the trail, best methods of travel by land and water, with other particulars that may be of service to future travellers or to any Government Department. Through the agency of the Mounted Police, who thus acquaint themselves with the unsettled, or only sparsely settled, regions of the great north-west, a mass of material is acquired every year which throws a vivid light upon the back-blocks of Canada. The Police, in fact, to-day are as much the pioneers of civilisation as they were thirty-six years ago, when they entered upon that historic march westward.

As an illustration of what a special patrol is, and what kind of report is returned, it will be instructive to study one in full. An interesting example is to be found in the patrol made by Inspector E. A. Pelletier from Norway House (Lake Winnipeg) to Sandy Lake, some 400 miles

ON A PATROL

to the east. This trip was undertaken as a sequel to a sensational murder case in which several Indians of the Fiddler, or Sucker, band were implicated. The guilty parties, who were arrested by two constables, Cashman and O'Neill, had strangled a young sick woman according to a superstitious custom of the tribe, and thus came under the notice of the Police. In Inspector Pelletier's patrol, the account of which is given below, one of the principal Indian witnesses was escorted back to his home at Sandy Lake, and advantage was taken of the opportunity afforded to deliver a homily on good living to the tribe in general.

"REPORT OF INSPECTOR E. A. PELLETIER, ON PATROL FROM NORWAY HOUSE TO SANDY LAKE.

"NORWAY HOUSE, *March* 18, 1908.
" The Commanding Officer,
   " Dépôt Division,
      " Regina.

" SIR,—I have the honour to report that according to instructions received from you I proceeded on a patrol to Sandy Lake, leaving Norway House on February 19, and returning on March 16, having been twenty-seven days on the journey, and having travelled a distance of about 600 miles with dogs.

" I left Norway House on the date mentioned above, accompanied by the following : Constable Cashman driving one team of dogs, Special Constable W. T. Towers as guide, Indian ex-prisoner Angus Rae, an Indian of Red Deer Lake near Sandy Lake, Mr. Donald Flett, a Hudson's Bay Company man, as interpreter, with his train of dogs; myself driving one train of dogs.

" Angus Rae came as far as Sandy Lake, where I left him with sufficient provisions to reach his home about two days' distance. We were obliged to carry him on the sleighs most of the way, as he was completely played out. Before the first day was over his feet got bruised, and he got in very bad shape. On his account we were delayed considerably, as in those places where riding on the sleighs was impossible we had to wait for him, as he could not go faster than a slow walk. However, he proved useful from Island Lake to Sandy Lake, where he acted as guide.

" We reached Oxford House on Sunday noon, the 23rd, after having travelled short days to spare the dogs. The distance from Norway House to Oxford House is 160 miles, time $4\frac{1}{2}$ days. While at Oxford I heard three complaints, two of which were settled there and then, amicably, and one of which I could not attend to, as the party was away on his hunting-ground.

" The first was a case of house-breaking with no intent to steal, but to borrow; the defendant claiming that the informer had given him permission to go into his house and use his stores while he was away hunting. This happened in the winter of 1906–7. A compensation was given by the defendant, and both were satisfied. Second complaint was about a man from Island Lake who was keeping from its mother a child of his late brother's. The mother wanted the child back. After making inquiries, I found that she was a good worker and able to provide for the child, and when at Island Lake I told the chief to make that Indian ' Adam Harper No. 1,' return the said child to its mother as soon as possible. Adam No. 1 was away on his hunting-grounds a couple of days from Island Lake.

" Third complaint was about an Indian beating his wife. I could not see the Indian, as he was away to his traps, but I left word that if I heard any more of this

ON A PATROL

about him, 'he would feel very sorry for it.' This expression is about the only one which can convey the meaning intended. This Indian, I heard, is very much addicted to beating his wife.

"The country traversed between Norway House and Oxford House is mostly lakes and rivers; some portages are encountered, the longest of which is not over 8 miles. The last one is just before getting into Oxford Lake. There are also two about 4 or 5 miles long. The others are short.

"From Norway House we go down the Nelson for about 14 miles, until near Sea Falls, then cut across into a big swamp which drains into Lake Nelson, known as 'Lake Winnipegosis' by the Indians. This is a large lake of about 30 miles and of good width. From the lower end of the lake we followed the watercourse into Oxford Lake, making such portages as are required to avoid bad places and rapids.

"The general appearance of the country seems unfit for agriculture, mostly muskegs and sandy soils with small jack pines; very few poplar or birch bluffs are met; in few places it is solid rock, and at others the ground is covered with boulders. There are patches of timber, but none of any commercial value.

"SETTLERS.

"Those four white men who left last fall for Churchill early in October got frozen about 70 miles from Norway House on their way to Oxford. Two of them left for the outside, the remaining two are still there; they built a good-sized cabin, and are comfortable for the winter. They brought ample provisions and are not in need of any help. They expect to make a new start in the spring, coming back to Warren's Landing to procure a new outfit. These are the only white men between Norway House and Oxford.

"GAME AND FUR.

"Is very poor this year all over.

"GENERAL HEALTH.

"There has been a great amount of sickness this winter among the Indians of Oxford Lake. A sore throat and bad cold is the general complaint, mostly due, I believe, to the mild winter. On Monday, the 24th, it was very stormy, and as it was still raging at night we decided to lay over Tuesday. We left Oxford on the morning of the 26th with a special guide for Island Lake. The weather was very cold and all the trails filled in. The guide was to come as far as Beaver Hill Lake, 70 miles. Considering the state of the trails, it was expected it would take us three days to the lake. We made it in two days, getting there late the evening of Thursday, after having some difficulty in locating the last portage. We left next morning, and arrived at Island Lake early in the afternoon of the 28th, distance of 20 miles. Total distance between Oxford House and Island Lake, 90 miles.

"The country traversed between Oxford and Beaver Hill Lake is just a river across the points of which there are some short portages, then into a lake and a succession of portages and lakes; mostly lakes.

"The country gets more and more broken, and some steep hills are encountered, but not of any great elevation. On one we had to take the dogs out and drop the sleighs down by hand. There is no timber of any value along the road. There are some few patches of burnt timber, none of any great extent, and few are recent. Between Beaver Hill and Sandy Lake the country is more broken and there are fewer lakes, the trail being mostly portages.

ON A PATROL

There are fewer muskegs and the timber growth is better.

"Game and fur is scarce. Fish is not plentiful at this time of the year, and the Indians in general, being very improvident, some of them have a hard time, having next to nothing to eat. Rabbits are scarce.

"Indians rely on game at this time of the year, but they have been very unsuccessful in their hunt this winter on account of the light fall of snow.

"INHABITANTS.

"We only came across two Indian camps between Oxford and Sandy Lake. On my arrival at Sandy Lake I immediately sent word to the chief and a few of his Indians that I wanted to see them. These Indians are very little enlightened, and their knowledge of the laws concerning this country is very slight.

"I spoke to those that came, about a dozen in number, and asked them if they had anything to bring before me. They had nothing. I explained to them a few of the laws that affected them the most, such as murder, poisoning, assault, theft, about making false statements, laziness, and gave them some advice about looking forward to the future, and not to live from hand to mouth as they do. I spoke to them about their superstitions, that as long as they were harmless we would not interfere, but that as soon as they became serious and dangerous they were unlawful. They seemed to be attentive. I believe this lecture will bear good results.

"The only white men living at Island Lake are the Hudson's Bay Company's agents, and a young Methodist schoolteacher. I am told there are about 600 or 700 Indians at Island Lake, as many if not more than the Oxford and

God's Lake Indians combined. The language spoken is 'Saulteux,' the same language as spoken at Sandy Lake.

"Island Lake is a large lake, full of islands, mostly small and heavily timbered. Good-sized timber is to be had here in many places. The soil seems to be better than any other place I have seen this journey; in ordinary years potatoes and garden vegetables ripen, also oats. Fish is very plentiful and of good quality; white fish is the staple fish. I have seen some trout about 25 lbs., large, deep-water trout; some are said to be a great deal larger. While I was at Island Lake I discovered that dog food was a problem there this year, and that we would have to take our dog food from Island Lake for the return journey. To make the trip effective I sent Constable Cashman on Monday, the 2nd, with a guide to Sandy Lake. He carried a letter written in Saulteux that was to be sent to the chiefs of the Suckers and Cranes, requesting them to come to Sandy Lake where I wished to see them, and to bring only their most important people with them, as provisions were short at Sandy Lake. Consequently I left the following Thursday with Angus Rae as guide. We reached Sandy Lake on Saturday afternoon, distance of 90 miles, 60 miles of which is portage.

"COUNTRY TRAVELLED.

"From the Hudson's Bay Company's post we cross the lake about 25 miles, then enter into the long portage about 45 miles long, when we come into some lakes and portages leading to the Hudson's Bay Company's post, this part being about 20 miles. The country between Island and Sandy Lake is poor in timber, mostly jack pine on the benches and black spruce of stunted growth on the lower lands or muskegs. The country is hilly, but none of any

ON A PATROL

height. One or two would reach from 200 to 300 ft., slope gradual. It is more broken than in any other section of this district, there being two divides on the long portage. We saw no deer tracks and only two fur tracks, one otter and one wolverine. We found no Indians living on or near the trail. On my arrival at Sandy Lake I found that Indian runners had been to the Suckers and Cranes, who had their camp two days out in different directions, and they were expected to arrive at any time.

" On Monday morning the Cranes came in. I spoke to them in the afternoon. The Cranes are a good band. I spoke to them as to the Island Lake Indians. They expressed their pleasure as to our coming into the country; that they were glad to hear the laws of the white man, and they would remember and do as the law asked them to do. The chief seemed to be a nice, middle-aged man, and very sincere.

" The Fiddler, or Sucker, band came in to us in the afternoon about supper-time. I spoke to them in the evening. The Sucker Indians are recognised as the worst band in the district. They are murderers, liars, and very crooked. I gave them good strong talk through the interpreter, and I feel sure they will remember for some time to come what I told them. I spoke to them about two hours explaining the law, and to what they were rendering themselves liable in each different charge. I told the chief that if he did not change his ways I would put another chief in his place; that a good chief had usually a good band, and otherwise; that we were the friends of the good Indians, and that the bad Indians need fear us as we were numerous, and when we were after one man we always got him, no matter how long it took. They were not to think that because they were living in an isolated place

THE RIDERS OF THE PLAINS

we would not hear of their doings, nor take steps to punish them in case they were against the law. I said that I hoped that the next time I shook hands with him I would be able to say, ' I shake hands with a good chief.'

" He seemed to be quite affected with what I told him, and assured me he would do better in the future, and try to make his people ' live better ' ; that they were very ignorant and were glad to hear the laws ; that his band was bad, and that it would be a lot of work to make them good. He then turned to his people and told them to remember what they heard and to try to live better, so they would become the good friends of the ' soldiers.' The Indians have us as soldiers all through this district. This meeting, I believe, will be of good results. I must say that if I had not been accompanied by a good interpreter I would never have been able to speak to them the way I wanted. Mr. Donald Flett, who accompanied me on the journey, made it possible to explain the law to the Indians and make the patrol an efficient one.

" One Indian woman that belonged to the Suckers asked to be transferred to the Island Lake tribe. She said that the Suckers did not live right, and she wanted to go and live at Island Lake. I found that she was related to some of the Island Lake Indians, and I allowed her to do so. An Indian, ' Paul,' employed by the Hudson's Bay Company, made the same request on the same ground. I found it could be done, and I told him to consider himself an Island Lake Indian from that on.

" I profited by this to point out to the chief of the Suckers that some of his people were ashamed of their own brothers, that the life they led was such as to make them wish to live in another part of the country away from them. I gave Angus Rae sufficient provisions to

ON A PATROL

reach home, and warned the Suckers that Angus was now a friend of ours, and that if they molested him in any way they would feel very sorry for it afterwards.

"My mission to Sandy Lake being completed, I left on my return journey on Tuesday morning, March 10.

"We made Island Lake in two days. After resting the dogs one day, we left on the 13th and came direct to Norway House, reaching the latter place on the 16th. The distance between Sandy Lake and Norway House is 270 miles ; this made six days of actual travelling.

"The trails were heavy in many places between Island Lake and Norway House, and the weather was bad, being very cold and stormy. We had strong head winds nearly every day. The country between Island Lake and Norway House *via* Beaver Hill Lake is mostly lakes, except that 20-miles' stretch between Beaver Hill Lake and Sandy Lake which is described previously. On leaving Beaver Hill Lake we travel along a small river and fair-sized lakes until the divide near Molson's Lake.

"The general country is flat ; one or two portages are fairly rough, full of large boulders ; but they are not of great length. The country is about the same as around Norway House, the timber of no value, and no agricultural land of any extent. Between Island Lake and Norway House only three Indians are near the trail, one on Beaver Hill and two on Molson's Lake. The party reached Norway House without accident, and none the worse for the journey.

"GENERAL.

"To make Police work effective at Island Lake and Sandy Lake, it is necessary for us to build a post at the former, and maintain it for a sufficient period to enable the Indians to gather the right and wrong of things generally.

"Island Lake is in a central place, from where patrols could be sent to God's Lake, Oxford Lake, and Sandy Lake, all of them being about 90 miles distant in different directions. A good location is to be had; dog food is plentiful and of good quality; good building timber is handy, the only drawback is that it is hard to get provisions in, and on that account they are a high price, some three or four cents a pound dearer than Split Lake prices. Otherwise the location is good, and in a district where a post is needed. There would be difficulty in the performance of our duties, and the suppression of unlawful practices, such as killing old people or sick people. The missionary at Island Lake told me that he had warned them against the custom with good result at Island Lake, but with little result at Sandy Lake, principally with the Sucker tribe, who seem to be in dread of punishment in this world rather than the next. They are with very few exceptions a very dirty lot, all of them very improvident, and this year will suffer, as the rabbits are nearly extinct. Still, there is not much destitution among them. There has been much sickness all through this winter; if they would be cleaner, and of cleaner habits, a great deal of sickness would be suppressed, which is mostly throat and chest trouble.

"Our pack of dogs proved most effective this winter, and I believe it is due to the good care we gave to them. I had two pups one year old this May, raised and bred by ourselves, which did good work on this patrol, and returned in splendid condition.

"I have the honour to be, Sir,

"Your obedient servant,

"E. A. PELLETIER, Inspector.

"*Commanding Norway House Sub-District.*

POSTSCRIPT.

"*Re* NORMAN OR OWL RAE.

"He is now at Island Lake totally deaf; he is sickly, and I believe in consumption. He has been supplied with charity nets and charity goods when required. He was unfit to be taken to Sandy Lake, and it was also his wish to remain at Island Lake.

Re JACK FIDDLER.[1]

"I made inquiries at Sandy Lake to find out how the Suckers took the news *re* suicide of Jack Fiddler. They seem to have never talked about it. It is a known custom amongst the Indians of the Territories never to mention the name or refer to an Indian that is dead. Nevertheless, I repeated the news to them, and said that we ourselves were very sorry to find that he had taken his own life, that we were treating him well and that we never thought he would do such a thing.

"*Re* JOSEPH FIDDLER.

"I told them that he had been taken into the white man's country, where he would be kept till the great chief of the white people thought it proper to send him back; that perhaps they would never see him any more. He was well looked after, and if he died it would be a natural death."

A far more lengthy patrol was undertaken by Inspector Pelletier in June 1908, its objects being (1) to establish Canadian jurisdiction over portions of the far north, (2) to report upon the country and possibility of the route from Hudson's Bay to the Mackenzie River; (3) to report upon

---

[1] This Indian, an old man of seventy, committed suicide while being conveyed to Norway House for trial. Chief Joseph Fiddler was sentenced to imprisonment for life. Norman, or Owl, Rae was a witness in the case.

THE RIDERS OF THE PLAINS

the number, the location, and condition of the natives; and (4) to ascertain whether any permanent detachments of Police should be stationed there.

Leaving Fort Saskatchewan on 1st June with three companions, Corporal Joyce, Constable Walker, and Constable Conway, Inspector Pelletier proceeded partly by steamer and partly by canoe to Fort Resolution on Great Slave Lake. Thence the party travelled *via* Artillery Lake, Hanbury River, and Thelon River to Hudson's Bay and Chesterfield Inlet, where they arrived on 31st August. At this point they were met by a party in the coast-boat *MacTavish*, specially chartered by Superintendent Moodie, but unfortunately the vessel was wrecked on the way to Churchill, and the party was obliged to proceed to Fullerton, the R.N.W.M.P. Post at the north of the Bay, and await the freezing-up.

By the end of November the trails were fit for travel, and the party started with dog trains overland for Fort Churchill, which was reached on 11th January. This Post was left on 7th February, and the route taken to Gimli, Lake Winnipeg, the journey ending on 18th March 1909.

On this remarkable patrol the total distance covered was 3347 miles. No natives or guides were employed from Great Slave Lake to Hudson's Bay, and owing to Inspector Pelletier's great experience in canoe work this portion of the trip was made without any mishap. The most difficult and dangerous part was that from Fullerton to Churchill, when the party were joined by Sergeant M'Arthur and Corporal Reeves. The cold was extreme, the days were very short, there was a lack of fuel, and towards the end the men were reduced to eating raw deer meat.

"We had two dog sleds, 18 ft. long and 2 ft. wide," says Inspector Pelletier, "there being nine dogs on

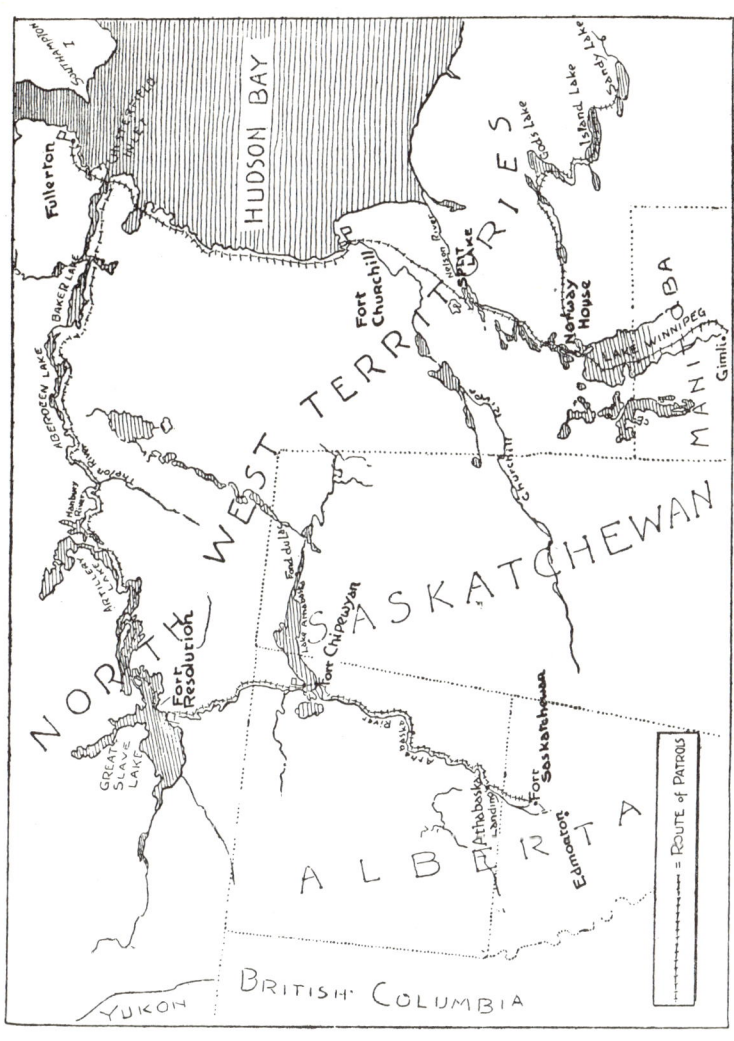

SKETCH MAP SHOWING ROUTES OF PATROLS UNDERTAKEN BY INSPECTOR E. A. PILLETIER, 1908-09.

each, with a load of about sixteen hundred pounds divided between the two sleds. The party consisted of Sergeant M'Arthur, Corporal Reeves, Special Constable Ford, natives Pook and Tupearlock, and myself, six in all." A later note in his diary throws light on the rough side of travelling in the Arctic at this time of the year. " The worst feature of a long journey like this (we were 43 days) in a country where no fuel is to be procured, is the absolute impossibility of drying clothing, bedding, etc. The moisture from the body accumulates, and there are no means to dry clothing to get rid of it in any way. Every day sees it harder to put on in the morning, and the bed harder to get into at night, until both clothing and bedding become as stiff as a board from the ice. It is a very uninviting task and disagreeable procedure getting into an icy bed at night, and the same thing in the morning getting into icy clothes. Sleeping with one's clothes on only makes matters worse. There is no fuel to be procured all the way between Fullerton and Driftwood Point, near Churchill, and even there it is only by chance that a stray piece is picked up."

Among the important results of this trip was the discovery of gold and copper out-croppings in some districts, which brings to mind the fact that on all such patrols as this the collection of scientific data is one of the duties of the officer in charge. Geological, meteorological, and other records have to be made for the information of different Government departments. A leader of a long-distance patrol, in addition to endurance, resourcefulness, and other qualities essential to Police work, must thus possess keen powers of observation, and be well trained in more than one branch of science.

CHAPTER XX.

IN BARRACKS.

To join the R.N.W.M.P.—Taking the oath—At the dépôt, Regina—Riding and drilling—Police horses—A day's routine—Instructional classes—The ideal and the real—Target practice—A special course—General duties—The lighter side—Punishable offences—An attractive life.

BEFORE the active life of a Royal North-West Mounted Policeman can be entered upon, a recruit has to undergo a period of instruction in many departments at the dépôt at Regina. Here he must spend some six months in learning to ride and shoot, and in the acquisition of as much knowledge respecting the varied duties of a constable as can be crammed into him in that space of time. The present low strength of the Force makes it inevitable that a man may be drafted from the dépôt to another division before he can be considered really an efficient Policeman. Six months is none too long a period for the course of instruction to be followed, but it is necessary that the total number of all ranks should be raised to 1000 if fuller attention is to be paid to the training of recruits.

In the preceding chapters we have seen the Mounted Policeman at work as soldier and peace officer in all parts of the north-west and in all conditions. It will be instructive now to go behind the scenes and watch the different stages of his development from the raw product into the finished article.

To join the Police a man must be between the ages of 22

and 40, must be sound in health and of good character, must be able to read and write either the English or French language, and must both ride well and understand the management and care of horses. These are the chief qualifications; fuller particulars as to enlistment are given elsewhere.[1] A very strict medical examination is held, for only the best men are wanted. The nature of Police duties makes this important. The Force has always been one into which entrance is purposely made difficult, and rightly so. There is no room in it for the weak and incompetent, for the coward or waverer; its traditions demand picked, resolute men who shall uphold its name and honour worthily. The Police themselves may resent a great deal of the sentimental " guff " that has been written in their praise, presenting them in an altogether false light, but they are very justly jealous of their reputation, of being styled " a corps that is unique in the military history of the world."

Let us follow a recruit from the date of his acceptance and his signing on for the required engagement of five years. In the first place he will take the oath of allegiance, together with the oath of office, which runs as follows :— " I, A.B., solemnly swear that I will faithfully, diligently, and impartially execute and perform the duties required of me as a member of the Royal North-West Mounted Police Force, and will well and truly obey and perform all lawful orders and instructions which I shall receive as such, without fear, favour, or affection of or toward any person. So help me, God." Then—if he be not there already—he will be sent to the headquarters at Regina, to be supplied with his kit and started on the road to acquire a Police education. Henceforward he will be

[1] See Appendix H.

IN BARRACKS

known as "Regimental Number 00123, John Jones," or whatsoever his name may be.

The kit, which is a free issue to every recruit, is a complete cavalry man's outfit, with, in addition, a supply of warm underclothing, fur cap, fur coat, buckskin mitts, moccasins, etc. For service in the Yukon and far northern districts an extra kit is of course provided.

Riding and drilling at the first mostly occupy the recruit's attention. In both of these departments he commences in the "awkward squad," and must work his way up to No. 1 squad or No. 1 ride. The question of horsemanship is of the greatest importance, as so much of his time will be spent in the saddle. Up to the end of last year this part of the curriculum was in the hands of the late Inspector Frank Church, than whom no better riding instructor could be found. An army man of sound experience (he was formerly Rough-riding Corporal-Major in the Royal Horse Guards, "the Blues"), Inspector Church took over the riding school at Regina shortly after enlisting in the Mounted Police in 1897, and worked his way up through all ranks to a commission.

The horses used in the Force are almost entirely plains-bred, the original "broncho" of the country having been improved by a thoroughbred strain. From four to five years is the age when they are taken on, and they spend a full year (if possible) at headquarters to be thoroughly broken in and trained before being sent out to other stations. Tough and wiry animals, standing about fifteen hands, these bronchos come mainly from the Albertan ranches. Very few horses of Eastern stock have been bought for years past, as these have not been found equal to the Western bred horses in endurance and hardiness.

THE RIDERS OF THE PLAINS

To comprehend to what a perfection of training bronchos can be brought one must see them in the field, lying down at the word of command while their riders use them as covers whence to fire, or performing intricate evolutions in a "musical ride." It has been said that an exhibition of a musical ride by a picked squad of the Mounted Police is equal to any that a cavalry regiment of the Imperial service can furnish, and indeed it would be hard to beat. In their scarlet tunics, brown "Stetson" hats, with lances topped with bright fluttering pennons, and mounted on glossy, well-groomed horses, blacks, browns, and greys, the troopers make an effective picture as they circle and form sections in the various movements of the ride.

More prosaic and uninteresting duties connected with his horse that the recruit must perform will be the grooming of his mount and, on certain days, having to act as stable guard. The stables are seen to regularly three times a day. He must learn, too, how to clean all harness, how to saddle and unsaddle a horse, how to shoe it, and how to care for it in the various conditions of his work in and out of barracks. A smattering of veterinary knowledge is essential, and this is imparted to him by the veterinary inspector on the instructional staff.

It may be noted here that the Mexican stock saddle is now used exclusively in the Force, this type, after experiment, having been found to be most serviceable. The bit that has been adopted is the Whitman, which is fastened to the bridle with two snaps. This can be whipped out of the animal's mouth, to allow him to feed, without removing the bridle. The picket rope is thirty feet long, giving the horse a circle with a diameter of sixty feet.

A day's routine at Regina in brief is as follows:

IN BARRACKS

Revéillé, 5.30 a.m.; stables, 6 to 7; breakfast, 7.15; rides and drills, 8.30 to 11.30 (including lectures on various subjects); mid-day stables, 11.30 to 12.30; dinner, 12.45; rides, drills, and lectures, 1.30 to 4.0; tea, 4.15; evening stables, 4.45 to 5.30. "Lights out" is sounded at 10.15 p.m. Extra duties that are entailed are, escorts on prisoners who are employed in various ways in the barracks; night-guard, from 6.30 p.m. till revéillé; and night-guards over the prison and stables. All the gates at the Police posts are closed at sundown, those at Regina being three in number, the north, south, and west gates.

In the acquirement of his training as a Police constable the recruit has to pass through the hands of other instructors besides the riding master and the adjutant who exercises him in drills. There are courses of musketry instruction to be gone through, and daily lectures on all manner of Police duties to be attended. For this purpose a capable staff is provided at headquarters.

"The efficient training of a recruit," says the Commissioner in an official Order, "requires twelve months. He must be drilled, set up, taught to ride (cavalry fashion), to shoot with a carbine and revolver, acquire a knowledge of his duties and powers as a Police officer, be instructed in simple veterinary knowledge, understand how a horse should be taken care of, and become an efficient prairie man, by which is implied a smattering of cooking, and the ability to find his way about and to look after the comfort of himself and his horse."

This is the ideal. In practice the recruit more often than not has to leave the dépôt with less than six months' service to his credit. Time does not allow of the full measure of training being undergone. This is an unfortunate state of things, and can only be remedied, as has been pointed out, by an augmentation of the Force.

A further comment of the Commissioner with regard to the class of recruits desired is very much to the point. He says : " The men of this force are now largely employed on independent duty, free from the immediate control of their superiors. They have important duties to perform, and the public rightly expect from them a high standard of conduct. We therefore must have trustworthy, trained men, full of energy and of sound judgment. I am forced to the conclusion that our present system of recruiting does not altogether secure that class. Although we get many excellent men, there are too many ' wasters.' There are three reasons : the long engagement of five years, the rate of pay, and the severe discipline. The term of service should be reduced to three years, and such a substantial increase made to the pay of efficient men as will persuade them to join and serve out the full term of their engagement. The bonds of discipline cannot be relaxed, for it is the solid foundation on which our efficiency rests, but with a more universally reliable class of recruits, better paid, and under shorter conditions of service, the disciplinary powers of the Act would be less required, and the possibility of dismissal a greater deterrent. A reduction in the wastage means a better trained force of longer service and increased efficiency."

The course of lectures which a recruit attends during his residence at Regina embraces a wide range of subjects. He is instructed on the duties of constables generally, the Criminal Code and other Federal laws which apply to the Territories, such as the Indian Act, Customs Act, Fisheries Act, Railway and Dominion Lands Acts, and the ordinances passed by the local legislature of each

A "MUSICAL RIDE" SQUAD, REGINA.
The late Inspector F. Church, riding instructor, in foreground.

IN BARRACKS

Province. An important feature is the procedure of a Magistrate's Court and the conduct of a prosecution. Constables are carefully coached in the handling of a case, being shown how to question witnesses and bring out the salient points.

In itself the criminal law requires considerable expounding, for the Policeman must be well posted in his powers as a peace officer. Whenever possible a demonstration of an imaginative character is given, in order to fix the lesson more firmly in the hearer's mind. Thus, a supposed crime is reported, and constables are asked to say what action they would take. The whole thing is followed up step by step, and under the guidance of the Inspector in charge of the class they are shown what should be done in such circumstances.

Under some of the Ordinances of each Province the Police are given *ex officio* positions by virtue of being members of the Force. These ordinances are very thoroughly explained to them, so that they know what they may and may not do. Every constable on entering the service is given a Manual, from which he learns all the elementary part of his duties; the instructional classes perfect him in this knowledge, and train him to the further use of his powers.

So much for class work. The recruit will find relief from this side of his training in target practice on the rifle range. Having learnt the mechanism of his weapon, he is next taught to shoot at given distances—200, 500, 600, and 800 yards. Disappearing targets are used for the purpose. In the mounted squads the constables are taken a mile away from the targets (which appear for one minute) and started towards them at a gallop. They then have to dismount, judging the distances themselves, fire, remount, and gallop on again to repeat the same process. The targets appear and disappear four times in the mile at unknown ranges.

In revolver practice, no less important than the carbine, the recruit is taught how to use it on foot, and how to shoot while mounted, at a walk, full gallop, and sudden halt. These four methods are taken consecutively in one lesson, the target being from twenty-five to thirty-five yards distant.

The importance of proficiency in rifle and revolver shooting is a point upon which the present Commissioner has laid much emphasis. He himself, it may be said, is a crack shot with both weapons, and has headed the list in the annual target practice of the Dépôt Division. Regular target practice is encouraged at all the divisional posts, and for some years past regimental matches have been held to stimulate marksmanship among members of the Force. At these meetings several valuable trophies are competed for. One of these is a silver cup presented by the Earl of Minto, the Honorary Commissioner.

As a further step in instructional work, the experiment was tried a few years ago of bringing in to headquarters two non-commissioned officers from each division. These underwent a course in general and veterinary knowledge. The former course included : a summary of constables' duties, detachment duty, discipline, duties in barracks, interior economy of the Force, the preparation of reports and vouchers, etc., correspondence, equitation, map sketching, the making of rough plans, travelling by compass, watch, and stars, drill (mounted and on foot), musketry, driving, first aid, and gymnastics. The veterinary course covered the care and management of horses in barracks, in camp, and on the line of march, the knowledge of the

IN BARRACKS

parts of a horse and the treatment of simple ailments, the fitting of saddlery and harness of all kinds, single, double, and four-in-hand, and the forming of picquets, guards, and Royal Escorts. These special classes proved very successful, and they have been continued with advantage.

Both non-commissioned officers and men are initiated early into the mysteries of a pack outfit, such as is needed for a long patrol. The outfit that a pack pony carries includes tent, bedding, cooking utensils, rations, and forage. All these articles require to be carefully arranged and skilfully fastened. The " diamond " and " squaw " hitches are used for securing the rope, the former taking two men to put it on effectively. The " squaw hitch " can be managed by one man.

What with drilling, riding, both in and outside the large riding-school, and attending lectures, the newly enlisted Policeman does not find time hang heavy upon his hands. In the intervals of duty there is always a good deal of kit cleaning, polishing, and burnishing to be done, for all his accoutrements have to be kept as spick and span as those of a line soldier. There are, moreover, such extra duties as have been referred to. The escort of prisoners while at work round the barracks calls out a number of men daily. Two or three have to be in attendance on each party, who wear the regulation black-and-white check prison trousers of a large draughtboard pattern. These are civil prisoners, be it noted, serving light sentences in the Police cells ; [1] military defaulters are kept quite separate, and given different work to do.

On its lighter side life at Regina has many attractions

---

[1] Convicts in the North-West Territories, sentenced to long terms of imprisonment, are sent to the Stony Mountain Penitentiary, near Winnipeg.

to offer the recruit. The dépôt is a complete establishment, with administrative buildings, officers' quarters, barracks for the men, riding-school, stables, guard-house, and church, and conveniences for recreation have not been overlooked. There is a good-sized concert hall, where entertainments are given; a well-equipped gymnasium; a large ground for cricket, football, and baseball in their seasons; while in the canteen are billiard tables and a piano. There is, in addition, a reading-room, well stocked with magazines and papers, and a library of several hundred volumes.

In the evening, should he be free from guard duty, the recruit may obtain leave to visit the town of Regina, about two miles from the barracks. For this he is required to wear the walking-out dress of scarlet tunic, yellow-striped blue trousers, and "Stetson" hat, and to carry a military cane. The small forage cap is for use in the barracks only. On Saturdays, with the riding-master's permission, he may take out a horse from the stables and enjoy a gallop on the prairie, which stretches far and wide round the post. Here he is at liberty to go in whatever direction he chooses, the town itself being alone barred to him.

As the headquarters of the Force, Regina is the best equipped divisional post in the Territories, but everything that is possible is done to bring the other posts into line with it. Canteens are provided, with reading-rooms and libraries, billiard tables, and apparatus for various games, with which the men may occupy their leisure hours. Such fines as are inflicted for breaches of discipline are devoted to a fund which is applied to the establishment of libraries and recreation rooms, and other objects of benefit to the Force.

IN BARRACKS

The offences for which a non-commissioned officer or constable of the R.N.W.M.P. is liable to arrest and trial are numerous, and indicative of the rigid discipline imposed. They are :—

1. Disobeying or refusing to obey the lawful command of, or striking, his superior.

2. Oppressive or tyrannical conduct toward his inferior.

3. Intoxication, however slight.

4. Having intoxicating liquor illegally in his possession, or concealed.

5. Directly or indirectly receiving any gratuity, without the Commissioner's sanction, or any bribe.

6. Wearing any party emblem, or otherwise manifesting political partisanship.

7. Overholding any complaint.

8. Mutinous or insubordinate conduct.

9. Unduly overholding any allowance or any of the public money entrusted to him.

10. Misapplying or improperly withholding any money or goods levied under any warrant or taken from any prisoner.

11. Divulging any matter or thing which it is his duty to keep secret.

12. Making any anonymous complaint to the Government or the Commissioner.

13. Communicating, without the Commissioner's authority, either directly or indirectly, to the public press, any matter or thing touching the Force.

14. Wilfully, or through negligence or connivance, allowing any prisoner to escape.

15. Using any cruel, harsh, or unnecessary violence towards any prisoner or other person.

16. Leaving any post on which he has been placed as sentry or on other duty.

17. Deserting or absenting himself from his duties or quarters without leave.

18. Scandalous or infamous behaviour.

19. Disgraceful, profane, or grossly immoral conduct.

20. Violating any standing order, rule, or regulation, or any order, rule, or regulation hereafter made.

21. Any disorder or neglect to the prejudice of morality or discipline, although not specified in this Act,[1] or in any rule or regulation.

Offences that are committed by commissioned officers are tried summarily by the Commissioner, who is empowered to compel the attendance of witnesses.

Although there are many pitfalls in his path, the recruit who goes to Regina to be moulded into an efficient Mounted Policeman has nothing to fear if he keeps his head and "runs straight." He will learn that his officers are gentlemen, one and all, and are prepared to treat him as such provided he conducts himself well. And if he develops quickly into a smart, soldierly constable he may find himself favoured by being selected as some officer's body-servant, in which case he will enjoy certain privileges, as relief from guard and other duties. If, again, he have a useful trade at his finger-ends, such as carpentering, harness-making or repairing, it is quite likely that he will add to his pay.

But, whether this be the case or not, he may rest assured that the life before him for the five years of his engagement will be one eminently suited to a healthy,

[1] "The Mounted Police Act" of 1894, which consolidated all prior legislation on the subject. Members of the Force are not subject to the Army Act and Militia Act, except when serving with regular troops, or "the Active Militia in the Field."

IN BARRACKS

vigorous young man. It will be a life of continuous employment and considerable variety, now in the township, now on the open prairie, exchanging the dull routine of garrison work for the more congenial atmosphere of the trail and the camp; it will be a life, too, which may expose him to no little hardship and peril in the course of duty. In all careers, however, there are drawbacks, and if the would-be Mounted Policeman is content to take the rough with the smooth, one can wish him no happier lot than service in this finest of all irregular corps.

CHAPTER XXI.

THE POLICE OF TO-DAY.

Distribution and strength—Network of posts—A divisional station—More men needed—Multifarious duties—" No complaints "—Present constitution — Comptroller Fred. White, C.M.G. — Equipment — Notable changes in uniform—Arms, past and present—Little-known phases of duty—More relief work—In the Yukon again—The north-west to-day—In the future.

AT the present time, thirty-seven years since their formation, the Royal North-West Mounted Police of Canada are 651 strong, all told—51 officers and 600 non-commissioned officers and constables. They are distributed over Alberta, Saskatchewan, the North-West Territories, and the Yukon Territory, an area which embraces 2,600,000 square miles.[1] The furthest-flung detachments are those at Herschell Island, on the shores of the Arctic Ocean, 2500 miles from headquarters, and at Fullerton, on the north-west corner of Hudson's Bay. That such a small force is scarcely adequate to the heavy demands made upon it will be admitted, but even if the authorised full strength of 800 officers and men were attained, the task of controlling so immense a tract of country would no less compel our admiration.

Looking at the distribution of the Force from a bird's-eye point of view, we see that the provinces and territories in question are covered with a network of posts of varying magnitude. They are divided into twelve main districts,

[1] See Appendix I.

INTERIOR OF CHAPEL, REGINA BARRACKS.

each of which is commanded by an officer who has under him a number of inspectors and other officers stationed at important points. Each one of these divisional posts is thus a centre which maintains communication with its own sub-divisional posts and detachments, and is responsible for the control of the same to the chief dépôt at Regina. So far as human endeavour can make it, the system is perfect.

A divisional post is a self-contained " fort," much on the original principle, with quarters for officers and men, a guard-room which generally serves as the common gaol, stables, storehouses, and other necessary buildings. The minor posts are most of them well-built and well-equipped stations, where once were only rude " shacks " or huts hastily knocked together. Detachments of lesser importance, ranging in number from a single constable to a squad of three or four men under a sergeant, may be quartered in farms or private houses. As a district grows in size, and the need for Police supervision increases, these isolated outposts will develop into bigger and more permanent stations.

The rapid settlement of the north-west in the past few years has brought with it a continuous demand for more particular Police supervision in special areas. This was only to be expected, but to reach the ideal aimed at the strength of the Force would have to be doubled. " I have many pressing applications from points all over the provinces," notes the Commissioner in his latest report to the Government. " I am anxious to meet every reasonable request, especially those from isolated places. I have often felt in refusing that I am doing an injury to the Force, because it tends to create a sentiment in the locality that the Police are not doing their full duty, and that as far as their particular locality is concerned they are of no value. This is a mistaken view to take, but I am bound to say a natural one."

The call for an increase of men, in the circumstances, is not only reasonable—it is urgent. Few will be found to dispute this. The Police have never shirked their share of the work in the development of the western country. On the other hand, one may concede that they have taken on their shoulders many duties which should be performed by other bodies. Much has been said on this point already. In addition to what may be termed regular police duties, they are responsible for the maintenance of common gaols, the escorting of prisoners to trial, the attendance upon all criminal courts, the service of all criminal processes, and the escorting of lunatics to asylums.

Besides all this, they render to certain departments of the Government valuable assistance, which imposes no light work upon the weaker detachments. They still furnish escorts for the payment of treaty money to the Indians, and attend all such distributions of money and rations. On these occasions the presence of a few constables is more or less imperative, as at these times the Indians are apt to quarrel among themselves and grow dissatisfied with their allowances.

In the Department of Agriculture, some of the work of the quarantine branch devolves upon the Police. Owing to the large importation of stock a great deal of vigilance is needed, and the Police Veterinary staff are constantly employed. Up to July 1907, these officers were charged with the duty of enforcing the Animals Contagious Diseases Act, but since that date the Department has appointed its own inspectors for the purpose.

THE POLICE OF TO-DAY

There is much, however, to be done in preventing the grazing of American cattle on Canadian soil, such encroachments frequently leading to trouble among stock-owners. The Police further assist the authorities by making detailed reports upon the crops and cattle in various districts, and the suitability of land for development in farming or ranching, and by distributing seed grain among new settlers, while they also see that the game laws are obeyed, to prevent the wanton destruction of deer, wood buffalo, and other animals.

For the Department of the Interior they supply patrols to collect timber dues in the absence of proper agents, and to guard against the depredations of timber thieves. At the big forest reserves at Rosseau River, Riding Mountain, and Moose Mountain, and in the entire Prince Albert district, R.N.W.M.P. officers are always on the alert to see that no infringement of the law takes place. They also receive application for permits to cut timber, and forward the same with affidavits to the Dominion Lands Agent.

What help has been, and still is, afforded the Customs Department need not be recapitulated here. The heaviest part of this duty naturally falls to those posts on or near the international boundary line, where smuggling is so prevalent. Some outposts, such as Marienthal (formerly Dupuis), Wood Mountain, Willow Creek, Pendant d'Oreille, and Twin Lakes, are ports of entry, and the members of the Force stationed there are acting customs officers. Nor is the collection of revenue the only task these perform. Pack-trains and travellers crossing the frontier have to be taken note of and, if needed, " let passes " issued to them. All along the border there is constant patrolling, so that rarely does a newcomer into Canadian territory escape the notice of the Police. If a fresh trail is observed a constable will quickly follow it up, overhaul the travellers, and examine them and their baggage, to assure himself that all is in order before the party is allowed to proceed.

Along with this rigorous inspection of strangers goes the regular patrol of all districts wherever there are settlers. All over the prairie country, at stated intervals, mounted constables ride from homestead to homestead to see that all is well with their inmates. Each is provided with a patrol sheet, on which the settler is required to enter any complaint that he may have to make. If nothing has happened that deserves to be brought under the notice of the Police, the constable fills in the form "No complaints," and the other signs it. These patrol sheets are duly handed in to the officers of the posts, and matters requiring investigation are promptly attended to. To foreign settlers especially, who are new to the conditions of the country, the occasional visit of a Mounted Policeman is doubly welcome. The constable, more often than not, is a man of considerable experience, and out of his fund of knowledge he can advise and help the homesteader in the building of his shack, the herding of his stock, the planting of his land, and in a score of other ways of which the outside world is little cognisant.

Every month the Superintendent of a district makes a return to headquarters, giving full information as to the work performed by his command in these various respects. By this means the Commissioner is put into possession of a complete knowledge of all that is transpiring in the divisions, and, so to speak, is enabled to keep a tight hold upon the reins. Every report thus sent in to him may be taken as a comprehensive history of the area affected, nothing being considered too insignificant for note. In

THE POLICE OF TO-DAY

the whole of these *dossiers*, therefore, ranging over a period of twelve months, we have a fairly exhaustive record of the country's progress in that time. Too much emphasis can hardly be laid upon this side of Police work.

As it stands to-day, the Royal North-West Mounted Police Force has changed little, if at all, from its original constitution. Although many people regard it as a military body, it remains still a civil one, being a branch of the civil Government of the Dominion. In this respect it resembles the Royal Irish Constabulary, a corps on which to some extent it was modelled. Directly under the control of the Premier and President of the Privy Council, the Right Hon. Sir Wilfrid Laurier, it has for its permanent official head the Comptroller of the Force, Lieut.-Colonel Frederick White, C.M.G., who has been associated with the Force since its inception.

Mr. White, as he then was, was appointed to the charge of the Mounted Police by Sir John Macdonald, to whom he acted as Private Secretary, and retained his position under all the successive administrations. To him in a great measure is due the deservedly high reputation for efficiency which the Force enjoys. In 1883 he was given the rank and status of a deputy head of department, a further recognition of his long and valued service being accorded to him in 1901, when he received the rank of Lieutenant-Colonel in the Active Militia. In the following year he was honoured with the decoration of a Companion of the Order of St. Michael and St. George.

The executive command of the R.N.W.M.P. is held by the Commissioner, who ranks as a lieutenant-colonel. Below this officer is the Assistant-Commissioner, with the rank of a major and, after three years' service, with that of a lieutenant-colonel. Next in order come Super-

THE RIDERS OF THE PLAINS

intendents (ranking as captains), in command of divisions, and Inspectors (ranking as lieutenants).[1] The former were originally styled Inspectors, while the grade immediately beneath them in rank were known as Sub-Inspectors. This last title was abolished many years ago, and the above nomenclature instituted. These, together with the medical staff of Surgeons, Assistant-Surgeons, and Veterinary Surgeons, comprise the commissioned officers. The non-commissioned officers are, as in the regular army, sergeant-majors, staff-sergeants of various kinds, sergeants, and corporals. The troopers, as is well known, are called constables, the grade of sub-constable having disappeared.

Offices that have become obsolete or that have been merged into others are those of Paymaster and Quartermaster. Since 1877 the duties formerly carried out by these have been relegated to the officers commanding divisions. In the same year, 1877, the post of Veterinary Surgeon was abolished, but it was revived later when the need for such an official arose, and in due course an addition was made to this branch of the service by the appointment of several veterinary staff-sergeants.

It is in the equipment of the Mounted Police that most changes have taken place. As the nature of their work has altered with the growth of the country, so has there been a gradual evolution in their uniform and arms. This is a matter which has been dealt with in part in previous chapters ; it will be well now to sketch the development of these features in full.

The full-dress uniform as originally worn by the Police

[1] Superintendents, and a certain number of Inspectors who are appointed, act as Justices of the Peace. The Commissioner has the powers of a stipendiary magistrate.

THE POLICE OF TO-DAY

in 1874, and for many years after, was a very showy one. It was something like that of an English dragoon, consisting of scarlet tunic, of the loose Norfolk jacket pattern once in vogue in the army, and without facings, grey (later blue) cloth breeches with a broad yellow stripe down the side, long brown riding-boots, and a white helmet with a glittering brass spike. For undress head-gear the trooper wore the smart-looking " pill-box " forage cap, which was at one time so popular in the regular service. There was also provided a brown duck fatigue suit for summer use, and for cold or wet weather a long blue cavalry cloak and cape. In the winter the regulation dress included fur cap, buckskin mitts, moosehide moccasins, and long woollen stockings. While on outdoor duty the Policeman was protected by a thick buffalo coat, until this was superseded by one of black Russian lambskin.

The officers' full dress was at first the same as that of the troopers, with the addition of gold lace. As a result of representations made to headquarters a more elaborate uniform was sanctioned. The commissioned ranks were now resplendent in a scarlet cloth tunic of the hussar pattern, with handsome trimmings of gold lace and braid, and a gold lace belt. On the helmet were long drooping plumes of horse-hair similar to those of a Lifeguardsman, while black " jack " boots, white gauntlets, a cavalry sword, and sabretache richly ornamented with gold lace, heightened the effect. The sabretache was further adorned with the corps' badge, which consists of a buffalo's head encircled by maple leaves, and bearing the motto " Maintiens le Droit " beneath. The breeches were at first of yellow cord, then blue cloth, with a yellow stripe running down the side. At about the time the tunic coat was adopted, this pattern took the place of the

" frock or Norfolk jacket " type worn by non-commissioned officers and men. It was considered to be smarter and neater in appearance.

As time went on the uniform of both officers and men gave rise to a great deal of discussion. For one thing, the helmet was considered too heavy and cumbersome, and its disadvantages were felt to outweigh any compensating effect of " dressiness " which it might be thought to possess. All ranks joined in the request that this headgear should be done away with. In 1880 Colonel Macleod, the retiring Commissioner, wrote in his annual report: " The uniform, clothing, and boots supplied to the Force last year were very good ; the underclothing particularly so. I think that a light grey felt hat would be preferable to the helmet. Very few wear the latter unless obliged to. On trips they are almost invariably carried in the waggons, and get greatly damaged by the knocking about. The men always wear felt hats when they can." It was to be some time, however, before the helmet was to be officially discarded.

The desirability of the red coat for general Police wear was also a much debated question. One Commissioner after another commented on this. In the early days, when the hardest pioneer work in the north-west was being undertaken, the significance carried by the " soldier dress " was of the highest importance. The impression it conveyed to the Indian mind, as has been said before, was the principal reason for its adoption. Where it failed to give satisfaction was in its usefulness as a working dress. Commissioner Irvine saw no necessity, he said, to do away with the tunic entirely — it could be used still on full-dress parades ; but he suggested that for general wear a working suit of brown duck should be

THE POLICE OF TO-DAY

adopted, such as was then being worn by some of the troops in South Africa.

The need for radical alterations in the field dress became more and more urgent. Divisional officers and others added their voices to the general protest. One pattern, which was considered to be the best fitted for Police work, was what was termed a " prairie dress," which was to consist of " dark brown cord or velveteen breeches, long boots and spurs, a heavy flannel shirt, over which a stable jacket could be worn when required, and a broad-rimmed hat of soft felt to complete the outfit." The regular uniform could be saved for parade, and for duty in settled districts where less rough work was entailed.

About 1898 a brown duck service suit was issued for wear about barracks, but this did not give universal satisfaction. It was of little use in prairie work, except for short trips in summer. In the following year Superintendent Cotton was again hammering the point into the authorities, urging the adoption of a really serviceable uniform. "I would renew," he wrote, "my previously made recommendation in favour of a prairie suit of some neutral colour. A loose Norfolk jacket (with plenty of pockets) made of light, soft cord, with riding breeches of the same material, would answer our purpose admirably."

These insistent demands at length had the desired result. By an Order in Council the following changes came into force on 1st January 1901: Discarded—helmet, forage cap, white gloves and gauntlets, tunic, black boots, cloak and cape, black fur cap, black lambskin coat, moccasins. Adopted—felt hat, service cap, brown gloves and gauntlets, brown boots (Strathcona pattern), brown ankle boots, field service jacket, field service pantaloons, fur cap

(Klondike pattern), elk mitts, with woollen mitts worn inside, felt boots and black stockings, pea jackets, slicker and sou-wester. The object in view was of course to make the uniform of more practical utility and adapted to the service throughout the Territories. Pipeclay and blacking were to be done away with. Gloves and boots of brown leather could be more easily cleaned.

In dispensing with the forage cap, as well as with the helmet, the authorities showed wisdom. Outside fatigue work in and about barracks it was of very little use. In the summer, on the open prairie, it afforded its wearer no shade from the hot sun, and in wet weather it gave no protection from rain. Also, when soaked, it speedily lost its shape. The forage cap, indeed, was suited for fatigue work alone, and it is only for this purpose that at the present day its use is sanctioned.

That most important—and, it must be admitted, picturesque—hat, the "Stetson," eventually solved the problem of a suitable headgear. This hat is of the well-known "cowboy" pattern, broad-rimmed and light and comfortable to the head. For summer wear it is in general use, both for practical work and for parade.

To-day, then, the summer field service uniform of a Mounted Policeman consists of a khaki suit, with brown belt and high-laced brown boots, breeches of navy blue, having a 2-inch yellow stripe down the side, a Stetson hat, and brown, or russet, gauntlets. The scarlet serge tunic, with black gorget patches, is worn for dress parades and for walking-out purposes. For winter, fur caps and coats, with pea jackets if required, and moccasins, with thick woollen stockings, form the customary dress.

Owing to the heavy expense incurred by their former elaborate uniforms, those of officers have similarly undergone

THE POLICE OF TO-DAY

many changes. The gold lace was considerably reduced, and a plainer tunic of the dragoon officer's pattern adopted for full dress. Among other things, the sabretache has disappeared. For hat, the Stetson is often used in the field, but for other occasions a cap of the Guards' type, with peak and gold band, embroidered according to rank, is worn. Officers of the medical and veterinary staff have a red, instead of gold, band to their caps.

For undress, officers still wear the blue patrol jacket with braided breast and hanging tabs that was instituted in the early days of the force.

From the earlier chapters of this book the reader has already learned that the arms used by the Mounted Police were originally the Snider carbine and the Adams revolver. For some years these proved equal to the rough work for which they were wanted, but in the course of time yielded to Winchester carbines (of ·45 calibre) and Enfield revolvers of a more accurate pattern. The carbine was later much improved upon, and continued to give satisfaction until certain defects made themselves obvious.

In 1890 Commissioner Herchmer made the following report upon the small arms in use : " Our Enfield revolvers are in excellent order, and answer the purpose very well, but the ammunition is too strong, and they shoot rather high, at short distances particularly. The small revolvers in use at railroad stations are also very good, and I have asked for some more. The Winchester carbines are still employed, and are still complained of. They, however, answer our purpose very well, and with close supervision and a considerable number of new barrels, which are being put in, will last for some time longer.

"Last winter (1889–90) Morris tubes were sent to Regina, and during the winter months the recruits derived great benefit from using them, and many of them in the spring proved excellent shots with the Winchester."

Five years later experiments were made with the Lee-Metford rifle, with the result that some of these weapons were introduced into the Force. Writing at the end of 1896, Commissioner Herchmer said: " Our Winchester carbines are in about the same condition as last year. By providing new barrels and parts worn out they will last some time, and for short ranges, up to 400 yards, they are well adapted for our work. Beyond this range the Lee-Metfords are very much more accurate; in fact, beyond 500 yards, the Winchesters are of little use. The sighting of the Winchester carbines is most defective, they nearly all shoot too low, and paper, or some other substance, has to be placed under the backsight to ensure any accuracy at target practice. We used American Winchester ammunition entirely, and it was of good quality."

The chief faults of the Winchester were its liability to get out of order, its tendency to break off at the stock, and the temptation it offered young recruits to waste their fire.

In 1900, when Commissioner Perry succeeded Colonel Herchmer in the command of the Police, the question of re-arming the Force was again taken up. In his first annual report (1901) he wrote: " D Division alone has the Lee-Metford carbine, all others being armed with the obsolete Winchester carbine and Enfield revolver. Carbines and revolvers have been in use a long time, and the rifling is worn out." Some of the Winchesters in the Yukon Territory were reported to be badly honeycombed. " If the corps is to be armed," continued the Commissioner, " it ought to be well armed. Without accurate arms there cannot be good shooting; without good shooting

THE POLICE OF TO-DAY

carrying arms is an anomaly. A change of the arms will call for a change in equipment. At present, when the revolver is worn, ammunition for the carbine must be taken whether the carbine is carried or not."

In 1903 such progress had been made that the Commissioner was able to announce that the Government had decided to re-arm the entire Force with modern weapons. Sir Charles Ross had submitted for trial two rifles, one with 28-inch barrel, and one with 25-inch barrel, the action being the same in each. The essential difference between the Ross rifle and the Lee-Metford, which was the pattern used in the Imperial service, lay in the bolt action. In the Ross the bolt is withdrawn and closed by a straight pull, whereas in the Lee-Metford the bolt is revolved through a quarter circle, either in opening or closing. Both have the same barrel and use the same ammunition.

After comparisons had been made with Winchester carbines, Lee-Metford and Mauser rifles, the Board of Officers which sat to inquire into the matter recommended the adoption of the Ross weapon, subject to certain minor alterations. The new rifle was of the following pattern: Length, from heel of butt to muzzle, 3 ft. $9\frac{1}{4}$ in.; length of barrel, 25 in.; distance between fore and back sights, $20\frac{3}{16}$ in.; length of stock, $14\frac{1}{5}$ in.; weight, 7 lb. 8 oz. Since then the Ross rifle (of calibre ·303) has continued to be the standard weapon of the Force, an improved pattern having been recently issued, but in some divisions the Lee-Metford and Winchester carbines are still used. In late years the ·45 Colt revolver has taken the place of the Enfield, and proved highly serviceable.

A new pattern of equipment also has been issued, its advantage being that the weight of the revolver is properly adjusted, and the rifle ammunition is not carried in the belt. For the latter a bandolier is worn.

Two arms that were recommended for use in the Force on its organisation in 1873 were the lance and the sword. A certain number of the former weapon were issued to the men on the occasion of the great march into the west under Colonel French, but the lance never found favour. At the present time it is employed only in drill and in the musical rides. The sword, similarly, was condemned soon after the Police arrived in the Territories.

It was felt that this weapon would be too much of an incumbrance to a Policeman in the exercise of his duty, and it was, of course, requisite that the number and weight of arms carried by each man should be reduced to a minimum consistent with efficiency. The only swords, therefore, in use now are those which officers are entitled to wear, these being of the familiar English cavalry pattern.

On the heavier side of its armament the Force possesses several 12-pounder and 7-pounder mountain guns, of which some are at Regina and some at Calgary. The old 9-pounder M.L.R. guns are practically obsolete. At Fort Macleod in the old days were two small mortars, but these were rarely, if at all, called into service.

Enough has now been said to give the reader a fairly clear idea of what the Royal North-West Mounted Police of to-day are, and what they do. It remains only to touch upon one or two sides of their work that have not yet received full attention. Little, perhaps, is known to the public of how the Police relieve distress when cases of a more or less acute nature are brought under their notice. In the olden days, when settlements were few and far between, the Police hospitals were filled with civilian patients, and Police surgeons were called upon to do the bulk of

THE POLICE OF TO-DAY

their work outside the Force. In the Yukon, as we have seen, in the first years of the rush, they were ever to the fore to render assistance to the destitute and sick ; in the Territories to-day this duty, especially in the winter-time, frequently devolves upon them. At Battleford, one severe winter, a large number of settlers' families were relieved, but for which the suffering must have been very great.

Some cases of destitution spring from the utter ignorance and incompetence of settlers who are new to the country. While out with a relief patrol in a district about a hundred miles north of the Saskatchewan, where much distress was reported to be, Inspector Knight found one Scottish family, consisting of a man, his wife, and three children, in a terrible state. It was mid-winter, and the new arrivals had made absolutely no provision for the bad time they had to face. They had no winter clothing, no fire, and little food. The youngest of the children, a baby about a year old, was almost dying. Thanks to the care of the Police patrol the lives of all were saved, and the settler was given a good start for the future.

Here, too, is a characteristic instance quoted by Superintendent M'Gibbon, of the Battleford District, in his report for 1907 : " On 17th December Inspector Genereux and Constable Tasker, with guide, left for the south of Tramping Lake to investigate the reported shortage of fuel, and destitution. On the trip he found a family consisting of Jas. Tait, wife and sister and seven children, without food or firewood, not even an axe to cut wood. They were supplied with what provisions could be spared by the Police. This family was actually starving. On this being reported to me, I sent a party from here on 27th December, Constables Burke, Townsend, and Foster, with provisions and clothing. This party returned on 8th January, travelling being slow, some days only eight miles could be made on account of the snow. On arriving at Tait's they found the family entirely out of food and firing; they had given up all hope, and were huddled together in the centre of the floor, trying to keep one another warm. There was wood to be got three miles off, but they had no means of hauling it, and the snow was too deep to get at it. Constable Burke and party hauled them a supply of firewood."

A new phase of duty that has arisen in recent years is the patrolling of certain lakes and rivers, which has necessitated the use of steamers and other craft. The R.N.W.M.P. steamer, the *Vidette*, has done good service on the Yukon River for many years, being usually the first boat to pass between White Horse and Dawson on the breaking up of the ice. In the same Territory there are two launches, the *Jessie* and the *Gladys*, which render valuable service on the Yukon, Hootalinqua, and other rivers. One of these is a gasolene launch, the other being propelled by steam. A duty which these craft have to perform is the convoy of the fleet of small boats that pass down the river in the spring, following the ice as it goes out. The Police officers on board have to lend a hand if a boat gets into difficulties, see that all camp fires are extinguished on the banks before the campers move on, and preserve law and order among the new-comers.

Another Police boat is maintained on Lake Winnipeg, in order to protect the fisheries. Regular patrols are made round this big sheet of water, and a very useful service to the Government is thus rendered.

With regard to the Police detachments in the Yukon, it is interesting to note the variety of duties that until recently fell to their lot. A summary of their work

"NO COMPLAINTS."

A settler on the prairie signing a Policeman's Patrol Sheet.

(From the picture painted by Paul Wickson for the Dominion Department of Agriculture.)

THE POLICE OF TO-DAY

included the following: Patrols, rescue work, care of asylums, penitentiaries, and prisoners, bailiffs for the sheriff, court bailiffs, patrolmen in Dawson and other towns, health officers, mining recorders, mining inspectors, timber agents, royalty collectors, customs-house agents, gold-dust inspectors, baggage inspectors, magistrates, coroners, mail carriers to many outlying camps, including such distant places as Kluahne, Livingstone Creek, Duncan and Glacier, and postmasters at the smaller posts on rivers and trails. Most of these extraneous duties consumed more than half the time and attention of all ranks, and until the Police were relieved of them the reduction in the Yukon Force that has since taken place could not be accomplished. The strength in the Territory is now 74, and but little aid is rendered other departments. In a few places, however, the detachments continue to act as mining recorders and Crown timber and land agents, while civil processes are still served everywhere by the Police.

In the north-west the troublous times are over. There is peace among the Indian tribes, a sense of security among the settlers far and wide. The provinces of Alberta and Saskatchewan are on the high road to prosperity, but the day when they will be able to stand alone without the assistance of the Mounted Police is still far distant. According to arrangement the employment of the Force within their borders will expire on 1st April 1911, but the governments of both provinces have petitioned that it shall be continued for another five years, that is, until 1916.[1] This request will be granted without doubt, and that it should be made is highly indicative of the value placed upon the services of the Police.

[1] In Alberta there are five divisional posts and sixty-four detachments; in Saskatchewan four divisional posts and seventy-eight detachments.

THE RIDERS OF THE PLAINS

In view of this condition of things, and the fact that the disbandment of the Force has been contemplated before, the question may well be asked : How long will the Mounted Police be required in the north-west ? To this there can be but one answer, and it is an answer which the provinces and territories have given unanimously. So long as the settlement of the western country goes on, so long will the presence of the Police be needed. Certainly no other body, civil or military, could so efficiently and so economically carry out the same duties. The bulk of the work has been done, perhaps, but many years of strenuous labour have still to be faced before Finis can be written to this chapter of Canadian history, and the Mounted Police may be relied upon to complete the task which they so bravely began. In this their high prestige will stand them in good stead. And even when the end is reached, and the yet un-unbroken prairie is covered with flourishing homesteads and fields of waving grain, it may be safely assumed that the Force will survive, symbolical representatives of the law and order which it has been their mission and their destiny to create.

APPENDICES

APPENDIX A.

LIST OF N.W.M.P. OFFICERS EMPLOYED ON THE WESTWARD MARCH OF 1874.

Lieut.-Colonel George A. French, Commissioner.

Major James F. Macleod, C.M.G., Assistant-Commissioner.

Staff: J. G. Kittson, M.D., Surgeon; Dr. R. B. Nevitt, Assistant-Surgeon; W. G. Griffiths, Paymaster; G. Dalrymple Clark, Adjutant; John L. Poett, Veterinary Surgeon; Charles Nicolle, Quartermaster.

  A Division: W. D. Jarvis, Inspector; Severe Gagnon, Sub-Inspector.

  B Division: G. A. Brisebois, Inspector; J. B. Allan, Sub-Inspector.

  C Division: W. Winder, Inspector; T. R. Jackson, Sub-Inspector.

  D Division (Staff Division): J. M. Walsh, Inspector; J. Walker and J. French, Sub-Inspectors.

  E Division: J. Carvell, Inspector; J. H. M'Illree and H. J. N. Le Caine, Sub-Inspectors.

  F Division: L. N. F. Crozier, Inspector; V. Welsh and C. R. Denny, Sub-Inspectors.

APPENDIX B.

THE TREATY WITH THE BLACKFEET, NUMBER SEVEN.

Articles of a Treaty made and concluded this twenty-second day of September, in the year of our Lord one thousand eight hundred and seventy-seven, between Her Most Gracious Majesty the Queen of Great Britain and Ireland, by her Commissioners, the Honourable David Laird, Lieutenant-Governor and Indian Superintendent of the North-West Territories, and James Farquharson Macleod, C.M.G., Commissioner of the North-West Mounted Police, of the one part, and the Blackfeet, Blood, Piegan, Sarcee, Stony, and other Indians, inhabitants of the territory north of the United States boundary line, east of the central range of the Rocky Mountains, and south and west of Treaties Numbers Six and Four, by their head Chiefs and minor Chiefs or Councillors, chosen as hereinafter mentioned, of the other part;

WHEREAS the Indians inhabiting the said territory have, pursuant to an appointment made by the said Commissioners, been convened at a meeting at the "Blackfoot Crossing" of the Bow River, to deliberate upon certain matters of interest to Her Most Gracious Majesty, of the one part, and the said Indians of the other;

AND whereas the said Indians have been informed by Her Majesty's Commissioners that it is the desire of Her Majesty to open up for settlement, and such other purposes as to Her Majesty may seem meet, a tract of country, bounded and described as hereinafter mentioned, and to obtain the consent thereto of her Indian subjects inhabiting the said tract, and to make a treaty, and arrange with them, so that there may be peace and goodwill between them and Her Majesty, and between them and Her Majesty's other subjects; and that her Indian people may know and feel assured of what allowance they are to count upon and receive from Her Majesty's bounty and benevolence;

AND whereas the Indians of the said tract, duly convened in council, and being requested by Her Majesty's Commissioners to present their head Chiefs and minor Chiefs, or Councillors, who shall be authorised, on their behalf, to conduct such negotiations and sign any treaty to be founded thereon, and to become responsible to Her Majesty for the faithful performance by their respective bands of such obligations as should be assumed by them, the said Blackfeet, Blood, Piegan, and Sarcee Indians have therefore acknowledged for that purpose, the several head and minor Chiefs, and the said Stony Indians, the Chiefs and Councillors who have subscribed hereto, that thereupon in open council the said Commissioners received and acknowledged the head and minor Chiefs and the Chiefs and Councillors presented for the purpose aforesaid;

AND whereas the said Commissioners have proceeded to negotiate

APPENDIX B

a treaty with the said Indians; and the same has been finally agreed upon and concluded as follows, that is to say: the Blackfeet, Blood, Piegan, Sarcee, Stony, and other Indians, inhabiting the district hereinafter more fully described and defined, do hereby cede, release, surrender, and yield up to the Government of Canada for Her Majesty the Queen and her successors for ever, all their rights, titles, and privileges whatsoever to the lands included within the following limits, that is to say:

Commencing at a point on the international boundary due south of the western extremity of the Cypress Hills; thence west along the said boundary to the central range of the Rocky Mountains, or to the boundary of the Province of British Columbia; thence north-westerly along the said boundary to a point due west of the source of the main branch of the Red Deer River; thence south-westerly and southerly following on the boundaries of the tracts ceded by the Treaties Numbered Six and Four to the place of commencement; and also all their rights, titles, and privileges whatsoever, to all other lands wherever situated in the North-West Territories, or in any other portion of the Dominion of Canada:

To have and to hold the same to Her Majesty the Queen and Her successors for ever:

And Her Majesty the Queen hereby agrees with her said Indians, that they shall have right to pursue their vocations of hunting throughout the tract surrendered as heretofore described, subject to such regulations as may, from time to time, be made by the Government of the country, acting under the authority of Her Majesty; and saving and excepting such tracts as may be required or taken up from time to time for settlement, mining, trading or other purposes by her Government of Canada, or by any of Her Majesty's subjects duly authorised therefor by the said Government.

It is also agreed between Her Majesty and her said Indians that reserves shall be assigned them of sufficient area to allow one square mile for each family of five persons, or in that proportion for larger and smaller families, and that said reserves shall be located as follows, that is to say:

Firstly.—The reserves of the Blackfeet, Blood, and Sarcee bands of Indians shall consist of a belt of land on the north side of the Bow and South Saskatchewan Rivers, of an average width of four miles along said rivers, down stream, commencing at a point on the Bow River twenty miles north-westerly of the "Blackfoot Crossing" thereof, and extending to the Red Deer River at its junction with

THE RIDERS OF THE PLAINS

the South Saskatchewan; also for the term of ten years, and no longer, from the date of the concluding of this treaty, when it shall cease to be a portion of the said Indian reserves, as fully to all intents and purposes as if it had not at any time been included therein, and without any compensation to individual Indians for improvements, of a similar belt of land on the south side of the Bow and Saskatchewan Rivers of an average width of one mile along said rivers, down stream; commencing at the aforesaid point on the Bow River, and extending to a point one mile west of the coal seam on said river, about five miles below the said " Blackfoot Crossing "; beginning again one mile east of the said coal seam and extending to the mouth of Maple Creek at its junction with the South Saskatchewan: and beginning again at the junction of the Bow River with the latter river, and extending on both sides of the South Saskatchewan in an average width on each side thereof of one mile, along said river against the stream, to the junction of the Little Bow River with the latter river, reserving to Her Majesty, as may now or hereafter be required by her for the use of her Indian or other subjects, from all the reserves hereinbefore described, the right to navigate the above-mentioned rivers, to land and receive fuel and cargoes on the shores and banks thereof, to build bridges and establish ferries thereon, to use the fords thereof, and all the trails leading thereto, and to open such other roads through the said reserves as may appear to Her Majesty's Government of Canada necessary for the ordinary travel of her Indian and other subjects, due compensation being paid to individual Indians for improvements, when the same may be in any manner encroached upon by such roads.

Secondly.—That the reserve of the Piegan band of Indians shall be on the Old Man's River, near the foot of the Porcupine Hills, at a place called " Crow's Creek."

And Thirdly.—The reserve of the Stony band of Indians shall be in the vicinity of Morleyville.

In view of the satisfaction of Her Majesty with the recent general good conduct of her said Indians, and in extinguishment of all their past claims, she hereby, through her Commissioners, agrees to make them a present payment of twelve dollars each in cash to each man, woman, and child of the families here represented.

Her Majesty also agrees that next year, and annually afterwards for ever, she will cause to be paid to the said Indians, in cash, at suitable places and dates, of which the said Indians shall be duly

APPENDIX B

notified, to each Chief, twenty-five dollars, each minor Chief or Councillor (not exceeding fifteen minor Chiefs to the Blackfeet and Blood Indians, and four to the Piegan and Sarcee bands, and five Councillors to the Stony Indian bands) fifteen dollars, and to every other Indian of whatever age, five dollars; the same, unless there be some exceptional reason, to be paid to the heads of families for those belonging thereto.

Further, Her Majesty agrees that the sum of two thousand dollars shall hereafter every year be expended in the purchase of ammunition for distribution among the said Indians; provided that if at any future time ammunition became comparatively unnecessary for said Indians, her Government, with the consent of said Indians, or any of the bands thereof, may expend the proportion due to such band otherwise for their benefit.

Further, Her Majesty agrees that each head Chief and minor Chief, and each Chief and Councillor duly recognised as such, shall, once in every three years, during the term of their office, receive a suitable suit of clothing, and each head Chief and Stony Chief, in recognition of the closing of the treaty, a suitable medal and flag, and next year, or as soon as convenient, each head Chief, and minor Chief, and Stony Chief shall receive a Winchester rifle.

Further, Her Majesty agrees to pay the salary of such teachers to instruct the children of said Indians as to her Government of Canada may seem advisable, when said Indians are settled on their reserves and shall desire teachers.

Further, Her Majesty agrees to supply each head and minor Chief, and each Stony Chief, for the use of their bands, ten axes, five handsaws, five augers, one grindstone, and the necessary files and whetstones.

And further, Her Majesty agrees that the said Indians shall be supplied as soon as convenient, after any band shall make due application therefor, with the following cattle for raising stock, that is to say: for every family of five persons, and under, two cows; for every family of more than five persons, and less than ten persons, three cows; for every family of over ten persons, four cows; and every head and minor Chief, and every Stony Chief, for the use of their bands, one bull; but if any band desire to cultivate the soil as well as raise stock, each family of such band shall receive one cow less than the above-mentioned number, and in lieu thereof, when settled on their reserves and prepared to break up the soil, two hoes, one spade, one scythe, and two hay forks, and for every three families, one plough and one harrow, and for each band, enough potatoes, barley, oats, and wheat (if such seeds be suited for the locality of their reserves) to plant the land actually broken up. All the aforesaid articles to be given, once for all, for the encouragement of the practice of agriculture among the Indians.

And the undersigned Blackfeet, Blood, Piegan, and Sarcee head Chiefs and minor Chiefs, and Stony Chiefs and Councillors, on their own behalf and on behalf of all other Indians inhabiting the tract within ceded do hereby solemnly promise and engage to strictly observe this treaty, and also to conduct and behave themselves as good and loyal subjects of Her Majesty the Queen. They promise and engage that they will, in all respects, obey and abide by the law, that they will maintain peace and good order between each other and between themselves and other tribes of Indians, and between themselves and others of Her Majesty's subjects, whether Indians, half-breeds, or whites, now inhabiting, or hereafter to inhabit, any part of the said ceded tract; and that they will not molest the person or property of any inhabitant of such ceded tract, or the property of Her Majesty the Queen, or interfere with or trouble any person, passing or travelling through the said tract or any part thereof, and that they will assist the officers of Her Majesty in bringing to justice and punishment any Indian offending against the stipulations of this treaty, or infringing the laws in force in the country so ceded.

In witness whereof Her Majesty's said Commissioners, and the said Indian head and minor Chiefs, and Stony Chiefs and Councillors, have hereunto subscribed and set their hands, at the "Blackfoot Crossing," the day and year herein first above written.

(Signed) David Laird.
  Gov. of N.W.T., and Special Indian Commissioner.
James F. Macleod,
  Lieut.-Colonel, Com. N.W.M.P., and Special Indian Commissioner.

Chapo-Mexico (or Crowfoot)	His **X** mark.
Head Chief of the South Blackfeet.	
Matose-Apiw (or Old Sun)	„ **X** „
Head Chief of the North Blackfeet.	
Stamixotocon (or Bull Head)	„ **X** „
Head Chief of the Sarcees.	
Mecasto (or Red Crow)	„ **X** „
Head Chief of the South Bloods.	
Natose-Onistors (or Medicine Calf)	„ **X** „

APPENDIX B

Pokapiw-otocon (or Bad Head)	His	**X** Mark.
Sotenah (or Rainy Chief)	,,	**X** ,,
Head Chief of the North Bloods.		
Takoye-Stamix (or Fiend Bull)	,,	**X** ,,
Akka-Kitcipimiw-otas (or Many Spotted Horses)	,,	**X** ,,
Attistah-macan (or Running Rabbit)	,,	**X** ,,
Pitah-pekis (or Eagle Rib)	,,	**X** ,,
Sakoye-aotan (or Heavy Shield)	,,	**X** ,,
Head Chief of the Middle Blackfeet.		
Zoatze-Tapitapiw (or Setting on an Eagle Tail)	,,	**X** ,,
Head Chief of the North Piegans.		
Akka-Makkoye (or Many Swans)	,,	**X** ,,
Apenako-sapop (or Morning Plume)	,,	**X** ,,
*Mas-gwa-ah-Sid (or Bear's Paw)	,,	**X** ,,
*Che-ne-ka (or John)	,,	**X** ,,
*Ki-chi-pwot (or Jacob)	,,	**X** ,,
Stamix-osok (or Bull Back Fat)	,,	**X** ,,
Emitah-Apiskinne (or White-Striped Dog)	,,	**X** ,,
Matapi-Komotziw (or the Captive or Stolen Person)	,,	**X** ,,
Apawawakosow (or White Antelope)	,,	**X** ,,
Makoye-kin (or Wolf Collar)	,,	**X** ,,
Aye-stipis-simat (or Heavily Whipped)	,,	**X** ,,
Kissoum (or Day Light)	,,	**X** ,,
Pitah-otocon (or Eagle Head)	,,	**X** ,,
Apaw-stamix (or Weasel Bull)	,,	**X** ,,
Onistah-pokah (or White Calf)	,,	**X** ,,
Netah-kitei-pi-mew (or Only Spot)	,,	**X** ,,
Akak-otos (or Many Horses)	,,	**X** ,,
Stokimatis (or The Drum)	,,	**X** ,,
Pitah-annes (or Eagle Robe)	,,	**X** ,,
Pitah-otsikin (or Eagle Shoe)	,,	**X** ,,
Stamix-ota-ka-piw (or Bull Turn Round)	,,	**X** ,,
Maste-Pitah (or Crow Eagle)	,,	**X** ,,
†James Dixon	,,	**X** ,,
†Abraham Kechepwot	,,	**X** ,,
†Patrick Kechepwot	,,	**X** ,,
†George Moy-any-men	,,	**X** ,,
†George Crawlor	,,	**X** ,,
Ekas-kine (or Low Horn)	,,	**X** ,,
Kayo-okosis (or Bear Shield)	,,	**X** ,,
Ponokah-stamix (or Bull Elk)	,,	**X** ,,

* Stony (Assiniboine) Chiefs. † Stony Councillors.

Omaksi-Sapop (or Big Plume)	His **X** mark.
Onistah (or Calf Robe)	,, **X** ,,
Pitah-siksinum (or White Eagle)	,, **X** ,,
Apaw-onistaw (or Weasel Calf)	,, **X** ,,
Attista-haes (or Rabbit Carrier)	,, **X** ,,
Pitah (or Eagle)	,, **X** ,,
Pitah-onistaw (or Eagle White Calf)	,, **X** ,,
Kaye-tapo (or Going to Bear)	,, **X** ,,

Signed by the Chiefs and Councillors within named in presence of the following witnesses, the same having first been explained by James Bird, Interpreter :—

 (Signed) A. G. Irvine, Assistant-Commissioner, N.W.M.P.
     J. M'Dougall, Missionary.
     Jean L'Heureux.
     W. Winder,
     L. N. F. Crozier, Inspectors.
     E. Dalrymple Clark, Lieut. and Adjutant, N.W.M.P.
     A. Shurtliff,
     C. E. Dening,
     W. D. Antrobus, Sub-Inspectors.
     Frank Norman, Staff-Constable.
     Mary J. MacLeod.
     Julia Winder.
     Julia Shurtliff.
     E. Hardisty.
     A. M'Dougall.
     E. A. Barrett.
     Constantine Scollen, Priest, witness to signatures of Stamix-osok and those following.
     Charles E. Conrad.
     Thos. J. Bogg.

ADHESION TO TREATY NUMBER SEVEN.

We, the members of the Blackfoot tribe of Indians, having had explained to us the terms of the treaty made and concluded at the Blackfoot Crossing of the Bow River, on the twenty-second day of September, in the year of our Lord one thousand eight hundred and seventy-seven;

Between Her Majesty the Queen, by her Commissioners duly appointed to negotiate the said treaty and the Blackfeet, Piegan, Blood, Sarcee, Stony, and other Indian inhabitants of the country within the limits defined in the said treaty, but not having been present at the Councils at which the articles of the said treaty were

APPENDIX B

agreed upon, do now hereby, for ourselves and the bands which we represent, transfer, surrender, and relinquish to Her Majesty the Queen, her heirs and successors, to and for the use of her Government of Canada, all our right, title, and interest whatsoever, which we and the said bands which we represent have held or enjoyed, of in and to the said territory described and fully set out in the said treaty ; also, all our right, title, and interest whatsoever to all lands wherever situated, whether within the limits of any other treaty heretofore made or hereafter to be made with Indians, or elsewhere in Her Majesty's territories, to have and to hold the same unto and for the use of Her Majesty the Queen, her heirs and successors for ever ;

And we hereby agree to accept the several benefits, payments, and reserves promised to the Indians under the Chiefs adhering to the said treaty at the Blackfoot Crossing of the Bow River, and we solemnly engage to abide by, carry out, and fulfil all the stipulations, obligations, and conditions therein contained on the part of the Chiefs and Indians therein named, to be observed and performed and in all things to conform to the articles of the said treaty, as if we ourselves and the bands which we represent had been originally contracting parties thereto and had been present at the Blackfoot Crossing of the Bow River, and had there attached our signatures to the said treaty.

In witness whereof, James Farquharson Macleod, C.M.G., one of Her Majesty's Commissioners, appointed to negotiate the said treaty, and the Chief of the band, hereby giving their adhesion to the said treaty, have hereunto subscribed and set their hands at Fort Macleod, this fourth day of December, in the year of our Lord one thousand eight hundred and seventy-seven.

    (Signed)   James F. Macleod,
                     Lieut.-Col., Special Indian Commissioner.
                Meanxkistomach (or Three Bulls)   His **X** mark.

Signed by the parties hereto in the presence of the undersigned witnesses, the same having been explained to the Indians by the said James Farquharson Macleod, one of the Commissioners appointed to negotiate the said treaty, through the interpreter, Jerry Potts, in the presence of

    (Signed)   A. G. Irvine,
                     Assistant-Commissioner.
            E. Dalrymple Clark,
                Lieutenant and Adjutant, N.W.M.P.
            W. Winder, Inspector.

APPENDIX C.

LIST OF NON-COMMISSIONED OFFICERS AND MEN OF THE NORTH-WEST MOUNTED POLICE KILLED OR WOUNDED IN THE SUPPRESSION OF THE NORTH-WEST REBELLION.

Reg. No.	Rank and Name.	Engagement.	Date.	Remarks.
			1885.	
—	Supt. Crozier, L. N. F.	Duck Lake .	Mar. 26	Flesh wound in cheek.
—	Inspector Howe, J.	,,	,,	Wound in right leg.
532	Corp. Gilchrist, T. H.	,,	,,	Left thigh fractured.
935	Const. Millar, A.	,,	,,	Wounded.
1117	,, Gordon, S. F.	,,	,,	,,
1048	,, Wood, J. J.	,,	,,	,,
1045	,, Manners-Smith, A.	,,	,,	,,
1003	,, Gibson, T. J.	,,	,,	Killed in action.
1065	,, Arnold, G. P.	,,	,,	Died from wounds.
852	,, Garrett, G. K.	,,	,,	,, ,,
635	,, Cowan, D. L.	Fort Pitt .	April 13	Killed by Indians.
925	,, Loasby, C.	,,	,,	Wounded.
565	Corp. Sleigh, R. B.	Cut-Knife Hill	May 2	Killed in action.
907	,, Lowry, W. H. T.	,, ,,	,,	Died from wounds.
402	Const. Burke, P.	,, ,,	,,	,, ,,
973	,, Elliott, F. O.	,, ,,	,, 14	Killed by Indians.
363	Sergt. Ward, J. H.	,, ,,	,, 2	Wounded.
333	,, Fury, W.	Loon Lake .	,, 28	,,
716	Const. M'Rae, D.	Frenchman's Butte	,, 28	,,

APPENDIX D.

LIST OF COMMISSIONERS OF THE R.N.W.M.P., 1873–1910.

                Name.   Appointed.

1. Lieut.-Col. George Arthur French . . . October 1873.
2. Lieut.-Col. James Farquharson Macleod, C.M.G. . July 1876.
3. Lieut.-Col. Acheson Gosford Irvine . . . November 1880.
4. Laurence W. Herchmer (afterwards Lieut.-Col.) . April 1886.
5. Lieut.-Col. A. Bowen Perry, C.M.G. . . . August 1900.

APPENDIX E.

LIST OF OFFICERS OF THE R.N.W.M.P. AT THE BEGINNING OF THE PRESENT YEAR, 1910.

Name.	Present Rank.	Date of Appointment.
Perry, C.M.G., Aylesworth Bowen	Commissioner	1st Aug. '00.
*M'Illree, John Henry	Assist.-Commr.	1st Nov. '92.
Wood, Zachary Taylor	,, ,,	1st July '02.
Deane, Richard Burton	Superintendent	1st April '84.
Constantine, Charles	,,	1st Sept. '97.
Sanders, D.S.O., Gilbert Edward	,,	1st July '99.
Primrose, Philip Carteret Hill	,,	14th Oct. '99.
Snyder, Arthur Edward	,,	1st July '01.
*Cuthbert, Albert Edward Ross	,,	1st Sept. '02.
Wilson, James Osgood	,,	1st Mar. '03.
Bégin, Joseph Victor	,,	1st Mar. '03.
Moodie, John Douglas	,,	1st Dec. '03.
*McGibbon, John Alexander	,,	1st Aug. '06.
*Routledge, Walton H.	,,	1st April '07.
*Starnes, Cortlandt	,,	1st Dec. '09.
Howard, Donald Macdonald	Inspector	1st Nov. '90.
*Jarvis, C.M.G., Arthur Murray	,,	16th May '93.
Demers, Francois Joseph A.	,,	3rd June '98.
Horrigan, Fitzpatrick Joseph	,,	4th Nov. '99.
*McDonell, Albert Edward Crosby	,,	1st Aug. '00.
*West, Christopher Harfield	,,	1st Aug. '00.
*Walke, William Mackenzie	,,	1st Oct. '00.
Pelletier, Ephrem Albert	,,	1st Jan. '01.
Worsley, George Stanley	,,	1st April '01.
*Heffernan, John Herbert	,,	15th May '01.
Taylor, John	,,	1st July '01.
Douglas, Richard Young	,,	20th May '02.
*Knight, Reginald Spencer	,,	1st Mar. '03.
*Richards, John	,,	1st Mar. '03.
*Parker, William	,,	1st Mar. '03.
*Duffus, Arthur William	,,	1st Mar. '03.
*Stevens, George	,,	31st Oct. '03.
*Tucker, Robert Edward	,,	1st April '04.
*Ritchie, James	,,	1st April '04.
*Genereux, John Horace	,,	1st April '04.
*Pennefather, Percival William	,,	29th June '04.
Allard, Alphonse B.	,,	1st July '04.
*Camies, Ernest Joseph	,,	1st Oct. '05.
*Belcher, Thomas Sherlock	,,	1st Aug. '06.

THE RIDERS OF THE PLAINS

Name.	Present Rank.	Date of Appointment.
Jennings, George Leslie	Inspector	1st Aug. '06.
*Junget, Christen	,,	1st April '07.
*McDonald, John Alexander	,,	1st April '07.
M'Carthy, William Offley	,,	1st June '09.
*Sweetapple, Charles Henry Heath	,,	1st Dec. '09.
*Raven, Charles Cummings	,,	1st Dec. '09.
*Fitzgerald, Francis Joseph	,,	1st Dec. '09.
Lindsay, William Pentland	,,	1st Jan. '10.
Paré, M.D., Louis Alphonse	Surgeon	1st Jan. '04.
Bell, M.D., George Pearson	,,	1st July '05.
Fraser, M.D., Samuel Martin	Assistant-Surgeon	1st May '89.
Thompson, M.D., William Ernest	,, ,,	12th July '98.
*Burnett, V.S., John Frederick	Insp. and Vet. Surg.	1st July '90.
*Wroughton, V.S., Theodore Ambrose	,, ,, ,,	1st Mar. '98.

* Promoted from the ranks.

APPENDIX F.

R.N.W.M. POLICE DISTRICTS AND OFFICERS ATTACHED THERETO.

PROVINCES OF ALBERTA AND SASKATCHEWAN, AND NORTH-WEST TERRITORIES—HEADQUARTERS, REGINA.

Commissioner—A. Bowen Perry, C.M.G.
Assistant-Commissioner—J. H. M'Illree.

REGINA DISTRICT (HEADQUARTERS, REGINA).
Superintendent—W. H. Routledge.
Inspectors—R. S. Knight, J. H. Heffernan, E. A. Pelletier, A. B. Allard, John Richards, C. Junget, J. Taylor, C. C. Raven, W. O. M'Carthy, W. P. Lindsay.
Surgeon—G. P. Bell, M.D.
Veterinary Surgeon—J. F. Burnett, V.S.

A DIVISION, MAPLE CREEK DISTRICT (HEADQUARTERS, MAPLE CREEK).
Superintendent—C. Constantine.
Inspector—J. Ritchie.

C DIVISION, BATTLEFORD DISTRICT (HEADQUARTERS, BATTLEFORD).
Superintendent—J. A. McGibbon.
Inspectors—J. H. Genereux, F. J. A. Demers.

APPENDIX F

D Division, Macleod District (Headquarters, Macleod).
Superintendent—P. C. H. Primrose.
Inspectors—T. S. Belcher, E. J. Camies.
Assistant-Surgeon, S. M. Fraser, M.D.

E Division, Calgary District (Headquarters, Calgary).
Superintendent—R. Burton Deane.
Inspectors—A. W. Duffus, A. M. Jarvis.

F Division, Prince Albert District (Headquarters, Prince Albert).
Superintendent—J. V. Bégin.
Inspectors—W. M. Walke, P. W. Pennefather.

G Division, Edmonton District (Headquarters, Fort Saskatchewan).
Superintendent—A. E. Ross Cuthbert.
Inspectors—G. S. Worsley, A. E. C. McDonell, R. E. Tucker, C. H. H. Sweetapple.

K Division, Lethbridge District (Headquarters, Lethbridge).
Superintendent—J. O. Wilson.
Inspectors—W. Parker, C. H. West.

M Division, Hudson's Bay District (Headquarters, Fort Churchill).
Superintendents—J. D. Moodie, C. Starnes.

N Division, Athabasca District (Headquarters, Athabasca Landing).
Superintendent—G. E. Sanders, D.S.O.
Inspectors—G. L. Jennings, D. McD. Howard, F. J. Fitzgerald.

YUKON TERRITORY—HEADQUARTERS, DAWSON.
Assistant-Commissioner, Z. T. Wood.

B Division, Dawson District (Headquarters, Dawson).
Inspectors—T. A. Wroughton (commanding), F. P. Horrigan, R. Y. Douglas.
Assistant-Surgeon, W. E. Thompson, M.D.

H Division, Whitehorse District (Headquarters, Whitehorse).
Superintendent—A. E. Snyder.
Inspector—J. A. Macdonald.
Surgeon—L. A. Paré, M.D.

THE RIDERS OF THE PLAINS

APPENDIX G.

LIST OF OFFICERS OF THE R.N.W.M.P. WHO HAVE LEFT THE FORCE FOR VARIOUS REASONS BETWEEN 1873 AND 1909.

Name.	Rank.	Date.	Remarks.
Breden, John	Sub-Inspector	11-5-'74	Resigned.
McLennan, D. B.	,,	— '74	,,
Forget, Joseph	Quartermaster	20-6-'74	
Young, Chas. F.	Superintendent	28-7-'74	
Richer, Theodore	,,	11-9-'74	
Le Cain, H. J. N.	Sub-Inspector	20-5-'75	
Nicolle, Chas.	Quartermaster	15-7-'75	
Carvell, Jacob	Superintendent	28-10-'75	Resigned.
French, Lt.-Col. G. A.	Commissioner	22-7-'76	,,
Brisebois, E. A.	Superintendent	1-8-'76	,,
Griffiths, W. G.	Paymaster	31-10-'76	Office abolished.
Poett, V.S., J. L.	Sub-Inspector	1-8-'77	Retired with gratuity.
Allen, Edwin	,,	10-9-'78	Resigned.
Welsh, Vernon	,,	1-10-'78	,,
Nevitt, R. B.	Surgeon	1-10-'78	,,
Jackson, Thomas R.	Sub-Inspector	5-10-'78	
Fortescue, L.	,,	28-2-'79	Resigned.
Macleod, C.M.G., James F.	Commissioner	1-11-'80	Appointed stipendiary magistrate.
Walker, James	Superintendent	1-2-'81	Retired with gratuity.
Winder, William	,,	1-4-'81	,, ,,
Denny, C. R.	Inspector	6-6-'81	Resigned.
Jarvis, W. D.	Superintendent	13-8-'81	
Kittson, M.D., John	Surgeon	24-1-'82	Resigned.
Frechette, Edmund	Inspector	1-11-'82	Retired with gratuity.
French, John	,,	1-7-'83	,, ,,
Walsh, James M.	Superintendent	1-9-'83	,, ,,
Prevost, H. R.	Inspector	23-1-'84	
Shurtliffe, A.	Superintendent	31-12-'84	Retired with gratuity.
Dowling, Thomas	Inspector	31-3-'86	Resigned.
Dickens, F. J.	,,	1-4-'86	Retired with gratuity.
Irvine, A. G.	Commissioner	1-4-'86	,, ,,
Crozier, L. N. F.	Assist.-Commr.	30-6-'86	,, ,,
Kennedy, G. A.	Surgeon	30-6-'87	Resigned.
Rolph, J. W.	,,	2-7-'87	

APPENDIX G

Name.	Rank.	Date.	Remarks.
Riddell, V.S., R.	Vet. Surgeon	31-12-'87	Resigned.
Mills, S. G.	Inspector	29-2-'88	,,
Baldwin, H. Y.	Surgeon	30-9-'88	,,
Brooks, W. A.	Inspector	30-11-'88	Retired with gratuity.
Powell, F. H.	Surgeon	31-5-'89	Resigned.
Williams, V. A. S.	Inspector	28-9-'89	,,
Likely, H. D.	,,	30-9-'89	Retired with gratuity.
Neale, P. R.	Superintendent	31-7-'90	,, ,,
Wattam, Thomas	Inspector	30-9-'91	,, ,,
Drayner, Frederick	,,	15-7-'92	Resigned.
Antrobus, W. D.	,,	1-11-'92	
Chalmers, T. W.	,,	30-4-'93	Resigned.
Jukes, M.D., A.	Surgeon	31-7-'93	Superannuated.
Matthews, W. G.	Inspector	31-10-'93	Resigned.
Hopkins, E. G. O.	,,	1-5-'95	Retired with gratuity.
Olivier, Hercule	,,	1-5-'95	,, ,,
Macdonell, A. R.	Superintendent	1-5-'95	Superannuated.
Norman, Frank	,,	1-5-'95	,,
Aylen, M.D., Peter	Assist.-Surgeon	1-7-'95	Retired with gratuity.
MacPherson, D. H.	Inspector	30-9-'97	,, ,,
White-Fraser, M. H.	,,	30-9-'97	Superannuated.
Wills, M.D., A. E.	Surgeon	15-2-'98	Resigned.
Bonnar, H. A.	,,	12-7-'98	,,
De Cou, D. M'G.	,,	30-6-'99	,,
Allan, J. B.	Inspector	31-12-'99	Superannuated.
Herchmer, L. W.	Commissioner	1-8-'00	,,
Gagnon, Severe	Superintendent	31-3-'01	,,
Harper, Frank	Inspector	31-5-'01	
Paradis, E. C.	,,	9-10-'01	
Scarth, W. H.	,,	15-4-'02	Resigned.
Baker, Montague	,,	31-10-'02	,,
Steele, S. B.	Superintendent	1-2 '03	Retired with pension.
Moffatt, G. B.	,,	1-3-'03	,, ,,
Cosby, F. L.	Inspector	27-8-'03	Resigned.
Griesbach, A. H.	Superintendent	1-12-'03	Retired with pension.
Crosthwait, S.	Inspector	31-12-'03	Resigned.
Cartwright, F. L.	,,	9-3-'04	,,
Wickham, W. C.	,,	26-3-'04	,,
La Rocque, H. C.	,,	1-4-'04	,,
Williams, W. M. de R.	,,	30-5-'04	
Brunton, H. G.	,,	14-7-'05	Resigned.

THE RIDERS OF THE PLAINS

Name.	Rank.	Date.	Remarks.
Irwin, W. H.	Inspector	1-7-'06	Retired with pension.
Macdonell, D.S.O., A. C.	Superintendent	— '07	Resigned.
Grant, J. W. S.	Inspector	— '08	,,
Davidson, H. J. A.	,,	— '08	Retired with pension.
Belcher, C.M.G., R.	,,	— '08	,, ,,
Shaw, A. E.	,,	30-6-'09	Resigned.
Lacroix, M.D., Octave	Assist.-Surgeon	30-11-'09	,,

The following Officers have died during the same period :—

Name.	Rank.	Date.
Clark, E. Dalrymple	Superintendent	2-10-'80.
M'Kenzie, Alex.	,,	18-5-'82.
Gautier, Arthur	Inspector	29-12-'85.
Miller, Robert	Surgeon	6-9-'87.
Bradley, Ernest	Inspector	16-7-'91.
Herchmer, W. M.	Assistant-Commissioner	1-1-'92.
Dodd, Henry	Surgeon	1-1-'93.
Piercy, William	Inspector	13-3-'93.
Huot, C. F. A.	,,	23-3-'93.
Jarvis, E. W.	Superintendent	26-11-'94.
Cotton, John	,,	7-5-'99.
Howe, Joseph	,,	17-8-'02.
Haultain, M.D., C. S.	Surgeon	20-5-'03.
Casey, H. S.	Inspector	26-3-'04.
Brown, E. Gilpin	,,	20-12-'04.
Morris, W. S.	Superintendent	4-4-'05.
M'Ginnis, Thomas	Inspector	4-3-'06.
Madore, M.D., G.	Assistant-Surgeon	— '07.
Flood, M.D., W. S.	,, ,,	— '07.
Strickland, D'A. E.	Inspector	— 3-'08.
Church, Frank	,,	15-12-'09.

By the Mounted Police (Dominion of Canada) Pension Acts, members of the Royal North-West Mounted Police may retire on superannuation after twenty years' service, or after fifteen years if incapacitated through ill-health. Officers receive pensions after twenty years' service, or a gratuity if owing to ill-health they are compelled to leave the Force before a pension is earned.

APPENDIX H.

HOW TO ENTER THE FORCE.

APPLICANTS who write for particulars as to joining the Royal North-West Mounted Police are sent a form which gives general information respecting the standard of requirements and terms of engagement for service. They are also advised to be examined, at their own expense, by a doctor to ensure their being free from certain specified complaints and defects which are the most frequent causes of rejection. This examination, of course, would be only a preliminary one, every applicant having to be again examined by the Police Surgeon. The official medical examination is very strict and searching, and the would-be recruit is warned not to incur the expense of the journey to Regina unless he is convinced that he is "thoroughly sound and fit for Police Service."

ROYAL NORTH-WEST MOUNTED POLICE FORCE.

Ottawa, 19

MEMORANDUM FOR THE INFORMATION OF APPLICANTS FOR ENGAGEMENT IN THE ROYAL NORTH-WEST MOUNTED POLICE.

1. Applicants must be between the ages of twenty-two and forty, active able-bodied men of thoroughly sound constitution, and must produce *certificate of exemplary character.*

2. They must be able to read and write either the English or French language, must understand the care and management of horses, and be able to ride well.

3. The term of engagement is five years.

4. The rates of pay are as follows :—

4 Staff-Sergeants	$2.00 per day.
Other Staff-Sergeants	$1.50 to $1.75 per day
Other Non-Commissioned Officers	$1.10 to $1.25 per day

THE RIDERS OF THE PLAINS

		Pay.
Constable—1st year's service	. . .	60c. per day.
2nd ,,	. . .	65 ,,
3rd ,,	. . .	70 ,,
4th ,,	. . .	75 ,,
5th ,,	. . .	80 ,,
6th ,,	. . .	85 ,,
7th ,,	. . .	90 ,,
8th ,,	. . .	95 ,,
9th ,,	. . .	$1.00 ,,

Extra pay is allowed to a limited number of blacksmiths, carpenters, and other artisans.

5. Members of the Force are supplied with free rations, a free kit on joining and periodical issues during the term of service. Kit to be kept in serviceable condition at the expense of the N.-C. Officer or Constable.

6. Married men will not be engaged.

7. The minimum height is 5 feet 8 inches, the minimum chest measurement 35 inches, and the maximum weight 175 lb.

8. Application to join the Force must be made to the Commissioner, Regina, Sask., or to the Comptroller, Ottawa.

9. No expenses, travelling or otherwise, of applicants can be paid from public funds.

10. Section 38, chapter 91, of the Revised Statutes, 1906, provides as follows :—

"Every person who, by concealing the fact of his having been "dismissed from the Force or by false or forged certificates or false "representations, obtains admission into the Force, or obtains "any pay, gratuity or pension, shall, on summary conviction, be "liable to a fine not exceeding eighty dollars, or to imprisonment, "with or without hard labour, for any term not exceeding six "months, or to both fine and imprisonment."

APPENDIX I.

DISTRIBUTION STATE OF THE FORCE, BY DIVISIONS, SEPTEMBER 30, 1909.

Division.	Place.	Commissioner.	Asst.-Commissioner.	Superintendents.	Inspectors.	Surgeons and Asst.-Surgeons.	Veterinary Surgeons.	Staff-Sergeants.	Sergeants.	Corporals.	Constables.	Special Constables.	Total.	Horses.
Dépôt.	Regina	1	1	1	6	1	1	7	5	4	78	15	120	85
	Arcola	...	...	...	...	...	...	...	1	...	2	...	3	1
	Balcarres	...	...	...	...	...	...	...	1	...	1	...	2	2
	Broadview	...	...	...	...	...	...	...	...	...	1	...	1	...
	Big Muddy	...	...	...	...	...	...	...	...	1	1	1	3	6
	Canora	...	...	...	...	...	...	...	...	...	1	...	1	1
	Craik	...	...	...	...	...	...	...	1	...	...	...	1	1
	Carnduff	...	...	...	...	...	...	...	...	...	1	...	1	1
	Carlyle	...	...	...	...	...	...	...	...	...	...	...	...	1
	Esterhazy	...	...	...	...	...	...	...	...	...	1	...	1	1
	Estevan	...	...	...	...	...	...	...	1	...	...	...	1	1
	Fort Pelly	...	...	...	...	...	...	...	...	...	1	...	1	1
	Fort Qu'Appelle	...	...	...	...	...	...	...	...	...	1	...	1	1
	Fillmore	...	...	...	...	...	...	...	...	...	1	...	1	1
	Grenfell	...	...	...	...	...	...	...	...	...	...	...	...	1
	Indian Head	...	...	...	...	...	...	...	1	...	2	...	3	3
	Kamsach	...	...	...	...	...	...	...	...	1	1	...	2	2
	Lanigan	...	...	...	...	...	...	...	...	1	...	...	1	1
	Lumsden	...	...	...	...	...	...	...	...	...	1	...	1	1
	Melville	...	...	...	...	...	...	...	...	...	...	...	...	1
	Moosomin	...	...	...	1	...	...	...	...	1	3	...	5	4
	Moosejaw	...	...	...	...	...	...	...	1	...	4	...	5	2
	Mortlack	...	...	...	...	...	...	...	...	...	1	...	1	1
	Milestone	...	...	...	...	...	...	...	...	...	1	...	1	1
	Marienthal	...	...	...	...	...	...	...	...	1	1	...	2	3
	Norway House	...	...	...	...	...	...	...	1	...	1	1	3	...
	North Portal	...	...	...	...	...	...	...	...	...	1	...	1	1
	Ottawa	...	...	...	1	...	...	3	1	...	1	...	6	...
	Outlook	...	...	...	...	...	...	...	...	1	...	...	1	1
	Oxbow	...	...	...	...	...	...	...	...	...	1	...	1	1
	Punnichy	...	...	...	...	...	...	...	...	...	1	...	1	1
	Sheho	...	...	...	...	...	...	...	...	...	1	...	1	1
	Strassburg	...	...	...	...	...	...	...	...	...	1	...	1	1
	Split Lake	...	...	...	...	...	...	...	...	1	1	1	3	...
	Town Station	...	...	...	...	...	...	...	...	1	1	...	2	1
	Wolseley	...	...	...	...	...	...	...	1	...	...	...	1	1
	Wood Mountain	...	...	...	1	...	...	...	...	1	6	1	9	15
	Willow Bunch	...	...	...	...	...	...	...	...	...	1	1	2	5
	Weyburn	...	...	...	...	...	...	...	...	...	1	...	1	1
	Windthorst	...	...	...	...	...	...	...	...	...	1	...	1	1
	Wynyard	...	...	...	...	...	...	...	...	...	1	...	1	1
	Whitewood	...	...	...	...	...	...	...	...	...	...	...	...	1
	Yorkton	...	...	...	1	...	...	...	...	1	4	...	6	6
	Yellow Grass	...	...	...	...	...	...	...	...	...	1	...	1	1
	On command	...	...	...	...	...	...	...	...	1	...	...	1	...
	On leave	...	...	...	...	...	...	...	...	...	1	...	1	...
	Total, Dépôt Division	1	1	1	10	1	1	11	13	15	128	20	202	162

THE RIDERS OF THE PLAINS

Division	Place	Superintendents	Inspectors	Assistant Surgeons	Staff-Sergeants	Sergeants	Corporals	Constables	Special Constables	Total	Horses	Dogs
A	Maple Creek	1	1	...	1	1	2	8	2	16	15	...
	East End	...	...	...	...	..	1	1	1	3	4	...
	Herbert	...	...	...	...	...	...	1	...	1	2	...
	Montgomery's Landing	...	...	...	...	...	1	1	...	2	1	...
	Pelletier's Lake	...	...	...	...	...	...	1	...	1	2	...
	Sask. Landing	...	...	...	...	...	...	2	...	2	3	...
	Gull Lake	...	...	...	...	...	...	1	...	1	1	...
	Swift Current	...	...	...	...	1	...	2	...	3	5	...
	Town Station	...	...	...	...	...	1	...	...	1	1	...
	Ten Mile	...	...	...	...	...	1	1	1	3	4	...
	Willow Creek	...	...	...	...	1	...	1	1	3	4	...
	On command	...	...	...	...	...	...	...	...	...	...	...
	On leave	...	...	...	...	1	...	1	...	2	...	...
	Total, A Division	1	1	...	1	4	6	20	5	38	42	...
C	Battleford	1	...	...	2	1	1	6	3	14	17	...
	,, North	...	...	...	...	...	...	1	...	1	1	...
	Jackfish	...	...	...	...	...	...	1	...	1	2	...
	Lloydminster	...	...	...	...	...	...	1	...	1	2	...
	Lashburn	...	...	...	...	...	...	1	...	1	1	...
	MacKinnon	...	...	...	...	...	...	2	...	2	2	...
	Onion Lake	...	...	...	...	1	...	...	...	1	2	...
	Paynton	...	...	...	...	...	...	1	...	1	1	...
	Radisson	...	...	...	...	...	...	1	...	1	1	...
	Scott	...	...	...	...	...	...	1	...	1	1	...
	Unity	...	...	...	...	...	1	1	...	2	2	...
	Wilkie	...	1	...	...	...	1	2	...	4	5	...
	On command	...	...	...	...	...	1	4	...	5	...	...
	Total, C Division	1	1	...	3	1	4	22	3	35	37	...
D	Macleod	1	1	1	3	3	2	15	5	31	31	...
	Big Bend	...	...	...	...	...	1	1	...	2	3	...
	Boundary Creek	...	...	...	...	...	...	...	...	...	...	...
	Coleman	...	...	...	...	...	...	2	...	2	1	...
	Cardston	...	...	...	...	1	...	1	1	3	5	...
	Claresholm	...	1	...	...	...	1	1	...	3	4	...
	Frank	...	...	...	...	...	1	1	...	2	2	...
	Kipp	...	...	...	...	...	...	1	1	2	2	...
	Kootenai	...	...	...	...	...	...	...	...	...	...	...
	Lille	...	...	...	...	...	...	2	...	2	1	...
	Nanton	...	...	...	...	...	...	1	...	1	2	...
	Pincher Creek	...	1	...	...	...	...	2	...	3	4	...
	Peigan	...	...	...	...	...	...	1	1	2	2	...
	Stand Off	...	...	...	...	...	1	1	2	4	5	...
	Staveley	...	...	...	...	...	...	1	...	1	1	...
	Twin Lakes	...	...	...	...	...	1	1	1	3	4	...
	On command	...	1	...	...	...	...	1	...	2	...	...
	On leave	...	...	...	...	...	...	...	...	...	...	...
	Total, D Division	1	4	1	3	4	7	32	11	63	67	...

APPENDIX I

Division.	Place.	Superintendents.	Inspectors.	Assistant-Surgeons.	Staff-Sergeants.	Sergeants.	Corporals.	Constables.	Special Constables.	Total.	Horses.	Dogs.
E	Calgary	1	2	...	2	...	3	15	4	27	23	...
	Banff	...	...	...	...	...	1	1	...	2	2	...
	Bankhead	...	...	...	...	...	1	...	...	1	1	...
	Berry Creek	...	...	...	...	...	1	1	...	2	4	...
	Canmore	...	...	...	...	...	...	1	...	1	1	...
	Cochrane	...	...	...	...	...	...	1	...	1	1	...
	Gleichen	...	...	...	...	1	...	1	2	4	4	...
	High River	...	...	...	...	...	1	...	...	1	1	...
	Innisfail	...	...	...	...	...	...	1	...	1	1	...
	Olds	...	...	...	...	...	...	1	...	1	1	...
	Okotoks	...	...	...	...	...	...	1	...	1	1	...
	Red Deer	...	...	...	...	...	...	1	...	1	2	...
	Strathmore	...	...	...	...	...	...	1	...	1	2	...
	Trochu	...	...	...	...	...	...	2	...	2	4	...
	On command	...	...	...	...	...	...	...	...	...	...	...
	On leave	...	...	...	...	...	...	...	...	...	...	...
	Total, E Division	1	2	...	3	1	6	27	6	46	48	...
F	Prince Albert	1	1	...	1	1	1	4	4	13	15	...
	Asquith	...	...	...	...	...	...	1	...	1	1	...
	Barrows	...	...	...	...	...	...	1	...	1	...	...
	Birch Hill	...	...	...	...	...	...	1	...	1	1	...
	Bonne Madonne	...	...	...	...	...	...	1	...	1	1	...
	Duck Lake	...	...	...	...	...	...	1	1	2	3	...
	Green Lake	...	...	...	...	...	...	1	...	1	...	...
	Hudson's Bay Junction	...	...	...	...	...	...	1	...	1	...	...
	Hanley	...	...	...	...	...	...	1	...	1	1	...
	Humboldt	...	...	...	...	...	1	...	...	1	2	...
	Isle à la Crosse	...	...	...	...	...	...	1	...	1	...	...
	Melfort	...	...	...	...	1	...	1	...	2	1	...
	Rosthern	...	...	...	...	...	1	...	...	1	1	...
	Saskatoon	...	1	...	...	...	1	3	...	5	5	...
	Tisdale	...	...	...	...	...	...	1	...	1	1	...
	The Pas	...	...	...	...	...	1	...	...	1	...	...
	Vonda	...	...	...	...	...	...	1	...	1	1	...
	Wadena	...	...	...	...	...	1	...	...	1	1	...
	Warman	...	...	...	...	...	...	1	...	1	1	...
	Zealandia	...	...	...	...	...	1	1	...	2	2	...
	On command	...	...	...	...	...	...	...	...	...	...	...
	On leave	...	...	...	...	...	...	...	...	...	...	...
	Total, F Division	1	2	...	2	2	6	21	5	39	37	...

THE RIDERS OF THE PLAINS

Division	Place.	Superintendents.	Inspectors.	Assistant-Surgeons.	Staff-Sergeants.	Sergeants.	Corporals.	Constables.	Special Constables.	Total.	Horses.	Dogs.
G	Fort Saskatchewan	1	...	...	2	1	...	10	3	17	15	...
	Andrew	...	...	...	...	...	...	1	...	1	1	...
	Brosseau	...	...	...	...	...	...	1	...	1	1	...
	Camrose	...	...	...	...	...	...	1	...	1	1	...
	Daysland	...	...	...	...	...	...	1	...	1	1	...
	Edmonton	...	1	...	...	1	1	2	2	7	4	...
	Entwistle	...	1	...	...	...	2	2	...	5	10	...
	Hardisty	...	...	...	...	...	...	...	...	...	1	...
	Morinville	...	...	...	...	...	...	1	...	1	1	...
	Provost	...	...	...	...	...	...	1	...	1	1	...
	St. Albert	...	...	...	...	...	...	1	...	1	1	...
	Stony Plain	...	...	...	...	1	...	...	...	1	1	...
	Stettler	...	...	...	...	1	...	1	...	2	1	...
	Tofield	...	...	...	...	...	...	...	...	...	...	...
	Vegreville	...	...	...	...	...	...	1	...	1	...	...
	Vermilion	...	...	...	...	...	...	1	...	1	...	...
	Viking	...	...	...	...	...	...	1	...	1	1	...
	Wetaskiwin	...	...	...	...	1	...	...	...	1	1	...
	Wainwright	...	...	...	...	...	...	1	...	1	1	...
	On command	...	1	...	1	...	2	11	...	15	16	...
	On leave	...	...	...	...	...	...	...	...	...	...	...
	Total, G Division	1	3	...	3	5	5	37	5	59	58	...
K	Lethbridge	1	1	...	1	3	1	9	2	18	16	...
	Coutts	...	...	...	...	1	...	3	...	3	8	...
	Grassy Lake	...	...	...	...	...	...	2	...	2	2	...
	Irvine	...	...	...	...	...	1	1	1	3	3	...
	Medicine Hat	...	1	...	...	...	...	3	...	4	6	...
	Medicine Lodge	...	...	...	...	...	...	2	1	3	3	...
	Magrath	...	...	...	...	...	...	1	...	1	1	...
	Pendant d'Oreille	...	...	...	...	...	1	1	1	3	3	...
	Stafford Village	...	...	...	...	...	...	1	...	1	1	...
	Taber	...	...	...	...	...	1	...	...	1	1	...
	Writing-on-Stone	...	...	...	...	...	...	2	1	3	3	...
	Warner	...	...	...	...	...	...	1	...	1	2	...
	Wild Horse	...	...	...	...	...	...	2	1	3	3	...
	On command	...	...	...	...	...	1	1	...	2	1	...
	On leave	...	...	...	...	...	...	...	...	...	...	...
	Total, K Division	1	2	...	1	4	5	28	7	48	53	...
M	Fort Churchill	1	...	1	...	1	2	6	2	13	}	35
	Fullerton	...	...	...	...	...	1	2	...	3	}	
	Total, M Division	1	...	1	...	1	3	8	2	16	...	35
N	Athabasca Landing	...	1	...	...	1	1	2	2	7	4	...
	Chipewyan	...	...	...	...	1	...	...	1	2	...	6
	Herchell Island	...	1	...	...	...	...	2	...	3	...	8
	Macpherson	...	...	...	...	1	...	2	1	4	...	14
	Peace River Crossing	...	...	...	1	...	...	...	...	1	2	...
	Lesser Slave Lake	...	...	...	...	1	...	1	2	4	10	...
	Sawridge	...	...	...	...	...	...	1	...	1	2	...
	Smith's Landing	...	...	...	...	...	1	2	1	4	...	5
	Vermilion	...	...	...	...	1	...	...	...	1	4	4
	On command	1	...	...	...	...	...	1	...	2	...	...
	On leave	...	...	...	1	...	...	1	...	2	...	...
	Total, N Division	1	2	...	2	5	1	12	7	31	22	37

APPENDIX I

Division	Place.	Commissioner.	Assistant-Commissioner.	Superintendents.	Inspectors.	Surgeons and Assistant-Surgeons.	Veterinary Surgeons.	Staff-Sergeants.	Sergeants.	Corporals.	Constables.	Supernumerary Constables.	Total.	Horses.	Dogs.
B	Dawson	...	1	...	3	1	...	2	2	1	16	8	34	13	...
	Town Station	...	...	...	...	...	...	...	1	4	...	5	...	...	
	Forty Mile	...	...	...	...	...	...	1	...	1	...	2	...	6	
	Selkirk	...	...	...	...	...	...	...	1	...	...	1	...	...	
	Grand Forks	...	...	...	...	...	...	...	1	...	...	1	1	...	
	Granville	...	...	...	...	...	...	...	...	1	...	1	1	...	
	Total, B Division	...	1	...	3	1	...	2	3	4	22	8	44	15	6
H	White Horse	...	...	1	1	1	...	1	...	1	12	5	22	14	...
	Town Station	...	...	...	...	...	...	...	1	...	2	...	3	...	...
	Carcross	...	...	...	...	...	...	1	...	...	...	1	2	...	...
	Champagne's Landing	...	...	...	...	...	...	...	1	...	...	...	1	1	...
	Livingstone Creek	...	...	...	...	...	...	...	1	...	1	...	2	2	...
	Total, H Division	...	...	1	1	1	...	2	3	1	15	6	30	17	...

RECAPITULATION.

Place.	Commissioner.	Assistant-Commissioner.	Superintendents.	Inspectors.	Surgeons and Assistant-Surgeons.	Veterinary Surgeons.	Staff-Sergeants.	Sergeants.	Corporals.	Constables.	Special Constables.	Total.	Horses.	Dogs.
Regina District	1	1	1	10	1	1	11	13	15	128	20	202	162	...
Maple Creek District	...	...	1	1	...	...	1	4	6	20	5	38	12	...
Battleford District	...	...	1	1	...	...	3	1	4	22	3	35	37	...
Macleod District	...	...	1	4	1	...	3	4	7	32	11	63	67	...
Calgary District	...	...	1	2	...	...	3	1	6	27	6	46	48	...
Prince Albert District	...	...	1	2	...	...	2	2	6	21	5	39	37	...
Fort Saskatchewan District	...	...	1	3	...	...	3	5	5	37	5	59	58	...
Lethbridge District	...	...	1	2	...	...	1	4	5	28	7	48	53	...
Hudson's Bay District	...	...	1	...	1	...	...	1	3	8	2	16	...	35
Athabasca and Mackenzie District	...	...	1	2	...	...	2	5	2	12	7	31	22	37
Dawson District	...	1	...	3	1	...	2	3	4	22	8	44	15	6
White Horse District	...	...	1	1	1	...	2	3	1	15	6	30	17	...
Total strength, Sep. 30, 1909	1	2	11	31	5	1	33	46	64	372	85	651	558	78

THE RIDERS OF THE PLAINS

The following Table gives the distribution by Provinces and Territories :—

	Commissioner.	Assistant-Commissioners.	Superintendents.	Inspectors.	Surgeons and Assistant-Surgeons.	Veterinary Surgeons.	Staff-Sergeants.	Sergeants.	Corporals.	Constables.	Special Constables.	Total.	Horses.
Alberta . . .	...	...	5	12	1	...	12	18	25	132	35	240	248
Saskatchewan . .	1	1	4	14	1	1	17	19	29	188	31	306	278
North-West Territories	...	...	1	1	1	...	...	3	5	15	5	31	...
Yukon Territory .	...	1	1	4	2	...	4	6	5	37	14	74	32
Grand total .	1	2	11	31	5	1	33	46	64	372	85	651	558

APPENDIX J.

STATISTICS OF CRIME UNDER ROYAL NORTH-WEST MOUNTED POLICE JURISDICTION.

SCHEDULE OF PRISONERS COMMITTED TO AND RELEASED FROM MOUNTED POLICE GUARD-ROOMS between Nov. 1, 1908, and Sept. 30, 1909.

	Saskatchewan.						Alberta.							North-West Territories.			Grand Total.	Remarks.
	Regina.	Moosomin.	Yorkton.	Maple Creek.	Battleford.	Total.	Macleod.	Calgary.	Fort Saskatchewan.	Lethbridge.	Athabasca Landing.	Lesser Slave Lake.	Total.	Norway House.	Barrows.	Total.		
Total number of prisoners serving sentence and awaiting trial on Oct. 31, 1908	22	5	6	2	6	42	21	51	39	33	...	...	144	...	1	1	187	
Total number of prisoners received	218	77	76	57	116	544	231	543	233	340	36	4	1,387	1	8	9	1,940	
Total number of prisoners discharged	229	79	71	52	111	542	220*	558†	229	346	36	4	1,393	1	9	10	1,945	*1 executed. †2 died while in Guardroom.
Total number of prisoners serving sentence or awaiting trial on Sept. 30, 1909	11	4	11	7	11	44	32	36	43	27	...	...	138	...	...	...	182	

COMPARATIVE STATEMENT OF PRISONERS RECEIVED IN MOUNTED POLICE GUARD-ROOMS between Years 1900 and 1909.

	1909.‡	1908.	1907.	1906.‡	1905.	1904.	1903.	1902.	1901.	1900.
Total number of prisoners received	1940	2105	1676	1515	1467	1505	1039	779	759	541

‡ Eleven months.

THE RIDERS OF THE PLAINS

Classified Summary of Cases entered and Convictions made in North-West Territories, from Nov. 1, 1908, to Sept. 30, 1909.

	Cases entered.	Convictions.	Dismissed, etc.	Awaiting Trial.
Offences against religion and morals— Drunk and disorderly	2	2	...	...
Offences against the North-West Territory Ordinances— Illegally importing intoxicants into prohibited territory	7	5	2	...
Illegally in possession of intoxicants in prohibited territory	4	4	...	...
Total	13	11	2	...

Recapitulation of Summary of Cases entered and Convictions made in the Provinces of Saskatchewan and Alberta and the North-West Territories, from November 1, 1908, to September 30, 1909.

Cases entered in	Cases entered.	Convictions.	Dismissed, etc.	Awaiting Trial.
Province of Saskatchewan	3,464	3,031	381	52
Province of Alberta	3,411	2,807	510	94
North-West Territories	13	11	2	...
Grand total	6,888	5,849	893	146

Comparative Statement of Convictions between Years 1900 and 1909, under General Headings.

Offences against	1909.*	1908.	1907.	1906.*	1905.	1904.	1903.	1902.	1901.	1900.
The person	804	882	729	590	478	386	317	189	144	109
Property	1,603	1,066	877	632	630	605	367	248	132	96
Public order	57	53	66	61	42	27	32	31	11	9
Religion and morals	1,909	2,212	2,208	1,533	1,379	1,312	923	494	500	350
Misleading justice	5	6	3	6	3	4	7	...	...	3
Corruption and disobedience	60	47	44	56	26	27	33	17	13	16
Railway Act	83	169	60	34	69	86	32	5	49	45
Customs Act	18	18	4	17	11	...	...	...	2	...
Indian Act	273	265	336	259	229	228	296	236	180	143
Animals (Contagious) Diseases Act	9	3	6	28	24	9	...	...	...	...
Fisheries Act	21	28	11	11	6	...	...	...	...	...
Dominion Lands Act	...	...	...	2	...	...	...	...	...	...
Election Act	3	...	...	4	2	...	...	...	...	...
Rocky Mountain Park Regulations	34	10	20	25	1	...	...	...	...	...
Militia Act	...	...	...	...	...	4	...	...	...	...
Inland Revenue Act	...	...	2	...	...	...	...	...	...	...
Penitentiary Act	...	...	1	...	...	...	...	...	...	...
Lord's Day Act	18	12	10	...	...	...	...	...	...	...
Manitoba Grain Act	11	2	...	...	...	...	...	...	...	...
Trades Union Act	...	1	...	...	...	...	...	...	...	...
Provincial Statutes and Ordinances	1,470	1,569	1,308	1,000	865	777	606	298	219	165
Convictions made in N.-W. Territories	11	10	...	...	...	...	...	...	...	...
Total	5,849	6,377	5,685	4,256	3,767	3,465	2,613	1,520	1,250	936

* Eleven months.

INDEX

Aberdeen, Earl of, 164; Governor-General, 172.
Adamites, 232.
Age of enlistment raised, 90.
Alberta, Province of, formed, 276; employment of Police in, 353.
Allan, Inspector J. B., 177, 248.
Almighty Voice tragedy, 174.
Arms and equipment, early, 28; changes in, 93, 117, 347.
Artillery, 115, 350.
Assiniboine Indians, 52; known as "Stonies," 53.
Athabasca, opening up of, 172, 229, 236, 260; Police district, 277.

Baker, Inspector M., 248.
Barracks, life in, 331.
Batoche's Ferry, battle of, 145.
Battleford, siege of, 141.
Bégin, Inspector J. V., 248.
Belcher, C.M.G., Inspector R., 191, 244, 248, 256.
Benevolent work, 217, 350.
Bennett, 191, 197, 203, 215.
Big Bear, 124, 128; at Fort Pitt, 140; capture of, 153.
Bill of Rights drawn up by half-breeds, 124.
Bison, or buffalo, the, 8.
Blackfeet Indians, 12, 52; daring and strategy, 54; atrocities, 56; repel Sioux overtures, 74.
Blackfeet Treaty, 62; full text of, 355.
Blackfoot Confederacy, 53.
Blood Indians, 53.
Bond, illicit liquor trader, captured, 36.
Bond Robbery, great, 241.
Bouthillette and Beaudoin murders, Yukon, 222.
Bow and Belly Rivers, 30.
Bowell, Hon. Mackenzie, 166.

Buck-jumping exhibition, a, 254.
Burns, Constable, 224.
Butler, Sir William, 6, 11, 56; meets Louis Riel, 122.

C.M.R. contingents in Boer War, 247.
"Cache-breaking," 194.
Calgary, Police post and origin of name, 46.
Canadian Pacific Railway, 99, 102; Pie-a-pot trouble, 104; strikes, 107; completion of, 120.
Cape Fullerton, 267.
Cartwright, Inspector F. L., 191, 214, 248, 256.
Cashman, Constable, long patrol, 272.
Cattle thieves, 95, 300.
Chalmers, Lieutenant, 250.
"Charcoal" Case, 182.
Chilkat Indians, 206, 220.
Chilkoot Pass and Summit, 194, 197.
Chippewa Indians, 52.
Chippewyan Indians, 54.
Christie and Crick, bond robbers, 241.
Church, the late Inspector Frank, 231, 248, 325.
Claim-jumping, 206.
Clark, Superintendent E. Dalrymple, 75.
Cody, Colonel, 9.
Colebrook, Sergeant C. C., 174.
Commissioners of Force, list of, 364.
Conradi, Constable, 282.
Constantine, Superintendent C., 173, 189, 277.
Cosby, Inspector F. L., 226, 248.
Cotton, Superintendent John, 88, 149, 181.
Cowan, Constable, killed, 140.
Cree Indians, 52, 84.
Crime statistics, 379.
Crosthwaite, Inspector S., 226.

Crowfoot, chief of Blackfeet, 39, 63, 68, 74, 83, 106.
Crow's Dance, Chief, incident, 81.
Crozier, Inspector L. N. F., 83, 127, 130.
Cumberland House post, 172.
Curtis, Sir Arthur, 210.
Custer massacre, 72.
Customs Duties, 98, 339.
Customs work in the Yukon, 200.
Cuthbert, Superintendent A. E. R., 226, 248.
Cut-Knife Hill, assault on, 144.

"D——," "Old man," 206.
Dalton Trail, 197.
Davidson, Inspector H. J.A., 248.
Dawson, M.P., S. J., Indian Commissioner, 60.
Dawson City, 197, 215.
De la Verendrye, Sieur, 3.
Deane, Superintendent R. B., 165, 168, 239.
Death-roll of officers, 370.
Death-roll, South African War, 258.
Demers, Inspector F. J. A., 248.
Dewdney, Hon. Edgar, Lieut.-Governor, N.W.T., 122.
Dickens, Inspector Francis, and Bull Elk, 82; after horse thieves, 95; defence of Fort Pitt, 139.
Districts and Posts, R.N.W.M.P., 44, 51, 89, 108, 170, 234, 277, 366, 373.
Divisional Police post, 337.
Dog trains, 212, 228.
Donkin, Corporal J. G., 154, 163.
Doukhobors, 230.
Dreamers, 233.
Duck Lake, fight at, 130.
Dufferin, 23, 32.
Dumont, Gabriel, 131.
Dyea, 197.

Egan, Sergeant, 298.
Eskimo, 263, 271; faith cure, 265.
Executive officers, 341.
Explorers in the north-west, early, 3.

Farm established, Police, 95.
Fiddler murder case, Indian, 309.
Field, Sergeant, 236, 285, 292.
Fish Creek, battle at, 145.
Fitzgerald, Inspector F. J., 261.
Foreign immigrants, 229.
"Fort," use of term, 31 (footnote).
Fort Benton, U.S.A., 12, 31.
Fort Buford, U.S.A., 84.
Fort Carlton, 133.

Fort Chipewyan, 260, 286.
Fort Churchill, 267; special patrol to, 320.
Fort Constantine, 189.
Fort Edmonton, 13, 17.
Fort Ellice, 17, 31, 44 (footnote).
Fort Garry, 20; old-time dog train from, 213.
Fort Macleod built, 35; abandoned, 114; new Fort Macleod built, 115.
Fort Macpherson, 261.
Fort Pelly, 31, 44 (footnote).
Fort Pitt besieged, 139.
Fort Regina, R.N.W.M.P. headquarters, founded, 90, 323.
Fort Rouge, site of Winnipeg, 4.
Fort Saskatchewan, 46.
Fort Selkirk, 208, 210.
Fort Walsh built, 46; in olden days, 48; condemned, 90; abandoned, 114.
Forts Carlton and Pitt Treaties, 61.
Fournier, Yukon murderer, 224.
Fraser, M.D., Assistant-Surgeon S. M., 41, 191, 197, 205, 214.
French, Inspector Jack, 252.
French, Lieut.-Col. G. A., first Commissioner, 20; leads march into the west, 25; resigns, 51.
"Fresh-killed meat," 158.
Frog Lake massacre, 137.
Fur traders, 2; warfare between, 5.
Fury, Sergeant W., 110.

Gagnon, Superintendent S., 130.
Galicians, 230.
Genereux, Inspector, 308.
Golden, railway strike at, 108.
Grey, Earl, Governor-General, 276.
Griesbach, Superintendent A. H., 20, 149.
Groseilliers, Sieur des, 3.

Half-breeds, grievances of French, 7, 121.
Harper, Inspector F., 191, 248.
Heffernan, Inspector J. H., 241.
Herchmer, Lieut.-Colonel L. W., appointed Commissioner, 162; resigns, 235; in Boer War, 248.
Herchmer, Superintendent W. M., 118, 142.
Herschell Island post, 261.
Hogg, Corporal, 281.
Honours gained in South African War, 256.
Horrigan, Inspector F. P., 226.

INDEX

Horse-stealing, 95; by Indians, 158, 295.
Horses, Police, 94, 325.
Howard, Hon. Thomas, Indian Commissioner, 61.
Howard, Inspector D. M., 226, 248, 266.
Howe, Superintendent J., 248.
Hudson's Bay Company, 4.
Hutton, General, 249, 254.
Hynes, D.C.O., Sergeant J., 256.

Illicit liquor traders, 12, 36, 157; in the Yukon, 190.
Indian Department, work performed for, 98.
Indian Scouts, 160, 185.
Indian tribes in the north-west, 52; treaties with, 59; oratory, 67; later prosperity, 69 (footnote), 171.
Indians, politic treatment of, 38; contrast in American and Canadian methods, 84.
Instructional staff at headquarters, 92, 327.
Irvine, Lieut.-Col. A. G., appointed Assistant-Commissioner, 51; and Sitting Bull, 75; Commissioner, 86; in the field against half-breeds, 129; defence of his enforced inactivity, 146; resigns, 162.
Ives, Hon. W. B., comment on Police, 171 (footnote).

Jarvis, Inspector A. M., 183, 191, 197, 214, 248, 256.
Jarvis, Inspector W. D., 29, 43.
Join the Force, to, 323, 371.

Kayak, Eskimo, 266.
Keewatin, meaning of name, 52.
King George medals prized by Indians, 53, 66.
King murder case, 272.
Kodik, case of boy, 221.

Labelle, Yukon murderer, 224.
Laird, Hon. David, Lieut.-Governor of N.W.T., 50; Indian Commissioner, 63.
Lake Bennett, 201, 215.
Lake Winnipeg patrol, 278, 352.
Lance, use of, 350.
Land Survey and half-breeds, 121.
Lansdowne, tour of Lord, 162.
Laurier, Sir Wilfrid, 279, 341.
Leeson, Constable, 221.
Lett, Constable, and desperado, 114.

Liquor law difficulties, 157.
Lorne, tour of Marquess of, 118.

Macdonald, Sir John, 12; formulates scheme for Police Force, 18; resigns office, 20; again Premier, 86; death of, 170.
M'Donald, Sergeant, and Sitting Bull, 79.
M'Donell, Inspector A. E. C., 220, 248.
M'Ginnis, Inspector, 308.
M'Illree, Assistant-Commissioner J. H., 149; and Almighty Voice, 180.
M'Kay, J.P., Mr. Thomas, 130, 146.
Macdonell, D.S.O., Inspector A. C., 84, 256.
Mackenzie, Alexander, 4.
Macleod, C.M.G., J. F., appointed Assistant-Commissioner, 23; at Fort Whoop Up, 31; Indian name of, 39; Commissioner, 51; Indian Commissioner, 63; stipendiary magistrate, 86.
M'Neill, General, on Sitting Bull Commission, 78.
Madore, M.D., Assistant-Surgeon G., 214.
Mail-carrying in Yukon, 204, 218, 228.
Manitoulin Island Treaty, 59.
"Mavericks," 301.
Medicine Pipe Society, 239.
Middleton, Major-General, and North-West Rebellion, 135.
Miners' meeting, a, 195.
Minto, Earl of, Governor-General, 275; Honorary Commissioner, 276.
Moodie, Superintendent J. D., 194; long patrol, 208, 248, 260, 267.
"Moose that Walks," story of, 57.
Mormons, 233.
Morris, Hon. Alexander, Lieut.-Governor of Manitoba and N.W.T., 60; Indian Commissioner, 60.
Morris, Inspector W. S., 141.
"Murder Island" mystery, 222.
Musical Ride, 326.

Neale, Superintendent P. R., 144.
Norman, Superintendent F., 166.
North-West Angle Treaty, 59.
North-West Company, 5.
North-West Mounted Police, organisation of, 19; Government control of, 20, 50, 86; augmentation of, 88, 161, 235.
North-West Rebellion, first, 7.

THE RIDERS OF THE PLAINS

North-West Rebellion, second, 120.
North-West Territories under separate government, 50; division into Police districts, 92, 336.
Norway House post, 271, 280, 308.

Offices, obsolete, 342.
Ojibbeway Indians, 52.
O'Neill, Constable J. A. W., long patrol, 91, 271.
Otter, Colonel, and North-West Rebellion, 136; attacks Poundmaker, 143.

Paré, M.D., Surgeon L. A., 214.
Parker, Inspector W., 233, 237, 248.
Patrols on Boundary Line, 166; on prairie, 340.
Patrols, special, 307.
Payment of officers and men, 19, 279; in Yukon, 218.
Pedley, Constable A., 286.
Pelletier, Inspector E. A., 226, 267, 308.
Pension Bill, 275.
Perry, C.M.G., Commissioner A. Bowen, in North-West Rebellion, 150; in Yukon, 200; 226; Commissioner, 235; receives C.M.G., 235.
Personnel of the Force, 163.
Pie-a-Pot, Chief, and C.P.R., 104.
Piegan Indians, 53.
Potts, Jerry, Interpreter, 39, 41; death of, 187.
Poundmaker, Chief, 128, 143, 153.
Prairie Chicken Old Man, 41.
Prairie fires, 168, 282.
Primrose, Superintendent P. C. H., 191, 214.
Prince and Princess of Wales' visit to N.W.T., 243.
Prince Albert, volunteers from, 129; base of operations, 133.
Provencher, Lieut.-Colonel, Indian Commissioner, 60.

Qu'Appelle Treaty, 60.

Radisson, Pierre, 3.
Recruits, training of, 325.
Red coat, significance of, 26, 49.
Red Crow, chief of Blood Indians, 41, 81, 239.
Reid, J. Lestock, Indian Commissioner, 61.
Richards, D.C.O., Sergeant-Major, 257.

Richardson, V.C., Sergeant A. H. L., 251.
Riel, Louis, 7, 122; capture of, 153; execution of, 154.
Robertson-Ross, report of Colonel, 12.
Robinson Treaties, 59.
Ross rifle, 349.
Ross's Scouts, 252.
Routledge, Superintendent W. H., long patrol, 207, 214, 224.
"Royal" conferred on Force, title of, 275.

Saddlery, 28, 93, 117.
Salteaux Indians, 52.
Sanders, D.S.O., Superintendent G. E., 186, 248, 250, 256.
Sandy Lake, patrol to, 308.
Sarcee Indians, 53.
Saskatchewan, Province of, formed, 276; employment of Police in, 353.
Scarth, Inspector W. H., 191, 214, 248.
Selkirk, Earl of, and Scottish settlers, 5, 6, 59.
Seller's patrol, Constable, 270.
Sheep Camp, 193, 195.
Sioux Indians, origin, 53; claim to be British subjects, 53; early settlers in Canada, 70.
Sitting Bull, war with Americans, 72; Custer massacre, 73; crosses border, 73; negotiations for surrender, 75; "Sitting Bull Commission," 78; formal surrender, 84.
Skagway, 192.
Sleigh, Corporal B., killed, 144.
Smith, Corporal, 280.
Smyth, Major-General E. Selby, inspects Force, 44.
Snyder, Superintendent A. E., 213, 248.
"Soapy Smith," 193.
South African War, 235, 246.
Spicer, Sergeant, 96.
Split Lake post, 271.
Stanley of Preston, Lord, Governor-General, 165.
Starnes, Superintendent Cortlandt, 190, 214.
Steele, Superintendent S. B., 43; railway strikes, 108; North-West Rebellion, 150; in Yukon, 190; in Boer War, 248, 256.
Stikine River trail, 197.

— 384 —

INDEX

Stone Fort and Manitoba Post Treaties, 59.
Strange, General, and North-West Rebellion, 136.
Strength of Force, 21 (footnote), 51 (footnote), 89, 108, 170 (footnote), 234, 277 ; in the Yukon, 214.
Strickland, Inspector D'Arcy E., 191, 200, 205, 214.
" Sun Dance," Indian, 237.
Sweet Grass Hills, 31.
Sword, use of, 28, 350.

Taylor, Inspector J., 226, 248.
Terry, General, 72 ; on Sitting Bull Commission, 78.
Thompson, M.D., Assistant-Surgeon W. E., 191, 214.
Timber dues, collecting, 339.

Umiak, Eskimo, 267.
Uniforms, early, 28 ; changes in, 116, 342 ; " Klondike uniform," 219.

Veterinary Surgeons, 338.
Vidette, steamer, 352.

Waite, D.C.O., Constable A. S., 257.
Walsh, Inspector J. M., 31 ; and Sitting Bull, 49 ; Chief Crow's Dance incident, 81 ; good opinion of half-breeds, 125.
Wascana Creek, Regina, 90.
White, C.M.G., Lieut.-Col. Fred., Comptroller, 135, 341.
White-Fraser, Inspector M. H., 147, 248.
White Pass trail, 197.
Wilde, Sergeant, 184.
Wilderness murder, 272.
Winnipeg, fort on site of, 4 ; recruiting dépôt at, 116.
Winnipeg Treaty, 61.
Witchcraft, case of, 221.
Wood, Assistant-Commissioner Z. T., 191, 198, 214, 226.
Wroughton, Inspector T. A., 226, 248.

Yukon Territory, 173, 188 ; variety of Police duty in, 205, 226, 352.